UNDERSTANDING MARRIAGE, FAMILY, AND INTIMATE RELATIONSHIPS

ABOUT THE AUTHOR

Jerry D. Lehman, Ed.D., is professor of psychology at the University of South Carolina Upstate, where he has been a teacher, counselor, mentor, and friend to students for over thirty years. He and his wife, Faye, are parents of two daughters, Lynn and Leigh, both of whom were instrumental in nurturing this project along. Leigh allowed dad to escape for some quiet writing time to her place in Florida during a sabbatical and Lynn was helpful, especially with computer problems—even buying dad a new laptop when his old one crashed.

UNDERSTANDING MARRIAGE, FAMILY, AND INTIMATE RELATIONSHIPS

By

JERRY D. LEHMAN, Ed.D.

Professor of Psychology
University of South Carolina Upstate
Spartanburg, South Carolina

CHARLES C THOMAS • PUBLISHER, LTD.
Springfield • Illinois • U.S.A.

Published and Distributed Throughout the World by

CHARLES C THOMAS • PUBLISHER, LTD.
2600 South First Street
Springfield, Illinois 62704

©2005 by CHARLES C THOMAS • PUBLISHER, LTD.

ISBN 0-398-07606-5 (hard)
ISBN 0-398-07607-3 (paper)

Library of Congress Catalog Card Number: 2005048564

Printed in the United States of America
CR-R-3

Library of Congress Cataloging-in-Publication Data

Lehman, Jerry D.
     Understanding marriage, family, and intimate relationships / by
Jerry D. Lehman.
        p. cm.
     Includes bibliographical references and index.
     ISBN 0-398-07606-5 -- ISBN 0-398-07607-3 (pbk.)
     1. Family. 2. Marriage. 3. Couples. I. Title.

HQ728.L494 2005
306.872--dc22

                                                                   2005048564

Dedicated to my wife, Faye,
and my daughters, Lynn and Leigh—
they each taught me in their own way
what many of the words in this book really mean.

PREFACE

The idea for this book took shape in the recesses of my mind soon after I started teaching a course on marriage, family, and intimate relationships. There were many topics I wanted to share with my students–topics that I felt would be relevant to their experience. I believed then and still believe today that there is no knowledge more important to the personal lives of students than knowledge about why intimate relationships succeed and fail. As the idea for this book went from thought, to pen, to paper, my enthusiasm never wavered. And as I wrote, I assigned the material as readings in my course. It was then that I realized that students also shared my enthusiasm for the course and the material. One student commented on how relevant the course was to her life. Another noted how pleased he was that the course had encouraged him to think about family and relationship issues in a new way; still another hoped that she could use her learning to improve her marriage.

Thus, the comments of students reinforced my thinking and my writing and it became something of a mission to introduce this material to interested students. And since they continued to sign up for the course, I continued to explore with them the emerging knowledge that makes up the field of relationship science. I feel very fortunate that I have had the opportunity to introduce students to the work of researchers, theorists, and therapists who have contributed to our knowledge base concerning marriage, family, and relationship issues. The work of these scholars' spans a number of different disciplines and is significant because it has the potential to impact lives in many positive ways. This book was written because of the significant work of these individuals; without their research, knowledge, and insight, there would be no book.

If you are a student using this book, my hope is that you will find this material as fascinating and exciting as I have. A Study Guide and other resources are available at www.understandingrelationships.net for assisting you in learning and understanding this material. As you read and discuss the book's content, I also hope that you will find ways to enhance your family life and intimate relationships. Much has been written about the breakdown of the family in our culture today. Many believe that the problems of crime, drugs, poor performance in education, and many of the other woes we see around us have their roots in the family. If this is so, how do we address these problems? The answer I believe is—one family and one relationship at a time. What Barbara Bush said in the 1990s is still pertinent today, "What happens in your house makes more difference than what happens in the White House."

If you are an instructor teaching a relationship course, I hope this material will allow you to shape a meaningful learning experience for your students. You will note that the content of this book is not as encyclopedic as many other texts; I have attempted to focus on issues and topics that are more family and relationship specific. This has allowed me to write about some topics in greater detail and I believe this depth allows students to better relate the material to their lives. Those of us who teach family and relationship courses usually want to go beyond just imparting knowledge; we want to help our students improve their family and intimate relationships. This is a noble but daunting challenge. If you have found ways that have worked for you in accomplishing this task, I would welcome hearing from you at jlehman@uscupstate.edu. In addition, if you use or are thinking about using this book in a course you teach, information about instructional resources is available at www.understandingrelationships.net.

I would like to thank my friend and colleague, Dr. Karen Macrae, who read portions of this manuscript and gave me valuable feedback. Also, this book would not have been possible without the support of the professionals at Charles C Thomas. I would like to thank them for their valuable help and assistance.

CONTENTS

UNDERSTANDING MARRIAGE, FAMILY, AND INTIMATE RELATIONSHIPS

Chapter 1

INTRODUCTION

It is 8:45 a.m., just fifteen minutes before a new semester begins. I am about to meet my marriage, family, and intimate relationship class for the first time. The class roll indicates that the class is full. Sophomores, juniors, and seniors from many areas across our campus have enrolled. As I make my way toward the classroom, I wonder why students have chosen to take a class on relationships. Of course, there are many reasons: the course is being taught at a convenient time, a friend had taken the course and recommended it, the course will count as elective credit, or perhaps they want to better understand intimate relationships in their lives. I know that relationships are central to students' lives–their satisfaction and happiness are often closely related to the well-being of their relationships.

MY STUDENTS' EXPERIENCES

First classes are usually difficult. Instructors struggle with how to be interesting, yet at the same time communicate necessary information about the course. I frequently ask students to write questions that they have about relationships or specific relationship problems. If they are allowed to do this anonymously, they usually share quite candidly. If this class is like others, students will have a variety of questions and problems to share. In the past the following comments have been typical.

3

- I have been married for six months. So far it has been wonderful. We are still in a kind of honeymoon stage and the newness of our intimacy and sharing is still fresh. But how can we keep it this way? When I look at my parents' marriage, I don't see happiness. How can I keep my marriage from becoming like their marriage?
- My boyfriend and I are living together or, as they say, cohabiting. We both thought that it would be a good idea. But now I'm not too sure! I seem to be giving more than I am getting in return. My expectations of what it would be like living together have not panned out. Were my expectations too high? Should I settle for less than I envisioned or say that the experience taught me that we are not right for each other?
- I am in the first serious relationship of my life. It feels good to be so close to another person. But I am fast losing my ability to think rationally. Yet when I do try to think about "us," I realize that we are very different, so different it's scary. Should I be concerned about these differences or will they make our relationship more exciting and keep us from being bored? I have seen so many married couples who seem to be bored with each other.
- My girlfriend and I argue constantly. Sometimes I wonder what we see in each other. But we cannot seem to break up. When we have tried, I can't get her off my mind and she says she feels the same way about me. So we get back together and before long we are arguing again. Do marriages between two people like us ever work out?
- I am thinking about filing for divorce. I have been married 12 years, have two children, and am married to a workaholic husband. He provides well but is never home and rarely helps with the children. I don't know what happened to our relationship. It seems like we woke up one morning and what we had was gone. Could we get our relationship back? I hate thinking about rearing the children by myself, but that looks like what may happen.
- Sometimes I wonder what's wrong with me. I am living with a man who has a violent temper and tries to control my every move. He is extremely jealous and believes that I have been unfaithful to him. He has not actually hit me, but I'm afraid that he might. Why did I fall for a man like this? Is there any chance he might change?
- I am shy and can't seem to meet anybody. My roommate and I are so different; she never meets a stranger and is out with friends all the time. I am not comfortable with having anyone too close to me. I'm not even sure I ever want to get married, but then it's depressing to think I might be alone all my life. Is there any hope for someone like me?
- My daughter is fourteen and right now we are having a lot of problems with her. She is threatening to run away if we don't let her do what she

wants. She has gotten in with a bad group at school and they have more influence with her than her dad and I do. We argue constantly with her about her room, her friends, her tattoos, her music, and just about everything else. I am really worried. We don't know what to do; certainly what we are doing is not working. Help!

• I have a beautiful marriage and a wonderful family. I realize how fortunate I am to have a loving husband and two healthy, happy daughters. We do a lot of things together as a family and I just hope that we are spared major problems down the road. We have strong religious beliefs and I think this has drawn us closer as a family.

• We have just had our first child. She has a difficult temperament and cries constantly. We have lost more sleep in the last month than I would have thought possible. We asked the doctor whether this would ever end. He recommended a book about children who cry a lot and are difficult. When are we going to find time to read a book?

• My father and mother never married so I never really knew my father very well. My mother was a single mother struggling with all of the problems that single mother's experience. She did the best she could under the circumstances, but it was hard for her and for me. I feel that I have somehow been cheated. I would daydream that my father would come and take me away and love me so all the hurt would go away. What I am wondering is this: how will the absence of a father affect me? Will I always be distrustful of men like I now seem to be? I desperately want a relationship, but at the same time, I am suspicious of every male's intent.

Of course, answers to questions like these do not come easily. However, throughout the semester, the course material and class discussion will address many of their concerns.

SOME CONCLUSIONS AT THE BEGINNING

I believe that there are things that students interested in relationships should know even before beginning their study. These things are not earth shattering; many of my students have probably already drawn these conclusions on their own.

• Humans have a need to love and be loved. We seek out companionship with others. And there is something special and deeply satisfying about an intimate love relationship.

• Yet close loving relationships, while highly rewarding and satisfying, can also be the source of great pain. Some of our greatest joys and heartaches take place in the family since it is in marriages and families where we love most deeply and run the risk of experiencing the greatest heartaches.

• No matter how hard partners try, no intimate family relationship is perfect. All couples will experience problems, as will parents and children and siblings with siblings. Expect problems occasionally and don't conclude that your marriage and family cannot make it because problems exist. According to William Doherty (2001), a prominent family life educator and therapist, married couples do not share their marital experiences with other married couples and therefore do not realize that many of the problems encountered in marriage are common to all marriages. Couples talk to each other about shopping, sports, the latest TV program, or the accomplishments of their children, but marriage is often a taboo topic. In sidestepping discussions about their marriages, couples isolate themselves from information and support that could be helpful as they navigate through their marital waters.

• The romantic love that was so wonderful in the beginning of your relationship will not be enough to sustain a marriage over time. The strong passionate feelings will fade. Then the couple will need certain skills in communication and conflict resolution, as well as a deep friendship and commitment if they are to sustain a strong marriage. It is after romantic love diminishes that a couple discovers if their relationship has the qualities that are necessary for a lasting, stable, happy marriage.

• Expect highs and lows in your close relationships and family life. That bundle of joy you brought home from the hospital will become that infant who constantly needs attention, that child who has a will of his/her own, and that adolescent that you may hardly recognize. That intimate talk that you shared with your spouse in the early days of your relationship may be replaced by gaps of silence as you struggle to find things to talk about other than the children.

• You will see traits in your partner that you previously overlooked. Some of what you see may be very satisfying while other things may be quite upsetting. For example, a wife may find that her husband is much more helpful or unhelpful around the house than she thought he would be. Or she may find that he is more of a workaholic than she realized. A husband may find that his wife is good with the children, but with her work and child responsibilities she finds very little time for her husband. Or he may find that her talkative nature is an irritant to his desire for solitude or that her emotionality makes him uncomfortable. And traits may appear that were not present before marriage—a drinking problem, a severe depression, migraine headaches, a nasty temper, or an inability to break away from the family of origin. Such are the realities of marriage and family life. It is like a journey down a winding road with unexpected joys and hazards along the way.

TOOLS THAT SUCCESSFUL COUPLES USE

Does this mean that a satisfying marriage and family life is impossible? Certainly not! Many couples and families cherish the good times and weather the storms of bad times as they negotiate their journey. Families often become stronger as they look back on their shared experiences together. They come to realize that marriage and family life changes and evolves. They learn to be flexible and take a long-term view. While an experience may seem tragic today, in time it will be woven into the fabric of life to create a complex mosaic involving both negative and positive experiences. But sustaining a happy marriage and family life is not easy; if it were, there would be far fewer divorces. So as you experience the highs and lows of marriage and family life, perhaps you should develop what Parrott and Parrott (2001) refer to as the tools that couples in good marriages use: ownership, hope, empathy, forgiveness, and commitment.

Ownership. Problems in families and relationships are not just due to the other person. Marriage counselors constantly hear that it is the other person's fault; if s/he would only change, then things would improve. The husband blames the wife, the wife blames the husband, and they get nowhere in solving their problems. Couple and family relationships are systems. Marriage partners and family members respond to each other as they each create their environment; they interact as if life were a dance—your move is followed by your partner's move which is followed by your move and so on. Therefore, it is not who is wrong or who is to blame; it is how the dance you are both engaged in and responsible for contributes to your problems. When couples take this viewpoint, they stop blaming each other and start examining their own role in the dysfunctional dance; then it becomes possible for each partner to take responsibility for what is happening in the marriage.

Hope. Research shows the benefits of an optimistic attitude; hope is a characteristic of such an attitude. When individuals begin to lose hope, fear sets in as they imagine the worst. When couples keep an optimistic attitude and their fears in check, they stay hopeful; when their fears rise, their hope diminishes. Parrott and Parrott are not suggesting that some bad marriages should not be abandoned. Rather, they are suggesting that many marriages and families that have experienced hard times have been saved and thrive today because partners have not given up hope.

Empathy. Empathy is the ability to see things from another's perspective, to understand from another's point of view without blaming or criticizing.

Therapists often tell partners that the differences they have are usually disagreements about preferences and points of view. If partners can understand and respect the dreams and circumstances upon which their partner's perspective is based, this understanding can help soothe anger and frustration. Get good at this type of understanding because research (Gottman, 1999) shows that 69 percent of the problems couples face are perpetual problems—problems that cannot be resolved. Yet, if couples can continue to discuss the hopes and dreams upon which their differences are based, they are more likely to respect their partner's position.

Forgiveness. Partners need to be willing to forgive and ask for forgiveness because in a marriage, both partners do things that hurt each other. Some slights are minor and may even fall under the category of honest mistakes. If so, apologize, forgive, and move on. However, some transgressions are major and hurt so deeply that rebuilding the relationship is difficult. Lost trust is regained slowly over time. If you care about your relationship, don't subject it to things that do great harm. Do as happily married couples do: limit your mistakes, be quick to apologize and willing to forgive.

Commitment. No marriage would last without commitment. The level of a couple's commitment will determine the length of their marriage. What does your "I do" mean in terms of commitment? Those who have been happily married for many years take commitment seriously; they have confronted just as many obstacles to happiness as most other couples, but they remain committed to each other and to their marriage.

A MARRIAGE AND FAMILY STORY

Couples who stay married often have heroic stories to tell. Their stories are often like the stories of happiness found, then lost, and then found again since they experience the highs and lows that are typical of marriage. The case of Troy and Dot Howard is an example.

Troy and Dot met in college, dated for a year, and were married soon after they both graduated. They were very much in love and thought they would sail through life successfully meeting whatever challenges came their way. Before the birth of their first child, they defined themselves as happily married. Their first child, Todd, was temperamentally difficult; he cried much of the time during the first year. They became very child focused, doing almost anything that would bring on a happy mood or cause the crying to cease. Because they had always wanted two children they had Ben when Todd was two. Ben had some health problems during those first months and Troy and Dot spent most of their time worrying about test results, doctor's visits, and tending to Ben's health needs. All the while, Todd was still fussing and screaming and so in only a few years, the Howards had gone from being a happy couple to distressed, harried parents of two difficult children. Over the next ten years, they focused on their children while neglecting their marriage. Both children were diagnosed as ADHD and had learning and behavioral difficulties consistent with this diagnosis. In the process of working, worrying, and caring for their children, the Howard's gradually lost their marriage. And although at times they could see what was happening, they could not stop overattending to their children. Thus they drifted apart, rarely made time for each other, and had very little to talk about except their children. Troy said he had accepted the loss of his marriage and felt that some day he and his wife would find each other again.

However, Troy did not realize that their troubles were far from over. By the time Todd was in the sixth grade, he was in trouble at school and with the police. He had broken into another student's locker and stolen some CD's and jewelry. And Ben was not far behind. A year later, they were partners in crime, stealing cigarettes from a convenience store. And a few years later when Troy and Dot thought they could take no more, both boys were arrested for possession of drugs. Over the next few years, this family and these boys were in and out of therapy and drug treatment programs many times. By this time, Troy and Dot were asking what they had done to deserve all the grief and pain. Answers did not come easily! They were both well educated, successful in their professions, and had provided many advantages for their children. They were deeply religious, had a strong sense of ethical values, and had modeled ethical behavior for their children.

One day during the middle of their turmoil, when the boys were in high school, Troy was driving home from work. A careless driver crossed the median and hit Troy head-on. Troy was seriously injured and for the first few nights after the accident, he was not expected to live. He spent weeks in intensive care, three months in the hospital, and a year out of work. When he returned home for nine months of recuperation, the boys were still in trouble (one was in a juvenile facility during part of this time) and Dot was left to struggle with the responsibilities of the children and now with Troy's recuperation. And Troy was not very helpful. His anger, grief, and bitterness seemed too much to overcome. He wondered what had happened to his marriage, his children, and to their lives. And in the middle of his recuperation, he lapsed into a deep depression. After about eight months, he finally got medical help for his depression, but his bitterness toward his wife and children were much harder to overcome. At one time, Dot and Troy blamed each other for what had happened to their boys and to their marriage, but therapy taught them that laying blame at the other's doorstep did no good. They were both involved in the process that had engulfed them. On an intellectual level, Troy could understand this, but on an emotional level, he could not turn off the bitterness and anger directed mostly toward his wife.

You might think that a couple like Troy and Dot would not stay together. They had too many strikes against them and had neglected their relationship for too long. Even their therapist had doubts about whether they would make it and could rebuild their relationship. Troy and Dot occasionally thought back to their good times together. They could still fondly remember the time they first met, their walks in the park together, their wonderful days after their marriage, and all their hopes and dreams. Somehow these positive memories never faded. It was their hope that some day they could recapture a little of that spark that had burned so brightly so long ago. Yet they crossed each other's paths like emotional zombies. They had been so badly hurt by their bitter words to each other and by their experiences with their children that it seemed their anger would consume them. There were times when Troy wanted to reach out and hold his wife in his arms and comfort her and say he was sorry, but he could not. The invisible barrier separating them seemed like too great an obstacle.

Yet Troy and Dot still believed they were in this together. They had a job to do; the boys still needed help and it was their responsibility to try to rebuild their marriage. They gradually began to turn their wrath toward the forces that had attacked their marriage; they would not stand and watch these forces win out over them. They simply would not let life beat them down any more. But they knew that it would take time. What had taken years to destroy could not be rebuilt in a day. Gradually they began to turn toward each other again in little ways and with little acts of kindness. Over months, then years, they found that they still loved each other. Gradually the bitterness began to fade and they thought about how hard they had tried to do the right thing. Oh they had made mistakes, but they respected each other's determinism and good intentions. Powerful circumstances had gotten the best of them at times, but they had not intended to do harm.

Today, this couple is still together and they will tell you that they have a strong marriage. It's a very different marriage than in the beginning. Now they are like two old warriors who have triumphed over the forces that had the audacity to attack their love, their marriage, and their family. When I saw Troy again the other day he greeted me with a smile, thanked me for my friendship, and said, "You may not believe this, but Dot and I now take time for each other everyday and Todd just graduated from college and Ben is in the honors program at a nearby school." As he walked away, I felt a deep respect for him, for his wife, for their marriage, and for their family. They had encountered life and they had survived. No, they had done more than survive! They had encountered hardships and it had strengthened them in a way that only struggle can. And it had drawn them closer together.

There are many survival stories in marriage like Troy and Dot's story. These stories are not frequently told; instead news about divorce, domestic violence, and unhappy marriages dominates the headlines. Yet there are many couples and families that have lived through good times and bad times and have been able to sustain and strengthen their love for each other.

MY HOPE FOR THE READER

My hope is that this book and the thoughts it initiates will provide valuable knowledge that can be used to strengthen marriage, family, and intimate relationships. One of the most frequent comments older students' make after reading this material is, "I wish I'd known these things years ago." Their assumption is that they could have used this information in constructive ways to create better relationships. I too make this assumption. Just as coaches believe that they can prepare their team beforehand to play better in the game, I believe that preparation for marriage and family life can have beneficial outcomes. However, even if the coach prepares the team well, players will still make mistakes, but this does not mean that prior instruction was of no value. Everyone will make mistakes in their relationships, but the hope is that with knowledge, individuals will make fewer mistakes and that they will recover more quickly from the mistakes that are made. So beware, the information in this book can be powerful. It has been used by students to effect change: one student called off her engagement, another talked with his wife about what he had read and they implemented some changes in their marriage, another student took steps to get out of an abusive relationship, another gained a whole new perspective on his relationship problems, still another decided to apply to graduate school in marriage and family therapy.

THE CONTENT

Each of the following chapters has been written with the belief that in each topic area there is content that the student of relationships should know about and understand. I have selected material that I believe you will find interesting and hopefully helpful, yet is basic to the content area. There is much that must be omitted in an introductory text, but there are references at the end of each chapter that can lead to further exploration of important topics. I have also included questions throughout the text that will help you think about your life in relation to the material. My goal has been to write in a style that is readable, down-to-earth, and engaging. I even hope that this is a textbook that you look forward to reading.

I have gone to three types of sources for the material selected: (1) to relevant theories that so often guide our thinking, (2) to good research that undergirds our knowledge, and (3) to the writings of marriage and family therapists who are on the frontline in the process of helping bring about change. Each of these sources has contributed valuable knowledge to the growing and important field of marriage and family studies. A brief description of Chapters 2 through 10 is presented below to help you get an overview of the content areas that will be the focus of your study.

Chapter 2, Theory and Research: Our Search for Understanding, presents material on the prominent psychological perspectives with an emphasis on each theory's relevance for understanding behavior in families. This discussion is followed by an introduction to family systems theory–an approach specifically relevant to understanding behavior in a family context. Then, since much of the text material is based upon current research, the last part of this chapter addresses the importance of research in the field of family studies and the different methods used in the research process.

Chapter 3, Family Rules, Structure, and Development, examines the importance of rules in family and intimate relationships. Rules provide the basis for a family's structure–the interactional patterns that are relatively stable over time. Since rules and structure are basic to the family systems approach, this chapter will emphasize the following: how rules develop, the nature of healthy rules, how rules create dances in families, how rules reflect a family's beliefs and ideology, and how rules and structure both remain stable and change over the course of a family's development. In discussing these topics, two things are emphasized: rules remain relatively stable over the short term, but can change over time as families and relationships change.

Chapter 4, Important Transitions in Family Life, deals with some major events that produce change in relationships and families. This chapter focuses on the changes produced by three fairly predictable events: marriage, the birth of the first child, and a child reaching adolescence. In this chapter, readers will realistically examine the joy and pain associated with these life-changing events. For those contemplating marriage or starting a family, this chapter should serve as a guide to the terrain ahead.

Chapter 5, Family Influence and Generational Connections, is about the lasting influence that families have on their members. No other connections are more powerful or long lasting as those created by the family. Our genetic makeup and our family of origin experiences create these connections. In this chapter, attachment and object relations theories are discussed along with information on how one's upbringing influences adult relationship patterns. Also, material on role theory is presented as well as information on how the family of origin influences emotional style. The theme of this chapter is that both genetic and family of origin influences cast a broad shadow over our development. Yet the chapter ends with information on becoming a transitional character–someone who is able to overcome the negative influences of the past and pass along a healthier lifestyle to his or her children.

Chapter 6, Emotions in Family Life, explores the important role of emotions in the family. Attention is given to the following: emotional intelligence, emotional management, male and female differences in emotional styles, positive and negative affect in marital interactions, and extreme emotional reactions. This chapter also presents material on how to nurture and strengthen healthy emotional connections as well as information on viewing the family as an emotional system. The theme of this chapter is that the health of family and intimate relationships depends on how partners and family members deal with their emotions.

Chapter 7, Love and Happiness in Intimate Relationships, examines myths about love, theories concerning why we choose a particular mate, and common mistakes individuals make in the mate selection process. Then, different definitions and types of love are examined; this discussion helps readers see that love is more than a romantic feeling. It helps them answer the question: When the romantic feeling wears off, what characterizes a happy marriage? The chapter ends with a discussion of family love and the things that characterize attitudes and feelings in loving families.

Chapter 8, Communication in Families, describes the complexities of the communication process. Common communication mistakes are analyzed and gender differences in communication style are addressed. The chapter concludes with a discussion of how to effectively communicate when couples experience conflict.

Chapter 9, When Couples and Families Struggle, examines some troubling signs that may exist even before a couple marry and discusses a premarital preparation program designed to prepare couples for marriage. Then the research of John Gottman, Diane Vaughan, and Karen Kayser is presented to help readers understand the process that unfolds as relationships deteriorate. The views of several marriage and family therapists are also discussed to help readers understand the process from the therapists' perspective. Then, a discussion of the characteristics of struggling families provides insight into the despair that often exists when family relationships break down and family members become alienated from each other.

Chapter 10, Helping Couples and Families, begins with a discussion of the attitudes that need to exist in order for partners to make positive changes in their relationship. Also in this chapter, three different approaches to marital therapy are presented: the Seven Principles Approach, the Imago Therapy Approach, and the Divorce Remedy Approach. The chapter ends with a discussion of family therapy and what happens when the client is a dysfunctional family. In this section, the goals of family therapy are presented and the characteristics of healthy families are described.

SUGGESTED READING

Doherty, W. (2001). *Take back your marriage: Sticking together in a world that pulls us apart.* New York: The Guilford Press.

Parrott L., & Parrott L. (2001). *When bad things happen to good marriages.* Grand Rapids, MI: Zondervan.

Chapter 2

THEORIES AND RESEARCH
OUR SEARCH FOR UNDERSTANDING

Psychologists and family scientists have benefited from both theory and research. The first comprehensive theory of personality originated from the work of Sigmund Freud. As Freud listened to his patients in therapy, he developed some tentative explanations for their behavior. These explanations were later developed into an integrated set of principles that he used to explain personality. Thus, the psychoanalytic theory was born. However, since Freud's explanations were based on his observations of patients, his theory was not based on rigorous scientific research that systematically tested the validity of his ideas. Yet Freud's theory provided direction for others who were interested in explaining behavior, and many early theorists followed the path set by Freud.

Today, Freud's psychoanalytic theory is just one of many psychological theories used to explain behavior. Since behavior is exquisitely complex, it is understandable why there are many different perspectives. Freudian psychologists examine early childhood experience, intrapsychic characteristics, and the nature of the unconscious. Biological psychologists attempt to determine the genetic and biological determinants of behavior. Behavioral psychologists seek understanding by analyzing environmental determinants such as reinforcement and punishment, while humanistic psychologists emphasize the effect of environmental conditions on the development of the self. In this chapter, we will first look at these psychological theories; then we will turn our attention to family systems theory—a theory developed specifically to understand behavior in a family context.

Yet theories of personality and behavior are not enough to satisfy the questioning mind of the scientist. For the scientist, theories often provide direction by suggesting what questions should receive further study. Then, using the tools of science, the scientist attempts to determine if theoretical explanations have support. Thus, in this chapter, we will not only look at theories but we will also look at the tools of science as we attempt to understand how these tools can be used to answer important questions. In future chapters, we will examine both theories and research as we attempt to understand the complexities of relationships.

The attempt to understand marriage, family, and intimate relationships is a relatively new field of study involving scholars from many different fields, including psychiatry, psychology, sociology, counseling, and family life education. The work of these scholars on family and relationship issues encompasses a relatively new field known as family science.

THEORIES: APPROACHES TO UNDERSTANDING

Freud's Intrapsychic Approach

Early psychological theories attempted to explain personality by examining internal characteristics. A person's internal motivations were often referred to as intrapsychic processes; these processes were mostly unconscious and thought to be strongly influenced by early childhood experience. These early theories paid lip service to the importance of the family but then turned away from the actual study of the family and focused on these internal, intrapsychic characteristics. It was these internal characteristics that needed to be understood if the mystery of behavior was to be unraveled. Freud's theory is an example of such an approach. Freud (1901, 1924) proposed that behavior is driven by powerful biological instincts; thus individuals are motivated from birth to satisfy powerful innate needs that are a part of their biological makeup. Interestingly, Freud selected two of these needs to be the central focus of his theory–sexuality and aggression. Many later psychoanalytically oriented theorists criticized his heavy emphasis on sexuality, thinking that other needs were more important. Freud also has been criticized for including aggression as a biological need. Many present-day psychologists are more likely to study aggression as a learned response.

As these powerful innate needs interact with environmental demands, Freud also believed that personality develops a structure; that is, it is made up of different components like a building is made up of bricks and mortar. However, the components of personality are abstract; they are within us but cannot be seen or touched in a physical sense. Rather they are intrapsychic structures that predispose us to think and behave in different ways. The three structures upon which Freud built his intrapsychic theory were the id, ego, and superego.

Id, the only personality structure present at birth, is very powerful and individuals struggle to contain its power throughout life. Id is self-centered, seeking to satisfy basic needs in ways that produce immediate satisfaction and the greatest amount of pleasure. Thus, id is governed by the pleasure principle. The id does not take into consideration the needs of others since its focus is only on self-satisfaction. Anyone who has observed an infant has probably noticed this self-focus. If an infant is hungry s/he may cry, demanding immediate satisfaction of this need regardless of the time of day or environmental circumstances. If an infant desires an object, s/he may reach for it even if it belongs to someone else or may be harmful. This is the nature of the id-dominated infant; s/he demands immediate need satisfaction without regard to the environmental situation or the feelings of others.

Freud believed that if humans were to become socialized they must learn to satisfy the innate needs of the id in acceptable ways, taking into consideration the teachings of family and culture. This socialization process usually begins during the second year of life when parents attempt to teach children that the immediate gratification of needs in just any way is unacceptable. We eat at certain times, not when we first experience the pangs of hunger; we relieve ourselves in the bathroom, not on the living room floor; we don't hit and kick sister to get her toy. As the child matures, parents become less tolerant of these infantile ways and they begin to communicate rules, often punishing or showing unhappiness when the rules are not followed. The child learns that the consequences of satisfying id impulses in unacceptable ways are sometimes painful, often unacceptable, and frequently punished. As parents teach these important lessons, the ego begins to develop. The role of the ego is to help satisfy id impulses in ways that are acceptable within the rules of family and culture. When ego develops, the child is better able to take the reality of the situation into consideration and redirect id impulses in desirable directions. Thus, ego is governed by the reality principle. Ego requires a type of thinking Freud called secondary process thinking. This thinking requires some problem solving strategies, a knowing that takes into consideration certain realities about when and how to express a need. The ego considers external reality: will I get caught, will I be punished, and will I be able to satisfy needs within the guidelines specified by the rules of family and culture?

Yet there is more to mature behavior than simply containing id impulses to avoid negative consequences. Freud believed that parents play an important role in helping children internalize a value system—an internalized sense of right and wrong. This internalization of values serves as an internal compass, attempting to guide behavior regardless of the external situation. The structure of personality containing these internalized values is the superego. This structure begins developing around the age of four and five and is the source of both pride and guilt; pride when we follow our values and guilt when we fail to live up to our internalized standards. When the superego is in charge, we pay attention to our internalized values or conscience and are steered toward behaviors that are consistent with our value system. Thus a child may resist his or her temptation to cheat not because of a fear of getting caught but because of the internalized belief that cheating is wrong. Going against this internalized belief would result in the psychological pain of guilt.

When id, ego, and superego have developed, individuals experience internal conflict. The id seeks immediate gratification of needs based on pleasure, while the ego directs attention to the reality of behavior, prodding the id to satisfy needs in ways that meet family and cultural standards so that negative consequences can be avoided. And the superego directs attention to internalized values regarding right and wrong. The strength of these three internal forces is greatly influenced by how parents respond to their children during the first five years of life. Faulty child-rearing practices, especially extreme frustration or overindulgence, in regard to the powerful innate needs, are likely to be harmful to the developmental process. Thus, faulty child-rearing practices may result in imbalances in the personality structures that result in immature adult behavior.

Although Freud wrote about powerful innate needs and the family's socializing influence, he never directly studied families. Instead, he inferred that the family left its mark on personality but then theorized about intrapsychic forces. At one point, Freud pointed an accusing finger at the family when he concluded that his female patients' recollections of sexual abuse as children were due to actual abuse by their fathers. After presenting this conclusion to his colleagues, negative reaction was so strong that Freud later concluded that these recollections were simply false memories, brought about by his patients' normal childhood sexual desires for their fathers. Family therapists Napier and Whitaker (1978), analyzing Freud's influence, lament Freud's failure to observe the nature of his patients' family lives. They write: "If he would have only interviewed the parents! If he had only looked harder, he would certainly have confirmed not just the power of early family incidents, but the continuing influence of the family throughout the individual's life cycle" (p. 42). Because of this omission, Freud's theory leaves many questions concerning the role of parents and the family unanswered, providing very little guidance for parents grappling with child-rearing and family issues.

Erikson's Psychosocial Approach

A number of early theorists disagreed with Freud over certain aspects of his theory, especially his strong emphasis on sexuality. These theorists broke away from the traditional psychoanalytic movement to develop their own theories. One of these theorists, Erik Erikson, developed a psychosocial theory, focusing more on the role of the social environment than on sexuality. Erikson (1963) proposed an eight-stage theory of development spanning the entire life cycle with each stage having a central crisis that must be resolved. A positive resolution leads to characteristics that are needed for mature, healthy social development while a negative resolution makes healthy adjustment more difficult. This psychosocial theory emphasizes the role the social environment plays in determining whether a crisis is resolved in a positive or negative way. Since parents play a crucial role in a child's early life as shapers of the social environment, Erikson's early stages are especially relevant to parents with young children.

The crisis of the first stage occurs during the first year of life and relates to the development of trust versus mistrust. This crisis is crucial during the first year since the child is dependent on others for survival. If parents provide for their child's needs in a loving, consistent way, trust emerges, resulting in the development of optimism and hope. If parents are harsh and unloving and neglect the child's needs, mistrust develops, resulting in discouragement and pessimism. Events that take place during the second and third years influence the child's learning during the second stage—autonomy versus shame and doubt. Children at this age have a budding curiosity and are more capable of initiating independent action. This often leads to behavior that parents consider "off limits." This curious tendency coupled with the child's obstinacy often creates the impression that the two-year-old is difficult, thus the term "terrible twos." When a young child initiates behavior that leads to success and approval by parents, the child becomes confident; when the child's behavior is defined as inappropriate and met with disapproval, the child learns to feel shame and doubt. The task for parents is to allow for the healthy expression of autonomy and independence within reasonable limits. Limits are important because at the same time children are learning to express their will and independence, they must also begin learning self-control. Parents who are overly harsh and critical or who do not set and enforce reasonable limits in a loving way increase the likelihood that children will experience shame and doubt, characteristics that impede healthy social development.

Erikson's third stage is a logical extension of the second stage. The crisis of this stage involves initiative versus guilt. Children at age four and five are now more mature physically and cognitively and enjoy taking the initiative with these newly developed skills. Caretakers must provide social environments that provide opportunities for healthy initiative without providing an overabundance of negative feedback that produces excessive guilt. If this and the previous crises are resolved in a positive way, trust, autonomy, and initiative develop and the child is better prepared to meet the crisis of the elementary school years—the crisis of industry versus inferiority. The major task at this age is to develop a sense of competence in regard to mastering the new challenges and demands of a school-age child: reading, writing, mastering arithmetic, and developing healthy social relationships with peers. Experiencing success produced by effort and work (being industrious) allows children to feel competent, while failure leads to discouragement and a sense of inferiority.

This theory has important implications for parents and families. Since parents are the major providers of a child's social environment during these early years, how parents interact with their children is crucial. It is the quality of this interaction that largely determines whether a crisis will be resolved in a healthy or unhealthy way. A positive resolution to these crises establishes a sense of trust and optimism, a confidence in initiating autonomous behavior, the beginnings of the ability to control inappropriate impulses, and a belief that with work and effort, success is possible and relationships can be meaningful. With such a positive start, the young person is better prepared to face the challenges of adolescence.

It is during adolescence that the search for identity begins. At this time, the crisis of identity versus role confusion reflects the young person's struggle to further separate from parents and form a strong, independent self. Although this search is a process that will take years to complete, it begins during the adolescent years. This adolescent struggle is an attempt to find what is comfortable and what fits the young person's developing personality. It involves important defining issues relating to career choice, relationship decisions, and a philosophy of life. This struggle is experienced differently by each adolescent and certainly requires much patience and understanding on the part of parents and teachers. If the young person cannot work toward a positive resolution of identity issues, then discouragement and confusion may set in, leading to unhappiness, rebellion, depression, or apathy. Working toward a positive resolution concerning identity issues establishes the foundation for a healthy identity in adulthood.

The young adult years bring other turning points that relate to maturity and competence as an adult. Erikson referred to the crisis of these years as intimacy versus isolation. His theory suggests that mature intimacy occurs when individuals have struggled with and conquered identity issues and can share with each other what their struggles have taught them without feeling threatened by their differences. It is interesting that the stage emphasizing intimacy follows the stage involving identity. Marriage counselors frequently suggest that individuals delay marriage until they have established a healthy sense of self and identity. Often couples marry at a young age, before they have grappled with the struggles of life that help shape identity and character. Some couples even marry expecting the marriage to resolve all of their identity issues. While this may work for a time, it usually fails since discovering authentic identity must come from within. Depending on one's partner for completion in regard to identity issues is a risky venture since it places responsibility for one's development on another. Peck (1978) suggests that mature intimacy in a marriage relationship occurs when two individuals have developed strong independent identities and are very capable of living without each other yet choose to be together. Since the issues of identity and intimacy are important to healthy relationships and successful marriages, these issues will again be addressed in later chapters.

In middle adulthood, the developmental crisis centers on generativity versus stagnation. During this stage, mature adults realize that many individuals have contributed in a positive way to their development. Thus, mature adults attempt to give back by being generous with their time, energy, and resources as they help others find a positive direction and purpose in life. Those who do not resolve this crisis in a positive way become stagnated, self-centered, and self absorbed; they are unable to reach out and support the growth of others. Then the final stage, the stage confronting older adults, is ego integrity versus despair. As the elderly review their lives, they may either feel satisfaction at having made the best of their opportunities (ego integrity) or disappointment due to unrealized potential and unfulfilled dreams. Those experiencing generativity and ego integrity are those who have resolved the crises of the earlier stages in a positive way. It is also these individuals who are best able to provide healthy, nurturing environments for their children and grandchildren so that the young of the next generation have healthy environments that foster positive growth.

Erikson's theory has greatly influenced our thinking about development. Yet, like Freud, he stopped short of actually studying family interactions; he did not observe entire families working together to solve problems. Had he done so, he might have been able to describe what parents and families do to promote or inhibit psychological growth. Therefore, we must look elsewhere to find a more family-oriented approach to understanding family processes.

The Object Relations Approach

Another group of theorists who modified Freudian thinking developed object relations theory. These theorists believe that interactions with parents and other significant individuals (objects) during infancy and early childhood instill powerful mental representations that are stored in unconscious memory. These early mental representations concerning what our caregivers were like influence how we view the self and others in adulthood. Thus our view of self and others, created largely by childhood experiences that are stored in unconscious memory, plays an important role in our adult relationships, especially close intimate relationships. Therefore object relations theorists focus on early bonds, usually the mother-infant/child bond, believing that the quality of this bond influences development far into the future. A similar view is held by a group of theorists known as attachment theorists. In later chapters, both of these theories will be discussed as we attempt to understand how the past influences behavior in marriages and families.

In summary, psychoanalytically oriented theories have greatly influenced our thinking about behavior. The proponents of these theories often elaborated on how childhood experiences impact adult behavior. However, these theorists rarely studied the complex interactions that take place in families as family members interact as family.

The Behavioral Approach

Another perspective that has important implications for the family is behavioral theory. Although much of this theory developed out of research with animals, many early researchers in this field assumed that the laws of learning extrapolated from animal studies also applied to humans. The early work of B. F. Skinner is especially noteworthy. Skinner (1953) noted that environments influence learning through either reinforcement or punishment. If something satisfying or the removal of something aversive followed behavior, the behavior was likely to reoccur or increase in frequency. This increase in rate of responding was called reinforcement. If behavior was followed by something unpleasant/aversive, then the behavior was likely to decrease in frequency. This decrease in rate of responding was called punishment. A response might also decrease in frequency due to extinction–the withdrawal of reinforcement.

Since research demonstrated that behavioral principles have relevance to human behavior, the application of behavioral concepts to families and family life soon followed. Parents should reinforce their children for appropriate behavior and ignore or mildly punish inappropriate behavior. In the 1960s, books began to appear advising parents on how to implement these behavioral management strategies with children. A book written by Patterson and Gullien in 1968, entitled *Living with Children: New Methods for Parents and Teachers,* was often recommended for parents struggling with child-rearing concerns. As behavioral psychology became more popular, these principles were also used in counseling couples. Partners were told to reinforce each other as they learned new ways of interacting in order to enhance their relationship. In one influential book, *Mirages of Marriages* (1968) by Lederer and Jackson, these authors reported that in good marriages, partners exchanged positive behaviors and in bad marriages, there was a breakdown of this positive exchange. This led to a behavioral contracting approach to marriage counseling where each partner was taught to reinforce his or her spouse and keep score of the positive reinforcements he or she received. This mutual reinforcement exchange model, which was seen by behaviorists as the model for a happy marriage, was later found to have little support (Murstein, Cerreto, & MacDonald, 1977). Rather, it was unhappy couples who kept score of positives and negatives whereas happy couples exhibited love (positives) unconditionally.

The Social Cognitive Approaches

As the behavioral movement became more influential, some researchers began exploring other learning models. Albert Bandura (1963, 1977) soon reported his findings on observational learning. Children did not need to be directly reinforced or punished to learn, but could learn vicariously by simply observing models. This finding had important implications for families. What children observe can have a powerful influence on the learning process. Since the most important models for children in the early years are parents, it is important that parents are cautious concerning the behaviors they model. Also, this research suggested that parents, as managers of the home environment, should be concerned about the models their children are exposed to through television, movies, and other media sources.

Bandura's research also opened the door to other possibilities. Children could observe a model, store learning from this observation in memory, and later use this learning to affect behavior. Therefore, the cognitive effects of learning (thoughts, perceptions, expectancies, and beliefs) could be stored in memory and influence thinking and behavior even days, weeks, or years later. This expanded the scope of behaviorism; it was now appropriate to study cognitive variables and the impact these variables had on behavior. It also made it more likely that therapists and researchers would study thinking, beliefs, and expectancies and attempt to change these variables when distorted thinking created problems in marriage and family relationships.

Cognitive behavioral therapists and marriage counselors often focus much of their attention on distorted and faulty thinking variables. Aaron Beck, a pioneer in the development of cognitive therapy, has studied many of the cognitive errors and distortions that struggling couples make. An example of such a thinking error is overgeneralization. Suppose a husband is critical of one of his wife's ideas concerning how to manage the children. She may think and say, "You always put my ideas down and never listen to me." The words "always" and "never" are probably generalizations that are not consistent with actual experience. Although this conclusion may seem very plausible to the wife in the heat of the argument, when this conclusion is later examined, she realizes that frequently her husband does listen to her and is often complimentary of her ideas. Since distortions in thinking are often the cause of problems in relationships, family members would benefit from understanding and avoiding cognitive errors. Beck (1988) has attempted to help couples who are struggling due to these misunderstandings. His book, *Love Is Never Enough: How Couples Can Overcome Misunderstandings, Resolve Conflict, and Solve Relationship Problems through Cognitive Therapy*, has been used by couples who are struggling in their relationships due to cognitive distortions. Chapter 4 will examine some unrealistic expectations about marriage and child-rearing; then in Chapter 8 the discussion will examine how thinking errors can result in communication problems in marriage.

The behavioral and cognitive behavioral perspectives have contributed to our understanding of how individuals influence each other in families. They have focused on how behaviors and ways of thinking are learned and how faulty thinking and learning can be modified. However, behaviorists did not develop their theories after observing family interaction, but rather applied concepts derived from other observations to the family. Thus these theories are not truly familial and do not directly address many of the issues that are of concern to family scientists.

The Humanistic Approach

The humanistic perspective is another approach used to explain and understand behavior. This approach developed as a reaction to the psychoanalytic and behavioral perspectives and became popular in the 1960s. Humanistic theorists believed that the earlier approaches did not adequately address issues that were important in explaining and understanding human behavior. The most influential humanistic theorists were Carl Rogers and Abraham Maslow. Since Rogers' approach has important implications for child development and family life, numerous family life educators have been influenced by his work.

Rogers (1951, 1961) believed that individuals are born with an actualizing tendency. This innate tendency provides the motivation and desire to become the best that an individual can become. Since Rogers viewed human nature as innately positive, the actualizing tendency propels individuals in the direction of goodness and cooperation based on the common good rather than toward a self-centered perception of what is good for the individual. Rogers also theorized that humans are born with an internal mechanism called the organismic valuing process. This mechanism allows individuals to evaluate their experience and know which experiences are growth enhancing and which are detrimental to positive growth. If individuals can get in touch with this innate aspect of their being, the choices that they make will be consistent with the actualizing tendency and will lead to healthy adjustment.

Although getting in touch with the organismic valuing process may seem simple, in reality, it is quite difficult. Early in life and throughout life, there are those who wish to dictate how others think, feel, and behave. Often parents attempt to tell their children how to be by communicating love and acceptance only if their children develop interests, values, and ways of being that are consistent with parental desires. Although a parent may see this as a natural part of the socialization process, carried to an extreme it can have serious drawbacks. Rogers believes that young children have a strong need to be regarded positively by others, especially parents. If this need for positive regard from parents takes precedence over the organismic valuing process (looking inward to find direction and guidance), then the child becomes what others want him or her to become rather than what is consistent with the valuing process from within. Since outside influences are strong, an individual may struggle to find the true self and to behave in ways that are consistent with this self.

Rogers worked with clients in therapy who were struggling with issues of self-determination and who were attempting to forge a new self. Since an unhealthy environment characterized by conditional love was the source of a client's problem, Rogers believed that providing a growth-producing environment in therapy was essential for positive change. Three things characterized this growth-producing environment.

1. The therapist must be real and genuine in the relationship with the client. Therefore the therapist should not pretend or put up a false front. If a therapist experiences a thought or feeling, s/he should be aware of this thought or feeling and even verbalize it if it is relevant to the client.
2. The therapist must communicate unconditional positive regard and acceptance. This is not necessarily approval of the client's thoughts or actions but is respect for the client as a person, regardless of what the client may be saying, doing, or experiencing.
3. The therapist must exhibit empathy for the client's problems and situation. Empathy involves listening to what the client is expressing and attempting to see the world the way the client sees the world without being judgmental or critical. Then this empathic understanding must be communicated to the client. Listening and communicating in this way has often been referred to as active listening.

Rogers believed that when therapists provided these conditions over time, this environmental exposure would allow clients to examine the false self that had developed and cast off the aspects of this self that were not consistent with the organismic valuing process.

Psychologists soon began to apply the principles of this approach to family life. One authority, Thomas Gordon (1970), whose book, *Parent Effectiveness Training,* was widely read and discussed in the 1970s, advised parents on child-rearing practices and on how to provide growth-producing environments in the home based on the expression of genuineness, empathy, and unconditional positive regard. Later family life educators began using some of the empathic, active listening principles to help couples improve listening skills, express empathic understanding, and aid in conflict resolution. The book *Fighting for Your Marriage*, by Markman, Stanley, and Blumberg (1994), and their PREP training (Prevention and Relationship Enhancement Program) provide a program for relationship enhancement and conflict resolution based on some of the concepts made popular by Rogers and Gordon. Chapter 8 will provide further discussion of this program.

The humanistic approach provides some interesting insights concerning the nature of healthy and unhealthy environments that can be utilized in work with families. However, this approach falls prey to the major drawback of the other theories discussed so far; it did not develop from the study of the family nor did it emerge from an orientation that had the family as its central concern. Because of this, many issues of interest to family scientists are not adequately addressed by this approach.

The Biological Approach

For many years psychologists have debated how important genetic factors are in determining behavior and personality. Recently, the biological approach has literally exploded with new findings that support the significance of biology in almost every aspect of our lives. In the field of personality psychology, recent studies (Segal, 1999) with twins strongly suggest that personality is influenced by genetics. Identical twins develop when a sperm cell fertilizes an egg cell or ovum; then the ovum splits creating two separate ova. This splitting involves a replication of genetic material leading to the development of two embryos with the same genetic makeup. Fraternal twins, however, develop when two different sperm fertilize two different ova, creating two genetically different embryos. Thus fraternal twins are no more genetically similar than siblings within a family. Twin researchers have been interested in studying the similarities and differences between identical and fraternal twin pairs. If they find that identical twin pairs are more similar than fraternal twin pairs, this suggests that the greater similarity is due to genetic factors.

However, twins, both fraternal and identical, are usually reared in the same environment; how then can one determine what is due to genetics and what is due to the environment? To answer this question, researchers have studied twins who have been separated through adoption soon after birth and reared in completely separate environments. Frequently these twins are unaware that they have a twin sibling until they are adults. This research has addressed some interesting questions: Will identical twins reared apart have similar personalities? Will identical twins reared apart be more similar than fraternal twins reared together?

Some interesting findings have emerged. First, identical twins reared apart are very similar in many ways, including personality. If one identical twin has an upbeat, happy disposition, usually the other twin does also. If one is outgoing and highly sociable, so is the other. Furthermore, identical twins reared apart are as similar or about as similar as identical twins reared together. And identical twins reared together are also very much alike. This tells us that even if identical twins are reared in different environments, many similarities still exist in regard to their personalities. Genetics then must be a powerful force behind these similarities. Fraternal twins, even when they are reared together, are not nearly as similar in their personality traits as identical twins reared apart. This tells us that even if fraternal twins are reared in the same family environments, these environments are not powerful enough to shape great similarities in personality.

Using twin and adoption studies in this way has helped researchers identify traits that have a powerful genetic basis. Findings suggest that three such traits are introversion-extraversion, emotionality or emotional stability-instability, and positivity and negativity in mood tendencies. There is also some evidence (Wheeler, Davidson, & Tomarken, 1993) that differences in regard to these traits are based on differences in the brain and the nervous system. For example, individuals with a positive, upbeat mood have higher brain activity in their left cerebral hemispheres, while individuals who are more negative in mood have higher brain activity in their right hemispheres. Furthermore, these differences in nervous system activity are present soon after birth and persist over time. As researchers begin to understand more about brain functioning, they are more likely to continue to associate different personality tendencies with nervous system functioning. Panksepp (1998) recently wrote about seven emotional command centers in the brain that relate to emotional functioning. Panksepp suggests that we inherit different levels of need activation in these seven areas and this creates important individual differences. As knowledge advances, further research will provide greater insights into the relationship between brain functioning, personality characteristics, and inheritance.

Longitudinal studies of infants and children have also enhanced our understanding of the influence of biology on personality. These investigations begin by studying infants soon after birth and follow the same group of individuals through childhood, into adolescence, and sometimes even into adulthood. This research attempts to answer several questions: Do infants, soon after birth, differ in how they respond? If so, how do they differ? If they differ soon after birth, are these differences consistent over time? These are important questions because if infants differ soon after birth in the ways they respond this suggests that these differences may be inborn, possibly genetic since environmental factors have had very little time to influence these tendencies. And if these unique behavior patterns persist over time, this may mean that they are somewhat resistant to modification, as they would be if they were inborn, genetic differences. This research suggests that there are differences soon after birth in response tendencies and that these differences are somewhat consistent over time. These unique behavioral tendencies that emerge soon after birth have been referred to as a child's temperament. Thus, children are born with different temperaments.

One comprehensive longitudinal study was begun by Thomas, Chess, and Birch (Thomas & Chess, 1977) in the 1960s. This study, known as the New York Longitudinal Study, found noticeable differences in how infants and young children respond soon after birth and in their early years. These differences are often referred to as the dimensions of temperament. These dimensions included the following:

Activity Level	General level of motor activity
Approach or Withdrawal	Initial response to new stimulation

Adaptability	Ability to adjust to new experience after initial response
Intensity of Reaction	Amount of energy utilized in a response
Quality of Mood	The amount of pleasant, friendly behavior vs. unpleasant, unfriendly behavior
Rhythmicity	Regularity of eating and sleeping
Threshold of Responsiveness	Stimulation needed to evoke response
Distractibility/Attention span	Persistence in attention focus/ease of distractibility

Further analysis of the data led these investigators to identify three basic temperament patterns in babies and young children. These patterns were:

Easy	Approaches rather than withdraws from new experience
	Is adaptive and has a pleasant quality of mood
Slow to Warm Up	Withdraws from new experience, slow to adapt
	Somewhat negative quality of mood
Difficult	Withdraws from new experience, slow to adapt
	Highly intense with negative quality of mood

Furthermore, these researchers found that 40 percent of the children in their study were easy babies, 15 percent were slow to warm up, 10 percent were difficult, and 35 percent were mixed types—not easily categorized into any of these three groups.

These and other temperament studies have contributed to our understanding of individual differences in children and have helped parents realize that powerful influences other than parenting style play an important role in child development. It is important to note that these studies do not suggest that parents are unimportant and that their interaction with their children is of no consequence. Parents do impact child development by the ways they respond to their child's uniqueness. For example, they can provide experiences that strengthen assertive tendencies in the withdrawing child and dampen the intense, negative responses of the difficult child. As you would expect, soon after the findings from temperament studies became known, books (Chess & Thomas, 1987; Turecki & Tonner, 1985) began to appear giving parents access to information about inborn, temperamental differences and suggesting strategies for dealing with the different temperament types.

* * * * *

In summary, all of the theories discussed so far have provided insight into behavior, even behavior that occurs in families. Yet none of these theories had the family as their central focus. Thus there was something lacking–a piece of the puzzle was missing when it came to understanding behavior that occurred in families. Family systems theory provides this missing piece.

The Family Systems Approach

Family systems theory is an extension of general systems theory, a theory that proposes that elements or parts of systems are interconnected and strive to maintain balance as a system operates to maintain itself and achieve goals. General systems theory is very broad and applies to all systems from one-celled organisms to complex systems such as the human body or large corporate organizations such as a Fortune 500 company. Many scholars studying and working with families believed that there was a need for a more specialized systems approach related to the unique characteristics of the family. Such an approach would view the family as a social system made up of interacting parts that influence each other in an on-going process. Thus, family systems theory evolved in order to better understand the powerful influence of the family. This approach has been very useful to theorists, researchers, and therapists, providing a new way of conceptualizing, understanding, and studying the family.

Applying Systems Concepts to the Family

Systems and Rules. The focus in the family systems approach is on the system itself. Previously each member of a family had been studied as if knowing each individual member would somehow help understand the family. The family systems approach rejects this idea. The word "system" implies that interrelated parts or elements interact in regular, persistent, and enduring ways as the system maintains itself. Without something to regulate and govern how the system functions, there is no system. What produces the regular and enduring patterns that are seen in families? From a systems perspective, these patterns are created by rules since rules govern interactions. However, when family members are asked to write their rules, they may write only five to ten short statements. In comparison, employee handbooks of corporations or student handbooks of universities have hundreds of rules. Why the difference? Are there fewer rules in families? Probably there are just as many rules in families as in other complex groups. However, the important rules in families are often outside the family's awareness. Yet it is still these rules that regulate the repetitive behaviors that make up the routine of family life. There must be family members to have a family, but to the systems theorist, the individuals standing in isolation from each other do not make up the family. There is no family in a systems sense until you have a regular and enduring pattern of behavior that governs the interaction of family members. These patterns are created and governed by rules. Thus, rules are important to family systems theory and their role will be examined more closely in Chapter 3.

Wholeness. In a systems sense then, the family is more than the sum of its individual parts and more than a collection of individuals standing in isolation from each other. As family members come together, they interact and as they do, they create a uniqueness that is far more than just the sum of each individual member. When we describe the Smith family, we are describing a complex group, organized around a set of rules, acting and reacting to each other in many ways as they communicate and function as a family. They are more than the sum total of Mr. Smith, Mrs. Smith, Beth Smith, and Jimmy Smith. To understand the Smith family, you must understand the dynamic relationships that exist among family members as they interact and function as a family.

Using this perspective, how does one get to know the Smith family? If you are their neighbor, you may have talked to Mr. Smith many times. You may know what he believes about politics, child-rearing, religion, and many other issues. You may have met Mrs. Smith and consider her a close friend. You may have even coached their children in soccer and occasionally taken them to school in the carpool. But do you know the Smith family? From a systems point of view, you do not. The best way to get to know the Smith family is to observe them interacting as family in many different situations and on many different occasions. Observing in this way leads to an awareness of the complex patterns that characterize interactions and the subtle ways that family members influence each other when they are together functioning as family.

Interdependence. With this wholeness focus, family systems theorists emphasize that movement or change in one part of the system influences every other part of the system. Thus, the system is dynamic, constantly changing, acting and reacting to input of various kinds. Virginia Satir (1972) used the example of a child's mobile to illustrate the changing nature of a system. A tug on the mobile at any point affects every other part; no part of the mobile is unaffected. Similarly, any input or change in one part of the family system will influence the entire system. For example, the birth of a child does not just increase the size of the family, but actually changes the nature of the entire family, creating a new entity as relationship and interaction patterns change. Since a change in one part of the family or in one member of the family triggers a change in other members, systems theory focuses on behavioral patterns that reverberate throughout the family unit rather than on any one individual member and his/her behavior.

Homeostasis and Feedback. The family, then, viewed as a system, consists of complex patterns of interactions between family members. These interactions are governed by rules that are often subtle and outside awareness. The patterns that develop over time make family activity predictable so that each member knows what to expect. Deviations from these patterns that are outside a preferred range are monitored and responded to so that the customary balance and equilibrium within the family can be maintained. This tendency to maintain balance and equilibrium and to seek stability is called homeostasis. The process of monitoring stability and balance is referred to as feedback.

The body is an example of a homeostatic system. It is involved in self-regulating so that body temperature is maintained around 98.6 degrees. If the outside temperature changes, then various regulating processes within the body go to work to maintain the desired temperature. We may be unaware of these changes and only occasionally notice the more obvious results such as perspiration or shivering.

A home heating system is regulated in a similar way. The thermostat set at 70 degrees is sensitive to changes in temperature. This sensitive mechanism monitors feedback from the air. When the temperature falls below the desired level, the heating system is activated. This results in the room temperature reaching the desired level and this higher temperature is sensed by the feedback mechanism, which turns off the heat. Therefore, there is an ongoing process based on constant feedback, which maintains the temperature around the desired level.

The systems approach views the family in a similar way. The family's rules and regulations tend to maintain a sense of balance and equilibrium, allowing the family to maintain itself and accomplish essential tasks with a sense of stability and predictability. When behavior deviates from what is acceptable, this deviation is sensed by the system and corrective measures are taken to bring the system back into balance. For example, in families, there are usually rules about how conflict can be expressed. These rules may dictate that family members may talk out their differences, even yell on occasion if the decibel level does not get too loud, storm out if talking is unsuccessful, but never hit or engage in any physical violence. Should physical violence occur, corrective measures are taken to bring behavior back within an acceptable range and restore balance to the system. If the fight is between two children, parents usually step in to make the necessary corrections. Mom and Dad may punish the children, send them to separate rooms, or encourage them to drop the issue for now and come back to it later. But whatever they do, it is intended to restore the family to a state of equilibrium. If the conflict is between husband and wife, words may be spoken, a hurt look may be expressed, or an emotion may be displayed, communicating that one partner has gone too far. These words, cues, or emotions are signs that disequilibrium exists and corrective measures are needed to bring the relationship back to a balanced state.

Some theorists contend that feedback constantly produces change so that rather than going back to the previous balanced state, the system seeks a steady state that is slightly different from the previous steady state. Therapists, working with troubled families, may not want the family to return to the balance of the past. Rather, they may want the family to look at new ways of interacting and relating so that a new, healthier equilibrium is established. Thus, the family is not a static system. Some feedback may push for change while other counterforces within the system seek the previous balance. How well the system can adjust and accommodate to various types of feedback is important to the health of the system. Positive feedback, or what Constantine (1986) calls amplifying feedback, pushes the system in order to produce change. Negative feedback, or what Constantine calls attenuating feedback, attempts to adjust the system back to the previous equilibrium or steady state. The teenager who comes home one hour later than the established curfew may be providing amplifying feedback that pushes the system to change. If being one hour late is a sufficient deviation from the normal balance, then parents may lay down the law in order to bring the system back into balance. If the teenager persists in coming home late, then the system may continually be taxed to the limit. This is similar to the heating system that must work harder and harder to reach the desired temperature. Minor tampering with the system, such as changing the air filter, may be all that is needed to restore the desired balance and stop the system from continually running. But minor tampering may not work and thus a major overhaul may be needed. For the teenager's family, perhaps a minor adjustment in the rules is all that is needed. Then again, a major change in rules may be warranted to accommodate the age level of the teenager. Decisions concerning change can be difficult. When is the teenager old enough to have a later curfew, drive the family car, or date without adult supervision? If changes are made to allow for a later curfew, then these changes reverberate throughout the entire system. Mom now worries more, which affects dad who also responds differently, thus the entire system is affected.

Input and Output. The system, then, is constantly monitoring input to see if this input is within the accepted range. Input (those things that are fed into the system either from within the system itself or from outside the system) includes a variety of things that the system is set up to monitor such as whether the teenage son is late or on time, whether money is spent appropriately or inappropriately, whether time is managed effectively or ineffectively, whether members are contributing the desired amount of work, and whether the school is using appropriate textbooks. While monitoring input, the system and members of the system are also producing responses; these responses are referred to as output. If a member's behavior (output) should fall outside the accepted range, then information concerning this behavior is fed back into the system as input and this produces responses (output) that attempt to bring the system back into balance.

Systems and Subsystems. The family system is also made up of subsystems that carry out certain functions. A number of subsystems develop in families; these involve alliances among family members as they carry out important tasks. The most noticeable and enduring subsystems in the family are the spousal subsystem, the parental subsystem, and the sibling subsystem.

The husband and wife as members of the spousal subsystem must communicate and cooperate in ways that enhance and maintain the marriage. The partners model marital behavior as they work as the spousal subsystem, teaching children about marital interaction, communication, intimacy, and commitment. If the spousal subsystem malfunctions, this reverberates throughout the system, spilling over in ways that affect the children.

The parents and others, such as grandparents who are assigned parental roles, make up the parental subsystem. Working together, the members of this subsystem function to rear children. Problems in this subsystem are evident when parents do not agree on child-rearing procedures or on how rules are implemented. Persistent rule violations by children may also reflect a breakdown in some aspect of the parental subsystem.

The sibling subsystem is made up of the children in the family. The give and take between siblings allows each child to learn how to compete, negotiate, cooperate, and function within their sibling group. Sibling interaction is important for learning relationship skills that will be needed when children venture out of the family. The sibling bond is one of the most enduring and longest lasting connections in life and some scholars (Bank & Kahn, 1982) have focused specifically on this family subsystem.

Other subsystems also exist but may not have as prominent a role as the spousal, parental, and sibling subsystems. For example, the male subsystem, the female subsystem, the father-daughter subsystem, or the mother-son subsystem may develop for carrying out specific functions within the larger system.

Boundaries. A boundary is a line of demarcation between two systems, subsystems, or entities. Boundary lines govern almost every aspect of our lives. We are familiar with property lines, state lines, and county lines that define the borders between different entities. In families, there are also lines of demarcation. Sometimes these lines, like property lines, are clear and apparent, but often these boundaries are more invisible and subtle. Yet their presence, whether clear or subtle, protects the family from outside invasion and from internal instability. When parents say to children, "we do it this way in our family," they are communicating that their family system is different from other family systems. They are also reinforcing the integrity of their system, protecting it from change, and controlling the flow of information coming into the system. Each family system protects itself to some extent from the invasion of outside information, ideas, and behaviors that would threaten the stability of their system. They do this by protecting and guarding their boundaries from unwanted influences that might corrupt their family system. This is what happens when parents put filters on computers, blocking access to certain websites, or when they limit access to certain cable channels and TV programs.

Boundaries also exist within the family, protecting the family's internal stability. Some of these boundaries may be physical, similar to property lines. Bart Simpson's sign on his door that states STAY OUT OF MY SPACE is an example of this type of boundary. Other boundaries are implied by statements like, "Don't mess with daddy's desk," "Stay out of mother's jewelry box" or "Leave daddy's tools alone." Boundaries may even dictate where family members sit at the kitchen table, who sits in a favorite chair in front of the television, and what side of the bed family members sleep on.

Some boundaries in families are governed more by feelings and emotions than by the regulation of physical space. Newlyweds often enjoy closeness based on feelings of attraction whereas older couples, feeling less romantic attraction, allow more space in their togetherness. Boundaries pertaining to children and closeness also change as children grow older. The hugs and kisses that were appropriate expressions of love when children were young are replaced by other ways of communicating as children mature. These examples indicate that boundaries are not static; they change as situations change. However, the emotional boundaries that exist in a family at any given time are important, for these boundaries regulate emotional expression in regard to closeness and distance and dictate how emotions are expressed.

Boundaries also differentiate, define, and separate subsystems within the family. Minuchin (1974) believes that this separation must be well defined if the family is to function effectively. Thus, the makeup, role, and function of the parental subsystem should be clear so that the autonomy of this subsystem is maintained. When this happens, other subsystems from within and outside the family will find it more difficult to infringe on the functions and responsibilities of this subsystem. However, the parental subsystem should be sufficiently open to allow contact with other subsystems so that information flows effectively from one system to another, allowing input to produce change when change is needed. Therefore, boundaries between subsystems should be somewhat flexible, not so rigid that they are never amenable to change. Having flexibility, for example, would allow a grandmother or perhaps an older sibling to temporarily be the authority figure and caretaker of the rules when mom and dad are out of town. Flexibility would also allow for some communication between subsystems concerning rules as children grow older and need more freedom.

The ease with which a system or subsystem allows information to flow in and out relates to the system's boundary permeability. The permeability of family boundaries tends to change over time as the family responds to input from within the family and input from external sources. The family that allows a high level of information flow both in and out of the system is considered an open system while a family that allows very little information flow is considered a closed system. No family's boundaries are completely open or closed; rather, families fall somewhere along a continuum between open and closed, permeable and impermeable. There are also many complexities to this process. For example, a family may be open to information from one source but not others. This would be the case when a family seeks guidance from a minister, rabbi, or priest but not from neighbors or in-laws. It is important that boundaries be clear and that rules relating to boundary maintenance be apparent to family members. Boundaries that are too rigid or too flexible invite frustration and confusion as family members struggle to find freedom and connectedness in their lives.

A Different View of Causality

A major difference between the family systems approach and older approaches that attempt to study and understand behavior relates to causality. Traditionally scientists have utilized linear causality in their attempt to understand cause and effect. Family systems theorists use a circular causality model.

Linear Causality. In science, it is often important to determine cause. In social sciences like psychology, it is important to determine cause and effect in relation to behavior. This means that behavior can be explained in terms of a series of events. A leads to B, which then is followed by C. The cause of behavior can be determined if we can just find the chain of events leading up to the behavior. A person takes a drug that causes certain physiological changes, resulting in dizziness. How do we explain this dizziness? It was caused by the drug, which produced certain physiological changes. The scientific method based on linear causality is important to science and has resulted in many significant findings that have increased our understanding and improved our lives. It is important to know that this drug had this effect on this particular person. However, the scientific method based on linear causality is not the only approach to understanding. Family systems theorists take a different viewpoint, one based on circular causality.

Circular Causality. While linear causality is appropriate in many cases, family systems theorists contend that where you have many parts that interact with each other in an organized but complex way, linear causality is inadequate. Linear causality is thought to be too reductionistic, not adequate for use in analyzing how parts are understood in relation to the whole. Also, the linear model assumes that forces move in one direction. However, in complex human relationships, forces influence each other in a bi-directional or even multi-directional way. In the family, a change in one person influences every other member in the family. This influence or change to others is then fed back into the system and influences every other part of the system and so it goes in a never-ending cycle. Thus, searching for the one true cause is pointless, since answers are not found in the individual parts but in the system itself. X does not cause Y, nor does Y cause X. Rather, X and Y interacting together cause each other. Thus, searching for a starting point in the chain is fruitless. When parents ask children, "Who started it?" each child blames the other. However, who started it depends on where in the chain of the feedback loop the search for cause begins. Thus family systems theorists do not look for "the cause" but rather turn their attention to process, attempting to discover the pattern of interactions taking place that influences the entire system.

An example will perhaps explain how circular causality works. Bob is spending more and more time at work. He says that when he goes home, his wife Betty complains about his lack of concern for her and their nine-month-old baby. If he was really concerned about them, Betty thinks he would be home more to help her with the baby. However, when Bob does come home and tries to help, he is criticized for his inadequate performance and lack of concern. Bob and Betty seem to go round and round. Bob says he stays away because of Betty's negative attitude and Betty says she complains because Bob stays away and performs poorly when he does help. Which comes first: Bob's staying away or Betty's complaining? Clearly, it is not one or the other, but it is both. Bob stays away; Betty complains. Betty complains; Bob stays away. It is useless to lay blame; they both are contributing to the problem.

From the family systems perspective, behaviors are the result of constant and complex interactions taking place within the system. Environmental forces outside the system may perturb the system, but these environmental forces do not determine what a system does. Becvar and Becvar (1993) use the example of a ball and what happens when someone kicks things that are in the shape of a ball. A rubber ball rolls after being kicked because of its makeup. A soap bubble ball bursts after being kicked whereas a large cannon ball may not budge. In each of these cases, the shape of the structure that was kicked was that of a ball. However, how the ball responded was determined by the specific makeup of each ball. Similarly, in a family system, the environment does not determine how the system responds but rather provides the context for allowing the system to respond in a way that its structure determines.

Just as the structure and makeup of balls differ, the structure of families differs. Families are made up of individual members who are unique just as each family's rule structure is unique; thus no two families are alike. Therefore, as families face different experiences, how they respond to these experiences is a function of the family's unique structural makeup. The environment may provide the context for family response, but how the family responds, evolves, and changes is a function of the makeup of the family. If a family seeks the help of a family therapist this therapist may provide the context or the kick, to use the ball example, but the therapist cannot predict what this family will evolve into or become. The therapist can only hope that the kick will perturb the internal structure of this family in a way that opens up new possibilities for growth and change.

Equifinality and Equipotentiality. The concepts of equifinality and equipotentiality relate to prediction and causality. The term equifinality suggests that many circumstances and events can be associated with the same outcome. This means that many different beginnings can be followed by the same consequences and outcomes. For example, both A and B can result in C. Thus a parent's overprotective behavior or a parent's overpermissive behavior may result in rebellious behavior on the part of a child. Furthermore, the concept of equipotentiality states that the same beginning can be associated with different outcomes. For example, A could be followed by B or C; thus a spanking may lead to more misbehavior or less misbehavior. Children of very strict parents may become either very strict or very permissive as parents. Thus from the viewpoint of family systems theory, knowing what causes C or predicting what effect A will have is fraught with difficulty; it should not be the major concern. Instead, the family systems focus is on studying the pattern of interactions that take place in the family as the system attempts to maintain itself.

Becvar and Becvar (1993) point out that the systems approach with its emphasis on what rather than why and its focus on the present rather than the past is very different from the traditional psychological point of view. From the systems approach, the objective is to observe the context in which family behavior occurs, to observe the family interactions that are associated with maintaining behavior, and then, if desired, perturb the family system in such a way as to change the context so that behavior changes. The family may have had their same old argument many times and it is clear that they are stuck. What is needed is new input in the form of information, ways of seeing the situation, and methods of communication that allow the family system to behave differently.

The Importance of Process

Rather than focus on cause, the family systems perspective attempts to examine process. This involves observing the interactions that take place as family members respond to each other. This interaction takes place through communication, both verbal and nonverbal. Family systems theorists ask "what" and "how" questions: "What is going on in the family?" "How do family members communicate as they interact with each other?" This is in contrast to "why" questions: "Why do family members say the things they do?" This "what" or process emphasis examines the sequence of behaviors that occurs as individuals communicate and as they are linked together through behavioral transactions. So at the heart of a process-centered approach is the "what" and "how" of communication.

In relation to behavioral transactions and communication it is impossible for individuals to "not" behave and to "not" communicate. Try not behaving? Even the act of trying not to behave is behaving. Try not communicating? Even if you sit still and remain quiet, you are behaving and this behavior has message value to an observer. So it is impossible not to behave and not to communicate, since whatever behavior you engage in is likely to have message value to someone else. When individuals are asked why they are having trouble in a relationship, they often blame their troubles on a failure to communicate. However, what they are describing is unsatisfactory communication since even if there is no verbal communication, communication at a nonverbal level is taking place since silence and the nonverbal cues that go along with silence have meaning to a partner. In recent years, a great deal of attention has been given to what is going on when couples communicate and the different meanings that are attached to verbal and nonverbal communication. Since messages can be interpreted in many different ways and what one meant to say is not necessarily what the listener hears, the complex nature of communication will be examined further in Chapter 8.

As systems theorists studied the process of interaction in families, they noticed that a series of behavioral transactions was often repeated many times in the course of a family's interaction. These interactions are sometimes called cycles since the steps in the cycle occur repeatedly in a predictable sequence and lead back to the same starting point. If they have a destructive influence, they are sometimes called vicious cycles. At times, they have been referred to as family dances since each participating family member has a role to play as members respond to each other. One such cycle or dance relates to pursuing and distancing. A wife may desire closeness and want to communicate feelings and have these feelings validated. Her husband may be uncomfortable with feelings, listening, and validating feelings so he may distance himself from these conversations. The more the wife pursues, the more the husband distances. So the wife, thinking it is hopeless, stops pursuing. This allows the husband to feel more comfortable around his wife, so he seeks a greater closeness. The wife, who is now enjoying this greater closeness, again begins to talk about those things that are important to her–feelings, relationships, and the details of what she is experiencing. The husband then becomes more uncomfortable, begins to distance, and the cycle begins again. Although partners are a part of this sequence process, they are often unaware of the sequence and its influence on family functioning. Since cycles are an important part of the interaction process in families and are rule governed, they will be examined in more detail in Chapter 3.

RESEARCH: FINDING SUPPORT FOR OUR HYPOTHESES

Theories are helpful because they provide different viewpoints from which behavior can be studied and understood. The theories we use determine what we pay attention to in our attempt to understand. However, if a theory is not supported by research, it cannot be taken too seriously in the world of science. Thus one characteristic of a good theory is that it is useful in providing predictions that can be tested through rigorous observation. These testable predictions are called hypotheses. At times, a researcher may test a hypothesis without working from a particular theory. This scientist believes that a question needs to be answered for the sake of knowing even though the question does not neatly fit a particular theoretical framework. Even though it is not necessary for a hypothesis to be generated by theory, it is important how the hypothesis is tested.

The scientist must provide empirical data–information that is systematically observed, measured, and recorded. In everyday life, the layperson casually observes without using the systematic and painstaking methods of science. A father may be asked how three-year-old children behave in nursery school. The father, who has a three-year-old, may be tempted to respond based on his casual observation of his three-year-old at home. Since the father has never systematically observed the behavior of nursery school children, his answer is based on his casual observation of his child's behavior at home and is nothing more than his best opinion. The scientist, however, answers the question quite differently. "I don't know, but it's a good question so let's go out to a nursery school and systematically observe, measure, and record the responses of the children." Or if such studies have already been conducted, the scientist may say, "Let's consult the scientific literature. We will find the answer there." Or a husband may be asked, "How do couples argue when they are in conflict discussion?" The husband who has just had an argument with his wife may answer based on his own experience. "They yell like hell." The question for the scientist poses a much bigger problem. How does the scientist systematically observe, measure, and record how couples argue in conflict discussions? The next section will help answer this and other questions posed by research scientists.

The Goals of Research

The methods of science help the researcher achieve three goals. These goals are: (1) to accurately describe what exists or what behavior is occurring, (2) to accurately predict the likelihood that something will or will not occur in the future, and (3) to provide an explanation for what has been observed. The method of research that is used to systematically observe, measure, and record may depend on which of these three goals the researcher is attempting to achieve. We will look at each of these three goals and the methods of research that are frequently used to achieve each goal.

Methods Used to Describe

The social scientist has three methods that are often used to help accurately describe what exists: (1) the survey, (2) naturalistic observation, and (3) the case study.

The Survey. The survey, in paper and pencil form, allows participants to answer a series of questions pertaining to the topic being studied. Usually there are a number of multiple-choice answers from which to select or a rating scale to use as the subject responds. At times, survey questions may be read to participants in person or over the telephone. Care must be taken in wording the questions, since stating questions using certain phrases and words may generate biased responses. It is not easy to develop good, unbiased questions for a survey instrument. After the survey is complete, the researcher must decide who will be asked to respond to the survey. Often the researcher wants the survey results to be representative of a larger population than those surveyed, especially if the researcher wants to infer that the findings reflect the attitudes of the larger group. Several years ago, a marriage satisfaction survey for wives was sent out to 100,000 women who were members of women's organizations. There was a 4.5 percent return–4500 responded by completing the survey. This population was not representative of all married women since only members of certain women's organizations received the survey. Nor were the 4500 completed survey responses representative of the 100,000 women to whom the survey was sent. The 4500 responders were self-selected; the researchers had no idea how the other 95,500 would have responded. What can be said about these results? One certainly should not generalize these findings by implying that the results apply to all married, American women since this was an unrepresentative, self-selected sample. However, a major news magazine reported the findings by implying that 70 percent of women married longer than five years were having affairs and that 95 percent felt that they were harassed emotionally by the men in their lives (Wallis, 1987). Sadly, other more scientific studies involving randomly sampled women did not come to the attention of the general public. These studies report a much greater incidence of happiness among married women–only 3 percent stated that they were "not at all happy" and over half reported being "very happy" or "completely satisfied" in their marriages (Peplau & Gordon, 1985). And far fewer were having affairs than the misleading data implies–only 10 percent in one study (Greeley, 1991).

If researchers want to be more certain the results of a survey accurately reflect a larger population, they must be concerned with the problem of sampling. If a researcher is interested in the marital satisfaction of doctors' wives, it would be impossible to have all doctors' wives respond to this survey–there are just too many, some probably wouldn't cooperate, others might be too busy, and others can't be located. The researcher would want to survey a randomly selected group of wives from the total population of doctors' wives. Even this would be quite difficult so the researcher might narrow the total population by selecting only doctor's wives living in one state or one city. In the random selection process, every person in the population the researcher is sampling (for example, doctors' wives in one city) would have an equal chance of being selected. When a random sample is drawn, the findings are much more likely to accurately reflect the larger population–all doctors' wives in the city where the researcher sampled the population. Getting a randomly selected sample from any population can be a difficult task. Usually serious scientists address issues involving their sampling techniques and how participants came to be a part of the sampled group when they report the findings of their research.

Another way that survey-type information is gathered is through a personal interview, which allows for a more open-ended response on the part of the participants. Responses to interview questions may even be recorded on audio or videotape, so that subject responses can be analyzed in greater detail. For example, a researcher may interview individuals about their marriages: How happy are they with their marriage? How frequently do they argue? What do they argue about? When conducting personal interviews to obtain data, researchers should realize that how questions are phrased and the interviewers tone and inflection can influence responses.

Naturalistic Observation. If researchers want to accurately describe how subjects behave in a particular setting, they may go to that setting and systematically observe. This is referred to as naturalistic observation because the participants' behavior occurs in the natural setting. As Yogi Berra might say, "you can learn a lot just by looking." And scientists have learned a great deal by observing behavior in natural settings—baboons in the wild, children at school, employees at work, and couples at home. When observing behavior in a natural setting, researchers must either go to the environmental setting and observe or place audio or video recorders in the setting to be the researchers' eyes and ears. The advantage of using audio and videotape is that observers who code the interaction as a part of their analysis can later review these tapes. Of course, it is important to get the participants' approval before you peer into their private lives. Some studies involving couples and families have involved setting up cameras in participants' homes and taping family interaction. This research has significant advantages since what is observed is actual interaction rather than a family member's after-the-fact verbal or written account of the interaction. After-the-fact verbal and written accounts sometimes vary from the feedback given by the objective eye of the camera.

A few researchers have even been able to provide apartments for couples to live in while data is being collected. These apartments not only provide comfortable living conditions but also allow video cameras and other instruments to measure and record the couple's responses. Of course, there are no video cameras in the bathroom and a couple's interactions are not monitored at specified times in the late evening and early morning. But are these observations in a natural setting and are couples likely to exhibit behaviors in these apartment settings that are typical of the behaviors they would exhibit at home? When they engage in conflict discussions, as they are sometimes asked to do, do they behave like they would if they were at home away from the eye of the camera? Scientists who view these tapes usually get the impression that couples soon forget about the cameras and behave in natural ways. Observing couples in their home or in an apartment provided for them while utilizing sophisticated equipment that is small and unobtrusive has provided researchers with a wealth of information for study. One prominent researcher, John Gottman, has used this approach for years to study couple interaction. Some of his fascinating findings will be discussed in later chapters.

At times, researchers may observe the same subjects at different times even extending over a period of years. In the discussion of the biological approach it was noted how researchers studied infants soon after birth and then at various times during their development. When one group of individuals is observed repeatedly over time, this is referred to as a *longitudinal* design. This allows researchers to observe and study the behavior of the same individuals again and again as they age. For example, if a researcher wanted to know if couples argue over the same problems throughout marriage, the couples could be observed at various times throughout their marriage. Do couples discuss and resolve their problem issues and go on to other issues or do the same problem issues occur again and again? Gottman (Gottman & Silver, 1999), using this longitudinal design, has found that the majority of problems couples face do not get resolved; they come up over and over throughout marriage. Thus, the longitudinal design allows researchers to observe and describe either consistency or change in the same group over time.

Sometimes rather than study the same group of individuals over time, the researcher studies the behavior of individuals in different age groups. For example, a researcher might study one group of couples in their early thirties, another group in their early forties, another in their early fifties, and still another in their early sixties to see what problem issues these couples confront. Such a study, sampling different couples at different ages within a specific period of time, makes use of a *cross-sectional* design. This design allows the researcher to compare different age groups to see if there is a different set of issues that confront couples in these different age groups. Remember that both *longitudinal* and *cross-sectional* designs assess what exists at various times and then allows for comparisons between the different assessments.

The Case Study. A third method of research used when the goal is to accurately describe is the case study. Sometimes a particular individual or a particular family will be studied in-depth over an extended period of time. Such an in-depth study provides much information about this one case but does not allow the researcher to generalize from this one case to other cases. Nor does the case study provide the necessary information to confidently explain why the behavior one has observed has occurred. Thus the case study researcher must be careful not to assume that other cases are similar or that the information gathered in this case can be used to explain behavior in this and other cases.

In summary, each of these approaches allows researchers to describe what exists. However, if researchers want to go beyond description and explain why something happened or predict future outcomes, other methods of research and analysis are more appropriate.

Methods Used to Predict

Another goal of the research scientist is to accurately predict. When this is the goal, a researcher will often collect information about two variables and then determine the relationship between the variables. Is there a relationship between a husband's expression of contempt for his wife (observed in conflict interaction) and the number of visits wives make to the doctor for health problems? The two variables in this case would be the number of times husbands expressed contempt toward their wives in conflict discussions and the number of visits wives made to see their doctor. Or is there a relationship between a husband's marital satisfaction level and a wife's marital satisfaction level? Here the two variables studied would be both husbands' and wives' satisfaction levels. To answer questions about relationships between variables, the researcher must collect data concerning each variable and then analyze this data. The analysis usually involves a correlation coefficient. This is a number that ranges from +1.00 to -1.00 and is used to depict the relationship between the two variables. This number is called the correlation coefficient.

If a researcher wanted to study the relationship between husbands' marital satisfaction levels and wives' marital satisfaction levels, the researcher would need to assess both the husband's and wife's satisfaction levels in many marriages. An assessment device would be used to determine each partner's level of satisfaction, perhaps ranging from a score of six, indicating extremely satisfied, to a one, indicating extremely dissatisfied. If you found that husbands who were extremely satisfied with their marriage had partners who were also extremely satisfied and conversely, husbands who were extremely dissatisfied with their marriage also had partners who were extremely dissatisfied, then the two variables (husbands' satisfaction and wives' satisfaction) are varying together. As one variable (husbands' satisfaction) goes up, the other variable (wives' satisfaction) goes up. In this case, there is a positive (+) relationship between these two variables and the correlation coefficient would be +1.00. A correlation coefficient that is close to +1.00 is very powerful, meaning that the researcher can be quite confident in predicting that if one variable is high the other will also be high and conversely, if one variable is low the other will also be low.

If, however, the correlational coefficient were close to -1.00, there would still be a great deal of power to predict. However, what the researcher would predict in this case is quite different; now the variables are inversely related. This means that if one partner's level of satisfaction is high, the other partner's level of satisfaction is likely to be low. But what if the correlation coefficient is 0 or close to 0. What would this mean? This means that for the couples for whom you have data, there are no tendencies that allow the

researcher to predict with any degree of certainty one variable from knowing about the other. For example, for all husbands who experience a high
level of marital satisfaction, their partners could have a satisfaction level that
is high, low, or somewhere in-between. It's simply impossible to predict from
the data. Therefore, the closer the correlational coefficient is to 1.00, be it
+1.00 or -1.00, the greater the power to predict one variable from knowing
the other variable. The closer the correlational coefficient is to 0, the less
power there is to predict one variable from the other variable.

When researchers conduct studies like this, to what degree can they predict one partner's level of satisfaction/dissatisfaction from knowing the other
partner's level of satisfaction/dissatisfaction? Will partners report the same
satisfaction level (high satisfaction/high satisfaction), (moderately satis-
fied/moderately satisfied), (moderately dissatisfied/moderately dissatisfied)
(low satisfaction/low satisfaction)? If satisfaction levels match, then the correlation coefficient will be close to + 1.00. Or will there be an inverse correlation with partners who have high levels of satisfaction having partners with
low levels of satisfaction (high/low)—a correlation coefficient that would be
close to -1.00? Olson and Olson (2000) recently reported the findings of a
study very similar to this example. The correlation coefficient between these
two variables (satisfaction levels reported by husbands and their wives) was
+ .56. This means that there is a tendency for partners to report similar satisfaction levels; however, the tendency is not so great that the researcher can
predict with great certainty how any one couple responded in regard to satisfaction level. The correlation coefficient would need to be closer to 1.00 for
great certainty. A correlation coefficient of +.56 leaves some room for variability. Even with this positive correlation, Olson and Olson (2000) conclude: "in many married couples, one person is much happier than their
partner" (p. 5).

Why is there not even more similarity in husband/wife marital satisfaction
levels? Why is it that in some marriages, one partner reports a higher level
of satisfaction than the other partner? Correlation research does not tell us
why the reported relationship between the two variables exists. Nor does it
indicate that one variable is responsible for or causes the other variable. It
would be easy to speculate about why there is not more similarity in satisfaction levels, but research scientists are not usually interested in speculation
unless this speculation is followed by research that attempts to answer spec-
ulative questions. Therefore, correlation studies often lead to further research
in an attempt to understand cause. Sometimes these follow-up studies are
surveys asking "why"-type questions. Yet one should remain cautious when
interviewing or surveying family members about why something has happened or why someone feels as they do. Ask a divorcing couple what went
wrong in the marriage or why they are divorcing and you may get one

answer from the wife and another from the husband. It is best to see such responses as the individual's present perception of why something has happened or why he or she feels as he or she does. Thus, the findings are descriptive of their perceptions and not necessarily accurate explanations for why something has occurred. Their perceptions may be correct, but they may also be incorrect, biased, or oversimplified. Therefore, whenever possible, investigators should use other methods of research when attempting to explain the cause of behavior.

Methods Used to Explain

Since descriptive studies and correlational studies do not allow researchers to be confident about cause, researchers need a more powerful approach to use when attempting to make statements about cause and effect. An investigator may conduct correlational research that shows that the more violence individuals have observed, the greater the likelihood that these individuals will engage in aggressive acts. This positive correlation between observed violence and aggression does not, however, indicate that observing violence actually causes aggression. The increased violence may have been due to other factors that were present when the violence occurred, such as the amount of alcohol ingested, the intelligence level of the individuals involved, the degree of frustration the individuals were experiencing, or the nature of their home backgrounds. You may even interview or survey inmates who are in prison for committing violent crimes. These inmates may tell you that they believe that observing violence led to their violent behavior. However, this does not mean that what these inmates believe is necessarily the case since they too may be searching for explanations to explain their behavior. In order to find a direct causative link between one variable (e.g., violence observed) and another variable (e.g., actual aggressive behavior), researchers conduct experiments.

The Experiment. An experiment is a study that takes place in a highly controlled environment where the experimenter can manipulate a variable, control for extraneous variables, and observe a response variable. In experiments, subjects are usually randomly assigned to different groups. Random assignment is important because it controls for differences in the group members, differences such as intelligence, interests, personality tendencies, and a whole host of other variables. These variables are referred to as extraneous variables because they have nothing to do with the experiment itself; yet these variables can influence the findings of the experiment if they are not controlled for through random assignment. If these variables were not controlled for or equalized throughout the different groups prior to the study, any one of them might influence the outcome of the study. In an experiment, it is important that the groups are equated on all differences except the one difference you are studying. This equalizing of groups before the experiment makes it unlikely that later observed differences in behavior are due to some preexisting differences. In a study to determine if observing violence leads to aggressive behavior, one of the randomly assigned groups would see a violent film and the other a nonviolent film. Thus the experimenter is manipulating a variable, in this case the type of film seen. The variable that is manipulated by the experimenter is called the independent variable. Then, after randomly assigning subjects to groups and manipulating the independent variable, the researcher observes the behavior being studied, in this case the amount of aggressive behavior subjects exhibit. Usually, if children are the subjects, the experimenter observes their behavior in a playroom situation; if adults are being studied, they may be told that pressing a button will deliver a shock to a person in the next room. The observed behavior in an experiment is called the dependent variable. Thus, in this example, you have the necessary ingredients for a controlled experiment: a highly controlled situation, the control of extraneous variables through random assignment, the manipulation of an independent variable, and the observation of the dependent or response variable. The advantage of the experiment lies in the amount of control over conditions and variables, making it possible for the researcher to be more confident about cause and effect.

Findings from experiments like the one above show that children exposed to an aggressive model are more likely to engage in aggressive behavior in a playroom situation than are children not exposed to such a model (Bandura & Walters, 1963); that angry college students are more likely to behave aggressively if they have seen a violent rather than a nonviolent film (Berkowitz & Geen, 1966); that delinquent boys seeing films depicting aggression behave in more aggressive ways (attacking other boys) than do delinquents viewing nonaggressive films (Parke, Berkowitz, Leyens, West, & Sebastian, 1977). These studies and others like them point to a causative link between watching violent programming and aggressive behavior. After reviewing this experimental research, one authority (Burger, 2000) writes: "In almost all cases, researchers find the participants who watched the violent program act more aggressively than those who saw the nonviolent program" (p. 434). Certainly there are enough studies like this to concern many parents. And our culture continues to find new ways to introduce children to violence. Many of the most popular video games for boys involve violence as a part of the game. However, a word of caution is in order about these experimental studies. The follow-up on subjects is usually only short-term and the opportunities to aggress are often artificial (pressing a button that will supposedly shock someone in the next room). These deficiencies have led some to wonder how much credence should be given to these studies and whether they tell us very much about real-life aggression. Certainly one should realize that aggression has many causes, not just one cause; however, findings suggesting any cause should be taken seriously.

It is important that researchers, when possible, conduct experimental research. This type of research is a powerful tool, allowing for more confident statements about cause and effect. Another example involving a topic of interest to many parents–the effects of exposure to pornographic material–has also been studied utilizing the experiment. With pornographic Internet sites easily accessible and many premium cable packages providing pornographic channels, many parents believe they have reason for concern. In these experimental studies, the research subjects are usually college students who have been told that exposure to pornographic material might be a part of the study. Thus, after being given this information and then agreeing to participate, they are more likely to complete the study and not be surprised by the graphic material. Students are then randomly assigned to a pornographic exposure group or to a non-pornographic exposure group. The pornographic exposure group usually sees a man force himself upon a female victim. First she fights him off, kicking and screaming; then she becomes sexually aroused, and finally in the end, she is depicted as enjoying the experience. This is often the theme of such material. These films usually ignore the horrific accounts of women who have experienced such attacks. Often several of these films are shown to the pornographic exposure group over several different days. The non-pornographic group sees the same number of films over the same number of days, but the film content is nonsexual. Random assignment is used to control for extraneous variables and the two types of films serve as the independent variable. The observed/dependent variables that the experimenter usually measures in these types of studies are aggressive behaviors, attitudes toward women, or perceptions of brutality. Comparing subjects in both groups after exposure to the different film types has shown that subjects in the pornographic group are more accepting of aggression and violence against women (Malamuth & Check, 1981), are more likely to administer harsher punishment to women but not men in a teaching situation (Donnerstein, 1980), and are more likely to be unsympathetic toward rape victims (Linz et.al, 1988, 1989). According to David Myers, (1993) a social psychologist who writes about this research, "viewing such fictional scenes of a man overpowering and arousing a women can (1) distort one's perception of how women actually respond to sexual coercion and (2) increase men's aggressiveness against women, at least in laboratory settings" (p. 442).

There are both advantages and disadvantages to the experimental method. The greatest advantage or strength is that these studies can help establish cause–that one variable can indeed cause another. However, these studies also have their limitations. Since they are conducted in a highly controlled laboratory setting, the findings may not be applicable to the real world. Also, there are some questions that controlled experiments cannot answer because some variables cannot be manipulated as independent variables (e.g., sex, birth order, most personality characteristics) and in other instances manipulating variables would be highly unethical. Suppose a researcher was interested in how husbands would respond to their wives' informing them that they want a divorce. How would you study this using the experiment? First the experimenter would need to identify a group of wives and then randomly assign some wives to a group that is told to inform their husbands that they want a divorce. The other group of wives might be told to inform their husbands that they want to go out to a fancy restaurant. Then the experimenter would observe how husbands respond to the requests of their wives. Would this be ethical? Certainly not! Most, if not all the wives who were asked to inform their husbands they wanted a divorce would object and the researcher would be chastised for manipulating subjects in an unethical manner. Therefore, if the researcher is to study this question, some descriptive approach is likely to be used. Thus, many questions of interest to the family scientist can only be studied using descriptive and correlational methods of research since it would be unethical or impossible to manipulate many of the variables a researcher might find interesting.

OBSERVATIONS OF MARRIAGE AND FAMILY THERAPISTS

Both theorists and researchers have contributed to the field of family science. Yet there is a third group of professionals who are interested in marriage, family, and relationship issues. These are therapists who see their main role as helping couples and families establish and maintain healthy relationships. These therapists are on the front line in the effort to help couples and families live more fulfilling lives. Some of these professionals have developed theories concerning relationship issues and a few have conducted research on the effectiveness of their models. Many of them have written with great clarity and insight about the therapeutic process and their attempt to bring about change in couple and family relationships. Their insights too are valuable and some will be included in later chapters.

As a student beginning your study of marriage, family, and intimate relationships, you embark on a journey that will introduce you to many of the ideas and findings of theorists, researchers, and therapists in the exciting field of family science. I hope you will find this journey fascinating and informative; it is about something most individuals care deeply about—their marriages, their families, and their intimate relationships.

IMPORTANT TERMS AND CONCEPTS

Family science
Psychoanalytic theory
Freud's intrapsychic theory
Erikson's psychosocial theory
Object relations theory
Skinner's behavioral theory
reinforcement
punishment
Bandura's social learning theory
vicarious learning
Roger's humanistic theory
actualizing tendency
organismic valuing process
unconditional positive regard
empathy
biological approaches to
    understanding
Family systems theory
wholeness
homeostasis
feedback
positive/amplifying feedback
negative/attenuating feedback

input/output
subsystems
boundaries
boundary permeability
linear causality
circular causality
equifinality
equipotentiality
process approach
hypothesis
research goals of scientists
methods used to accurately describe
survey
naturalistic observation
case study
methods used to predict
correlation
correlational coefficient
methods used to determine cause
the experiment
independent variable
dependent variable

SUGGESTED READING

Aiken, L. R. (2000). *Personality: Theories, research, and applications.* Springfield, IL: Charles C Thomas.

Shaughnessy, J. J., & Zechmeister, E. B. (1994). *Research methods in psychology* (3rd ed.). New York: McGraw-Hill.

Chapter 3

FAMILY RULES, STRUCTURE,
AND DEVELOPMENT

In the family, rules and structure are intertwined. The purpose of rules is to regulate behavior and family functioning. As rules fulfill this purpose, a predictable pattern of behavior and interaction develops. Once this predictability occurs, the family is organized around their rules–the family has an organizational structure. Family members sense who is in charge and what roles and behaviors are expected of each family member. As families organize around their rules family life becomes more predictable and less chaotic. Thus rules are necessary in order to produce the predictable patterns of behavior that determines a family's organizational structure.

Think for a moment about how the rules evolved in your family. Did you have planning and negotiation sessions? Did you have lengthy discussions about who would manage the money and who would cook the meals? Did you have a contract or prenuptial agreement specifying each partner's duties and obligations? Of course, each couple and family is different and there is not one way to establish rules and family structure. But there are powerful forces at work that influence the decisions a couple makes as they develop the rules that determine their family's structure.

FAMILY RULES AND STRUCTURE

The Origin of Rules

There are a number of variables that influence a family's developing rule structure. Three influences are especially powerful—culture, family of origin, and personality.

Cultural Influences

The cultures partners have experienced will have a powerful influence on their rules. If partners share cultural backgrounds, then some of their beliefs will be similar and the process of establishing rules will be easier. In some cultures, parents choose their son or daughter's partner to achieve a proper match. Although in these cultures the son or daughter has no choice in the mate selection process, partners get a mate from the same cultural background, thus reducing some cultural differences that might make establishing initial rules difficult. If partners come from different cultures, their feelings and perceptions concerning roles, religion, child-rearing, education, and even marriage itself may be very different. Can love conquer cultural differences? Books and movies often focus on this theme—can partners make it in marriage when their backgrounds are very different? Even if partners are from the same culture, some cultural background differences will still exist and play an important role in determining what rules evolve; however, their similar cultural backgrounds will likely allow them to agree on many things, making the rule establishment stage less difficult.

- If you have established your own family, were there cultural differences that made rule development difficult?

Family of Origin Influences

No two families, even from the same culture, are exactly alike. Therefore, another powerful influence affecting couples as they establish their rules is each partner's family of origin. Family therapists often believe that families transmit ways of relating, feeling, and coping from one generation to another. Thus, as two partners come together to establish their family structure they have important memories of how things were done in their family of origin. If childhood memories are positive, partners may want to replicate that "at home" feeling as they begin the rule creation process. If the "at home" feeling of each partner includes different memories, then conflicts may arise concerning which "at home" feeling should prevail. It may be that even the choice of a partner is influenced somewhat by the unconscious desire to marry someone who makes us feel safe in the same way our family of origin made us feel safe.

However, even if childhood memories are mostly positive, individuals usually have experienced enough frustration in their family of origin to desire some changes when establishing their new family. For example, if in one's family of origin, family members did not express positive emotions openly, individuals may strive to be more emotionally expressive in their new family. If memories of one's family of origin are mostly negative, then a person may strive to develop healthier rules in his or her own family. However, this is not always as simple as it may seem. Many couples have said that they would never be like their parents, but when the stresses of family life increase, they often find themselves doing the same things that were common in their family of origin. Some patterns are difficult to break even when one wishes to establish new patterns.

The process of transmitting ways of being from one generation to the next is referred to as the generational transmission process. Attitudes, beliefs, styles of relating, methods of expressing intimacy, ways of coping with stress, and ways of communicating are often thought to be a part of this generational transmission process. This process may pass along behavioral patterns that are healthy or unhealthy, affecting such things as the quality of marriage, loving or abusive behavior, and even mental health and illness (Burr, Day, & Bahr, 1993).

- If you have established your own family, were there family of origin factors that influenced the rules you created? Did you attempt to model after your family of origin? Were there instances where you set out to be different?

Personality Influences

As partners begin establishing their rules, they usually discover that they have different opinions and preferences. These differences are often due to basic differences in personality. Both partner's personalities have been shaped by heredity and environmental influences that are deeply ingrained and usually difficult to change. When partners come together to establish their rules, they often run head-on into these differences. Although research indicates that individuals marry partners whose needs and personalities are similar, there are always enough differences to make marriage challenging. Perhaps the partners have one or two areas where they differ. If these differences are important to them, then these areas may constantly involve conflict, making it seem that they are very different when in reality, their similarities far outweigh their differences. Dan Wile (1988), an author and marriage therapist, believes that when individuals choose a marriage partner, they are choosing a set of problems that they will grapple with for as long as they are married. The differences that create these problems are so much a part of each individual's personality that each is unwilling or unable to change. Gottman (Gottman & Silver, 1999) has found that 69 percent of the problems that couples grapple with are perpetual problems–problems that the couple will not be able to completely resolve. He believes that these perpetual problems are often rooted in personality differences or are due to needs that are basic to each partner's identity; these differences in personality and needs will be difficult to change. Gottman (1994) also has found that when partners are mismatched in their preferred conflict management styles, this mismatch may also put the marriage at risk. Such mismatches may also be rooted in basic personality differences. So as couples begin to hammer out the rules that will govern their relationship, they should expect some tension and disagreement.

- If you have established your own family, how did personality differences between you and your partner influence rule development? When differences of opinion occurred, how did you manage conflict? Did one partner demand power over the process or was power shared? Was their give and take that allowed for negotiation?

Is There an Ideal Family Structure?

Just as there are no two personalities exactly alike, there are no two families with exactly the same rules and structure. Healthy families come in many forms, as do unhealthy families. However, Nichols (1999) notes that healthy families are similar in three ways in regard to their structure. They have clear boundaries, a hierarchal organization, and a certain degree of flexibility.

Clear Boundaries

Boundaries in families serve several purposes. Clear boundaries protect individual family members from unhealthy infringement by others. This allows family members to be different; dad likes sports, mom likes chatting on the Internet, Marge likes reading, and Tim likes playing with his action figures. They all respect each other's differences without believing that they must all be alike. When conflict over differences occurs, they attempt to negotiate in a way that respects individuality. Thus there is respect for each individual's identity and the boundaries this identity establishes.

Clear boundaries also serve to establish lines between subsystems. Partners work together as the parental subsystem to rear their children. Therefore, it is the parents' responsibility to cooperate as they implement fair rules regarding the children's behavior. The partners also make up the marital subsystem, a subsystem that cooperates to establish and maintain the health of the marriage. Thus, the partners protect their marriage from infringements that lead to the deterioration of their relationship as a couple.

A family also must create clear boundaries between their family system and forces outside the system. Some outside influences are defined as consistent with the family's values and goals and the family allows these influences to penetrate the system; other influences are defined as inconsistent with the family's values and goals and the family protects itself from these influences. For example, there are some internet sites and TV programs that may be off limits to the children. The point is that boundaries should be clear and family members should know what the rules are in relation to boundary infringement.

Hierarchial Organization

When the first child is born, a three-person system is created. Now the parents form an alliance for the purpose of rearing their child. As the child matures, the question becomes—how much input should the child have in dictating family rules concerning such things as bedtime, TV time, and how much attention the child is to receive. It is best if parents agree on healthy child-rearing goals and how these goals are to be achieved. They need to speak with one voice as they work together as the parental subsystem, disciplining and teaching their children.

Therefore it is the parents' responsibility to establish reasonable rules for their children and expect the children to abide by these rules. Nichols (1999) states that in healthy families "there is an unambiguous hierarchy of power, with leadership in the hands of the parents, who form a united coalition" (p.

102). Some parents have the mistaken idea that their young children should have input in all decision making. Therefore, the parents ask; "Is it okay if mommy and daddy go out tonight and get a babysitter for you guys?" Or they ask, "Don't you want to go to bed now?" These parents often wonder why their home life is so chaotic and why they have such a hard time getting their children to cooperate. What they need to understand is that it is the parents' responsibility, working together in an alliance as the parental subsystem, to establish reasonable rules. Parents need to communicate these rules to their children—"every other week your mother and I go out together for the evening and you stay with a babysitter" or "it's 8:30, time for you to start getting ready for your bedtime at 9:00 o'clock." Children expect their parents to be the authorities, but if parents give up this authority to their young children, the children will attempt to impose their will and family life will become more chaotic. When the parental subsystem establishes and enforces reasonable and clear rules, this enhances the likelihood of healthy functioning. Of course, as children mature, their ideas and concerns need to be heard and seriously considered so that rules can be modified to become more consistent with the child's maturing developmental needs.

Just as parents should be concerned about creating a healthy hierarchial organization that strengthens the parental alliance, they should also be aware of breakdowns in organizational structure that lead to unhealthy alliances. Unhealthy alliances often develop when marriage partners have irresolvable conflicts or unmet needs. In an attempt to get one's way or satisfy an unmet need, one partner creates an alliance with a child that crosses over generational boundaries. The following examples illustrates how unhealthy alliances might develop.

- A mother disagrees with her husband about family rules and is critical of her husband in front of the children. While the husband is at work, she and the children create their own rules. Such an alliance undermines the parental subsystem and puts the children in an awkward position with their father. And the husband is upset with his wife for disregarding his authority, thus creating more spousal tension.
- A mother, desperate for friendship, tells her teenage daughter that they should be best friends and share the details of their lives. Thus the mother weakens an important boundary between mother and daughter, creating confusion for the daughter and making it less likely that the mother will make age appropriate friends.
- A father and daughter become especially close, enjoying long talks and activities together. Since the father's relationship with his wife is conflicted, they no longer talk and do things together. Thus a need that should be met in the spousal dyad is transferred to the father-daughter

relationship, creating a confusing situation for the daughter and resentment on the part of the mother.

- A father is an alcoholic and his twelve-year-old daughter is expected to take care of him during his bouts with the bottle. Thus she is expected to play the role of parent to her father. This forces the daughter into an unfair and unhealthy role with the father. Parents have a responsibility to care for their children, not thrust upon them adult roles that are inappropriate.
- A divorced mother is a single parent rearing her young son. The son is expected to be "the little man around the house." Thus the mother creates an alliance with the son, expecting him to fulfill an inappropriate and unhealthy role.

In each of these situations, important boundaries have been crossed, leaving the family and individuals in the family at risk. These cross-generational alliances do not deal with conflict and unmet needs in a healthy way and they impede the healthy development of the children involved.

Flexibility

Another characteristic of healthy rule structure in families is flexibility. As parents struggle to create clear boundaries and a healthy hierarchal organization, they must also have the ability to adapt. At times, boundaries and rules must be readjusted to meet the demands of special situations. For example, if a parent is hospitalized, an older child may need to carry out some functions of the sick parent until that parent recovers or other arrangements can be worked out. Also, normal development makes the family a changing, dynamic system—a system that must accommodate to the developmental changes of the family life cycle. Just when the rules seem to be worked out, things change. The children get older and the rules that were previously appropriate now become obsolete. Parents still need to be in charge, but rules may need to be modified to fit the new developmental needs of family members. Parents who cannot make these necessary modifications usually find themselves in trouble, especially when their children are adolescents. Parents should not see the rules and structure in the family as set in concrete; changes may even be needed when parents would prefer that things stay the same. The real challenge of parenthood requires a delicate kind of knowing, knowing when to be flexible, when to stand firm, and when and how to allow developing children to take part in the rule changing process.

- In your family of origin, were there clear boundaries, a proper hierarchial organization, and a healthy flexibility? Were there unhealthy alliances that made healthy adjustment difficult? If you have set up your own family system, have you struggled with any of these issues?

Healthy and Unhealthy Rules

Healthy families have rules that provide clear boundaries, exhibit a hierarchial organization that puts parents in charge of leadership functions, and allow for flexibility. Yet healthy rules also serve other functions. According to Virginia Satir (1964), healthy rules will support five freedoms, freedoms that everyone should enjoy. These include: (1) the freedom to perceive what one perceives (to have his/her own perceptions), (2) the freedom to think one's own thoughts, (3) the freedom to feel one's own feelings, (4) the freedom to choose what one desires, and (5) the freedom to develop in ways that are consistent with the actualization or positive development of the self. Of course, when children are young, parents must assume responsibility and make decisions for the child. But as the child matures, gradually the child becomes more autonomous. So, in one sense, parenting is the ability to nurture development while gradually giving up control and decision-making to the maturing child so that s/he comes to have more and more responsibility for decision making in regard to the five freedoms. This nurturing process is not easy. It requires patience, courage, insight, and skills that parents often find elusive. It also requires the establishment of a healthy rule structure.

If the five freedoms are important goals, then some rules are healthy while others are unhealthy. Healthy rules provide nurturing environments where the five freedoms are encouraged. Unhealthy rules discourage growth in regard to these freedoms. Some rules have even been labeled toxic because they attempt to deny the child the right to his/her feelings, thoughts, and perceptions. These rules are often observed in troubled families where children are told how to think, perceive, and feel. The following rule characteristics support and nurture healthy growth in families:

- Healthy rules encourage each person in the family to develop a sense of worth and dignity. For example, some families allow each family member an opportunity to be heard at the appropriate time because everyone's thoughts and feelings are important. Thus healthy families have rules that allow each family member to speak and be heard. Unhealthy families often live by the rule that the parents are to be heard; children have nothing valuable to say and should keep quiet.
- Healthy rules reflect the belief that family love is unconditional and feelings, both positive and negative, are acceptable and can be discussed. If a child hits his brother or sister, the parents may remind the child that

there are rules against hitting and negative consequences for the aggressor, but angry feelings are acceptable and can be openly discussed. And when discipline follows an infraction in the healthy family, parents implement discipline within an atmosphere of love. Unhealthy rules teach that love is conditional, that it will be withdrawn when a child breaks a rule.

- Healthy rules allow family members to be unique and different so that no one must fit the same mold. Although there will be rules that apply to everyone, if all rules dictate exact sameness, this does not allow for the development of individual differences. Unhealthy rules such as—you will take piano lessons because your sister took piano lessons—fail to recognize that children are different and what's best for one may not be best for another.

- Healthy rules generally benefit the entire family, not just one member or one group within the family. Therefore, the rules that are beneficial for the children are beneficial for the adults. Although there may be some rules, like bedtime rules that differ for children and adults, adults too have rules that govern when they go to bed. The difference is in the age-appropriate nature of these rules. Unhealthy families often have rules that imply—do as dad and mom say, not as dad and mom do.

- Healthy rules are realistic and attainable. Rules that violate realistic expectations are especially frustrating for children. Expecting children to do things they are incapable of doing sets them up for failure. Every child cannot be a sports star or make the honor roll; nor can children suppress natural emotions such as sadness and anger. Unhealthy rules demand behaviors that exceed the capabilities of family members.

Blevins (1993) believes that parents should ask certain questions about rules in an attempt to determine if their rules are appropriate.

1. Do rules strengthen relationships, facilitate communication, and encourage cooperation, understanding, and support among family members?
2. Do the rules reflect age-appropriate standards and are rules consistent with each child's developmental level?
3. Do rules allow for a healthy individuality in all family members?
4. Do rules sufficiently protect each person's boundaries?
5. Do the rules allow family members access to their thoughts, feelings, and opinions without pressure to believe as others believe and think as others think?
6. Do the rules help the family achieve healthy goal?

Rules that achieve these goals foster healthy development in family members. Although many factors determine outcome in families, a healthy rule system is among the most important.

- Do you agree with Satir that healthy rules support the five freedoms as the end-goal of development? Did rules in your family of origin support these five freedoms? Were there rules in your family of origin that you thought were unfair and unhealthy?

The Nature and Function of Rules

Family Rules Are Often Implicit

Individuals often think of rules as regulations that are intended to govern behavior and interaction. In most cultures, important regulations are written into law and are formally stated and made public. Even in organizations like businesses and schools, regulations are written down so that employees and students know what behaviors are appropriate and inappropriate. But family theorists make a distinction between regulations and rules. Regulations describe what is supposed to be; rules define what is. When family members are asked about their rules, they often talk about regulations that they expect and hope will guide behavior. It is more difficult for them to talk about rules. Nichols (1999) states, "family rules—what is, not what's supposed to be—are established through trial and error and are generally not carefully thought through. The rules may be products of our own creation, but because they are complex and unspoken, we often become caught in patterns not of our own choosing" (p. 95). Thus, since rules are often unspoken, they are difficult to examine.

Yet families have many rules since many predictable patterns of interaction occur in families. These rules can be envisioned on an implicit-explicit continuum. Explicit rules are known, clear to everyone, and possibly discussed and written down. These rules may be first stated as regulations that family members hope will be followed. If they are followed with regularity, they describe what is; therefore they fit the family theorists' definition of a rule. Less explicit rules may be completely outside awareness, never written down or discussed. Yet because these rules regulate a predictable pattern of behavior, they have a powerful influence on family functioning. A rule regulating where family members sit at the kitchen table for meals may be such a rule. Since this rule evolved without any discussion, family members are not aware of its presence even though they abide by it every day. Some family rules are so implicit that they may not even be consciously recognized, even after the predictable pattern is pointed out to the family. In a family therapy session, it was pointed out that a father and son only talked when the father found something to criticize about his son—his earring, his tattoo, his music, his friends. The father denied that this was the case and resisted any suggestion that his pattern of interaction with his son was rule governed. The son said, "Well I guess we could try to talk, but we don't." Destructive patterns in families are often rule governed; yet the family fails to recognize the rule behind the destructive pattern. Without recognizing the rule, the pattern is difficult to change.

When families experience problems, they often attempt to make their regulations more explicit. The teenager who comes in well after his 11:00 o'clock curfew is told in no uncertain terms never to do it again. After he has done it numerous times, his parents are reduced to screaming and yelling the curfew time as they attempt to lay down the law one more time. When families find that they must spell out their regulations with such fervor, the family is usually in trouble. Burr, Day, and Bahr (1993) state: "Families can only operate when the majority of the beliefs they use to govern themselves are shared, implicit, and affectively comfortable" (p. 223). Shared implies agreement; affectively comfortable means that the rules feel right. Implicit implies that well functioning families do not need to be constantly reminded of the rules or have the rules made explicit. Yet there are times when more explicitness is appropriate. Family life educators often suggest that more explicitness is appropriate during times of transition—for example, when a couple is newly married, when the couple experiences the birth of a child, when a child reaches adolescence, or when a family member dies. At these times, rules may surface, be discussed, and even need to be modified.

> • Do you agree that in families rules should usually be shared, implicit, and affectively comfortable? What were some explicit and implicit rules in your family of origin?

Rules Allow for Accountability

Rules stipulate appropriate and inappropriate behavior and when rules are in place accountability is possible. When rules are established, behavior can be monitored, providing feedback concerning how the family system is functioning. Parents often serve as the primary monitors of behavior, although children may also get in on the monitoring process. Did Dad pick up the children after school? Did the children do their homework before watching TV? Did mom make the appointment with the pediatrician? Families attempt to regulate and monitor a wide variety of activities and behaviors. Therefore, there are many different types of rules that are monitored, each having a specific regulatory function.

Rules Establish Physical and Psychological Boundaries

In families, many different boundaries exist. Some of these relate to physical space. The drawer in daddy's study is off limits to the children as are the gun and wine cabinets. Even chairs and sometimes rooms are set-aside just for certain people or certain activities. The telephone in the adolescent daughter's room may be solely for her use, while a son's video games may be off limits to everyone except him and his friends. Rules about physical space create problems especially if they are unclear or not agreed upon. Do parents have a right to go through an adolescent's room as they attempt to monitor his/her behavior? If so, under what conditions may parents do so and for what purpose? Disagreements and unclear rules about boundaries can become points of contention in families.

Rules also regulate behavior in regard to psychological space. Family members usually learn to be respectful of each other's psychological boundaries. Some topics raise anxiety levels and are off limits for discussion. Children learn what they can and cannot say in front of parents. They may even learn that they can say some things to mom but not to dad. Couples quickly learn their partner's hot button issues and the way these issues need to be addressed, if they can be addressed at all. Thus, there are invisible psychological boundaries that if crossed lead to negative consequences.

Rules Regulate Closeness and Distance

Some rules relate to distance regulation and the cohesion of the family unit. These are rules that regulate how much togetherness/closeness there will be within the family. Do members eat together; attend church, mosque, or synagogue together; watch TV together; or even talk to each other on a regular basis? Is the spousal dyad close or distant? Do partners frequently talk and do things together? Some families cherish closeness, while others rarely come together as a cohesive unit.

Rules Regulate Roles

Some rules relate to roles. Although at times, roles are shared, most families find that if tasks get accomplished on a regular basis, someone must take major responsibility for the task. Who is expected to cook most meals, bathe the children, pay the bills, cut the grass, do the grocery shopping, take the children to the doctor, go to PTA meetings, etc? Rules concerning role responsibility are usually needed for the efficient operation of the family.

Rules Specify Exceptions

In some families, rules are applied rigidly and there are very few exceptions. In other families, many exceptions are allowed. One adolescent states,

"My dad is a dictator and there are almost no exceptions to anything," while another comments, "In our family, if we make a good case, there are allowances made so I would say we are quite flexible." Every family may have a general rule about how allowable exceptions are and whether an exception is even brought up for discussion may depend on the family's general rule regarding exceptions.

Rules Pertain to Implementation and Violation

Rules of implementation specify how rules are to be carried out. Not only is the child to help clean up after dinner, but when washing the dishes, the child is to use a certain kind of detergent, pre-wash before putting things in the dishwasher, and stack plates and other utensils in an appropriate way. If a family member does not carry out assigned duties or does not perform a task appropriately, there may be rules that deal with the violation. These rules spell out consequences, what is to happen when violations occur.

- What a family is like is determined by the family's rules. Recall some rules from your family of origin that relate to the following: physical boundaries, psychological boundaries, closeness and distance, roles, exceptions, implementation, and violation.

Rule Sequences: Dancing in Families

A number of family scientists (Haley, 1976; Burr, Day, & Bahr, 1993) have written about rules sequences. These rule sequences dictate a series of behaviors in a complex pattern. Thus when one thing happens, this triggers a reaction that is followed by another reaction, then another, and so forth. For example, an implicit rule may dictate that when the children fight, mother may yell at them in an attempt to bring peace. When mother's reprimands increase in volume, a second rule may kick in–dad now can enter the fray, not only increasing the volume but also the intensity. This sets off another reaction-the younger child begins to cry. At this point, another rule comes into play; mother can now turn toward dad and scold him for screaming at the children. Dad now has the right to yell at mom, saying he was just trying to help, and after all, she yelled first. Now mom has a right to yell back, dad has a right to leave, mom must try to console the crying child, and the couple has reason to create distance in their relationship for a time. If this is a common pattern, we say that this behavior is rule governed and involves a series of rules implemented in a step-by-step sequence as the couple and family interact. The couple has not discussed the rules in this sequence, nor are they conscious of the sequence, yet this pattern may frequently occur. This particular rule sequence is not very effective in producing what the husband and wife desire, yet they seem unable to change since they understand so little about what is happening. When a sequence occurs that is negative or disabling in terms of family functioning, it is frequently referred to as a vicious cycle.

Not all rule sequences in families are negative and disabling. For example, many families have positive rule sequences that family members enjoy. For example, both the father and mother may have different rules that they use in creating closeness and warmth during the bedtime ritual. The father plays a game, imagining what his young daughter will dream about during the night. The father guesses, then the child guesses. After both have guessed, the father says "sweet dreams my pumpkin," the daughter kisses her father three times on the nose, then they both say together, "don't let the bed bugs bite" as they embrace before the father turns out the light. The mother's sequence may involve reading a story, followed by other behaviors that communicate closeness and warmth. Such sequences produce love and affection and perhaps positive memories that will last a lifetime.

Behaviors that have special meaning for family members and are repeated because of the satisfaction they bring are often called rituals. In a ritual, family members know their role and can predict the sequence of behaviors that characterizes the ritual. Rituals, if handled well, give the family a special identity, create closeness among family members, and provide comfort, predictability, and reassurance. Families frequently develop rituals concerning bedtime, mealtime, vacations, holidays, birthdays, graduations, and marriages. If rituals have been handled well, family members remember them fondly and may want to pass them down to future generations.

Rule sequences are often referred to as dances. Just as the rules that govern dancing dictate that one move follows another, in the family, often one behavior leads to another and to another in predictable sequences creating interactions that are so ingrained that the behavior resembles a dance. In the book, *The Family Crucible* (Napier & Whitaker, 1978), family therapists describe their work with a troubled family. Claudia, the teenage daughter, is engaging in many behaviors that are unacceptable to her parents. After talking with the family about family interactions, the therapists turn to Don, the eleven-year-old son, and ask him to describe the family's dance. The son, without hesitation, aptly describes the dance in the following way:

Well, Claudia will do something, like leave her room an extra-special mess, or leave her books at school, or stay out too late–this was in the days before it got this terrible–and mom will yell at her. And Claudia will sulk off to her room. Then dad will come home, and Claudia will be up in her room, and dad will try to go find out what is wrong with her. Then mom will say something to me about dad taking Claudia's side, or she will just get real quiet. Dad will come downstairs, and then in about a half an hour, Claudia will come down looking weepy, and nobody is speaking to anybody for quite a while. It makes for a wonderful dinner. (p. 17)

It is often difficult for family members to see the rule sequences that operate in their families. Although Don seemed especially perceptive, other family members may be far less perceptive. However, just knowing that these sequences exist in every family may help family members pay closer attention to them and help them root out destructive, vicious cycles.

- What rule sequences existed in your family of origin? Did these sequences have a positive or negative influence on family functioning? If you have established your own family, what rule sequences are occurring and how do these sequences influence family functioning?

Dances Couples Do

Although all families create rule sequences and perform dances, family scholars have frequently focused attention on dances couples do. Couples rarely talk about these patterns and may only vaguely be aware of their existence. Blevins (1993) identifies and discusses the following dances.

THE PURSUER-DISTANCER DANCE. If one partner seeks to deal with anxiety head-on by talking issues out while the other is uncomfortable with such a direct approach, the partners are likely to engage in the pursuer-distancer dance. The pursuer, who is comfortable with engagement, plunges headfirst into areas of disagreement, while the distancer, sensitive to anxiety-laden issues, makes a hasty retreat. This retreat may involve turning the head away from the pursuing partner, becoming silent, staring into space, or walking away from the confrontation. Pursuers often want to talk about issues so that barriers do not disturb the closeness that they desire. Distancers find it difficult to deal with emotion-laden issues and to talk about thoughts and feelings, so they put up barriers that their partners seek to tear down. Thus one partner pursues and the other withdraws. There needs to be some degree of flexibility in a relationship so that pursuers can back off when this is appropriate and distancers can draw close when this is needed. Couples need to find a comfortable way to handle issues so that the pursuer is not overbearing and the distancer is not severely threatened. If this dance is inflexible and rigid and no comfortable compromise can be found, the dance itself may become an irritant in the relationship. This is such a common pattern in relationships that it will be discussed further in later chapters.

THE DRIFTING COUPLE DANCE. Partners often drift apart due to a lack of similar interests and an inability to resolve conflict. These couples go their separate ways, rarely doing things together such as watching TV, going to a movie, or planning activities together. When they are together, there is little joy in the relationship. When the newness of their relationship wore off, these partners were left with many disagreements; yet they found the emotional intensity of their arguments so overwhelming that they became remote and disengaged. They live separate lives, without sharing much of themselves with each other. Perhaps they have a few interests that allow them to occasionally connect, such as their children or their work but over time this interaction becomes superficial. They rarely talk about their relationship or touch each other in affectionate ways. Their life together becomes quite predictable as they follow the same ritualized routine each day. Their marriage is adrift without much hope of finding a new course. Since they never address their problems and differences, the flow of their unhappy relationship remains the same and they are unable to get out of their rut and alter the dance.

THE CONFLICTUAL COUPLE DANCE. Just as the drifting couple avoids conflict, the conflictual couple uses conflict to help them deal with issues of closeness and distance. At times of uncomfortable closeness, they will find an issue to fight and bicker about; this allows them to disentangle from each other. After conflict, they both retreat perhaps into an icy silence. Over time, they calm down and one or both partners experience anxiety over their distance, wanting to repair any damage through closeness. They now come together, perhaps even using a previous disagreement as a reason to kiss and make up, drawing close once again. As in most dances, this cycle is repeated in the marriage with each spouse having very little knowledge of the pattern or why it is used.

THE CIRCULAR DANCE. Couples who engage in the circular dance connect with each other emotionally and intellectually, but they rarely resolve issues. Rather than locking horns like the conflictual couple, they use rationality to circle the wagon. If a wife brings up a grievance, the husband explains his point of view. They argue their positions in a rational way, saying virtually the same thing over and over again. They may even enjoy the debate, knowing exactly the position their partner will take since they have been over this ground many times before. Often they agree to disagree but continue to argue from time to time over the same issue. Another variation on this dance is for one partner to eventually say, "Oh, you're right, you're always right, you don't care what I think." On hearing this, the partner draws closer, trying to convince the partner of true caring. But the issue is never resolved, although for a time, caring is exhibited and closeness is regulated. This circular dance seems to keep the couple somewhat connected and helps them process some of their anxiety.

THE OVERFUNCTION-UNDERFUNCTION DANCE. The overfunction-underfunction dance relates to household tasks. As partners live together, they take on different roles in regard to chores. For example, wives often complain that their husbands don't do enough around the house. This complaint often emerges after the birth of the first child. If the husband seldom helps, the wife may begin to overfunction, taking on more and more of the childcare and household responsibilities. Of course, her overfunctioning allows her husband to underfunction and as long as he underfunctions, his wife feels she must overfunction. Although the wife blames her husband for being lazy, they are both responsible for this destructive dance. As long as they avoid coming together and agreeing on a fair distribution of duties, this dance continues to be a thorn in their relationship.

THE NATURE AND FUNCTION OF DESTRUCTIVE DANCES. Blevins (1993) makes several points about the nature of destructive dances. These dances usually help control some anxiety in the relationship. In this way, they are somewhat like the neurotic paradox. Neurotics experience high levels of anxiety, so to reduce this anxiety, they engage in behaviors such as obsessive cleaning or excessive work. This does temporarily reduce some of the anxiety but as long as they reduce anxiety, only in this way they continue to engage in behaviors that are thought of as neurotic and they fail to address the real source of the problem. As couples attempt to regulate anxiety in their relationship, they learn to do so by engaging in dances. Although these dances do protect couples from some anxiety, they can be destructive because they prevent couples from dealing with anxiety arousing issues in more healthy ways. In relationship dances, each partner stimulates and reinforces the behavior of the other. For example, the wife's overfunctioning sets the stage for the husband's underfunctioning. As she overfunctions, she reinforces his underfunctioning. Conversely, the husband's underfunctioning sets the stage for his wife's overfunctioning. As he underfunctions, his wife's overfunctioning is reinforced. It takes two to dance. Either partner can influence a dance. However, if one partner changes and behaves counter to the expected behavior, this is likely to result in a countermove by the other partner. These changes and countermoves may not always lead to a desired outcome, yet they always change the nature of the dance.

- In your relationship with your spouse or partner, what dances occur and what purpose do these dances serve? Would there be a more effective way for you to deal with relationship issues?

In summary, rules and rule sequences often just develop in families over time, without much thought or discussion and without family members consciously realizing what is occurring. At other times, rules may develop on the spur of the moment, dictated by circumstances. And occasionally, a rule may be painstakingly developed and frequently discussed. These are usually rules that require a great deal of cooperation to implement or involve problem areas for the family, making it necessary to work through the details so everyone is clear and there are no misunderstandings. Rules are so central to family functioning that they permeate every aspect of family life; they will in some way relate to every subsequent chapter in this text.

Two Important Dimensions Influenced by Rules

David Olson (1988) has described two important rule-regulated dimensions that influence family functioning—cohesion and adaptability. Each of these dimensions can be represented along a continuum. The cohesion dimension characterizes the closeness/separateness that exists in the family and the adaptability dimension characterizes the family's flexibility.

Cohesion

Cohesion refers to the forces that connect and hold a relationship together. At one end of the cohesion continuum are families that strive for a great deal of closeness, togetherness, and connection; these families are characterized as "enmeshed." Rules in these families tend to bind members together—they are overinvolved in the emotional lives of each other. Since there is little separateness and individuality allowed in these families, they have a suffocating quality to them. At the other end of the cohesion continuum are families that encourage separateness and individuality. These families are described as "disengaged" since they are loosely organized with few bonds of connection. Rules in these families tend to protect individuality rather than togetherness. The glue that bonds these family members together is weak, allowing family members to come and go without showing much connection and emotional closeness. Olson stresses the importance of a balanced or middle position on this continuum; this balanced position is represented by the words "separated" and "connected." Families in these middle positions tend to find the necessary balance between togetherness and individuality to function more adequately than those at the extreme ends of the continuum. This continuum can be depicted in the following way.

Cohesion

Disengaged ——— Separated ——— Connected ——— Enmeshed

Adaptability

The second dimension that Olson studied was adaptability. At one end of the adaptability continuum are families that are very rigidly organized. In these families, there are many rules that rigidly regulate every aspect of a family's functioning. These rules are difficult to change; thus predictability permeates these families and the word "rigid" is used to describe families at this end of the continuum. At the other end of the adaptability continuum are families that have very little organization. In these families, there is so much flexibility that there is little predictability or pattern to family interaction; family members seem to come and go as they please as if there were no rules that apply to everyone. Olson uses the word "chaotic" to describe these families. Again, Olson generally finds that a balanced position on this dimension, described by the words "structured" and "flexible," tends to characterize families, that function more adequately. In these families there is enough structure to provide reasonable limits but enough flexibility to allow for healthy change. The adaptability continuum can be depicted in the following way.

Adaptability

Chaotic ——————— Flexible ——————— Structured ——————— Rigid

Olson has combined these two dimensions, creating a circumplex or circular model that allows families to be viewed in relation to 16 different conditions. There are four inner conditions that are considered balanced–flexibly separated, flexibly connected, structurally separated, and structurally connected. There are also four conditions at the corners that are considered extreme–chaotically disengaged, chaotically enmeshed, rigidly disengaged, and rigidly enmeshed. The other eight conditions are considered mid–range-chaotically separated, chaotically connected, flexibly enmeshed, structurally enmeshed, rigidly connected, rigidly separated, structurally disengaged, and flexibly disengaged. Olson has devised an assessment instrument to measure family functioning in regard to these two dimensions and the 16 possible conditions. This assessment measure has been used extensively in his research on families. Some findings relating to this model (Olson, 1988; Olson, McCubbin, Barnes, Larsen, Muxen, & Wilson, 1983) are presented below.

1. Families that function at the balanced or innermost positions tend to function more adequately across time than those at the extremes.

2. Families that are balanced may also occasionally operate at the extremes when special circumstances warrant but most of the time, they operate in a moderate manner.

3. Families that operate at the extreme four corner positions tend to be too connected or too disengaged or too rigid or too loosely organized. These families have trouble finding a healthy balance between these extremes.

4. Most families float around somewhat on the circumplex as they experience developmental changes. During the establishment stage of family development, there is some flexibility. As children enter the family, there is a trend toward less change, then again with the coming of adolescence, there is often more flexibility.

5. Families also tend to float around during times of crisis. For example, when a family member dies a family may experience a renewed sense of closeness for a time as they adjust to their loss.

6. Families from different cultures vary in relation to the emphasis they place on togetherness/separateness and stability/change. For example, the Amish may stress high cohesion and be rigid with regard to change. However, these extreme families may function effectively when every family member is in agreement with the family's style. It is when someone in the family, perhaps an adolescent, is uncomfortable with the extreme style that problems arise. Therefore, when assessing a family's style, it is also important to assess each individual member's agreement or disagreement with that style.

Families differ in their desire for closeness and their ability to be flexible. Rules that regulate cohesion and adaptability usually involve things that family members feel strongly about, yet fail to understand in terms of their origin. In his marriage preparation program, Olson helps each partner analyze these dimensions in his and her family of origin, believing that often "in your couple relationship, you either repeat what you learned in your family or you tend to do the opposite" (Olson & Olson, 2000, p. 137).

- In your family of origin how close or separate were family members? Was there a healthy balance represented by the words "separated" or "connected" or was your family extreme as represented by the words "enmeshed" or "disengaged"? Relate your present family situation to the separateness-connected dimension.
- In your family of origin, how adaptable or rigid were family members? Was there a healthy balance represented by the words "structured" or "flexible" or was your family extreme as represented by the words "rigid" or "chaotic"? Relate your present family situation to the adaptability dimension.

Beyond Rules: Family Beliefs and Ideology

Specific rules are usually based on the beliefs and values that are important to family members. For example, if education is valued, rules about homework will be established. If order is a high priority, then rules concerning neatness will likely regulate behavior. If religion is valued, then rules about attending church, synagogue, or mosque will be important. Over time, families develop an ideology, a shared belief system that is central in guiding the family's rules, goals, and way of being. This belief system is made up of the assumptions that the family defines as important and serves as the family's basic guidance system. Some scholars use the term family paradigm when referring to a family's basic belief system.

Stephen Covey (1997) believes that a family's beliefs should be reflected in a family mission statement. He describes this as "a combined, unified expression from all family members of what your family is all about—what it is you really want to do and be—and the principles you choose to govern your family life" (p. 72). He suggests that family members work together to write such a statement and even hang it on the wall in some prominent location. Just as you would not start a journey without a destination in mind, Covey believes you should not start your family journey without a clear vision of what you want your family to be. Since the creation of a family mission statement is a shared effort, it is not one person's document, but it reflects the vision of the entire family. The mission statement serves as a family's compass; it provides direction and guides decision making.

Also Covey suggests that couples develop a mission statement for their marriage. This statement should set forth the guiding principles that shape the course of the couple's relationship. One couple, taking Covey's suggestion to heart, wrote the following mission statement and displayed it prominently in their home.

OUR MARRIAGE
In our marriage
we promise to work together and cooperate in love
rather than be pulled apart by our differences.
We realize that work, children, and other duties
will often come between us
but
we promise never to allow this for long
for
we realize that the foundation of our lives is our loving relationship.
So we pledge to honor our relationship,
Nurture our friendship and sustain our love
Forever

Another family wrote the following family mission statement.

OUR FAMILY
Our family is a place where we will
love, encourage, and nurture each other.
We will teach each other about our similarities and differences
and learn to appreciate and respect both.
We will teach each other about the world outside the family
so that we will be better prepared to meet the challenges of that world.
We know that the journey of life begins in closeness and involves
a gradual separation over time.
When we are close we will attempt to nurture and love
so that when we separate we will feel confident in making our own way.
So be it in our family.

- Write a mission statement that reflects what you want your marriage to be. Remember that such a statement would be a cooperative effort between you and your spouse but putting your ideas on paper will help you think about what is important to you.
- Write a mission statement that reflects what you want your family to be. Remember that such a statement would be a group effort but putting your ideas on paper will help you think about what is important to you.

Of course, most families do not write a mission statement. Families often give very little thought to what they want to be as a family. Instead, the basic beliefs that govern their interactions remain somewhat implicit. Family members may realize that education is important in their family because day-to-day actions support this belief–the trip to the museum, the parents' interest in the child's homework, the friendly chat with the child's teacher, the availability of books in the home, or the father reading and discussing an interesting story with his son or daughter before bedtime. Yet the belief itself may be rarely discussed. Perhaps if families did write a shared mission statement, family members would be more aware of how everyday actions are guided by a philosophy that the family has deemed important.

Different Ideology Systems

Some scholars (Constantine, 1986; Kanter & Lehr, 1975; Burr, Day, & Bahr, 1993) have attempted to describe different family belief systems that govern how families operate. These systems are sometimes called family paradigms. Although no two families have exactly the same governing systems or family paradigms, some families are similar. Because of this similarity, it is possible to describe some common ideological types. Keep in mind that just as rules are often implicit, so too is a family's paradigm. Most families have not given their belief system much thought; they are just the way they are. You might ask family members to describe their ideology or belief system and find that they have trouble doing so since this system is abstract and usually partly below the surface of awareness. Just as rules are best discovered by watching family members interact, paradigms may best be described by an outside observer who is able to watch a family interact over an extended period of time; then the observer may be able to infer the basic beliefs around which the family is organized and governed.

Three family paradigms that have been studied and described are the closed, open, and random paradigms (Constantine, 1986). See if your family of origin closely parallels one of these types.

The Closed Family Paradigm

These families value tradition and a "right" way of doing things. They follow established rules of society, develop traditional family rules, and expect adherence to these rules. Boundaries in these families are well defined and inappropriate behavior is quickly reprimanded. In these families, a child's friends may be closely scrutinized, TV programs closely monitored, and inappropriate websites placed off limits. The use of time in these families has a predictable pattern. They follow the family schedule as closely as possible and any deviation is frowned upon. This closed method of organization is often an attempt to preserve things that were valued in the parents' families of origin. In closed family paradigms, parental authority is important and this leads to an authoritarian, power-oriented system in which there is limited freedom to discuss new ideas and ways of doing things. Members are expected to fall in line because the family's way of doing things is traditional, time-tested, and right.

The Open Family Paradigm

The open family is more democratic in its operating methods. Members value input from each family member and a flexible give and take is encouraged. This family negotiates in order to find consensus and if consensus is not easily reached, family members continue to negotiate since each individual's view is valued. Much tolerance exists just as long as family members don't cause discomfort to others or violate the consensus of the group. Boundaries are less rigid in open families than in closed families, ideas are more freely expressed, schedules are more flexible, and time is less organized and patterned. The theme in these families seems to be—let's work together, find consensus, and encourage the free flow of ideas.

The Random Family Paradigm

The random paradigm is quite different from the open and closed paradigms. In random families, there are very few traditions and prescribed forms of behavior. Family members come and go as they please; there are very few set schedules and rules. Eating and sleeping patterns are left up to each individual and may vary significantly from day to day. In these families, individual freedom is the first priority as members do their own thing, set their own goals, and find their own course. There is very little family connectedness and cohesion; behavior seems to emerge from moment to moment experiencing rather than from family planning. The only rigidity in these families seems to be the insistence that individuality and personal freedom are of highest value. To many observers, the random family appears chaotic since there is so little predictability and cohesive activity.

What happens when families organized around these different paradigms confront problems and experience stress? Constantine (1986) believes that under stress, each family tries harder to implement its belief system and rules. As they try harder, they exaggerate their character. This tendency for families to rely on an exaggeration of their own paradigm during times of stress has been called the exaggeration principle. The closed family in times of stress reinforces its beliefs in tradition and authority. It lays down the law one more time, perhaps this time with more force and emotional intensity. Boundaries to the outside world become even more rigid as the family draws closer together to stave off the crisis. Open families, when exaggerating the nature of their character, try harder as they gather more information and again attempt to reason things through in order to reach a consensus. They become more frustrated when their way of management continues to fail, but having no back-up system, they continue their attempt to reason things out. As random families face crisis, they become even more chaotic. They continue to rely on creativity and individuality in hopes of finding a solution, often becoming more separate and isolated.

- What type of paradigm did your family of origin most closely resemble? Did you ever observe the exaggeration principle at work in your family? How might families learn new and more effective ways to deal with stress?

The Importance of Early Understandings

When partners marry, they begin the process of establishing the rules and understandings that will govern their relationship. During the courtship period, couples often talk about how they want things to be in their family, but it is not until they begin living together that they get to experience firsthand the joys and difficulties of meshing two different belief systems in a mutually satisfying way. Some couples say their agreements just happened, evolving without much discussion, while others say their rules were the result of long discussions. Regardless of how rules develop, these understandings are important–these are the rules that will shape the couple's relationship. Lyman Wynne (1984), one of the early pioneers in the family systems movement, developed a principle that reflects the importance of these early understandings. This principle, known as the epigenesis principle, states that what is done in the early stages of a relationship influences what can be and is done in later stages of the relationship. For example, if the husband establishes the position of authority early on in the relationship and makes most decisions with minimal input from others, this repetitive behavior establishes a rule that will influence future decision-making. However, if a couple begins consulting about most decisions and compromising when differences exist, then this pattern is likely to influence later decision making. Just think about all of the understandings and rules that develop in families. These rules govern every aspect of family life. If the epigenesis principle holds true, these initial understandings will become the foundation of the family's structure and will be somewhat resistant to change.

Why are the established patterns so difficult to change? Early in the family systems movement, it was recognized that forces within the system often oppose change in order to preserve the status quo. This concept has been referred to as morphostasis. This emphasis on preserving the status quo suggests that the form of a family system soon becomes set and that there is a tendency for the family to maintain its set internal environment. Haley (1964) referred to this as the "first law of human relationships"–when one family member pushes for change, another responds in a way that seeks to limit change. This can often be seen when children or adolescents push for change by violating rules or complaining about how unfair things are, only to be told in no uncertain terms that this is the way it is in "our family."

Burr, Day, and Bahr (1993) suggest three reasons why forces within the family resist change. First, the understandings around which families organize their lives are very important to certain members of the family; these understandings have significant meaning and are associated with deeply felt emotions. Perhaps this is why it has been difficult for some males to give up some of their decision making power and participate more equally in household responsibilities. If early childhood experiences have left the impression that males should have final authority in decision making and only limited responsibility for household tasks, then any deviation from this does not reproduce that "at home" feeling that is so important to comfort and well-being. And there are many things that relate to "home" about which we feel strongly. It's as if our growing up experience has left deep marks on our psyche, affecting how we think things should be done when we establish our family.

Another reason change is difficult is because many of the beliefs and feelings that we bring to the establishment stage of marriage are rooted in the unconscious. The partners may not know why they feel and behave as they do. Nor do they easily see their attitudes and behavior as extreme; their attitudes and behaviors are those of all responsible partners and parents. When the reasons for our behavior and strong feelings are rooted in the unconscious, it becomes difficult to examine the things that need to be understood in order to change.

A third reason that rules and established patterns are difficult to change is because a rule becomes a part of a complex web of rules and any attempt to change one rule has broad implications for many other established patterns. If dad must pick up the children after school because of a change in mother's work schedule, this can change many things. Dad does not fix the after school snack like mother did, so the children complain. Dad allows the children to play in their school clothes, which upsets mother. Dad does not get as much work done at home as he did at the office, which upsets dad. Thus, changing one thing can have broad ramifications for many other things, making what may seem like a fairly simple adjustment to the family schedule, a very difficult change to implement.

Burr, Day, and Bahr (1993) recognize how difficult it is to change the established rule structure. They state: "Anyone who thinks couples can go back and restructure the basic aspects of their relationship just does not understand the nature of family systems. A few parts of relationships can be changed later, but a large number of things cannot, and it usually takes a great deal of energy and effort to make even small changes" (p. 192). Perhaps this is why divorce rates are so high. One or both partners would like change, but they realize that restructuring their relationship in significant ways would be extremely difficult.

FAMILY DEVELOPMENT AND CHANGE

Early in the development of family systems theory, the emphasis was on stability–the family system was seen as resistant to change. However, later theorists realized that even though forces resist change, families do change. Change is often gradual, occurring over time and to different inputs. Many things produce change—the birth of a child, a teenager going off to school, your mother-in-law coming to live with you, or your son or daughter growing up and needing more freedom. The changes in rules and family structure brought about by life events like these may not come easily, but change does occur because the family system is never completely static. The change that takes place as the system adapts to input from various sources is called morphogensis.

Therefore, both morphostasis and morphogenesis occur in families. The push for change and the resistance to change is inevitable in the family system. A young daughter wants to spend the night at a friend's house even though there will be very little adult supervision; the parents object. The teenager wants full driving privileges at sixteen; the parents think the teenager is not mature enough for such privileges. The wife wants more help with the children from her husband; the husband only half-heartedly agrees. An elderly parent moves in with the family after experiencing health problems; the family struggles to adapt. When rules and patterns change, the family structure is modified. And so it goes in families until a new balance is found, only to be disturbed again by other inputs and demands.

Change Produced by Expected Events

Many things that produce change in families are predictable. These predictable changes are a part of the normal developmental process and are often associated with age-related developmental change. When couples marry, they begin the process of developing the rules and guidelines that will characterize their life together. If they decide to have children, the family system quickly becomes more complex and new guidelines and agreements must to be negotiated as the couple focuses on caring for the new arrival. As other children arrive, more change is inevitable as each new arrival adds another level of complexity. To some extent, expected changes can be planned for and discussed even before these changes occur. Fixing up the spare room as a nursery and taking a course at the hospital on childcare are ways of planning for expected change. However, it is difficult to prepare adequately for some of life's major events even if there is time to prepare. It is usually impossible to realize how tiring it can be caring for an infant, how much time it takes to meet the infant's needs, and how much the new arrival will disrupt the relationship the couple has established together. These realizations usually come through experience. When they occur, new guidelines and rules must be hammered out as the process unfolds. Each new agreement modifies the family structure, as the system becomes more differentiated and complex.

Then as children grow up, expected events produce other changes. Entering school leads to new rules about who picks the children up after school, who helps with homework, and how much time can be spent watching television. The adolescent years bring a push for new agreements and rules because of the increased maturity level of teenagers. When young adults graduate, move away, and struggle with their own independence the family must again redefine itself, finding rules that are appropriate for new circumstances. Then as parents retire, age, move into health care facilities, and eventually die, the remaining spouse must learn again to adjust.

There is often ambivalence associated with some of the expected events that produce change in families. A daughter's marriage may produce both a smile and a sigh; you are happy for the love she has found but saddened by the realization that your relationship with her will never be the same. You may also eagerly anticipate the birth of your first child but worry about the added responsibility associated with that birth. Even in death, there may be ambivalence. You are grief stricken by the loss but relieved that your loved one is no longer suffering.

Years ago when experts were thinking about families, they assumed that families were very similar in terms of the events they experienced. This led to the development of life cycle stages. Carter and McGoldrick (1989) have outlined the stages of the family life cycle. These stages include:

Stage 1: The single young adult
Stage 2: Marriage: The formation of a new marital system
Stage 3: Families with young children
Stage 4: Families with adolescents
Stage 5: Children moving out of the family
Stage 6: Families in later years

Some typical changes are associated with these life cycle stages. Three of these changes will be discussed in the next chapter–the change that occurs when partners marry, the change associated with the birth of the first child, and the change occurring when a child reaches adolescence.

In recent years, attention has focused on the variability which characterizes families: some couples choose not to have children, other marriages break up and partners remarry creating new families, and still others chart a life course that would never have been imagined fifty years ago. With the realization that it is difficult to predict events, scholars began using the term "life course." This term reflects the idea that there are many paths that individuals take as development unfolds; the choices one makes determine the future and create one's unique life course. Although there are still predictable sequences of events along the road (courtship usually precedes living together, birth usually precedes child rearing, sickness and old age usually precedes death), many life-changing and family-changing events are not so predictable.

Change Produced by Unexpected Events

Some events are unexpected and unpredictable. A young child becomes seriously ill at the age of four, causing the family to readjust their schedule and change their priorities. Such an event is unforeseen and unexpected. When this occurs, it sets in motion a number of changes as family members struggle to adjust. The mother and father spend more time at the hospital and less time at work. The other children must take on more responsibilities now that they receive less attention from their parents. Some rules must change, at least temporarily, and some of the usual patterns that have been established must be suspended for a time. Not all unexpected events are major crisis events nor are all unexpected events interpreted as negative. Winning the lottery may be seen as a positive change, yet winning may alter the way a family operates, not only in relation to money but also in other significant ways.

As you look at the following list, evaluate whether the unexpected event described would be significant or insignificant for the family and whether this event would have a negative or positive impact. Think of some changes that might be set in motion within the family as a result of the unexpected event.

- The birth of a mentally challenged child.
- An automobile accident, resulting in injuries to the husband/father requiring several operations and six months of recovery before he is able to resume normal work and functioning.
- A promotion at work that increases the family income by $50,000 but requires moving from a small midwestern town to the suburbs of Chicago.
- The loss of the primary wage earner's job due to a downsizing of the company.
- The father of two children stops paying child support because he is sentenced to jail; the mother must go on welfare.
- A mother goes back to work immediately after her first child is born due to unexpected financial hardship; her mother-in-law is recruited to care for the baby.

- A teenage daughter excels in school and earns a $25,000 scholarship to college.
- A sixteen-year-old son is apprehended for DUI in a stolen car.
- A wife leaves her husband and children, saying she is tired, depressed, and needs her freedom.
- A mother and father experience a religious conversion and start going to church regularly and taking the children.
- A six-year-old son wins an art contest at school and has his art displayed in the school library.
- A nineteen-year-old daughter announces that she is a lesbian and plans to move in with her lover.
- A teenage son has just been diagnosed schizophrenic. The parents are told that this is a major mental disorder with unknown outcome.

As you can see from this list, there are many types of unexpected events. Perhaps you needed more information about a family before deciding how a family might respond to these events. Since each family is different and has a unique structure, families will react to events differently. Some families will cope better than others. Some unexpected events will have a negative impact–the loss of the primary wage earner's job because of a downsizing of the company; others will probably be evaluated positively–a daughter earning a $25,000 scholarship. Yet others may even produce ambivalence. For example, the family with the possibility of significantly increasing the family income by moving to Chicago may be excited about the extra money but despise the thought of moving. If the money is needed but the move is upsetting to family members, an approach-avoidance conflict is inevitable. It is also interesting to note that almost any change, whether expected or unexpected, positive or negative, produces stress. This stress is fed into the family system and reverberates throughout the system as the family adjusts.

Perhaps the above list helps explain why parents sometimes feel blindsided by unexpected events. For example, research tells us that one in one hundred people will be diagnosed with schizophrenia-a major mental disorder. Yet before it happens, you never imagine it could happen in your family. It will always be someone else's child or spouse, not yours. When you add up all the unexpected things that can go wrong, you realize that very few families will remain completely immune to negative, unexpected events. Although prior to their occurrence, these unexpected events were not anticipated.

- What were some unexpected events that affected your family-of-origin? Would you evaluate these events as positive or negative? How did the event(s) influence change in your family of origin? If you have established your own family, what unexpected events have you encountered? How did the event(s) influence change in your family?

Comparing Stages and Transitions

Family scientists find it helpful to distinguish between stages and transitions. A stage is a time of relative stability when change is minimal and family life is calm. A transition is a period of fairly rapid change when the system is being pushed to reorganize in some way. Transitions usually follow times of stability. When a couple marries or starts living together, this is a change that requires adjustments by both partners. Working through this period of change and transition usually brings a period of stability and equilibrium. The couple defines what it means to live together and their relationship has a sense of predictability. If the couple has a child, this change disrupts their previous stability, bringing rapid change that will require new adjustments. As the couple works through the new agreements of this transition, their life becomes somewhat more predictable as they enter a new stage where the child is a central part of the family. Adding a second child will again upset this equilibrium and produce change. In time, the parents adjust to this change and a new predictability develops. The stability and predictability of stages does not necessarily imply health; rather, this stability and predictability mean that the family has adjusted to the way things are and is no longer in transition.

Both transitions and stages characterize family life. Marriage, the birth of children, graduation, children leaving home, and retirement are expected events each family must work into the fabric of life. Some preparation is possible when changes are expected and can be anticipated. Courses, books, and even this book attempt to educate about what marriage is like, what couples can expect when children arrive, and how happy and unhappy couples deal with conflict. This knowledge can help couples and families prepare for the typical transitions of family life, making it more likely that a healthy stability will develop after the transition.

Yet many events that produce transitions are unexpected; they are not a part of the normal developmental flow of life. Unexpected events produce some of the most difficult transitions since they are not anticipated and catch us unprepared. But in time, families usually develop new patterns that redefine their system, leading to less upheaval and more predictability.

WHAT WE LEARN AS LIFE UNFOLDS

Life teaches us many lessons. Often these lessons are learned in the context of the family. How we adapt to life's changing circumstances determines our level of maturity. Judith Viorst (1986), in her book, *Necessary Losses*, explains that in order to mature psychologically, individuals must give up some illusions and impossible expectations. It is in the process of giving up, of losing, that one finds the potential for healthy growth. The beliefs we must give up are closely tied to family life and occur at different stages of development. Viorst believes that a sense of loss occurs when we realize that mother cannot be with us forever; that hurts cannot always be soothed; that all relationships are flawed; that both good and bad, love and hate, exist in everyone including ourselves; that we cannot protect ourselves and those we love from danger and loss; that our options are limited; and that death is inevitable. Thus as we weave our way through family life from birth through old age, we learn that loss is an important part of life and that how we respond to loss will define our character.

Roger Gould (1978) has also written about the transformations of adult life. Gould explores how childhood learning influences adulthood in the form of unfinished business. He calls this unfinished business childhood consciousness. Individuals must confront, master, and break free from the immature, childhood thinking that has led to a number of false assumptions. These false assumptions must be surrendered and replaced with a more mature outlook; thus we must shed childhood consciousness for adulthood consciousness. This change usually occurs with age as individuals are exposed to the experiences of life. Although the false assumptions learned in childhood may be intellectually viewed as incorrect in the late teenage years, these false assumptions do not surrender their power over us until emotional experiences reveal them to be false. It is when personal experience hits home and our own emotions are affected that we truly begin the process of developing a more mature adult consciousness.

Young people first begin to question early learning and assumptions during the teenage years. Children have usually grown up seeing their parents as protectors—all-powerful and all knowing; so children assume that they will always follow their parents' way and believe as their parents' have believed. However, adolescents begin to question, even rebel against parental ways. They begin to question the following childhood assumptions: I must view the world the way my parent's view the world and I must accept my parent's idea of what is safe and appropriate if I am to survive and be successful. As adolescents challenge these assumptions, they may still be closely tied to their parents and dependent on them for support. Yet there is some truth to the adolescents' logic. Adolescents realize that parents are not as sure about their worldview as they pretend to be. The parents are like the Wizard of Oz and the teenager is like Dorothy who has exposed the Wizard as a tired old man manipulating a machine. In the adolescents' rebellion and struggle to throw off false assumptions and beliefs, there is the danger of going to an extreme, literally embracing the opposite. If we are lucky, "we finally come down someplace between our parents' safety advice which underestimates our ability, and our own unreasonable disregard for safety, which is our childlike wish for invulnerability" (Gould, 1978, p. 61). Wherever the young person lands, this landing is the result of challenging the parents' worldview. As this challenge occurs, the young person begins the process of developing adult consciousness.

Yet adult consciousness is not achieved overnight; it is the product of years of experience. Other false assumptions associated with childhood learning must be challenged. False assumptions usually addressed during the twenties include:

- Life is fair. Dreams will come true if we work hard. Effort will be rewarded if we engage in "right" behavior. Somewhere along life's road, these beliefs are challenged. Whether it was Vietnam, the World Trade Center disaster, the loss of a job, financial failure, a failed marriage, or the untimely death of a loved one, sooner or later, reality hits home. No matter how hard we try, dreams do not always come true and hard work does not always guarantee success.
- There is one right way; find this right way and things will be okay. Young adults often believe that there is one right career, one right marriage partner, one right time to have children, one right way to rear children, and one right way for just about everything. If we can just find the right way, our problems will be solved. The "right way" philosophy is usually challenged somewhere along life's path, usually in young adulthood when we learn that there are many acceptable ways and sometimes none of them will make things turn out right.
- Others, especially those close to us, can help when help is needed. Often this assumption relates to our view of marriage. We expect our partner to cheer us up, make us happy, entertain us, and endow us with characteristics that we do not possess. Sometimes we expect children to fulfill us and give life meaning when we cannot find meaning on our own. Usually somewhere in young adulthood, experience teaches us that these "others" cannot always do for us what we cannot do for ourselves.

Then in our late twenties and early thirties and beyond, just as we have grappled with the above false assumptions, life experiences force us to confront other immature beliefs. These include:

- When something is understood intellectually, it is fully understood. The brashness of young adulthood asserts itself in a kind of intellectual bravado. I am an adult now; listen to what I know. But true understanding does not come just through intellect. True understanding is honed through personal experiences that are laden with emotion. When we have these experiences, we realize that our previous understanding was superficial and shallow. Through the school of hard knocks, we discover that life is a struggle, that close relationships are full of love and hate, that evil sometimes wins out over good, that our way is not the only way, that you can't go home again, and that shattered dreams are not the end of the world. Often it takes a traumatic experience to gain these insights—perhaps a betrayal, a divorce, an illness, or a death. And after these experiences, we are never quite the same; childhood consciousness has given way to adult consciousness.

- Understanding the people close to us is not difficult. During our thirties, we often realize that life is more complex than we previously had thought. Early in marriage, couples often side step their differences for the sake of harmony and focus on the positive aspects of their relationship. But as time passes, differences are perceived, leaving us to wonder—who is this person I married? The partner we thought we knew now has a mind of his or her own. And thus the false assumption concerning how easy it would be to understand each other and make it in marriage must be revised.

- As adults, we are not like our parents in any way. When young people rebel, they often suppress any awareness that they are like their parents. Perhaps they are similar in a few ways in regard to their parents' admirable traits but certainly not in other ways. Yet as individuals get older and especially if they have their own children, they glimpse a part of their parents in themselves. As this happens, they often feel uneasy, as if forces beyond their control motivate their behavior. Yet if adults are honest, they usually see even some of their parent's undesirable characteristics in themselves.

- Threats to security are not real. This belief is usually challenged during the thirties. Often the threats to security at this time come from within. Is this the life I want? Is this the career I want? Is this the person I want to spend the rest of my life with? Because these thoughts come from within, they seem all the more perplexing. Didn't we have it all figured out; now we're back to questioning again.

Then in the mid-life decade (35-45) still other struggles force us to abandon false assumptions for a more mature outlook. These struggles cause us to question some of the following assumptions:

- Illness and death happen to others but not to me and my loved ones. This assumption usually vanishes with the illness or death of a parent or loved one. Reality sinks in; we are now next in line. Accompanying this reality is the feedback from the mirror and the body. Gray hairs, wrinkles, and other physical changes take their toll on our consciousness; we can no longer deny reality. We too are vulnerable.
- It is not possible to experience life beyond what exists in one's present marriage and family. In mid-life, the pattern to a couple's marriage has been established. The ruts that exist may seem so deep that no amount of effort will be sufficient to bring about change; even attempts to renegotiate things may be fraught with peril. There are three choices: (1) Stay the same and forego any attempt at growth and change. (2) Attempt to renegotiate and come to new understandings in order to grow in the marriage. This may be dangerous since any attempt may fail, leading back to sameness or forward to separation. (3) Move away in separation with the hope that there is life beyond the marriage. The last two choices seek something new and force the couple to confront the question—is there life beyond our present marriage and family situation?
- Others are to blame; it's not our fault. As adults reach middle age, they are likely to confront their darker side. Now there is a new realization that what is happening and has happened in our life is not all the fault of others. We too are guilty of selfishness, greed, hatred, and a desire to control. We are not innocent.

As individuals give up childlike thinking and false assumptions, they gradually move toward a more mature adult consciousness. They are able to cast aside immature beliefs and meet life head on as adults. Learning these lessons may be painful, but this learning is necessary if adults are to perceive life in a mature, realistic way. Individuals must put aside the false assumptions developed in childhood and experience life as adults.

- As you have matured have you noted any of the changes that Gould wrote about? If so, elaborate on the change that seemed most significant to you.

IMPORTANT TERMS AND CONCEPTS

rule	adaptability dimension
family structure	family ideology
implicit rule	closed family paradigm

explicit rule

implicit-explicit rule continuum

rule sequence

vicious cycle

ritual

pursuer-distancer dance

drifting couple dance

conflictual couple dance

circular dance

overfunction-underfunction dance

circumplex model

cohesion dimension

open family paradigm

random family paradigm

exaggeration principle

epigenesis principle

morphostasis

morphogenesis

stage

transition

childhood consciousness

adult consciousness

false assumptions

SUGGESTED READINGS

Blevins, W. (1993). *Your family: Your self.* Oakland, CA: New Harbinger.

Covey, S. (1999). *The 7 habits of highly effective families.* New York: Franklin Covey.

Gould, R. L. (1978). *Transformations: Growth and change in adult life.* New York: Simon and Schuster.

Nichols, M. (1999). *Inside family therapy: A case in family healing.* Needham Heights, MA: Allyn and Bacon.

Satir, V. (1964). *Conjoint family therapy.* Palo Alto, CA: Science and Behavior Books.

Chapter 4

IMPORTANT TRANSITIONS IN FAMILY LIFE

- Providing Information about Marriage
- The Transitions of Married Life
- Providing Information about Child-Rearing
- The Transitions of Family Life
    - Parenthood: What Happens to the Marriage
    - Six Domains and their Importance
    - What Couples Fight About
    - Rearing Children and Adolescents in a Toxic World
    - How Parenting and Adolescence Have Changed
    - What's a Parent to Do

There are several predictable transitions in adult life. Each of these transitions requires family members to adjust and change. Family life educators often attempt to help couples and families through these times by dispelling myths and half-truths about the transition and providing accurate information concerning what the transition has been like for others. Although family life educators usually cannot provide real-world experience, they can provide information and training that can be beneficial when real world experience arrives. This training helps family members anticipate and prepare for what lies ahead. In this chapter, three predictable transitions will be discussed–the transition to married life, the transition to parenthood, and the transition associated with children becoming adolescents.

PROVIDING INFORMATION ABOUT MARRIAGE

Family life educators and family counselors often attempt to dispel unrealistic expectations young people have about marriage. Do partners know that romantic love will wane? Are they aware of the types of love that sustain marriages after romantic love fades? Do they realize that disagreements are inevitable? Are they aware of how much their relationship will change over time? Do they know the importance of commitment and compromise in the relationship building process? Are they aware of how children will change their marriage? Since many couples are naive about the realities of marriage, educators try to bridge the gap between unrealistic expectations and reality. Here is some information they would want young people to know.

Partners should strive to keep their own individual identities even through they will also develop an identity as a couple. Couples often make use of the unity candle in marriage ceremonies. The ceremony begins with two candles burning brightly; then during the ceremony, each partner takes one of the burning candles and together they light a single candle. They then extinguish their individual candles to symbolize their coming together as one. Certainly two people do come together in marriage, but allowing their two individual candles to burn brightly along with the third candle would better reflect the ideal. This would recognize how important it is for each partner to also retain a separate identity. Perhaps Kahlil Gibran (1923) stated it best when he wrote: "But let there be spaces in your togetherness, and let the winds of the heavens dance between you" (p. 16).

An individual should be able to survive and thrive with or without a partner. At times, a person may say that s/he just could not survive without his or her spouse. Peck (1978) calls this parasitism, not love. Each partner should be strong enough to survive and even thrive on his or her own because of a strong separate identity. Partners who have too much togetherness in marriage eventually feel suffocated because they lack room to grow as individuals.

Individuals should be able to find happiness from within without expecting their partners to make them happy. Each partner does have some ability to influence the mood of the other, but long-term happiness and contentment must come from within. When the newness of marriage wears off, a partner's ability to make his or her spouse happy diminishes. Partners must take responsibility for their own level of happiness and not expect a spouse to do for them what they cannot do for themselves.

Partners should not be expected to make each other whole and complete. This is similar to the belief about happiness. At times, an encouraging spouse may be able to reinforce his or her partner's strengths, but it is unrealistic to think that a spouse can produce a drastic makeover. Each individual must take responsibility for his or her change and not place this responsibility on others.

Love will not always come easily and seem natural. Keeping love alive will require work. Preventing negativity from overrunning positivity in marriage

requires effort. This is difficult for the young starry-eyed couple to understand. Yet if couples realize that work is required, they may be more likely to
do this work when it is needed.

*Just because partners love each other does not mean they know each other's every
need; needs must be clearly communicated throughout marriage.* Each partner perceives and thinks differently and if your spouse is to understand your needs,
you must communicate them clearly. Don't expect your spouse to be a mind
reader.

Even partners in loving marriages have things that they find difficult to talk about.
A partner soon learns that there are sensitive issues that are laden with anxiety. These issues often lead to conflict and are difficult to discuss. In order
to work through difficult issues, couples will need to learn how to effectively
communicate so that the difficult issues do not erode the foundation of the
marriage.

*Partners will not always be able to put their love and their relationship as the top
priority in their lives.* This is simply not possible in a complex world. The pressures of work, child-rearing, and personal interests will often supersede your
relationship. As marriage evolves, most partners begin taking their relationship for granted; kindness often falls by the wayside and harsh words are
common. Partners must occasionally remind each other that nurturing their
relationship is still important and daily acts of kindness and love are still
essential.

Partners will have disagreements and issues that will be difficult to work through.
Some of these differences will be very aggravating, while others will be only
mildly irritating. Partners must continue to love each other in spite of these
differences.

Marriage is ever changing; partners change and so does the marriage relationship.
Individuals and relationships are always dynamic. Ride the waves of change
with the knowledge that some waves will bring joy, while others will bring
pain and struggle.

- Have unrealistic expectations characterized your thinking about marriage? If so, what expectations have you had that turned out to be unrealistic?

THE TRANSITIONS OF MARRIED LIFE

To help couples understand the changing landscape of marriage, Dym and
Glenn (1993) have attempted to map the developmental stages of marriage.
These theorists, who also work as family therapists, believe that couples pass

through recognizable stages in their marriages and if couples know what to expect on their journey, relationship difficulties will seem more "normal." Dym and Glenn believe that couples pass through a recurring three-stage cycle.

The first stage in this recurring cycle is Expansion and Promise. This stage begins to take shape when partners come together to form a loving relationship. This initial stage is characterized by romance, hope, and optimism as partners promise their love to each other. It's as if they have an implicit contract to listen, to love, and to care for each other. In the initial stage of Expansion and Promise, excitement and high expectations abound as couples chart their course together and develop their identity as a couple. Partners in this stage feel accepted and loved as they open up and tell their stories to each other; they take time to talk and understand each other as they enjoy the intimate nature of their new relationship. Partners in this stage usually believe that they are lucky to have found someone so wonderful, so attractive, so caring, and so much like the person of their dreams. Yet, even as they enjoy the expanse of this new relationship, there are occasional glimpses of things to come.

These glimpses may first occur when partners notice a characteristic in the other that they had not seen before or perhaps had overlooked because of the initial elation of Expansion and Promise. Why is he so moody? Why is she so sensitive? Where did that anger come from? What happened to that confident person who seemed so secure and stable? With these glimpses and the conflicts that result from them, the partners make initial forays into the next stage—Contraction and Betrayal. These occasional glimpses, however, quickly give way to the positive feelings of Expansion and Promise, especially if the partners easily work through or minimize what they have seen. But with time, these characteristics occasionally reemerge and cannot be easily minimized, overlooked, or worked through. These troubling characteristics may be due to irritating personality traits or habits and are usually most annoying when one partner is tired, overworked, or upset. As these behaviors persist, the positive feelings of Expansion and Promise gradually give way to the negative feelings of irritation and disappointment. At some point, these forays into Contraction and Betrayal become more prevalent and the couple crosses a threshold; now negative feelings replace positive feelings as the prevailing tone of the relationship. When this happens, the couple enters the stage of Contraction and Betrayal.

The initial passage through Contraction and Betrayal can be frightening. Partners now ask—what happened to the good feelings they had, the promises they made, and the similarities they observed? Partners now see their differences more clearly and they wonder how such differences could have been overlooked. The initial, implicit contract implying that one's partner would always be the "perfect mate,"–always caring and understanding–now seems to be violated. As differences and disappointments are acknowledged, couples argue more, try to change each other, and attempt to turn the other back into the partner they thought they had married. This makeover usually fails, leaving each partner feeling angry, unaccepted, and unloved. Each partner believes that the other has betrayed the initial agreements made during Expansion and Promise.

As this process takes place, each partner contracts, reverting back to stereotypical patterns of behavior that were repressed, unexpressed, or unnoticed during Expansion and Promise. The husband may bully and demand; the wife may cry. The husband may withdraw; the wife may pursue. The husband gives advice; the wife desires a good listener. The husband leaves to spend time with his buddies; the wife pouts, calls her friends, or her mother. There are topics that are now difficult or impossible to discuss because of the tension in the marriage. Signs of affection are less apparent. Sex drops off in frequency and becomes more mechanistic. Often husbands continue to pursue their wives sexually, but wives, wanting the tenderness of intimacy, withdraw and shut down. Conversely, women may seek to repair the relationship by talking things out while men avoid talking about feelings and withdraw to a safe haven, perhaps work, sports, or television.

Even though this stage is profoundly difficult, Dym and Glenn (1993) believe that it is an essential part of couple development. It is during this stage that the "other" self, a self that has been hidden or ignored during Expansion and Promise, emerges and is on display. This imperfect, blemished self, although unsightly, is still an important element of each partner. Until partners can bring this self into the relationship, they will not feel real or whole as a partner in the marriage. This is a time of harsh honesty when partners must face their personal flaws and the limitations of their relationship. If couples can survive Contraction and Betrayal, they may realize that the promises of the initial stage of Expansion and Promise were too unrealistic; now they must forge a new relationship, one that is more honest, more accepting of the true self of the other, and more truly loving. Dym and Glenn believe that although this stage is not for the faint of heart, it is just as necessary for couples to experience as the other stages.

If couples persevere through their conflicts and differences and survive the initial stage of Contraction and Betrayal, they emerge in the stage of Resolution. Compromise and negotiation characterize this stage. Partners now see both the good and bad in their mate and they look for ways to make things better–a kind word, a thank you, a gift of roses, or an affectionate hug. They may sense in each other a desire to work things out–to tap into those repressed feelings of love upon which their relationship was created. Over time, a new more accepting relationship emerges based on reasonableness, tolerance of differences, and greater maturity. Partners are now able to be more flexible, less demanding of the other, and more capable of making adjustments. In this stage, partners are able to integrate the positive and negative feelings of the two earlier stages while emphasizing friendship, cooperation, and good judgment. Whereas Expansion and Promise was full of hope and optimism, and Contraction and Betrayal was filled with pessimism and doubt, the stage of Resolution is characterized by working things out.

Dym and Glenn believe that each couple cycles through these three stages many times throughout their marriage. Although the stages of each cycle may be experienced somewhat differently from the stages of the previous cycle, the stages and the general characteristics of each cycle remain the same. Also they suggest that a couple uses one of the stages as a Home Base, a place where they spend most of their time and energy. Couples will customarily begin and end the cycle in this Home Base stage.

Dym and Glenn are not the only therapists who have noted that marriages go through different stages. Davis (2001) has also written about this process, hoping that a marriage map will prevent unrealistic expectations. These two stage theories share many similarities. The following five stages depict Davis's analysis of the changing nature of marriage.

Stage 1: Passion. This stage is the falling in love stage where passion and romance prevail. Partners feel fortunate to have found their soul mate and believe that they will be together forever in a state of eternal bliss.

Stage 2: What was I thinking? During this stage, disillusionment sets in. Things that had previously been overlooked or were not apparent in one's partner are now difficult to ignore; now personalities, habits, and beliefs begin to clash. The partners no longer work as a team but seem like competing opponents. There are times when that loving feeling is gone and the partners wonder if they made a mistake on the way to their marriage.

Stage 3: Things will be fine if s/he changes. During this stage, partners desperately attempt to change each other. This change is perceived as important because they are in a battle to define the marriage. You are right; your spouse is wrong. You are rational and clear-headed; your spouse is willful and stubborn. Things are said, feelings are hurt, and frustration abounds. The choices in this stage are: to accept things as they are and stay together; to live somewhat separate, unhappy lives; to divorce–get out and cut your losses; or to put an end to conflict and learn healthier, more loving ways to respond to each other. Although the latter path takes great faith and courage, Davis believes that it can lead to the happiest, most fulfilling time in a couple's marriage.

Stage 4: My partner and I are different; that's just the way s/he is. In this stage, partners begin to accept their differences. They will never agree on everything, but they will find ways to live together and love each other in spite of their differences. Partners in this stage have some empathy for each other because they see that they are not faultless in the relationship. Forgiveness and compassion reappear. Partners choose not to go to war over things that would have led to conflict in the past. Rather than fighting as competitors, partners now attempt to cooperate as teammates. The changes in this stage make the next stage possible.

Stage 5: Together, at last. Like Dym and Glenn, Davis believes that marriage can reach a quieter, more harmonious place. In this last stage, partners reconnect and again begin to see the qualities they originally admired in each other. In essence, the marriage has come full circle–from love to disillusionment back to love.

Both Dym and Glenn and Davis believe that couples should be aware of the stages of the marital map even before marriage. If partners realize that all marriages have ups and downs, then they may be more willing to persevere through the difficult times as they hope for a better day.

- Have these theories about the stages of marriage changed your beliefs about what marriage is like? If you are married or have been married can you personally relate to the different stages?

PROVIDING INFORMATION ABOUT CHILD REARING

Just as therapists and family life educators provide information about marriage, they also provide information about children and childcare. Parenting is one of the most challenging tasks couples experience, yet there is no training required for the job. States require licenses to drive a car, run a business, and practice a trade, yet there are no licensing requirements for parents. The infant must make do with whatever parenting is provided. If parenting is drastically inadequate, social service agencies may intervene, but this is usually only after incompetence has been well documented. Therefore, family life educators must work to convince prospective parents that basic knowledge about children and child-rearing is crucial. Educators usually begin by addressing some commonly held beliefs that are either not true or are half-truths. These misleading beliefs include the following:

Being a good parent will come naturally; it will be fun and easy. Many parenting tasks require skills that do not come naturally. Some of the demands even go against what is natural. Do you enjoy losing sleep, being overworked, or hearing the incessant cries of a baby? Although some aspects of parenting will be enjoyable, other aspects of the job will be tedious and boring.

If parents love their children and are "good" parents, then their children will not have serious problems. Loving your child is certainly important, but love does not guarantee a positive outcome. Even parents who love their children and have adequate knowledge and training can have children with problems. Many non-parental factors, such as heredity, the peer group, and the mass media, influence development. There are simply no guarantees.

There is always one best solution to a child-rearing problem, find it and your problem will be solved. When things go wrong, parents look for solutions but often find there is no clear-cut best way to deal with the problem. Even experts may disagree on what is best. And sometimes, no matter what you try, positive results may be illusive.

Parents should never have negative feelings toward their children. Even parents who love their children often say they have negative feelings toward them. It is best not to be overburdened with guilt over such feelings. However, it is also important that parents not allow negative feelings to dominate the parent-child relationship.

If an infant or young child is difficult and fussy, the child is intentionally trying to give the parents a hard time. For the exhausted mother trying to care for a difficult child, it may seem that some ill intent is involved. Yet many children are born with difficult temperaments and fussiness is just an expression of this temperament. It is best to remember that all children exhibit a wide range of behaviors and they will do so regardless of who the caretaker is and what the circumstances are.

Children will always appreciate what parents do for them. Certainly many grown children do appreciate what their parents have done to foster their development. They often develop this appreciation when they begin rearing their own children. Yet many adults also remember the hurts parents inflicted and the mistakes parents made, while young children and adolescents are often too self-absorbed to see the sacrifices their parents make.

Having a child will improve the marriage. Having a child to improve a marriage is risky business. If a couple is having problems in the marriage, it is unlikely that a child will solve those problems. Having a child usually adds to the pressure and stress couples face.

One's partner will do his/her fair share in helping with the new baby and the housekeeping tasks. Although roles have changed somewhat and husbands are doing more than in the past, wives still complain that the bulk of the work falls to them. As one mother put it, "I seem to naturally know what to do and he doesn't. How come he doesn't know?" Whether it is a matter of not knowing or simply not doing, wives still end up with the bulk of the work. This often causes wives to end up exhausted, stressed out, and frustrated.

It will be easy to agree with your spouse about methods of child-rearing. Prior to having children, couples may talk in a general way about what rearing children will be like. However, couples cannot contemplate all the problems they will face rearing children, nor can they know for sure whether they will agree or disagree about how to resolve their differences. Disagreements will occur and these disagreements will likely add stress to your marriage. *As children get older, child-rearing problems diminish; when children leave home, your worries are over.* Child-rearing problems can be just as troublesome during adolescence as during earlier stages. Even though parental concerns are somewhat different during adolescence, feelings can be even more intense when disagreements arise. And don't expect your worries to end when your son or daughter leaves home. You will never stop being a parent no matter how old your children are.

- Has your thinking been characterized by any of the above misleading belief? Would you agree that these statements represent false impressions of what parenting and child rearing are like?

THE TRANSITIONS OF FAMILY LIFE

Some events in family life produce rapid changes in a couple's life. The birth of the first child is often such an event. Couples frequently find that even if they have planned and anticipated that "bundle of joy," they are still unprepared for the changes that occur. These changes are usually experienced in both positive and negative ways. There is the fulfillment, love, and joy that parents have as they proudly care for their newborn; yet there is also added work, lost sleep, new worries, and increased stress. The family now becomes a new system; it is no longer a system of two, but rather a system of three. This change is so dramatic that the couple's life as it has been experienced ends and a new structure of family life begins to take shape. Will this new structure be satisfying? Will the new parents be able to adequately meet the needs of their child and maintain a satisfying marital relationship?

This transition from couple of two to family of three has been the focus of two major longitudinal studies in the last twenty-five years. Carolyn and Phillip Cowan (1992, 2000) directed the Becoming a Parent Project at the University of California and Jay Belsky (Belsky & Kelly, 1994) lead the Penn State Child and Family Development Project. The Cowans studied ninety-six couples from pregnancy through their child's first kindergarten year and Belsky followed 250 couples from prebaby days to the child's third birthday. The findings of these two studies as well as others conducted more recently show that this transition is indeed a difficult transition for most couples. John Gottman, writing about this transition in the preface of Cowan and Cowan's book (2000) states: "Marital conflict increases, often by a whooping factor of nine (Belsky & Kelly, 1994), conversation and sexual activity decline dramatically, and in approximately 40 to 70% of these marriages, marital satisfaction, particularly the wife's, declines dramatically within the first year after the baby's birth" (p. xix-xx).

Parenthood: What Happens to the Marriage

As partners experience the baby transition, they immediately notice the changes in their marriage. These changes occur in almost every aspect of their life together–the way they communicate, what they communicate about, the rules of their relationship, their emotional experiencing, and even their sexual relationship. Cowan and Cowan (1992) note that after the baby arrives, there is just not enough time to attend to the baby, run the household, give time to one's job, and also nurture the marriage relationship. Even if a couple attempts to make time for their relationship, doing so is not easy; schedules must be coordinated and preparations made. By the time it all happens, there is little energy and spontaneity left to nurture their marriage relationship. One way to explain all of these marital changes is to focus on the many new stressors that couples experience as they become more child-focused. However, the Penn State study discovered an even more fundamental explanation–the natural polarizing effect that a baby had on the parents. This polarizing effect calls attention to the partners' differences–differences that existed before the baby's arrival, but during prebaby days, these differences could be minimized or avoided as the couple focused on their similarities and the positive aspects of their relationship. The arrival of the baby forces these differences to the forefront for all couples. Belsky and Kelly believe that what happens to the marriage–whether it becomes more or less satisfying–depends upon how a couple manages these differences. And how they manage these differences depends upon six characteristics and capabilities that each partner brings to the parenthood transition. The Penn State researchers referred to these characteristics and capacities as domains. For example, if a couple was strong in each domain, then their transition was smooth; if they were weak in each domain, then they had difficulty. Belsky and Kelly found that some marriages they studied were tested to the breaking point; 12 to 13 percent struggled to maintain their solidarity and their belief in the marriage. These marriages went into severe decline. Another 38 percent went into moderate decline with partners becoming more polarized, experiencing less marital satisfaction than before. Thirty percent experienced no change in marital satisfaction, while 19 percent actually improved in marital satisfaction. As life gets played out in the hectic routine of caring for baby, each spouse makes a series of discoveries about his or her partner. Will these discoveries draw the partners closer together or push them apart?

These discoveries relate to what partners learn about each other in regard to the six domains.

- If you are married and have had a child, did you notice a polarizing effect that influenced your relationship with your spouse after the birth of your first child?

Six Domains and their Importance

Although all parents experienced increased stress during the transition to parenthood, Belsky and Kelly (1994) observed that some couples navigated the transition to parenthood more smoothly than others. Whether there was improvement or decline in marital satisfaction depended on a couple's ability to successfully resolve differences related to the six domains.

The Domain of Self

The focus of this domain is on whether partners have the ability to work together as a team and give up some of their individual aspirations and needs. If partners have the capabilities needed to do this, then a smooth transition is more likely. There were several factors that influenced how well a couple could work together as a cohesive team. The first was how the couple balanced their needs for autonomy and affiliation. Belsky and Kelly note that women and men often differ in regard to this balance.

Women often have a strong need for affiliation, while men are more likely to value autonomy, independence, and be more self-focused. While these differences exist before the baby arrives, prebaby differences are likely to be minor irritants in the relationship because the partners have more time and energy to give to each other and to the satisfaction of their own autonomy/independence needs. After the baby is born, when the couple is tired, irritated, and overworked, autonomy/independence issues must be more balanced if the couple is to work together as a successful team. Belsky and Kelly (1994) write: "the man must now be willing to surrender not just a portion of his independence, as he did in prebaby days but nearly all of it. This will involve curtailing or giving up activities such as work, sports, and hobbies that are very important to someone who cherishes independence" (p. 103). In addition, the husband must be able to move away from his self-focus enough to help his wife not only with the increased workload but also with the varied emotions that naturally come with this transition. For the husband this sacrifice is usually not easy; he may be uncomfortable with this baby work and ill equipped to help with his wife's emotional needs.

The wife, too, usually needs to make some sacrifices. Because of her powerful affiliation need, she may feel drawn to the baby in a way that is difficult to control. This powerful connection to the baby makes her emotional experiencing dependent upon what the baby does. Any little upset the baby experiences may increase her anxiety and be a cause for alarm. As these alarm bells go off, her desire to talk about these concerns and connect with someone, usually her husband, increases. The mother's increased baby focus and her desire to talk about baby make it difficult for the couple to find time to be alone and nurture their marriage. Even if a night out is scheduled, the talk may focus on baby, not on the couple or their relationship. Belsky and Kelly ask: "Can a woman learn to regulate these emotions sufficiently to provide her husband with a measure of attention and affection? Can the woman regulate her dependency sufficiently to handle minor problems and upset on her own?" (p. 103-104). Partners during this time bid for each other's help, attention, and affection. The nature and frequency of these bids and how a spouse responds greatly influence the level of marital satisfaction.

Finding a healthy balance of autonomy and affiliation in marriage also depends upon another important characteristic of the self-domain. This characteristic is security. Does each partner exhibit enough self-confidence and self-esteem so that difficult circumstances are not a threat to individual security? If so, each partner can be flexible enough to change for the sake of the common good. For example, the husband can give up much of his self-focused activities to become sensitive to the emotional needs of his wife and the many ways he can help with household tasks. He may give up some TV, sports activities, and hobbies because he knows that these are not the essence of who he is. He is secure enough to feel good about himself without these activities and confident enough to feel content with his new role. A high level of esteem and security also allows partners to be more comfortable with decision making; secure parents more easily distinguish between minor and major upsets and thus know when to be concerned and when to let go. The confident parent can let go of minor worries, allowing energy to be directed elsewhere. For example, the secure wife realizes that the baby can survive in the care of others. Realizing this, she can spend worry-free time alone with her husband nurturing their love and their relationship.

Belsky and Kelly (1994) note that one characteristic of an insecure wife is to think that she is the only one who can provide adequate care for the baby; even her husband does not hold, feed, and respond to the baby's needs in the proper way. When the husband attempts to help, his efforts are criticized for being sub-par or deficient. An extension of this attitude is for the wife to believe that her husband should think and feel exactly the same way she thinks and feels about the baby. When he does not exhibit the same worry and concern she feels, her way of being has not been validated and this is a threat to her security. She then feels hurt and rejected and complains about her husband's insensitivity. Husbands, in response to complaints of deficient performance and insensitivity, often feel threatened. The wife's emotional neediness and the husband's inability to satisfy her bids for help result in a predictable response–fleeing into the safety of self-focus (more TV, sports, hobbies, or work). Seeing this, the wife may intensify her demands for help and support while the husband, thinking his efforts will be demeaned, retreats further into the safety of other pursuits. The estrangement that results from this cycle is not an immediate response to one situation, but usually develops over time. It involves one small incident after another, until the couple finally realizes that a fundamental change has taken place in their relationship.

Couples whose marriages improved after the birth of their first child exhibited a very different pattern. These couples brought characteristics to marriage that allowed them to cooperate and work together to reach mutual goals. They exhibited a confidence and security that allowed them to balance autonomy and affiliation issues in a mutually satisfying way. These couples were able to appreciate each other as they shared household chores, realistically evaluated the seriousness of situations, expressed sensitivity to their partner's needs, and found some time to nurture their relationship as husband and wife. They rated high on the domain of self and this made it more likely that they would come through this transition feeling positive about their relationship.

> • Comment on your marriage in relation to the domain of self. Do you and your spouse have a healthy or unhealthy autonomy/affiliation dimension? How healthy are you and your spouse in regard to security/insecurity issues?

The Domain of Gender Ideology

As the 250 couples in the Penn State Child and Family Development Project were studied, it became apparent that often partners had different gender ideologies. These differences reflected how partners defined male and female roles in relation to household chores. If these differences could not be worked through, they tended to disrupt the unity of the marriage. One reason for this disruptive influence was the constant day-to-day reminder of these differences. Other differences could be pushed aside or might not come up frequently, but issues of childcare and who does what around the house were a daily concern. Even if couples had talked about the importance of sharing childcare and household responsibilities prior to the baby's arrival, these researchers found that a large gender disparity still existed after the baby arrived. Men may be doing more, but women still carry the bulk of responsibility and work around the house. This disparity often led to arguments. In some cases, wives just gave up and did the task in question for the sake of time, energy, and peace. Disagreements about work and chores, regardless of how they were handled, served as constant reminders of the partner's marital differences. These differences eroded the sense of fairness and oneness that the couple valued. Even when there are small differences, some erosion occurred, but "in marriages where there are big disagreements about chores and work, the erosion rate can often be so rapid that by the end of the baby's first year, the husband and wife are left wondering if they have anything in common outside of the roof over their heads and the baby in the nursery" (Belsky & Kelly, p. 125).

Cowan and Cowan (1992) also noted this disparity in childcare and household work among the couples they studied. For example, when the babies were six months old, mothers were doing much more of the childcare duties than either partners had predicted before their baby arrived; thus expectations that fathers would do more to relieve their wives of some of the childcare responsibilities was not fully realized. Yet the couples did not understand why there was such a workload discrepancy; it seemed as if they had picked up some illness in the hospital that dictated a gender-related division of labor. Even though the men in this study wanted to be more involved parents, there seemed to be forces that made it difficult to have a more equal distribution of childcare and household tasks. These researchers came to believe that there were several significant obstacles that prevented a more shared division of labor. First, it is difficult to overcome the notion that caring for baby is mom's work, perhaps because there are too few models of male nurturing in the families of origin of new parents. Second, men feel less competent in caring for a young child and they turn to their wives, expecting them to be more skilled at childcare duties. Frequently, wives step in to relieve the new father of his discomfort and so the task is taken over by the expert. This occurs so frequently that it becomes a marital dance—the father's hesitancy giving over to the mother's competence. And if the mother breastfeeds her baby, it is all the more difficult for the father to share in the intimate moments of the feeding situation. Thus men back away from taking more responsibility, preferring to go back to more comfortable tasks. Then too, these researchers suggest that the dynamics of the workplace and the difficulty in finding adequate childcare make it more likely that women will stay home, at least during the first few months after the baby is born. This pushes fathers back into the role of breadwinner, making it more likely that fathers will play a secondary role in childcare during these early months.

Yet, there were a few fathers in the Becoming a Family Project who took a very active role in child-rearing tasks and household management. This became an interesting group to study—the more involved dads and their marriages could be compared to the less involved dads and their marriages. The active involvement of fathers when the child was six months old was associated with several things. First, these fathers and their wives had higher self-esteem and both rated their marriage as more satisfying. They felt less stress in their role as parents and described their families as a more cohesive unit. As these fathers continued to be involved in childcare duties, they continued to report lower stress regarding parenting tasks and were less likely to be depressed. Also this active involvement continued to be associated with their wives' attitudes. Cowan and Cowan (2000) write, "Women whose husbands took more of a role in the care of their child were more maritally satisfied and described their family as having greater cohesion than mothers whose mates were less involved with the children" (p. 102). Furthermore, these researchers found that when dads were less involved in childcare, the more likely both partners were to report unhappiness with the marriage.

- Do you and your spouse have different opinions about gender roles? If so how has this affected your marriage?

The Domain of Emotionality

Another domain that the Penn State researchers studied was the domain of emotionality; they were interested in how important this domain was to establishing a stable marriage during the early baby years. The trait of emotionality is often thought of as a characteristic of temperament—a biological predisposition to respond in certain ways in regard to emotional expression. The arrival of the first child provides many opportunities for emotional highs and lows. There are the highs of the child's smiles and coos, the child's first words, and the child's first steps; there are also the lows associated with spit-ups, sickness, crying spells, dirty diapers, and sleepless nights. Both partners will experience these highs and lows, but there are often differences concerning the amount of attention given to the positives and the negatives. How much mental energy will a parent spend raving over the positives and worrying over the negatives? Those who are predisposed to see the negatives often worry and imagine the worst-case scenario. Those who are predisposed to see the positive are more upbeat and optimistic.

Why is a predominance of worry and anxiety such a disadvantage in marital and parenting situations? The Penn State researchers found two contributing factors—the Velcro effect and the magnifying effect. Partners with negative emotionality often see problems and cannot move on. It's as if they get stuck (the Velcro effect) on anxiety and worry about what they perceive and imagine. Then they magnify the importance of the stressor (the magnifying effect) and the little concern becomes a big concern and the moderate concern becomes a large concern. The person who has a bent toward positivity is not as likely to be stuck on worry and magnification and can move on and expend mental energy in more appropriate ways. A spouse predisposed toward positivity may say, "Oh don't worry, it's just a runny nose," while the spouse with a bent toward negativity responds, "What do you know, it could be pneumonia and you would never know or care." Belsky and Kelly (1994) note that the domain of Emotionality is related to security. Just as highly secure individuals can regulate their autonomy and affiliation needs appropriately, they can also regulate their anxiety, worry, and concern in ways that are realistic to the situation. The insecure person has trouble doing this, tending to get stuck on their negativity and magnification.

If the couple's relationship is viewed from a systems perspective, then how each spouse responds affects the other. The secure reassuring spouse may have a calming influence on an anxious partner or may drive the anxious partner to distraction by calm reasonableness. Or the more secure, positive spouse may do both—at times calming the storm and at other times, lighting the fire. Many individuals exhibit an equal balance of positive and negative emotionality. When this was observed in study participants, it seemed to give these individuals an ability to pull back from a negative focus. It provided a self-correcting mechanism that allowed the couple to refocus from negative to positive before they became too unbalanced.

How did the Emotionality domain influence marriage? Not surprisingly, the marriages in which both partners were inclined toward positivity benefited the most and the marriages where both partners were inclined toward negativity suffered the most in terms of marital satisfaction. When one partner was inclined toward positivity and the other toward negativity, the outcome was more variable. These marriages could decline in satisfaction or possibly remain the same. Belsky and Kelly (1994) wrote, "If the positive partner stepped into the marriage and used his sunny disposition to navigate himself and his partner through the storm, a marital decline was usually forestalled" (p. 167). If this did not consistently happen, the marriage was likely to decline in satisfaction.

- Comment on the domain of emotionality in your marriage? Are you and your spouse similar or different in regard to emotionality? Has one partner's high level of emotionality been problematic in your marriage?

The Domain of Communication

One frequent complaint of couples who are having relationship difficulties is that they just don't communicate as they once did. The Penn State researchers were interested in studying communication as it evolved through the parenthood transition. They found that when partners talk about how marriage has changed after baby, they almost always lament the decline of quality communication. Practically all of the couples noted this decline and about half of the couples continued to experience this diminished quality of communication throughout the three-year follow-up period. This inability to regain quality talk influenced feelings of closeness and often led these couples to conclude that the baby had changed them in some irreversible way. Yet it need not be this way. Nineteen percent of the marriages actually improved in communication quality. A closer look at the researchers' analysis will help explain why some couples experienced an improvement, while others suffered a decline.

Two things became apparent as the study unfolded. Couples talked less after the arrival of the baby and their talk became less satisfying. It was as if the changes brought about by the baby inhibited meaningful couple talk. A major factor contributing to this diminished talk was lack of time. The new demands brought on by the baby were so overwhelming that partners rarely found time to talk with each other in a meaningful way. Also, it was not uncommon for one partner, usually the wife, to be so baby focused that talking about anything else became difficult. When one partner attempted to shift the conversation to other things, the baby-focused partner had trouble making the shift for an extended time and in a meaningful way. Many couples found that rather than expanding the number of things they had to talk about, the baby limited their focus; conversation now centered on baby, those things that concerned baby, and the routine of daily life with baby.

Another related problem that was common among study participants was a decline in activities which promote intimacy—a dinner out, a picnic in the mountains, intimate talks at breakfast on Saturday morning, and even making love. If the environmental settings in which intimate talk occurs are absent, then intimate talk declines. Although it was hard to verify, the Penn State researchers wondered if the lack of time and energy for sex that accompanied this transition had an important effect on intimate conversation. Since sex is the most intimate of shared relationships, a decline in lovemaking may create a subtle distance, making personal talk more difficult.

The researchers felt that the lack of intimate conversation about subjects other than baby had a negative influence on conversational skills. If skills are not practiced under somewhat ideal conditions, these skills diminish. And since there was no time for intimate talk and the sharing of personal feelings, new parents seemed to forget how to listen and show understanding. Many couples even admitted that since the arrival of the baby their ability to listen and understand had deteriorated. Along with this lack of intimate sharing and personal talk, another problem was noted. Belsky and Kelly refer to this as "a kind of inhibiting self-consciousness." Personal information that couples would have easily shared in the past now seemed difficult to share; it seemed too personal and private, almost embarrassing to bring up.

After gathering their data, the Penn State researchers attempted to pin-point differences between the couples who managed communication well and those who did not. Some interesting findings emerged. If partners side-stepped difficult issues before baby and fail to come to a satisfying "we" or "us" in their relationship, communication problems after baby were more likely. For some couples, discussing relationship difficulties, even before the baby's arrival, can be so difficult that they take the easy way out—one partner gives in and goes along for the sake of peace or both partners avoid the issue for the sake of harmony. Hashing out differences before the baby arrives allows partners to learn important communication skills—how to share feelings with each other concerning difficult issues, how to listen to each other when there are disagreements, and how to use communication to work through differences. When partners are successful at this, they find the "we" in their relationship and define that "we" as important. Even though agreement cannot always be found, these couples have experience in meaningful communication. If a couple has learned to communicate about difficult things during prebaby days, this will help them engage in meaningful talk during the baby transition. If couples have avoided this kind of meaningful communication and opted for the "I'll go along to keep peace" or "we'll avoid the issue" approach, they are less likely to successfully bridge the communication gap during the baby transition.

This continuity from prebaby to postbaby in regard to communication should not be surprising. The baby transition, although it brings change to couples' lives, does not turn husbands and wives into different people. Not only is there continuity in communication styles, Cowan and Cowan (2000) found that there is stability in personality traits before and after the baby transition. Those partners who felt good about themselves and their marriage before baby are likely to feel good about themselves and their marriage after baby; those partners who have negative feelings about themselves and their marriage before baby are not likely to feel drastically different after baby.

- Comment on the domain of communication in your marriage. Did intimate communication decline after the birth of your first child? Prior to having children, were you able to successfully resolve difficult issues? Did you get better or worse at this after starting a family?

The Domain of Expectations

As partners await the arrival of their first child, they have many expectations about how things will be after the baby arrives. What are these expectations? Will these expectations be violated by actual experience during the first few months and years after the baby arrives? If so, in what ways would expectations be violated? Would those partners who were realistic about this transition fare better during this time than those partners whose expectations were violated? The researchers decided to assess each partner's expectations in six areas before baby and then follow up after baby in order to see if expectations were realized. They assessed expectations in the following areas:

1. Expectations about the overall quality of the marriage–did partners expect the marriage to improve, stay the same, or deteriorate during the transition?
2. Expectations about the amount of conflict in the marriage–did partners expect more conflict or less conflict during the transition?
3. Expectations about self–did partners expect to perceive themselves differently in regard to adequacy, self-confidence, and happiness as the transition unfolded?
4. Expectations about the amount of shared care giving–did partners' expectations about how the work would get done bear any resemblance to reality?
5. Expectations about the relationship with extended family–did partners' expectations about the role extended family members would play during the transition come to fruition?
6. Expectations about relationships with non-family members–did partners expect to stay close to old friends and did they expect to make new friends easily?

These researchers found that overall expectations were only slightly out of line with reality. However, there were some variations in terms of the six assessment areas. Couples' expectations were most unrealistic in the area of shared caregiving. They were somewhat inaccurate in regard to how a baby would influence the marriage and marital conflict. They were only slightly inaccurate in regard to how the baby would change them and most accurate concerning relationships with family and friends.

Although occasionally a violated expectation was violated positively, this was not usually the case. Most often, expectations were violated negatively. For example, a wife expected her husband to be more helpful with the baby's care. Were there certain characteristics that seemed to predispose a person to vulnerability when an expectation was violated negatively? There indeed were! One characteristic was gender. When things did not go as expected, wives were more upset. When this occurred, wives suffered a 25 percent drop in marital satisfaction, while husbands experienced only a 10 percent decline. Also, certain individuals were more likely to be upset by dashed hopes of a certain kind. Working mothers were especially upset when expectations concerning the husband's shared caregiving did not work out. Usually, the mother was left holding the bag since it was her work schedule that had to be rearranged when the father did not fulfill his role. Individuals who were likely to be most upset about unfilled expectations regarding marital quality and conflict reduction were those who perceived the baby as a kind of therapy for a troubled marriage. A baby does not usually heal a troubled marriage; nor does a baby usually increase one's level of self-esteem, happiness, and fulfillment.

Are negatively violated expectations associated with decreased levels of marital satisfaction? The answer was a resounding yes. Averaging all the data for the 250 couples, the researchers found that those with unrealized expectations were much more likely to be dissatisfied with their marriages at the end of the study.

- Comment on the domain of expectations in your marriage. What were your prebaby expectations in regard to the six areas? What was the postbaby reality?

The Domain of Conflict Management

Another domain that made a difference in marital satisfaction during the baby transition was the domain of conflict management. All couples had hot button issues during the baby transition period. Belsky and Kelly reported that conflict increased 20-30 percent during this time. However, some couples experienced more difficulty managing conflict than others. Some couples withdrew from debate because they could not tolerate heated discussion and other couples could not pull back when conflict became too heated. Neither of these approaches was successful. Successful conflict managers were usually sensitive to the warning signs given by their partner that things were becoming too heated. In men, these cues included defensiveness and agitation and in women, sadness and fear. Sensing these warning signs, constructive fighters would back off rather than continue the attack. Thus, they did discuss their grievances (unlike avoiders who could not do so) but did not allow these discussions to get out of control (unlike the couples who could not pull back and went for the kill). The researchers suspected that the constructive fighters contained their conflict because of the deep affection and friendship they had for each other. This deep affection and high regard kept them from letting the fight cross the line between airing grievances and all out war. Also, the constructive fighters did not always need to win; it was just as important to find a way to stop the disruptive squabbling and get back to being happy. Thus, they frequently offered compromises, hoping to find common ground so that they could restore goodwill. The ability to handle conflict and restore goodwill in a marriage is so important that later chapters will examine how stable, happy couples manage conflict and what happens to marriages when conflict escalates and spirals out of control.

- Comment on the domain of conflict management in your marriage. Were you able to successfully manage conflict in prebaby days? Did having a baby seem to increase conflict in your marriage? How successfully did you handle conflict after the first baby arrived?

Longitudinal studies like the Penn State Child and Family Development Project and the Becoming a Family Project are important because they provide an in-depth analysis of what happens in marriages during the important baby transition. These studies help couples envision the road ahead, should they have children. Many couples find this road rocky while others navigate the terrain more easily. Perhaps knowing the differences between these two groups will help couples during their baby transition days.

What Couples Fight About

The ability to manage conflict successfully is essential in marriage. Many experts believe that all couples have significant differences; it is how these differences are managed that will determine the success of the marriage. There are some conflicts that are common to most marriages. The following discussion addresses these common conflicts.

Conflict over Household Chores

Disagreements over household chores often become more salient after the arrival of the first child. Cowan and Cowan (2000) reported that "the division of workload in the family wins, hands down, as the issue most likely to cause conflict in the first two years of family making" (p. 108). At this time, a mother's energy is often drained. If significant differences exist in division of labor and one partner is upset by these differences, this has an undermining effect on the marriage. As Belsky and Kelly (1992) noted: "each disagreement reminds the husband and wife that they have conflicting ideas about fairness, conflicting values, conflicting visions of their obligations to each other and to the marriage. . . ." (p. 124) Thus disagreement about what was equitable and fair caused problems. In some homes, husbands did little, but this was acceptable to the wife; in other homes, doing little was intolerable. Belsky and Kelly noted that it was not just differences in who should do what that led to erosion in the marriage; it was also the frequency in which these differences led to disagreement. Since these differences were confronted on a daily basis, it often felt as if the partners were not working together as a team.

Other researchers have also studied the gender issues in relation to household chores. Several findings stand out. Couples still divide work along gender lines and women still do more of the work. Thornton (1997) surveyed 555 couples and found that two-thirds of the women reported doing most of the housework. Wives also see housework as their domain and their husbands as helpers—someone who follows directions. Furthermore, wives often have higher standards for performance regarding household tasks than husbands; therefore, when husbands do help, their contributions often fall short of their wives' standards. Several things may happen at this point: a wife may criticize her husband for doing a poor job, she may actually do the job over since her husband's efforts were so deficient, and she may conclude that asking her husband to help is useless since he is so incompetent. The husband, feeling criticized and demeaned, decides to back off since his contribution is so unappreciated. There is even a joke among some husbands that goes like this: if your wife asks you to do a job around the house, never do it well; instead, do it poorly, then she will not ask again. But wives are usually not laughing. For them, inequity in household chores can seriously erode a sense of good feeling in the marriage.

Remember that it is not just how much a partner does around the house that is important, it is also whether partners believe that their spouse's contribution is a fair share. When one partner feels that the load is unfairly distributed, a slow resentment can build; a wife may come to believe that her husband just does not care that she is tired and overworked. However, the wife may have trouble expressing her concerns to her husband without creating more stress and turmoil.

- Have conflicts concerning household chores been problematic in your marriage? If so, have different expectations concerning roles been at the center of the conflict?

Conflict over Money

One recent study (Olson, Fye, & Olson, 1999) reported that over 50 percent of married couples disagree over how money should be spent. When you are single, you may make unwise money decisions, but at least you have no one to blame but yourself. When you are married, you become financially intertwined. This is why it is important for you to work out some agreements about money. Happy couples are much less likely to say they disagree about finances than unhappy couples. Also, Blumstein and Schwartz (1983) reported that when partners have an equal say in money decisions, they have a more peaceful marriage. These same researchers noted that couples seldom talk about money prior to marriage, but after marriage, money issues often become a major source of disagreement.

Why so much fuss about money? Nortarius and Markman (1993) believe there are two reasons. Couples are faced with financial decisions on a daily basis; therefore, if there is disagreement, it is constantly apparent. Then too, money issues often reflect deeper differences that are hidden and sometimes difficult to talk about. Arond and Pauker (1987) discuss four money orientations that may be the hidden differences behind money conflict–control, status, security, and enjoyment.

CONTROL. Matters of power and control often center on money. Husbands may believe that they should control the purse strings because that's the way it was when they grew up. In the old traditional marriage, this arrangement may have worked, but today wives are much more likely to work and make as much if not more money than their husbands. Therefore, why should wives not have equal access to money and an equal say in determining how money is spent? Partners who fail to discuss money issues before marriage will find that they cannot avoid such discussions after marriage.

STATUS. A person who views money as status is concerned with presenting the right image in the community and among friends. Money is valued for what it will buy because things impress others. One spouse may want a new car because a car represents more than a car; it makes a statement about one's status. Another spouse may be content to drive an old car, caring little about status and what other's think.

SECURITY. For those with high security needs, money provides security. A sufficient bank account or stock portfolio is essential for these individuals to feel safe in an unpredictable world. Financial security provides protection for the future. This view is in contrast to the person who believes in living for today. Why save money when you could die tomorrow; then what good is a large bank account and stock portfolio? These two opposing orientations often cause considerable conflict in marriage.

ENJOYMENT. Some individuals spend money for the enjoyment it brings to themselves and others. Money and the things money buys bring happiness and they enjoy being happy and making others happy. These individuals often spend money as an expression of love. One mother enjoyed spending money on her daughter because it was a means of expressing her love for her daughter. This had been the way money was used in her family of origin. For her husband, this was a frivolous use of money. From the father's perspective, his daughter already had plenty, thus why waste money? As you might guess, money had not been used in this way in his family of origin.

In many marriages, a conversation that couples should have but often avoid having is one about money—planning a budget, talking about their disagreements over money, and compromising so that each spouse feels s/he has fair input into money decisions.

- Have conflicts concerning money surfaced in your relationship? Do you and your partner have different orientations concerning money?

Conflict Involving Relatives and In-laws

Some have said that when individuals marry, they don't just marry a person, they marry a family. Many partners fail to understand this until they get married; then reality sinks in. The popular TV show, *Everybody Loves Raymond*, is based partly on the theme of intruding parents and in-laws. It is funny because we often see a little bit of ourselves in the lives of Raymond and Deborah. Then, too, it is funny because it is happening to them and not to us. In one program that focuses on in-law intrusiveness, Raymond's mother drives her car into Ray and Deborah's living room. This brings up all kinds of issues relating to Ray's mother meddling into Deborah and Ray's affairs. We laugh at what Ray and Deborah put up with in regard to his mother, but if we were in their situation, it would soon stop being funny.

Some research (Lauer & Lauer, 1986) shows that it is the mother in-law relationship that is most problematic. Other research (Arnstein, 1985) has found that 48 percent of mother in-law relationships are rated good, while 52 percent are characterized as poor. Young couples often fail to understand how important it is for them to establish reasonable boundaries around their relationship so that it is protected from the unhealthy intrusiveness of relatives and in-laws. Partners often regret that they did not establish firm and clear boundaries early in their marriage; had they done so, they might have avoided later problems. Husbands especially need to be firm in protecting their wives from an overbearing mother-in-law. Psychologists would tell husbands like Raymond to protect their wives from mother in-laws who constantly put their wives down, demean their wives' cooking and housekeeping, and generally disrupt the flow of family life. But this takes a strong husband! Does he anger his wife or his mother? In a healthy marriage, the husband's words and behavior firmly support his wife as he protects her and their relationship from overintrusive in-laws.

• To what extent have problems with relatives or in-laws influenced your marriage?

Conflict over Sex

Young couples wonder what this conflict is about. All they know is that sex is good. No, not good but GREAT! They cannot imagine a time when it will not be that way. So for them to learn that many couples have sexual problems seems almost unimaginable. Yet it frequently happens! In a survey of 26,442 couples, Olson et al. (1999) found that in 64 percent of these marriages, at least one partner had problems concerning the amount of affection they receive from their spouse. Furthermore, in 49 percent of these marriages, at least one partner was disinterested in their partner sexually; in 48 percent of these marriages, partners had difficulty discussing sexual matters; and in 46 percent of these marriages, partners had trouble keeping their sex life enjoyable. Another finding from this study revealed that 69 percent of the couples reported that one partner had more interest in sex than the other. As the previous discussion of Dym and Glenn's work indicated, as couples go through the stages of marriage, their differing needs become more apparent. Wives often complain that their husbands no longer talk and listen to them. For wives, talking, sharing feelings, and listening characterize emotional closeness. Wives often need this emotional sharing; it makes them feel cherished and loved. For a wife, this sets the stage for a satisfying sexual relationship since she is more likely to give of herself sexually when she feels fulfilled by the other parts of the relationship. Men are not as likely to need emotional talk and listening to enjoy sex. Sex for a man is often his way of experiencing intimacy with his wife. Although couples often do not talk about this difference or any of their sexual problems, these issues are often addressed in couple's therapy. The case study presented in the book, *The Family Crucible*, has the couple finally talking about their sexual differences. The wife complains that her husband's approach to her is unfeeling and degrading and in no way consistent with what a loving relationship should be. She angrily elaborates, "I think I have a *right* to expect some feeling from the person I share my body with! I just can't disconnect what I feel from what I do! But you, for God's sake, could make love in the midst of a furious fight" (Napier & Whitaker, 1987; p. 195).

Differences in sexual responsiveness are often misrepresented by media sources like MTV and pornographic films. This material, which is often produced by men, frequently depicts women as being perpetually available for the sexual pleasure of men whatever the circumstances. Sex is often performed without any talk or feeling, yet the female screams in ecstasy. Therapists and wives tell a very different story. If a husband wants his wife to be sexually responsive, it is important that he respond sensitively to her needs at other times in the marriage. A husband should let his wife know that she is loved and appreciated, not just during romantic encounters but also at other times. Gottman (1994) has even found that "men who do more housework and child care have better sex lives and happier marriages than others" (p. 157). It is what partners do when they are not making love that will determine if their sex life will be exciting and enjoyable. Keep the channels of communication open, respect each other's differences, become a good listener, and help each other on a daily basis. Perhaps with this effort, partners will continue to find satisfaction in their sexual relationship even after many years of marriage.

- How would you describe the sexual component of your relationship? Are there areas of both satisfaction and dissatisfaction? If so, what are these areas?

Conflict Involving Children

Disagreements over child-rearing issues do not usually emerge until after the arrival of the first child. From Belsky's study, we have seen what a large impact a child has on a marriage. Gottman and Silver (1999) have also studied married couples as they confront this transition. They believe that the secret to keeping a marriage strong during this time revolves around the attitude of the father. For the mother, having a baby is a life-changing experience; she is changed forever by her feelings for the baby and the impact of motherhood. But what will happen to the father? Will he be left behind or can he experience some of the same excitement and deep love for the baby that his wife feels? If he can also experience this excitement, the couple can go through this transition together, understanding and supporting each other along the way. If he cannot, the marriage will suffer and the husband may resent the baby's intrusion, leaving the wife disappointed that her husband cannot share her deep feelings. It is a critical time for the family and for the marriage.

Even if a couple handles the baby transition well, there still can be conflict over child-rearing issues. Often differences partners have regarding household chores and money get played out in situations involving the children. And at other times, partners find that their child-rearing philosophies are different. Both partners love their children, but the best way to express this love is in question. One may believe that children should be allowed to explore in a world with few boundaries and limitations; the other believes in a tougher love, where rules and boundaries help children learn responsibility. And husbands and wives often have different styles in dealing with children. Will each partner appreciate the other's style without insisting that one way is best? How the differences involving child-rearing issues get worked out will influence marital satisfaction during the child-rearing years.

- Are you and your spouse similar in terms of your child rearing philosophies? If there are areas of difference, what are these areas?

Conflict and Communication

Couples often cite communication problems as the prime reason for divorce. Communication difficulties usually surround the areas of conflict that a couple experience. Many couples, after initially trying to resolve differences, simply give up. Their previous attempts at discussion have been so heated and stressful that no discussion is better than more conflict. Since communication problems often encompass a variety of issues, communication will be addressed in greater detail in Chapter 8.

Rearing Children and Adolescents in a Toxic World

Rearing children has never been easy. When a child is added to the family, the family system changes; this creates new concerns that must be worked through if the new system is to establish a healthy balance. Then as children get older, there are new cultural and environmental influences that impact the child and the family. Some authorities believe that these influences are more powerful today than ever before. James Garbarino, director of the Family Life Development Center at Cornell University and author of the book, *Parents Under Siege*, (Garbarino, 2001) describes the North American culture of today as socially toxic. Just as physical environments can become contaminated with PCBs, anthrax, lead, or any number of other poisonous chemicals, the social environment can also be tainted with poisons that are harmful. Some of these toxins have been around for years but have become more powerful in recent years, while others are relatively new to the cultural landscape. A list of socially toxic agents that Garbarino believes parents should be concerned about includes:

- potentially harmful Internet sites and chat rooms
- degrading and harmful television and other media programming

- advertising that exploits children as consumers
- newer and more powerful illicit drugs
- media sources that depict parents as bumbling fools while kids are depicted as savvy
- gun and weapon availability and easy access to these weapons
- a culture that teaches that possessions define one's importance and worth

Internet Sites

The power of the Internet to influence culture and children is a recent phenomenon and is just beginning to be understood. Information that was previously unavailable or difficult to obtain is now readily available with the flip of a switch. Responsible parents must grapple with how to protect their children from pornographic websites and harmful conversations in Internet chat rooms. But it's an uphill battle. When a teenager was asked if it was possible to keep pornography out of the home, he responded by saying that parents try, but a kid is likely to see it at a friend's house either on video or the Internet, so why make such a big deal about it.

Television and Movies

Violence and sexual themes saturate movie and television programming. A 1993 report by an American Psychological Association Commission on Violence and Youth concluded that "there is absolutely no doubt that higher levels of viewing violence on television are correlated with increased acceptance of aggressive attitudes and increased aggressive behavior." And perhaps sexual themes are even more unsettling for parents. This generation is being exposed to graphic sexual content on TV, in music, and in the movies. Ron Taffel (2001) notes that hit songs like "Starfuckers" and the lyrics about oral sex–"wine dine 69 me"–are easily understood by the MTV generation.

The Advertising Culture

Advertising is now directed toward younger audiences. Even elementary school children know the brands they must buy to be cool. The advertising message says that you are important if you have the right things. Many parents have also succumbed to this message. It's not the quality of character that matters; it is the quantity and quality of one's possessions.

Drugs

Illicit drugs are still available and are easy to obtain. What has changed, however, is that the newer drugs are more potent and are readily available to many kids even in middle school and junior high. The drug culture is so much a part of the youth culture in some neighborhoods that explaining the downside of drugs falls on deaf ears, especially when the immediate benefit is pleasure and everybody else is doing it.

Portraying Parents as Bumbling or Vicious

Most movies and many television programs are targeted to young audiences and exploit themes that resonate with youth. One such theme is to portray parents and adults as cruel or incompetent while depicting young children or teenagers as savvy and smart. While many of these programs are meant to be humorous, there is also a message—parents are dysfunctional and cannot be trusted; kids know best.

Guns, Weapons, and Violence

Years ago we would not have predicted that children and teenagers would arm themselves and go on shooting sprees at home, at school, and in the community. Yet this is a reality in our time. In many schools, students must pass through metal detectors monitored by guards who are full-time employees of the school or police department. We should not be surprised! Guns are easily available in every community. Violent video games teach children to hunt down their prey and shoot to kill. Movies provide violent models for children to imitate. Parents seem to have good reasons to be concerned about the safety of their children.

While these concerns worry parents, there are also other changes that make it harder for parents to spend quality time with their children—an increase in the divorce rate, the rise of single parent households, the greater likelihood of children being born to unwed mothers with no father available for childcare help, and the increased pressure for both parents to work in order to pay the bills. As all of these changes have occurred, Garbarino believes that there has also been an increase in the number of difficult children who tax the limit of family and societal systems. He points to four trends to explain this increase in difficult to manage children.

1. Today there are more severely premature infants surviving than ever before. Some of these infants have been put at an even greater risk by

their mother's cocaine or alcohol abuse. When these vulnerable children are born they need special attention and resources to help them develop normally. When these resources are not available, perhaps because parents are young and lack income and social support, these children are more likely to become difficult.

2. More children are being reared in single-parent families. Often when this occurs, the single parent does not have the support needed to deal effectively with the stresses of child-rearing and s/he is overwhelmed by the persistent demands of a young child.

3. The quick pace of modern society does not allow for a lot of one-on-one parent/child interaction time. When options to disengage are available, such as TV, these options are often used to the detriment of child development.

4. There are too many things to do and not enough time. When this happens, something must suffer and it is frequently time spent with children. Garbarino (2001) states the following proposition: "The less time an individual has with a child, the more difficult it is to manage that child, the more assistance it takes to compensate" (p. 67).

• Do you agree that conditions today are more toxic for children than conditions in the past? If you are a parent, what adjustments have you made to protect your children from these conditions?

How Parents and Adolescents Have Changed

As cultural changes have evolved, both parenting and adolescence have changed. These changes have been the subject of Ron Taffel's book, *The Second Family*. After interviewing children and adolescents, Taffel (2001) concludes that many adolescents have turned toward their peer group as their second family. His insightful analysis of what has happened in the home and how changes have influenced children and adolescents deserves thoughtful consideration.

What happened to parenting? Taffel (2001) notes that parents, especially parents who both work, have less time to spend with their children. While mom microwaves supper, dad is watching TV and talking to a business partner on the phone. The teenage son is conversing with friends on the Internet and the eight-year-old daughter is watching a video while listening to a Jennifer Lopez CD. Everyone seems to be doing several things at once without giving undivided attention to each other. Taffel notes: "it's not just that parents are out of the house more often—it's that even when everyone's home, 'shared' family time is not what it used to be" (p. 18). A recent survey found that working mothers spend less than twelve minutes a day talking with their kids and fathers spend even less time doing so—about eight minutes. Taffel believes that what children want most from their parents is something they are not getting—their parents' undivided attention. Although the children are saddened and sometimes angered by this lack of attention, by junior high school they have accepted it as the way things are; their parents are just preoccupied with other things. It's not that parents are failing to provide in other ways for their children; they buy them things (CDs, videotapes, toys, games) and take them places (gymnastics practice, soccer camp, cheerleading practice) but fail to provide what Taffel says elementary kids want most—the individual, undivided attention of their parents.

Although these parents are often hardworking and are able to provide for their children's physical needs, they are confused about how to handle child-rearing problems. Is it Tough Love children need or is it unconditional positive regard? This confusion is not due to a lack of child-rearing information; there are more child-rearing books available now than ever before. Experts simply do not agree on how to handle the many problems that parents face. When Wendy William and Stephen Ceci (1998) gave child-rearing experts a series of family and child-rearing problems, they found that it was not uncommon for the experts to give very different advice. So what's a parent to do? With no consensus on what is best, parents are often bewildered, overwhelmed, and uncertain. And Taffel believes that parents relinquish too much of their authority. When every situation is judged on its own merits, there are no absolutes. Children soon learn that rules are flexible; they can be made up in the process of living. A kind of moral relativism exists—a live and let live philosophy. When adolescents in Illinois were asked about moral standards, they were hesitant to label any behavior as right or wrong and they could not see how adults could aid them in making moral decisions. In this "laissez-faire" kind of climate, Taffel believes that adolescents look outside the family for structure, comfort, and security. And they find this comfort with other adolescents who speak their language, wear the same brand of clothes, and face the same struggles.

- As a parent or family member have you observed some of the changes Taffel has noted?

What happened to adolescence? Adolescents have always separated themselves from their parents. But now, Taffel believes there are important differences. In the past, the purpose of adolescent rebellion was to separate from an oppressive parent who was standing in the way of new ideas and behaviors. However, today, by the time kids become teenagers, they already feel separated from their parents. They have been pushed out the door to dance classes, art classes, and gymnastics classes and have spent many hours apart from parents, immersing themselves in TV, MTV, the Internet, video games, and the pop culture. Taffel believes that if adolescents are angry, it is because they do not feel "held in their own families" and not because parents are overprotecting them or standing in the door holding them back. Nor is this generation as angry with their parents as past generations; rather they seem to be seeking attention as they struggle with detachment and emptiness. Usually they are not disdainful of their parents but rather think their parents don't know them and don't understand their inner lives. So they seek the companionship of those who have shared the same culture growing up—their peer group. According to Taffel, the pull of this second family begins early in life and the child's involvement spans three levels: Introduction, Exploration, and Comfort.

The Introduction Level begins early. Parents unwittingly introduce children to second family pursuits when the child is young. These pursuits include TV programming, advertisements, movies, video games, the fast food industry, and the latest toy craze. And the values of children are being shaped by the excitement, entertainment, and novelty provided by the things around them. Since television is so often the centerpiece of this excitement, it's as if there is a bond between the child, the television, and the things which television has to offer. Also, as children are sent off to daycare while parents work, they are introduced to children of the same age with whom they will go lock step through life, sharing the same space, entertainment, games, fads, and interests. As parents spend less time with their children, especially undivided attention time, children are pulled more and more into a culture dominated by the media and shared with their own peer group. As a result, Taffel (2001) believes that children develop the "gimmees"—a powerful desire for the *in* things that are promoted by advertisers and the peer group. The "gimmee" attitude assumes that things buy happiness. As parents spend more time at work, children spend more time with peers; this results in less parent-child time together and more time for children and adolescents to bond with peers. Thus parents become less influential as the influence of the second family begins to take hold.

The Exploration Level soon follows. During the elementary school years, media fads and the "gimmees" are in full swing. According to Taffel, *the tyranny of the cool* dominates children's thinking, especially in elementary school when they must have all the *in* things to be cool. Advertising has now paid off—being popular means wearing the right shoes, having the coolest backpack, and displaying the appropriate designer labels. In this world of the cool, there are immediate decisions that must be made regarding gratification: the level of difficulty of the video game, the channels on the TV, and the most interesting Internet sites. Today children often seek instant gratification, having low frustration tolerance for things that are difficult and boring. As homework gets harder, children are tempted to turn away from difficult academic tasks and turn to the comforts of a less demanding life reflected in the philosophy of the second family.

The Comfort Level takes hold in the teen years. Some young teenagers become fully immersed in the second family culture by the seventh or eighth grade. This is a culture that is more and more distant from parents. Young teens have had their fill of scheduled time and now enter a "live and let live" world dominated by their peers. This second family doesn't demand much; it simply provides acceptance as teenagers hang out together. *The tyranny of the cool* loses much of its power at the Comfort Level. Teenagers are now compelled to find their own *comfort zone*. During this time, teens break off into compatible subgroups–the skateboarders, the jocks, the intellectuals, or the heavy metal types. These groups often provide the structure, understanding, and nurturing that one would expect from a family. And within these groups, a teenager may exhibit behaviors, both good and bad, that are not openly exhibited in the family of origin. The teenager who is non-communicative at home may communicate effectively in the peer group. The teen who will not take part in family rituals enjoys the rituals of the second family; the young person who lies to his parents would never think of lying in his peer group. Since these young people have been exposed to a wide variety of talk in the media and on the Internet, they are more comfortable discussing taboo topics. And these teens frequently talk to their second family friends either online or when they are hanging out. They stay connected, provide support, create rituals, and generally are there for each other. Of course, not all teens find a group; some stay on the fringe, attempt to float from group to group, or get left out. Yet Taffel believes that adolescence has changed, with teens being more disconnected from parents and much more in touch with their second family.

As teens immerse themselves in the second family, they often have secret lives that parents know very little about, especially if parents are busy and see their teen for only a few minutes a day. Then too, teens are likely to protect their secret lives from anyone who is not a part of the second family. Since parents have very little outside contact with second family members and these members are highly protective of their privacy, parents may be clueless as to the thoughts and activities of their teenager.

This disconnection from one's real family and this immersion into the culture of the second family appear to be what happened in the affluent suburb of Conyers, Georgia, when many teens acted out sexual and aggressive behaviors in the late 1990s. This incident came to the attention of authorities due to an outbreak of syphilis among the teenage population and was depicted in the Public Television Program, *The Lost Children of Rockdale County*.

While most parents were at work, these teens gathered in malls, motels, and homes and acted out sexual behaviors, often imitating what they had seen on X-rated videos and movies. These teens were caught up in a culture that was unknown to their parents and even when it became known was difficult for these parents to comprehend. These parents had lost control of their children and could not understand the forces at work underlying their teenagers' behavior. Taffel (2001) suggests that parents, teachers, and administrators ban together, forming a network of individuals who stay on top of what teenagers are doing. These individuals should develop hot lines of communication, informing each other at the first sign that something may be amiss. But he warns parents to beware—"When a hot line is fully functional and effective, adults have to prepare themselves to hear information that will shock, even terrify" (p. 178).

- Have you noted the levels Taffel discusses? How relevant are Taffel's conclusions to your own experiencing?

What's a Parent to Do

Does the increase in social toxicity, the change in the home environment, and the increasing influence of the second family portend trouble for every child and adolescent? Certainly not! Studies (Furman & Buhrmester, 1992; Lempers & Clark-Lempers, 1992) still indicate that a great majority of high school students perceive their parents as sources of support and affection. Many follow a positive path by taking positions of leadership, volunteering in community agencies, and taking schoolwork seriously. Yet there is some evidence that more young people today are at risk than in the past. Garbarino (2001) reports that twenty-five years ago, 10 percent of kids were troubled enough to see professional counselors while today it is closer to 20 percent. And parents seem aware of how difficult parenting is today. In a 1999 *USA Today* poll, about 90 percent of parents questioned held the belief that it was more difficult to rear children today than it was twenty-five years ago. Seventy five percent of these parents mentioned the media and the pop culture as detrimental influences that have made child-rearing more difficult.

Can any parent predict with 100 percent certainty that their child will not become seriously troubled? Probably not! There are too many powerful and complex variables at work to reliably predict and control outcomes. For example, research indicates that one in one hundred individuals will develop schizophrenia, a major mental disorder that usually afflicts teenagers and young adults. If parents factor in all the other possible problems—autism, eating disorders, depression, addition to drugs, hyperactivity, etc.—they realize that escaping hardships involving children is very difficult. When attempting to predict what will happen or to determine what went wrong, parents and even experts must have knowledge that usually is not readily available. This knowledge would relate to the following questions. Does the child's genetic blueprint predispose illness? Does the child's temperament make the job of parenting more difficult? How resilient is the child? Can the child bounce back from difficult circumstances? To what extent is the social environment toxic and how susceptible is the child to the influence of the media, the peer group, and other influences? How prepared are the child's parents to provide nurture and support through both good and bad times? What are the risks and opportunities this child will face? Do the risks outweigh the opportunities? How will the child interpret the world–through the lens of optimism or the lens of pessimism? The world is not a simple place and there are no simple answers. Hopefully, we are beyond the time when all negative outcomes are attributed to faulty parenting and positive outcomes to superior nurturing. Outcomes are surely more complicated than this simplistic view suggests. Yet parents certainly need all the knowledge, understanding, resources, and support that can be made available so that every child will have the best opportunity to thrive.

IMPORTANT TERMS AND CONCEPTS

Dym and Glenn's marital stages
Davis' marital stages
Belsky's six domains
socially toxic environment
the second family
Taffel's three levels of second family involvement: Introduction, Exploration and Comfort
tyranny of the cool

SUGGESTED READINGS

Belsky, J., & Kelly, J. (1994). *The transition to parenthood: How a first child changes a marriage*. New York: Delacorte Press.
Dym, B., & Glenn, M. L. (1993) *Couples: Exploring and understanding the cycles of intimate relationship*. New York: HarperCollins.
Garbarino, J., & Bedard, C. (2001). *Parents under seize: Why you are the solution, not the problem, in your child's life*. New York: The Free Press.
Taffel, R., & Blau, M. (2001). *The second family: How adolescent power is challenging the American family*. New York: St. Martins Press.

Chapter 5

FAMILY INFLUENCE AND
GENERATIONAL CONNECTIONS

Powerful bonds develop in families. These bonds create connections that are unlike any other connections in life; these connections are created by daily experiences with mom, dad, and siblings as family life unfolds. Family experiences are etched in memory at an early age and influence life far into the future. Parents also influence their children through heredity, connecting family members through DNA. Therefore, parents influence their offspring by providing genetic material and environmental experience. This chapter will examine this influence and explore the ways connections with parents and family impact our lives.

PARENTAL INFLUENCE AND HEREDITY

Since we receive half of our genes from each parent, the influence of heredity casts a long shadow over our development. However, parents do not transmit an exact replica of their genes to their offspring. Each sperm from the male and each ovum from the female are made up of a unique combination of each parent's genes. New life begins when a unique combination of genes from the mother combines with a unique combination from the father, creating a child who "inherits a configuration of genes that is both similar and different from that of its parents" (Ambert, 2001). This means that there is much randomness to the inheritance process.

Furthermore, personality predispositions are thought to be polygenic, the result of a combination of several genes acting together. Thus, to inherit a tendency to be extroverted, a certain combination of genes from the mother must interact with a certain combination of genes from the father. Presently, scientists do not completely understand what combination of genes is needed to produce predispositions or how this combination process works. They do know, however, that unless you have an identical twin, your genetic blueprint stamps you as one of a kind—not completely different from others but certainly unique in your own way. So the old saying is correct—there's no one else in the whole human race with your kind of style and your kind of grace, no one else exactly like you, no one else like you. Heredity deals the cards while the forces of the environment and the individual's own initiative determines how this hand is played out in life.

Recent research (Segal, 1999) involving longitudinal studies, twin studies, and adoption studies has contributed to the understanding of the genetic hand. These studies strongly suggest that not only physical characteristics but also personality characteristics are linked to heredity. Some important traits that appear to have a powerful genetic basis include emotionality, introversion-extraversion, and sensation seeking. Once these tendencies emerge in personality, they then become the forces that guide the experience selection process. For example, the outgoing, sociable child will select experiences that are very different from the shy, reserved child and these different experiences continue to mold personality. Thus inherited tendencies affect us by influencing the behaviors we engage in and the experiences we select; these behaviors result in environmental consequences that further mold and shape personality. Therefore, there is an ongoing interaction between inherited tendencies and the environment with both playing an important role in shaping personality.

THE INTERACTION OF HEREDITY AND ENVIRONMENT

An interesting example of the interaction of heredity and environment is seen in the child who inherits a tendency to be a sensation-seeker. Individuals who inherit this tendency seek high levels of stimulation in order to reach their preferred level of arousal. Even though research (Zuckerman, 1991) suggests that this tendency is inherited, the direction sensation-seeking takes is influenced by environmental opportunities and the experiences the individual selects to satisfy this need. From a cultural perspective, there are both positive and negative directions sensation seeking can take. On the positive side, there are such things as rock climbing, skydiving, bungee jumping, or stock car racing. On the negative side, the young person might choose gang activity, stealing, running away from home, or any number of drug-related behaviors. If these negative experiences are the only exciting experiences available, the young person may satisfy this need in a negative way. However, if family members recognize this tendency, they may be able to provide positive alternatives, making it more likely that this tendency will be satisfied in a culturally acceptable way. Thus environmental opportunities are crucial in determining the direction a tendency such as sensation seeking will take.

Therefore acknowledging the importance of heredity does not completely negate the importance of parenting and the environment. Although we now know that parenting and environmental influences are not responsible for every aspect of an individual's personality and behavior, we also know that parenting plays a crucial role in determining how the genetic hands gets played out. In discussing the role of parenting in this process, Ambert (2001) mentions several important ways parents make a vital contribution. First, not all traits and behaviors are equally influenced by genetics. Certain characteristics such as beliefs, values, and manners may have little input from heredity. In regard to these characteristics, parents can have a powerful influence. Even in instances where there is high hereditability, a parent may be able to encourage, direct, or temper the inherited tendency. The case of the high sensation-seeking child serves as an example, as does the case of the child who is musically gifted and is encouraged by parents to develop this gift. However, a certain amount of cooperation from the child is also important in this process and this cooperation may be influenced by both genetic and environmental variables. Also, a supportive, healthy, loving environment can positively influence most every child regardless of genetic predisposition. Ambert (2001) notes that providing this type of environment "may well be parents' foremost contribution to their offspring" (p. 192).

Today, scientists emphasize the importance of both heredity and environment but still struggle to understand the role each plays in determining something as complex as behavior and personality. On an intuitive level, individuals often seem to understand the importance of both hereditary and environmental influences. Perhaps this is why so many adopted children attempt to find their biological parents. They want to establish contact with those who have contributed so much to their way of being. Yet these same children are grateful for their adopted parents who helped shape their inherited tendencies into their present form.

- If you were adopted in infancy, would you want to find your biological parents? Why or why not? What seems to be an important physical trait that has been passed down in your family? Although it is difficult to say if a personality trait is more due to hereditary or environmental influences, what personality tendencies do you possess that you suspect have a strong basis in heredity?

Couples who marry share none of their genes; only identical twins share the same genetic makeup. And even though partners may come from families that are similar, no two family cultures are exactly alike. Therefore, couples are faced with the task of creating their own family culture, one that is comfortable to both partners even though they are different in many ways. Since partners are so different, perhaps it should not be surprising that many couples divorce. Many of the problems couples confront have been found to be perpetual problems. Where do the strong feelings and entrenched attitudes that partners have originate? Do they come from inherited personality tendencies, the family of origin environment, the broader culture including the peer group and mass media, or some combination of all of these? To the struggling couple, it probably doesn't matter; they just experience their difficult issues as painful reminders that all is not well. Yet therapists often believe that helping couples understand the origin of their strong feelings in regard to their difficult issues is helpful; when partners understand the origin of their feelings and those of their partner, they are more likely to accept these feelings as legitimate. John and Julie Gottman (2001) work with couples to help them uncover the dreams behind their perpetual conflict issues. As couples uncover their dreams behind their conflicts, they often confront emotional memories that originated in their families of origin or long-standing personality traits that just seem to characterize each of them. The Gottmans (2001) provide a list of common perpetual issues that often surface in marriages. Examine some of the problem issues on their list and think about where a couple's differences in regard to these issues might originate? Are a couple's differences due to inherited tendencies, family of origin experiences, or some combination of heredity and environmental factors?

- One partner tends to be neat and organized; the other partner tends to be sloppy and unorganized.
- One partner tends to be emotional; the other partner very seldom expresses emotions.
- One partner wants closeness and togetherness in the marriage; the other partner values individuality and a greater degree of separateness.
- One partner enjoys spending money, seldom worrying about a budget; the other partner is more conservative, wanting to account for every penny.
- One partner wants a fairly equal division of labor regarding household chores; the other partner is content with doing very little.
- One partner is strict when disciplining children; the other partner is more lax and flexible.
- One partner frequently desires sex; the other partner prefers sex less frequently.
- One partner wants a close relationship with relatives; the other partner desires more separateness.
- One partner is religious; the other partner seldom seeks religious guidance.
- One partner is outgoing and prefers being with people; the other partner enjoys staying home, reading, or watching television.
- One partner is punctual, needing to be on time; the other partner is often late.
- One partner likes to talk, often about emotions and events of the day; the other partner is much less verbal, frequently turning away from such talk.

Often couples conclude that the way they are in regard to these issues is due to fundamental personality differences—differences that are based on innate temperament, experiences in one's family of origin, or possibly to some combination of these factors. And partners often conclude that their way of being is just the way they are—neither can easily change. Perhaps this is why 69 percent of the problems couples face are perpetual problems; these problems are never completely resolved (Gottman & Silver, 1999).

- Think of the way you are in relation to the items listed above. How did you acquire your tendencies? Do you think your tendencies are due more to innate temperament or to environmental influence? Have differences in regard to these issues caused problems for you in your intimate relationships?

THE FAMILY AND ENVIRONMENTAL INFLUENCE

Relationships in families and the bonds created by these relationships are influential throughout life. Family relationships and connections are not replicated in any other relationship setting: not at work, school, or any other groups. Think of the relationship that develops between a mother and child. The bonds that are established in this relationship are like no other bonds. These bonds have been forged by the many experiences the mother and child have shared over a lifetime. The mother is unique, the child is unique, and mother and child come together in this unique mother-child experience; there is nothing else that replicates this intimate relationship. Add to this the father-child experience; the sibling-sibling experience; and the experience with grandparents, uncles, aunts, cousins, and nieces and one realizes that this complex web of connections and relationships will never again be reproduced in this shape and form.

- As you think back on relationships in your early life, what do you remember about your mother, your father, and other family members?

Then, too, there is something more than the individual relationships that develop between family members; there is the experience of these individuals coming together as family. When we ask someone what their family was like, we are not asking what each individual in the family was like, but rather how the family functioning as a whole was experienced. When mom, dad, and children come together as family, they become something far greater than just the sum of each individual family member living together in close proximity. They become a unique entity we call the family. And people develop connections with this family entity. When a daughter moves over a thousand miles from home, she may return to see mom and dad, but she also may want to experience the warmth of family. When she establishes her own family, she may want to replicate that "at home" family experience. What our family of origin was like is permanently etched in our memory and these memories are usually laden with emotion, making them even more meaningful.

- As you think back on your family of origin, describe what your family was like.

Why are family connections and family relationships so meaningful? Burr, Day, and Bahr (1993) suggest several reasons. First, these connections and relationships begin to influence us during our earliest years when we are dependent and vulnerable. Parents and family pervade our early life and since we cannot select our parents or our family, the shadow of their influence is constant. Although a few adult children have attempted to divorce their parents, this severs ties in only a legal sense. It does not reverse the fact that the parents who brought these children into the world are their biological parents, nor does it erase past memories or undo the influence that these parents have had upon them.

Another reason that family connections and relationships are so important is due to the scope of that influence. Relationships in the family have the ability to influence thoughts and feelings about so many things. These include thoughts and feelings about self, others, religion, education, success, failure, money, power, sex, rules, and emotions. The family has the ability to influence attitudes about male and female roles, love, intimacy, anger, conflict, communication, and children. While other factors outside the family also influence one's attitudes and behaviors, the family usually gets there first, is dominant during the early years, and is often a continuing presence throughout life.

GENERATIONAL INFLUENCES THROUGH TIME

Attachment Theory and the Importance of the Past

Psychologists have often assumed that early childhood experiences have special importance–the child is father of the man. One theory that reflects this belief is attachment theory. The major proponents of this theory have been John Bowlby and Mary Ainsworth. Bowlby (1969) concluded that infants develop unconscious "working models" of attachment. This means that if a child experiences a healthy, nurturing love from early caregivers, the child will develop a positive attitude toward self and others; the child learns that s/he is lovable and trustworthy and that others can be counted on for support and nurturance. This working model of what self and others are like is carried into the future by way of a person's belief system; this belief system is ever present to influence future relationship experiences. However, if attachment needs are not meet by loving concerned caregivers, the child comes to believe that s/he is unlovable and that others cannot be trusted to supply needed nurturance. In developing this theory, Bowlby was especially interested in the responses of young children who were separated from their caregivers for short periods of time. He noted that some young children handled this separation well, as if they thought that mother would soon return. Other children were more upset by separation; they cried for long periods of time and seemed to exhibit deep despair. Still other children responded with detachment to both the separation and the return of the mother.

Mary Ainsworth (Ainsworth, Blehar, Waters, & Wall, 1978), who worked with Bowlby in the 1950s, developed a quantifiable way to measure security and attachment. Her assessment strategy developed in the following way. She would study mother-infant interaction in the home during the first year of life and then bring the mother and young child into a strange laboratory playroom where the environment could be more easily manipulated. In this playroom, the child stayed with the mother; later the mother left for a short time and the child was alone, and then the mother returned. It was believed that this strange situation episode would activate the child's attachment system. Ainsworth closely observed the children to determine how they would respond to the strange situation, to the mother's leaving, and to the mother's return. The child's response to the mother's leaving and return became an especially important indicator of attachment and this situation became known as the strange situation test.

Securely attached children in this strange situation environment begin to explore the playroom, exhibiting interest in the toys and other playthings. When the mother leaves, they show signs of missing her, often by crying. When she returns, they seek her out for comfort, are quickly soothed, and then they return to play. This reconciliation between mother and child seems to activate a sense of confidence in the child so that the world can again be explored. The mothers of this group were especially well attuned to their infants' needs and mental states and did not under or overreact to these states. They valued the attachment relationship with their children and seemed to know how to create a healthy, secure environment so that their children's attachment would be secure. Secure attachment was found in about 55 to 65 percent of the infants.

The ambivalently attached infants seemed wary and somewhat distressed even prior to separation. There was little exploration by these children even when the mother was present. They appeared anxious and were not easily soothed either before or after separation. When the mothers returned to the playroom, these children failed to settle down and gain a sense of comfort; instead they continued to cry and focus on their mother. They resisted soothing and had difficulty returning to play. These children had an excessive need to be close, yet closeness did not turn the attachment activation system off. In the home, these mothers were observed to be inconsistent in their treatment of their children in regard to both responsiveness and availability. It was difficult for these mothers to be properly sensitive, perceptive, and attuned to their child's needs. They might hug their child but at a time when a hug was not consistent with the child's state of mind. Thus, they tried to connect but in a way that was inappropriate to the child's behavior and mental state. Therefore, these infants were uncertain whether their needs at any given time were going to be appropriately attuned to and satisfied. Sometimes they were and sometimes not, leaving them anxious and distressed. Five to fifteen percent of the infants demonstrated this ambivalent attachment.

The avoidantly attached infants focused on the toys and the environment throughout the strange situation procedure. They continued to play as if nothing had changed even when the mother left and returned to the room. These children did not cry when the separation occurred and they overtly ignored the mother when she returned. They have a moving away or turning away stance and may even resist being picked up. However, studies reveal that these childrens' heart rates change when the mother returns, indicating that they are aware of the mother even though they do not overtly respond to her return. What parenting style would be associated with such a dismissing response on the part of the child? Ainsworth found that these mothers were neglectful, rejecting, and emotionally unavailable. Thus they were insensitive to their child's needs and unable to meet these needs. Surprisingly, 20 to 30 percent of infants were found to be avoidantly attached.

But do attachment styles become embedded in our character and carry over from childhood, influencing adult behavior and relationships? Many attachment theorists believe that such a carryover does occur. Remember Bowlby's "working model" for interpersonal relationships is a kind of mental representation of what a person believes about self and others. Can this mental picture or working model, which is thought to be formed in childhood, influence how one thinks and behaves as an adult? The first hint that this might be the case appeared in the *Rocky Mountain News* some years ago (Hazan & Shaver, 1987). A short "love quiz" was printed in the "Lifestyle" section of this paper, which readers were to complete and return. Readers were asked to check which of three love styles best described them in relationships. The first was a secure style, one in which a person easily gets close to others and can comfortably depend on others in relationships without worry of abandonment or overcloseness. The second was an avoidant style in which there was discomfort in closeness, an inability to trust others completely, and a tendency to be wary when others want to get close. The third was an anxious-ambivalent style in which there was an anxious urge to merge with a partner, combined with a concern that the partner will become uneasy and sever the relationship. Although the assessment was crude and the more than one thousand respondents were not a scientific cross section, the results were interesting. Fifty-six percent of the respondents were categorized as secure, 25 percent as avoidant, and 19 percent as anxious-ambivalent. A subsequent national survey (Mickelson, Kessler, & Shaver, 1997) found similar results–59 percent secure, 25 percent avoidant, and 11 percent anxious-ambivalent, with 5 percent unclassifiable. What was interesting about these findings is how closely they matched the percentages of the children in the attachment theory research.

But have adults who exhibit different attachment styles been exposed to parents in early childhood who were similar to the parents in Ainworth's studies? Since one cannot go back and observe these individuals and their parents during childhood, the next best thing is to interview them and ask about their memories of childhood, especially their memories of parents. The findings are consistent with Ainsworth's parental styles. Those adults who have secure attachment styles tend to remember parents who were warm and supportive in a trusting family atmosphere. Those adults who have avoidant attachment styles are more likely to recall parents who were distrustful and emotionally distant and those with anxious-ambivalent styles are likely to recall parents who provided very little support and encouragement (Brennan & Shaver, 1993; Hazan & Shaver, 1987; Levy, Blatt, & Shaver, 1998).

Do different attachment styles affect romantic relationships? A number of studies have found that individuals with secure attachment styles have more stable, happy, and satisfying relationships than do individuals characterized by the other styles. Also, adults with secure attachment styles are more likely to have partners with this same style (Brennan & Shaver, 1995; Pistole, 1989; Simpson, 1990; Collins & Read, 1990). In contrast, individuals with avoidant attachment styles are more likely to be fearful of intimacy and to report never having been in love (Hazan & Shaver, 1987; Feeney, Noller, & Patty, 1993). The anxious ambivalent individuals tended to fall in love many times but have difficulty keeping a long-term stable relationship. Perhaps this is because they are fearful of abandonment and try too hard to please (Hazan & Shaver, 1987; Pistole, 1989).

The Becoming a Parent Project

Attachment theorists suggest that family legacies are past down from generation to generation. Secure, self-confident parents create healthy, nurturing environments for their children. When these children grow up, they are secure and confident enough to provide healthy, nurturing environments for their young. Sadly, the opposite may also be true. Parents with problems may provide less than adequate nurturing; this less than adequate nurturing creates problems for their children, which later influences the type of care these children provide for their offspring. There is much anecdotal evidence that seems to support this belief. But is there any research support for this generational transmission effect?

In Cowan and Cowan's longitudinal study (The Becoming a Parent Project discussed in Chapter 4), these researchers followed couples from pregnancy through kindergarten. As they followed these couples, they studied four issues that related to the concept of generational transmission. These issues related to (1) problems with alcohol, (2) conflict in one's family of origin, (3) secure/insecure attachment relationships with parents in the family of origin, and (4) family distress and academic and social problems of children. Their findings are relevant to the question—Is their any support for the generational transmission principle?

Couples from Homes Where Alcohol Was a Problem

Many psychologists (Woititz, 1983; Ackerman, 1989) have written about the negative effects associated with growing up in a family where one or both parents abused alcohol. The Cowan's asked the couples in their study if any of their parents had struggled with alcohol problems. Surprisingly, 20 percent of the subject parents anticipating their first child had at least one parent who struggled with an alcohol-related problem. As these researchers accumulated data about how these couples coped with the parenthood transition, they examined the relationship between alcohol problems in the family of origin and coping effectiveness during the parenthood transition. Although none of the expectant parents reported having a problem with alcohol, other findings from this part of their study are troubling. Cowan and Cowan (2001) write: "On *every* index of adjustment to parenthood—symptoms of depression, self-esteem, parenting stress, role dissatisfaction, and decline in satisfaction with marriage—men and women whose parents had abused alcohol had significantly greater difficulty" (p. 142). So even if these new parents do not abuse alcohol, the legacy of alcohol may have a lasting effect. These researchers suggest that it may be the things that characterize the home life in alcoholic families—denial of problems, secret keeping, little expression of inner feelings, etc.—that lead to self-esteem and personality problems that are difficult to overcome.

Conflict in One's Family of Origin

The Cowans also asked the expectant parents in their study about the amount of conflict they remembered in their families of origin. Family conflict was measured by giving each partner a family environment scale that assessed family conflict. This allowed the researchers to group couples in regard to their similarities and differences concerning the level of conflict in their families of origin. Four pairings became possible: (1) both partners come from low-conflict families, (2) both partners come from high-conflict families, (3) the wife comes from a high-conflict family, the husband from a low-conflict family, and (4) the husband comes from a high-conflict family, the wife comes from a low-conflict family. The researchers then correlated the information about conflict levels in families of origin with the satisfaction levels in their marriages. The findings are interesting. When both husband and wife come from low-conflict families of origin, they report the least drop in marital satisfaction during the first eighteen months after the birth of their baby. These couples were more likely to sustain their satisfaction level. But what about the couples who both came from high-conflict families? The Cowan's (2001) write: "When both partners came from high-conflict families, they experienced a substantial decline in their satisfaction with marriage over the same period of time" (p. 144). Thus, when both couples came from high-conflict families, they simply could not sustain their level of marital satisfaction during the parenthood transition.

But what happened when partners were mix-matched in regard to the conflict levels in their families of origin? When the husband's family had low conflict and the wife's family had high conflict, they were able to avoid serious deterioration in their marital satisfaction. The Cowan's speculated that when wives in these pairings became irritable, their husbands did not respond with irritation; thus they did not escalate the tension, anger, and criticism in the marriage. This may have had a calming effect, allowing the wife to avoid a serious deterioration in marital satisfaction. However, the outlook for marriages where husbands perceived high conflict in their families of origin while wives perceived low conflict is not as hopeful. This pairing produced increased dissatisfaction in the marriage for both partners, with wives being especially dissatisfied in these marriages. The Cowans speculate that when these husbands expressed irritation and frustration during the early baby days, their wives, not having seen this in their families of origin, became distressed. This may have led to higher levels of marital dissatisfaction. The Cowans (2001) write: "In this case, the negative cycle from the husband's family gets replayed, overriding the wife's more benign early experience" (p. 144).

Secure/Insecure Attachment in the Family of Origin

The Cowans were also interested in gathering information about partners' recollections of their early childhood experiences. They were especially interested in whether their recollections of their parents were consistent with secure or insecure attachment styles. Mary Main's studies (1985) have indicated that when parents recall childhood experiences that are consistent with insecure attachment, these parents are more likely to create an insecure attachment relationship with their children. Therefore, researchers in the Becoming a Parent Project obtained information about the parents' early childhood relationships through interviews and questionnaires. Some of these new parents recalled loving, caring parents who nurtured in a comforting way, while others recalled parents who were neglectful and uncaring. Even if a subject recalled neglectful parents, this subject could be in the secure group if s/he had worked through childhood experiences and now had a healthy working model of relationships. These researchers used The Adult Attachment Interview developed by Main and her associates for classifying the type of relationship partners experienced and the working models they utilized. After assessing secure/insecure attachment relationships in the partner's families of origin and the partners present working model of relationships, they found that the majority of their couples could be divided into three groupings: (1) groups where both the husband and wife had a secure working model, (2) groups where both the husband and wife had an insecure working model, and (3) groups where the wife had an insecure working model of relationships and the husband had a secure working model. (Note: there were too few couples in the husband insecure/wife secure group for conclusions to be drawn.) After couples were classified in this way, the researchers observed the parents interacting both together and individually with their child and these interactions were rated.

The secure/secure partners displayed much more warmth and positive interaction toward each other in the observed situations; furthermore, they each were warmer and more effective at helping their children with problem tasks when observed individually with their child. The insecure/insecure partners were less cooperative and warm with each other and they exhibited more negativity toward each other in the presence of their child. While dealing with their child individually, "both parents with insecure models were much less warm, engaged, and structuring than other parents in the study" (p. 146).

But how would the couples react in the husband secure/wife insecure group? These findings are encouraging. In this pairing, couples were as positive with each other and their child as were those couples in the secure/secure group. When husbands have a secure working model of relationships and their wives have unresolved issues concerning parents and their growing up years, the Cowan's report that "the women's parenting was as warm, structuring, and engaged as that of the mothers described as securely attached" (p. 147). These findings suggest that in these marriages, something, perhaps it is the quality of the marriage relationship, allows the mother to keep unresolved issues of the past from negatively affecting her relationships with her husband and child.

Parental Distress and the Competence of Children

The Cowans (2001) were also interested in how the children of the parents in their study would adjust to kindergarten. Would children from distressed homes have more difficulty with academic and social skills? Children were given achievement tests measuring reading recognition and mathematics skills at the end of their kindergarten year and the kindergarten teachers rated the children's behavior twice during the year using an item checklist. The researchers found a relationship between family distress and academic scores and social ratings. These researchers write: "When families were in difficulty or distress in many aspects of their lives, their children were described by their kindergarten teachers as more aggressive or more shy and more likely to have problems concentrating in the classroom. These children also had lower reading and mathematics achievement scores at the end of their kindergarten year" (p. 160). These researchers suggest that marital conflict may have a disruptive effect on parent-child relationships, making parents less effective in helping their children manage developmental tasks. The teachers' ratings of these children—less able to concentrate on school work, more aggressive or shy—and their lower achievement scores may reflect this disruptive influence.

Since the Cowans' study involves correlations, other factors such as inherited predispositions may have been responsible for the relationships they observed. However, many family scientists believe that the family of origin environment is a powerful environment and that this environment is at least partly responsible for the relationships that exist.

Object Relations Theory and the Importance of the Past

For many years, psychoanalytic theorists have emphasized the importance of childhood experience. First Freud, then others modified Freud's ideas to create their own brand of psychoanalytic theories. These theories also emphasized the importance of childhood but often de-emphasized sexuality and focused more on the role of the social environment. Among these theorists was a group whose ideas became known as object relations theory. Although today, there are several different interpretations of object relations theory, theorists working from this framework hold common assumptions with each other and with attachment theorists. First, object relations theories assume that childhood experiences with significant others (objects) are crucial to development. Usually the significant object is the mother, father, or both parents. It is assumed that the child develops an unconscious mental representation of these significant objects (parental figures). Furthermore, this unconscious mental representation of the parents is used as a basis for interpreting how one thinks about and relates to others throughout life. Thus, the lens of childhood is used to interpret the world long after childhood has been left behind. Therefore, the kind of attachments and interactions the child has with significant others in childhood greatly influences the nature of future relationships. Some theorists even suggest that the person we marry and the way we perceive and interact with this person are determined by the interactions we had with our first significant caregivers during childhood. So both attachment theorists and object relations theorists believe that relationships in early childhood influence relationships in adulthood. An example will illustrate what some object relations theorists believe happens during the second year of life, which can impact future relationships.

According to Mahler, Pine, and Bergman (1975), when infants toddle away from their mothers to explore the environment for the first time, they realize their separateness from her. Mahler believes that just as this awareness of separateness is flourishing (between 15 and 24 months), the child can create a distance from mother. Also at this time, the child develops a special need for mother to share new experiences (closeness). The child, on the one hand, seeks closeness, only to move away for the excitement of new experience. It is a time of ambivalence; the child desires closeness but at the same time fears the engulfment that characterized the earlier months. The child cherishes the new freedom associated with leaving mother but does not want to lose sight of mother. It is a phase characterized by alternating desires—to push away from mother and to cling to her. It is the child's first experience with the paradox that everyone experiences in regard to intimacy—the desire to be close to another in relationships and the desire to develop an independent identity. A child's ability to sustain separateness will depend on how the mother is mentally represented in the child's mind. If the child holds a picture of mother as warm and loving, the tendency to sustain separation will be enhanced. The child knows that s/he can explore and then return to mother with the assurance that mother will be there to comfort and soothe. Mother becomes a consistent, positive mental image that the child can latch on to and use even to self-soothe. According to Mahler and other object relations theorists, this type of healthy emotional availability on the part of the mother is crucial during this time. If she is preoccupied or unavailable, too much of the child's energy is used to make contact with her and the child becomes preoccupied with wooing. If mother is overly anxious about separation, she may become intrusive, checking on the child's every move and the child cannot easily separate from her. Thus, if too much of the child's energy is bound up in trying to separate, it becomes more difficult for the child to return to her.

Note the similarities between attachment theory and object relations theory. Both theories propose that early maternal and parental bonds are important and that mental representations of early experience with caretakers can have a lasting influence on later development. In Chapter 6 these two theories will again be discussed in relation to the development of the abusive personality. But for now, our attention will turn to how object relations theory has been used to help couples understand marriage relationships.

Imago Theory

One theorist with an object relations bent, Harville Hendrix (1990, 1992), has spent many years helping couples understand how their relationships are influenced by the past and how they can overcome early psychological wounding to create healthier, more mature marriages. Hendrix's ideas illustrate how an object relations orientation can be used to explain adult relationship problems, especially problems in marriage.

Yearning for Completeness

Hendrix believes that we have an unconscious memory of a time during prenatal development when our needs were completely meet and we felt content. He believes we attempt to recreate the sense of contentment associated with this early time when all our needs were met. To some degree, this is what love is since falling in love stirs within us memories of this special time. However, in adulthood, it is our beloved who ignites these feelings within us, feelings that are unconsciously associated with our original caretaker and the time during prenatal development when all our needs were easily satisfied.

Impediments to Aliveness

Since the womb environment was an all-nourishing environment, the early years can never replicate this ideal state. Even with good nurturing, parents at times struggle to provide for their child's needs. Since the infant cannot understand what is happening and has little control, even minor deprivations and threats take on important significance. Instinctively, the infant is sensitive to situations that are associated with danger and safety. The birth process is the first threat, but other threats soon follow as the child attempts to adjust to an imperfect world. For the infant, each situation comes to be judged in terms of survival value. Is it safe or threatening? Is it smoothing or frightening? Does it feel good or produce pain? The primitive part of the infant's brain is already at work recording sensations and feelings regarding safety and survival. The primitive brain associates experience with pain and pleasure but is unable to make subtle distinctions in situations. These early experiences, although not consciously remembered, become deeply and permanently imbedded in the primitive brain. Years later when our experience with emotions and feelings is out of proportion to the present circumstances, the old brain may have instinctively responded as it did in childhood. It's as if the old brain unconsciously forces feelings and sensations upon us. This means the more recently developed rational part of our brain must explain these feelings and sensations without having access to the unconscious old brain material.

Psychological Wounding

During the early years, there are many threats to the child's safety and survival. These threats separate the child further from the idyllic aliveness and wholeness that is so desired. Hendrix (1992) believes that when needs go unmet, psychological wounding occurs and it is important to understand the nature of this wounding if individuals are to understand themselves. Hendrix writes, "Understanding the nature of your wound is the key to your healing, for it has affected all of your behavior, your decisions, and your life choices, especially in the area of intimate relationships" (1992, p. 52). Also, the severity of one's wound depends on the stage at which the wounding occurs and the seriousness of the deprivation. Generally, wounding in the earliest stages has the greatest detrimental influence and severe impoverishment is more problematic than minimal impoverishment.

Understanding Childhood Experience

Since everyone has been wounded to some degree in childhood, it is important to understand the nature of this wounding. Hendrix proposes that from birth to age nineteen, we progress through six stages of development. However, usually there is one stage that has been especially problematic; this is due to our innate temperamental characteristics and how our parents responded to us at that particular time. This problematic stage is where we are most "stuck" and the issues associated with this stage will continue to reappear throughout life. As care giving occurs, the child is creating a mental picture of the caregiver or caregivers. Hendrix (1990) calls this mental picture the "Imago" after the Latin word for "image." According to Hendrix, "your imago is a composite picture of the people who influenced you most strongly at an early age" (p. 38). This picture takes shape during early development, at a time when our impressions are not very accessible to conscious memory. Thus many early impressions were etched in our primitive memo-ry—how our caregivers seemed to us, how they met or failed to meet our needs, how they made us feel safe or threatened, their tone of voice, their facial expressions. And the experiences that made the most lasting impression were the ones where caregivers were unable to meet our needs and our survival seemed threatened. At this point, we were psychologically wounded. The primitive brain filed these experiences away under the heading caregiver/survival without making fine-line distinctions regarding the nature of the situation.

Harville Hendrix and the Developmental Process

Hendrix (1992) believes that individuals go through six stages of development from birth through the teenage years. With proper nurturing, the child can successfully learn the appropriate tasks of each stage and move on to the next with confidence, ready to meet new challenges. However, if care is deficient and needs go unmet, the child must adjust to these conditions. These adjustments are defensive moves for the sake of survival and establish maladaptive patterns that may carry over into the future. Although each stage is important, the early stages are especially important. It is during the early years that the child is most helpless, dependent, and impressionable. Thus this discussion will focus on the first two stages (birth to three years) to illustrate how Hendrix believes parents influence their child's development during these important years. Although not all object relations theorists agree on the content and nature of the developmental stages, each perceives the early years as important building blocks that influence the adult years.

The Stage of Attachment (Birth to Eighteen Months)

Hendrix's (1992) first stage of development, spanning the first eighteen months, is the stage of Attachment. At birth, the infant's environment drastically changes. The transition from the warm, nurturing womb, where needs were met, to the cold, outside world is the child's first separation. In this new environment, the child quickly learns that survival is dependent upon help from others. Thus the infant begins the crucial task of reconnecting and reattaching, for separation is a threat to survival itself. The first eighteen months can be difficult for both infant and parent. For the infant, there is no longer automatic warmth and nourishment; for the mother, there are the constant demands of a helpless child. These demands first center on food, but emotional and bodily contact provided by loving caretakers are also critically important. If needs are met in a caring, consistent manner over the first eighteen months, the child develops a secure attachment to its caretaker and learns that the world is a safe place. The development of this early, secure attachment cannot be overemphasized; it is the basis for other important learning yet to come and it will shape future behavior in important ways. Hendrix, like Ainsworth, estimates that about 50 percent of infants have the care they need to become securely attached.

But what happens to the infant who cannot securely attach? Of course, the need to feel whole, connected, and at peace with life's circumstances does not go away just because parenting is inadequate. Rather, the infant must struggle to adapt and make sense of the world. During this struggle, maladaptive methods of coping and viewing the world begin to emerge. In this process, the young child is taking in information about self, the caretaker, and the world. These images and impressions about self and others are often depicted as "good" or "bad" and influence the child's behavior and coping strategies. In response to threat and inadequate nurturing, the child, during the attachment stage, develops a predictable pattern of either clinging or detaching in relation to others.

If the caretaker is inconsistent in meeting the infant's needs, Hendrix (1992) believes the infant begins to cling. Some parents are present and comforting at times, present but emotionally cold at other times, and simply not present at other times. Such inconsistent nurturing is confusing to the infant. The question becomes: Will the caretaker be there? What must I do to assure my safety? Since this caretaker occasionally reinforces the child's attention-seeking efforts, these efforts continue. But the child becomes anxious and upset at this unpredictable mothering, coming to see both self and mother in a "good/bad" ambivalent way. The young child needs the comfort the caretaker can provide but even on the occasions when the child is comforted, there is anger over past failures to comfort. The infant suffers psychological wounds that become a permanent part of personality structure. In adulthood, these individuals present themselves in a needy, clinging way, desiring reassurance that the partner will always be there and exhibiting anxiety at the slightest doubt. Their fear is of abandonment and their response is to demand, cling, and pursue. A task these individuals find difficult is to be separate and to allow a partner to have space.

Other infants who are unable to securely attach become detached. This is likely to occur when the caretaker is not available emotionally for the infant and is only occasionally available physically. The infant may attempt to attach to this caregiver but be consistently thwarted due to the caregiver's emotional coldness and unavailability. Therefore, any attempt to attach leads to failure and pain and, in time, the infant withdraws, preferring withdrawal to the pain of rejection. The picture of "self" and "other" that begins to develop is that both are "bad" and need to be repressed. Therefore, the pattern of rejecting one's personal needs and rejecting the other (caretaker) is set in place. Yet on an unconscious level, the primitive brain is alarmed, for it is these very needs that are necessary for survival. In response to this alarm, the young child numbs feelings and withdraws, creating a false self. This self may look competent and independent but is only a façade that hides a deeper self that is desperately trying to avoid contact for fear of rejection. The detached infant learns to survive on what is given, to make do with the situation, and to hold back tears. If this established personality pattern does not change, Hendrix (1992) believes the detached child becomes an avoider and tends to withdraw in relationship situations.

Adult avoiders have trouble contacting feelings since early in life they rejected their feeling side. They are not giving of their emotional selves, preferring instead to stay aloof and distant; thus they avoid the pain caused by feelings and intimacy. Yet unconsciously, they too have needs for contact and emotional closeness and they are often attracted to a clinging, reaching out, expressive partner. With such a partner, they fulfill some of their denied need for contact without having to approach. Still, closeness is uncomfortable and the same approaching partner they are attracted to often demands too much closeness, causing avoiders to anxiously retreat. But the clinger, having married an avoiding partner who is similar to his/her childhood caregiver, has had much experience pursuing so the demand/withdrawal pattern will become an established part of their relationship. The challenge for the avoider is to become more comfortable with emotional expression and to stay in contact without fleeing to the safety of distance.

The Stage of Exploration (Eighteen Months to Three Years)

After children deal with attachment issues during the first eighteen months, they then awaken to the wonders of exploration. From eighteen to thirty-six months, a child's world becomes a fascinating place. With increased motor and cognitive abilities, opportunities for exploration seem limitless; although they still want to know that mother is there, they also want to march out into this exciting world. If they are allowed to explore confidently and then return to a secure base, life is both exciting and supportive. Parents who understand this stage attempt to allow exploration while setting reasonable limits for their child's safety. If parents are too restrictive and overprotective during this stage, the child struggles to break away and is hesitant to return to a stifling, possessive caretaker. Thus a pattern of distancing from the controlling parent begins. Some children, while returning physically for needed reassurance, turn away emotionally. In their attempt to resist the controlling influence of the caretaker, these children appear to comply but inwardly resent the parent's intrusive manner, thus establishing a pattern of outward compliance but inward resistance. The distancing child may have made it successfully through the attachment stage but is now thwarted in the attempt to explore. This child does not fear contact but rather fears control and absorption. For protection, this child carefully maintains boundaries to ward off intrusion. As adults, Hendrix (1992) believes the distancing children become isolators. They fear being consumed, controlled, and smothered by their partner. When relationship anxiety occurs, their established pattern is to withdraw and create distance. As adults, a distancing partner needs to become comfortable with closeness and learn to share feelings in intimate ways.

Another response parents make to the exploring child is to push the child away too soon or not be available when the child returns. This child is allowed to explore but upon returning, either finds the parent gone, psychologically unavailable, or preoccupied. Thus, the young child fears abandonment. Where were you? Why did you not respond? Why are you so unavailable? The fear engendered in such a child leads to attention-seeking behaviors. If these attention-seeking behaviors garner the parent's attention, the child is reassured of the caretaker's presence and availability. This pattern of pursuing the love object to gain reassurance can influence adult behavior. The adult pursuer fears loss and abandonment; when their partner seems unavailable, this stirs up old anxieties that initiate a pursuing response. They may talk, cry, complain, or engage in any behavior that reassures them that they are not alone. Their intrusiveness infringes on the boundaries of others. They often see their partners as distant, not realizing that their constant pursuit of closeness pushes others away. The challenge for this partner is to feel comfortable with separateness and to respect the boundaries of others.

- Perhaps everyone, to some extent, was psychologically wounded during development. Think about your nurturing. Were you psychologically wounded in any way? If so, how and by whom?

Minimizers and Maximizers

As individuals progress through the developmental stages, Hendrix (1992) proposes that children become minimizers or maximizers in the way they expend energy. Minimizers tend to withdraw into themselves in regard to thoughts and feelings. They do not share their thoughts and emotions easily but rather protect their boundaries from infringement. They tend to be self-focused, looking inward for direction, while at the same time, they may attempt to direct and dominate others. Maximizers move toward others as they express their thoughts and feelings. They share thoughts and feelings easily and may intrude on the boundaries of others while allowing others easy access to their inner world. The maximizer/minimizer difference is similar to the pursuit/withdrawal difference that has been previously discussed.

Hendrix (1992) notes that statistically more males tend to be minimizers and more females are maximizers. He believes that this is due to differences in the socialization process, especially the way parents treat males and females differently in regard to emotional expression. Yet he notes that in some marriages, this tendency is reversed, with the wife exhibiting minimizing tendencies and the husband exhibiting maximizing tendencies.

- Are you a minimizer or maximizer? Explain how this affects your behavior.

The Socialization Process

Another important factor that influences development, especially how an individual responds in intimate relationships, is the socialization process. Hendrix sees faulty socialization in much the same way as humanistic psychologists like Carl Rogers. According to Hendrix (1992), there are four behavioral areas that are especially sensitive to the influence of socialization—thinking, feeling, acting, and sensing. In each of these areas, families and cultures attempt to dictate what is acceptable. As this happens, children learn ways of being that are taught by parents, school, and society; thus, the child learns that certain ways of thinking, feeling, acting, and sensing are considered acceptable and others are unacceptable. However, the desire to engage in disapproved ways of thinking, feeling, and behaving does not go away but instead is suppressed. In attempting to be what others want, individuals lose touch with important aspects of their being. As this occurs, individuals are no longer whole but split off from themselves, unable to see themselves in all the ways that they truly are. Thus, when an individual's unacceptable characteristics begin to emerge into awareness, these characteristics must be denied or distorted in some way in order to protect the self from that which is threatening. Often, denied characteristics are things individuals disliked in their parent(s); recognizing these things in themselves would require them to admit that they are like their parents. Thus, Hendrix (1992) sees the socialization process as "a process of mutilation, of chipping away at our wholeness" and in this process, "we lose contact with the exquisite pleasure of our own pulsating life energy" (p. 161).

As individuals repress aspects of their nature, these aspects become a part of the hidden or missing self. Unable to look inward and find the missing self, individuals turn outward in their search. In their attempt to find happiness and satisfaction, they turn to things—money, clothes, cars, sex, and drugs. But true wholeness and aliveness are not to be found in things but rather in the struggle to find one's repressed, missing self. If we are fortunate, "we meet someone who brings us alive, someone who makes us feel that the journey is over. We fall in love—with our Missing Self" (1992, p. 162).

- Since the repressed aspect of self is difficult for us to see, it is hard to examine. Think about what you were taught as a child. Have these teachings resulted in behavior and ways of being that now do not seem right to you even though they may still guide your behavior? Have others told you things about yourself that you were not fully aware of and that you wanted to deny? What were these things? What traits did you dislike in your parents? Do you see these traits in yourself?

The Nature of Falling in Love

Falling in love is both wonderful and mysterious. It is wonderful because it makes us feel euphoric and alive; it is mysterious because it is difficult to understand. How is it that the person we love brings out our aliveness and so many others simply did not ring any bells? Individuals want to believe that free choice is involved in the mate selection process, but Hendrix disagrees. The falling in love process is dictated by the unconscious motives that reach far back into childhood. These motives relate to early memories of our caretakers—what they were like, how they treated us, and how and when we were psychologically wounded. These impressions, embedded in the primitive brain and inaccessible to consciousness, make up our imago and influence our search for a partner. Without realizing what is happening, individuals seek a match between what is stored in unconscious memory concerning their early caretakers and the traits and characteristics exhibited by the person who is their imago match. Since caretakers are a big part of what is stored in the primitive brain, individuals search for partners who resemble their caretakers in both positive and negative ways. And Hendrix (1990) believes that the negative traits outweigh the positive traits in their influence. It may seem illogical that individuals would be attracted to someone with the negative traits of their early caretaker(s) since those negative traits may have inflicted childhood wounds. However, the part of the brain directing the search for a partner is the unconscious old brain and its logic is different. The old brain attempts to reproduce the family of origin associated with one's childhood so that wounding experiences can be worked through and healed. Having received enough nurturing to survive but not enough to feel satisfied, the old brain motivates choices that reproduce the original frustration so an individual can resolve unfinished business. Thus, one important factor in mate choice is to find a partner who has both the positive and negative characteristics of your primary caretakers with the negative traits being especially important. This person—an imago match, is the person an individual falls romantically in love with and the euphoria of romantic love temporarily blinds the individual to this person's negative traits. Later, these traits will become more apparent, but for a time, the partners bask in the beauty of romantic love.

• According to this theory, how does the old brain influence our selection of a mate? What does it mean to say that we have met our imago match?

According to Hendrix (1992), two other unconscious factors are also important in mate selection. During the socialization process, individuals deny certain characteristics that are a part of the self. These characteristics may be undesirable characteristics individuals saw in their parents, characteristics that they also possess but fail to recognize. Thus, an individual unconsciously chooses a mate not only because the mate possesses negative traits that resemble those of the individual's parent(s) but also because these same traits are a part of his or her denied self. This allows the individual to feel "whole" without having to take responsibility for aspects of the self that produce discomfort. As this happens, the individual is likely to see these traits in his or her partner since it is common to project these denied traits onto one's spouse. Thus, an individual will marry someone who exhibits some of the negative traits of the individual's parents. These are characteristics that the individual may also possess but deny. Then the individual will project one of these denied negative characteristics onto his or her partner and respond to the partner as if s/he truly has this negative characteristic. This projection may actually provoke this negative trait in the partner. Hendrix quotes a colleague as having said that we "pick imago matches, project them, or provoke them" (1988, p. 75).

In summary, Hendrix believes there are several things occurring as we search for a mate, each operating at an unconscious level: (1) We search for a partner who was wounded at the same stage of development where we suffered our greatest wounding. However, you and your partner will probably have developed different coping styles in response to this wounding—one will be a maximizer and the other a minimizer. (2) We search for a partner who has both the positive and negative traits of our caretaker(s) with the negative traits being especially important. (3) We search for a partner who exhibits negative characteristics of our denied self; often these are traits that match our parents' undesirable characteristics. (4) We search for a partner who possesses characteristics that we lack, thus attempting to merge those missing characteristics into ourselves, hoping to become complete.

- If you are in a relationship, think about that relationship in terms of Hendrix's theory. As you examine that relationship, do any of Hendrix's ideas ring true?

No one is certain why we fall in love with one person and not another. Perhaps the process is so complex that it will never be fully understood. However, another therapist, Augustus Napier, also believes that experiences in the family of origin are important in the decision-making process. His ideas are similar to those of Hendrix, yet also different. Napier believes that although physical attractiveness may initially bring people together, this attractiveness will not be enough to sustain the relationship. Here are some of Napier's (1988) ideas about the mate selection process.

1. We marry someone who is similar to us in how s/he experiences the world. This similarity goes beyond race, religion, and social class. It involves similar experiences within our families of origin. It may be that partners come from families that have experienced similar types of struggles, similar goals and philosophies, similar methods of handling conflict, a similar tolerance for intimacy, or some other important similarity. But the point is—"we are drawn to someone whose family world is in several important ways similar to our own" (p. 220).
2. We are drawn to a partner "whose basic psychological 'situation' in his or her family of origin is similar to our own" (p. 221). It may have been that both were the oldest, the family helper, the responsible one, the caretaker, or perhaps both were wounded in a similar way. Yet in some important way, you will share something significant with your partner that goes back to early family experience.
3. We will also see in our partner a "shared vulnerability" that at times we will be unable to see in ourselves but will see clearly in our partner. And though it may take years for us to recognize, we will also share a similar type of traumatic experience with our partner that goes back to childhood experience.
4. We marry someone who has the ability to create in us a sense of security, warmth, and protection similar to that "at home" feeling we experienced in childhood. Since it is the mother who is the first provider of that warmth and security, often the person we marry reminds us in some way of our mother. Napier (1988) believes that this is more likely to hold true for men than for women. For women, the tendency is to marry someone who reminds them of both mother and father. So our

partner will remind us in some way of a loved person in childhood with whom we felt safe; this person will also have characteristics of many of the major players in our childhood.

5. The person we marry will also remind us of ourselves, especially that part of ourselves that we do not see clearly or like very well.

6. Yet we will also marry someone who is different from us and these differences will bind partners together. Although there is more support for the similarity hypothesis than for the opposites attract hypothesis, Napier (1988) still believes that "there are powerful forces that seem to compel us to seek out someone who is in certain respects different from us; and the same forces tempt us to 'specialize' within marriage, each partner playing a particular role or 'representing' a certain attitude to life" (p. 224). This may lead to implicit agreements in the marriage that one partner will be the adult, while the other will be the child or that one will be the caretaker, while the other will be the recipient of that care. Also, we are often attracted to someone whose family of origin offers us something that is different from ours—perhaps hers was highly organized and his chaotic. Nevertheless, Napier believes that the strongest forces that bind partners together come from their similarities rather than their differences. And at times, even surface differences are based on hidden parts of the self that are in some way recognized in the partner.

Napier believes that the complicated marriage partnership will eventually do several things: it will expose our weaknesses, make us examine ourselves, and uncover problems we have carried over from childhood. This confrontation with our past and ourself will be painful, so painful that at some time in the marriage, the relationship itself will seem threatened. If we learn from and survive this pain, it is possible to develop a mutually satisfying relationship.

As you can see from this discussion, both Napier and Hendrix believe that mate selection is a very complex process influenced by hidden motivations that are imbedded in childhood and family of origin experiences.

The Roles We Learn to Play

A great deal has been written about the roles that children from dysfunctional families learn to play as they attempt to cope with the stressful demands placed upon them. These roles are often adopted as coping mechanisms and represent a child's defense against a difficult home environment. Ford (2001) believes the following roles serve this purpose.

The Scapegoat

This child usually becomes a problem in some way. By taking on the family's pain, the child distracts the troubled parents from their conflicts and troubles. This forces the parents back together as they deal with their "troubled" child. These children see to it that they are triangled into a parental relationship to temporarily reduce tension.

The Superhero

These children believe that if they can just be good enough, try hard enough, and always say and do the right thing, then the family situation will improve. On the outside, they may appear strong, but on the inside, they feel hurt and lonely.

The Enabler

This child spends time and energy trying to work things out so that conflict is reduced and family members feel better. This person often cares for the "sick" member of the family so that things are smoothed over and the family's problem can remain hidden or seem less significant.

The Distractor

Children who adopt this role attempt to distract attention away from the problem by being humorous or entertaining. The strategy is an attempt to divert attention away from conflict and help the parents turn their attention elsewhere.

The Lost Child

This child uses withdrawal to avoid pain. The lost child spends time alone, perhaps reading books or watching TV. This strategy removes the child from the direct line of fire and may be based on the belief that if s/he is not around, things will get better.

Frequently, these coping roles get carried over into adulthood. The concept of wounding helps explain what happens. Wounded children do the best they can to adapt using various roles. Then in adulthood, when they experience stress, they fall back on these early coping styles. This is problematic because childhood methods of coping are often inappropriate and unhealthy in adulthood. Thus, individuals must learn new, more mature ways of coping as adults. Many counselors and recovery experts also believe that individuals must work to heal their childhood wounds if they are to fully recover.

- Did you take on any of the above roles in your family of origin? Have any of the roles you adopted as children carried over to adulthood?

Another View of Roles: To Bind and Push Away

Even if family of origin experiences are mostly nurturing and positive, family members still take on certain roles. Some children may be predisposed by innate personality tendencies to adopt certain roles; others may be forced by family situations to take on a role. Napier writes about different roles that family members play, stating that his ideas draw upon the work of Helm Stierlin. Napier (1988) describes two types of roles–those that bind to the family and those that push toward separation. Although family members experience forces that both bind and push away, one of these forces is usually dominant in a person's childhood and this force continues to influence adult life. Napier believes that to understand marriage, "we need a working knowledge of the 'dramatic structure' of the family we grew up in–particularly the roles we assumed, and how we came to occupy them" (p. 162). Napier discusses the roles that bind and the roles that push away.

Roles that Bind

THE PARENTAL CHILD ROLE. Some children are thrust into parental roles. These children are given and often willingly accept great responsibility–responsibility that in many families would be shouldered by parents. These children are expected to carry some of the workload and/or emotional responsibilities of the parents. This often happens in families where there is an overabundance of work, an absent parent, or a parent who exhibits a low level of functioning. On the surface, these children may seem especially competent, yet underneath, they are deprived and sometimes resentful. Their primary way of obtaining reinforcement is through being strong and useful. While this provides these children with a valued place in the family, it sets them up for difficulties in adulthood.

Oldest children and females are especially vulnerable to this role. As adults, they are attuned to the needs of others but have difficulty connecting with their own needs. They feel competent when caring for others and being helpful, but they are often exploited in relationships. They allow their children and others to take advantage of them and cannot set reasonable limits. In their relationships, they seem to choose people who underfunction so that they can continue this helping role as an adult. They often feel guilty for not doing enough or angrily criticize their spouse for underfunctioning. Yet they fail to see that their guilt and criticism are a projection of their own deep resentment over having no one to care for them. This resentment reaches far back into childhood where these individuals were caretakers and seldom had the care they needed.

THE COMPANIONATE CHILD ROLE. Companionate children take on the role of friend to one of their parents. If a parent is lacking in support or is especially needy, this parent may seek companionship from a child–often an older child. A daughter whose mother needs closeness frequently plays this role. It becomes a problem when the mother depends on this relationship too heavily and relinquishes her parental role. The child then crosses the parental boundary and is brought into the relationship to take on the role that a husband or friend should fulfill. If this companionate role hinders the child/adolescent from developing age-appropriate friends, then the young person may deeply resent the companionate role. However, at other times, this child may be flattered by the special attention received from the parent. Often, the companionship child lacks a strong parent to lean on, to depend on, to fight with, and to enforce limits. Although these children may have trouble recognizing the betrayal they feel, when they do gain insight, they realize that what they needed from the parent was a parental figure not a friend. Companionate children and the parent with whom they have bonded often have trouble separating. This parent may be intrusive throughout life and the adult companionate child may continue to feel overburdened, having difficulty pulling away from the needy parent.

THE MARITAL CHILD. The marital child role is played in families where a child is either directly or in subtle ways expected to satisfy a companionship or sexual need of the opposite sex parent. Although there is often a healthy banter between mothers and sons and fathers and daughters, there is a line that should not be crossed–a line where banter and teasing becomes unhealthy. Although children learn about sexuality by observing parents, at no time should a child be expected to play the role of marital partner by fulfilling the companionship or sexual needs of the opposite sex parent. Many times, the marital child role is not overtly sexual; instead, there is only subtle pressure for the child to fulfill a friendship need of the opposite sex parent–to be with, to be close, and to talk. The marital child role is most likely to be played out in certain situations: one parent is absent, the relationship between partners is seriously fractured, or a partner has serious mental health problems. Today, family situations often put children at risk. In divorce situations, mothers are often left alone to rear children, putting mothers in situations where they are overinvolved with their sons. In remarriage situations, daughters are especially vulnerable to abuse by stepfathers. Marital children often feel drained and uneasy about their overinvolvement with the opposite sex parent. And there are serious consequences for the child thrust into this role. As adolescents, they may be quite flirtatious and exploit their sexuality to their advantage or they may act out and allow themselves to be exploited by others. In adulthood they often have difficulty trusting their partners.

THE DEPENDENT CHILD ROLE. The dependent child role is often played out in families where a parent's overprotective attitude, excessive attention, and smothering concern are a dominant theme. Napier (1988) writes: "Such parents communicate that the world is a fearful place, and that this child needs special help and protection, thereby keeping the 'infantilized' child unnecessarily dependent and immature" (p. 178). Daughters and the youngest child are especially vulnerable to this role. To outsiders these parents may appear to be good parents; yet due to their upbringing, they are anxious and insecure. Thus, they bring a deprived inner self to the parenting situation and project it onto their child. "In overhelping their child, they are indirectly attempting to meet their own needs, trying to be for the child the kind of parent they wanted for themselves" (p. 179). However, these parents do not recognize their overconcern. If it is called to their attention, they are likely to become defensive, saying they are only doing what all good parents do or rationalizing their overprotectiveness by pointing out that is it a dangerous world and a parent cannot be too overprotective.

Napier believes that mothers are more likely to display this attitude. The typical picture is of the self-sacrificing mother who cannot do enough for a child she perceives as needy. However, Napier believes that there are frequently complicating circumstances. When mothers have the bulk of the child-rearing responsibilities, they feel the stress, loneliness, and lack of support that goes along with this role. In their attempt to get some of their emotional needs met, they develop an overcloseness and overconcern for their children. If fathers were more emotionally and physically present in the marriage and in rearing the children, perhaps wives could turn more to their husbands for the satisfaction of their emotional needs. Napier believes that mothers who bind their children through overprotection and concern often create problems in the lives of their adult children; they frequently become meddlesome mothers in-law.

Adult children who were bound to parents in an unhealthy way have a strong need for support. If they feel safe and supported, they are friendly and loyal; if security and support are withdrawn, they feel anxious and fearful. They usually do not express anger directly, but instead express it passively or turn it inward and become depressed. In the marriage selection process, they are likely to seek partners who were parental children; these partners will care for them and offer them a safe and secure environment.

- Did you take on any roles that were binding? Are these roles influencing your present relationships?

Roles that Push Away

There are also forces that push family members away from the family—outward toward separateness. The purpose of the family is to help members become more separate without completely losing a sense of healthy connection. As families attempt to manage this balance, members play different roles at different times. For example, a mother may establish an environment with a son that tends to bind, while a father creates an environment that pushes toward separation. Therefore, the concept of role taking is usually not simple and straightforward. However, just as binding roles propel family member inward, other roles propel outward. Whereas bound children are overinvolved in the family's life, children who are pushed outward and away from the family go outside the family for support. Napier discusses three roles that push outward—the rejected child role, the delegate child role, and the rule-breaker role.

THE REJECTED CHILD ROLE. The rejected child role is a cruel burden for a child to carry. A child's need to be loved is powerful; to experience rejection is especially debilitating. This role is often forced upon a particular child, perhaps because the child was literally unwanted, being born at a time when caretaking responsibilities were especially burdensome. Some parents make no attempt to hide their displeasure over a child's presence. Sometimes there is not a good fit between the child's temperament and the caretaker's personality. As the child fusses over this inability to mesh, the parent's irritability increases, eventually becoming rejection. In other homes, the parents should not have had children; they can barely take care of their own needs. Any of these situations can lead to problems for children—problems that negatively influence their developing sense of well-being. In an ideal world, only parents who desire children and have the ability to adequately love and care for them would have children, but the world is far from ideal.

Children who are cast in the rejected role often struggle in adulthood to please others. If they fall short, they often blame themselves or project blame onto others. As adults, they frequently struggle with their anger and may be vulnerable to depression. They don't like to displease for this leads to rejection, yet at the same time, they feel upset, angry, and unworthy without knowing the source of these feelings. These individuals often have difficulty establishing stable, intimate relationships; they keep others at a distance and have superficial relationship encounters. They seem to be attracted to those who also occupy the rejected role or to those who are parental, hoping to find the parents they never had.

THE RULE BREAKER ROLE. Some children take the role of rulebreaker. Napier (1988) believes that this is a courageous child who senses that something is amiss, usually in the parents' relationship. This child often rebels, acts out, and causes trouble to deflect attention away from parental bickering and tension. Rulebreakers sense the tension in the spousal dyad and breaking rules draws the parents' attention away from their conflicted relationship. These children often unconsciously sacrifice themselves to save the marriage but get no credit since the parents usually turn against them in anger and disgust.

At times, one parent will give the rulebreaker a subtle, underhanded permission to act out and rebel. This parent may not be able to stand up in defiance of the rules but unconsciously wishes s/he had such strength. For example, the child who misbehaves in a teacher's classroom draws the ire of the teacher and the school. The parents also lash out at the rulebreaker, wondering what has happened to their previously obedient child. Yet in earshot of the child, one parent may take up for the rulebreaker, criticizing the teacher for unfair treatment of the child. At other times, this same parent may betray the rulebreaker by siding with the other parent and those who criticize. Because of these mixed messages, rulebreakers often come to distrust words.

It takes a strong child to play the role of rulebreaker. Their behavior is frequently extreme—they act out sexually, get involved with drugs, break the law, and wear outlandish clothes. Their behavior makes a bold statement even though it is in direct opposition to parental desires. Thus these children seem to triangle themselves into their parents conflicted relationship. It is not unusual for rulebreakers to marry parental types; they can then rebel against their partner.

THE DELEGATE CHILD ROLE. The child cast in the delegate role feels pressure to succeed. This pressure may be directly expressed—be the best athlete, make the best grades, or win the top award. Sometimes this pressure is subtle; a father may have failed in some way and the son is implicitly encouraged to avoid a similar failure. In some families, there is an unhappy, unfulfilled mother and the daughter is to be different. For the delegate child, the pressure is to succeed in the outside world so the family can be proud and the world can see what a credit the delegate is to the family. There is often a "we will be proud of you if . . ." quality to these families. So the delegate may be the striver, someone who tries hard to please. In some ways, delegates are like parental children; they appear strong but have difficulty knowing what they really feel and want. Beneath the competent exterior they may be insecure and lonely, knowing that no success is quite good enough.

Delegates often marry partners who will cater to their wishes and help them appear successful. They frequently turn their energies toward work rather than family and have trouble seeing the emotional needs of others. They have difficulty getting in touch with their own emotional needs and thus may be viewed as unemotional by family members. The delegate's partner often struggles unsuccessfully to find out what the delegate is feeling. Yet delegates may complain that they are misunderstood and family members do not meet their emotional needs.

- Did you take on any of the roles that push outward from the family? Are these roles still influencing your present relationships?

Examining Determinants of Our Emotional Makeup

When partners attempt to connect emotionally, sometimes past experiences interfere. This was the case with Betty, a wife who could not work through conflict with her husband. At the first appearance of a complaint from him, she became hypersensitive, blaming herself with derogatory statements like, "I'm just no good! No wonder you hate me." If this didn't cause Betty's husband to back off, Betty would run to the bedroom and cry for the rest of the evening. In time, her husband stopped trying to reach her; it just made things worse. In therapy, the couple learned how Betty's mother had played an important role in this marital interaction. In childhood, Betty's mother had been extremely demanding, giving Betty tasks that were far beyond her abilities. Betty tried hard to please but often fell short and was scolded harshly for her incompetence; she would often run to her room and cry, thinking what an awful child she must be. Her mother would then call her a crybaby and tell her to "hush up." In her marriage, Betty tried hard to please her husband. But when the husband exhibited the least bit of irritation, Betty recoiled, becoming super-sensitive and blaming herself. What Betty did not realize was that at these times, she perceived her husband as she had perceived her harsh, scolding mother and she behaved accordingly–thinking she was no good and running to her room. Since Betty locked into her childhood emotional feelings, these feelings prevented the couple from dealing with conflicts in their marriage. For Betty, it was important to understand the roots of her feelings since understanding is often the first step toward change. But this history is not easy to examine; doing so often requires visiting old memories that are quite painful.

In an attempt to foster emotional understanding, Gottman and DeClaire (2001) encourage couples to examine the past. They believe that there are three elements that warrant examination: (1) one's emotional history, (2) one's emotional philosophy, and (3) one's vulnerabilities. In regard to emotional history, it is important to examine what was learned about emotions in the family of origin. Although genetic make-up may predispose an individual toward a certain kind of emotional responsiveness (e.g., excitability, caution, anxiety, distress, silliness, boredom), early experiences influence how these emotional tendencies get played out in life. Therefore, Gottman and DeClaire believe that feelings about emotions, like love, anger, sadness, and fear, are related to how these emotions were handled in the family of origin. Therefore, it is important to identify one's emotional response tendencies and examine the origin of these response patterns. For Betty, it was helpful to learn that her emotional response to her husband related to past experiences with her mother. She learned that her husband's disapproval and criticism caused her to become childlike; at these times she responded to her husband as she had previously responded to her mother. It was important for Betty to understand this projection for several reasons: she could now tell herself that she was not a child but an adult, that her husband was not her mother, and that it was okay to talk about their conflict issues.

Gottman's research (2001) indicates that families have a philosophy about emotions. This is the family's belief about feelings and how feelings should be expressed and dealt with in daily life. After studying many families over several years, Gottman and DeClaire (2001, 1997) concluded that families adhere to one of four broad categories in regard to their emotional philosophy: dismissing, disapproving, laissez-faire, and coaching.

The Emotion Dismissing Philosophy

Emotion-dismissing families often discouraged emotional expression. When a child did express an emotion like fear, the parents were likely to play down the importance of the feeling with an emotion-dismissing comment, such as "don't be afraid; you're a big boy now." These parents turn away from their children when they attempt to connect with them emotionally. In some families, this is especially true with regard to emotions that are defined as negative–fear, hurt, anger. Boys may especially be the targets of this dismissing philosophy; they are often told to "suck it up" or "get back in the game," as if the emotions were secondary to the situation.

The Emotion-Disapproving Philosophy

Emotion-disapproving parents have a similar philosophy. They too discourage negative feelings but do so by disapproving of these feelings.

Comments like: "turn that frown into a smile" and "don't let me hear another sound from you" or "don't let me see that lower lip, that's a no-no in this family," reflect this philosophy. Some families are especially disapproving of negative or sad emotions. They seem to believe that these emotions will magically go away if they are discouraged. These parents turn against their children's bids for emotional connection and miss many opportunities to teach children that both positive and negative emotions are a natural part of life.

The Laissez-Faire Philosophy

In homes where a laissez-faire philosophy is exhibited, parents allow the expression of all emotions, both positive and negative, but do not help their children learn how to deal with emotions or to self-soothe. These parents also have trouble setting limits in regard to emotional expression. Thus they turn toward their children with empathy but miss valuable opportunities for instruction.

The Emotion-Coaching Philosophy

Emotion-coaching parents encourage emotional expression by turning toward their children with empathy; they also set limits on their children's acting-out behavior and teach self-soothing and problem-solving skills. Emotion coaching is such an important philosophy for parents to have as they interact with their children, that it will be discussed in greater detail in Chapter 6.

Which philosophy best describes the prevailing attitude in your family of origin? Betty's was dismissing and disapproving, especially in regard to negative emotions involving hurt, anger, and fear. Therefore, she struggles to deal maturely with these feelings in her marriage. Understanding one's family of origin in regard to beliefs about emotional expression is a clue to understanding present emotional experiencing.

- What was the philosophy of emotion in your family of origin? Did your parents encourage or discourage the open expression of such emotions as love, anger, sadness, hurt, and fear? How did your parents help you cope with your feelings?

Gottman and DeClaire (2001) also believe that it is important to examine any long-standing, persistent vulnerability in regard to emotions. These vulnerabilities are often rooted in painful childhood experiences and affect our intimate relationships. Since we often project images and feelings from the past onto our present relationship partners, we may have hot issues that conjure up feelings that are out of proportion to the present situation. Betty's response is an example. Her husband was not being overly critical and harsh in the way he brought up difficult issues in their marriage; instead, it was Betty's hypersensitivity to any hint of dissatisfaction that kept her from exploring their difficult issues. These sensitive vulnerabilities can stem from a number of different childhood sources—mistreatment, loss, trauma, abandonment, emotional or physical abuse, harsh child-rearing practices, or a serious problem in the family due to illness, drugs, or alcoholism. Or a child may have been thrust into a role that was unfair, such as the role of rejected child, marital child, or dependent child. Why is it important to gain insight into the past? It is important because "Getting clear about the past allows you to separate yesterday's issues from today's reality" (Gottman & DeClaire, 2001; p. 167). This understanding can help break the past's hold, freeing the individual to behave in new and more effective ways.

- Thinking about painful past experiences can be difficult. However, you may want to give some thought to your present emotional vulnerabilities and the past experiences that have given rise to these vulnerabilities. If you find this especially difficult, perhaps talking with a counselor or therapist would be helpful.

CHANGING ONE'S FAMILY LEGACY

Undesirable characteristics are often passed from one generation to another. If the undesirable characteristic is genetic in origin, there may be little the family can do. However, many undesirable patterns are not entirely genetic; instead, they involve learned patterns that have negatively influenced the family line, perhaps over many generations. Many undesirable characteristics weave their way through a family's lineage (e.g., drug/alcohol abuse, child/spouse abuse, child-rearing styles, problems with anger, difficulties with intimacy, problems regarding commitment). When destructive patterns are passed from generation to generation, it is important that someone in the lineage break the cycle. Broderick (1988) calls the person who is able to do this a transitional character—a person who changes the course of family history in a single generation. Although becoming a transitional person is not always an easy task, certainly there are those who have successfully played this role.

Several scholars and researchers (Burr, Day, & Bahr, 1993; Bennett et al., 1987) have discussed what family members can do to replace negative family characteristics with positive ones. One approach is to make a deliberate attempt to change by carefully planning a change strategy. Covey (1997), in his book, *Seven Habits of Highly Effective Families*, advises family members to be proactive. He defines this as the ability to respond rationally based on principles and values rather than responding reactively based on emotion and circumstances. Humans are able to do this because of an ability to be self-aware. We can take a position outside ourselves and can observe our thoughts and actions somewhat objectively. Although this is difficult, when it happens, we open up the possibility of change. The angry father can tell himself that he does not like how he vents anger in the family; he will pull back and learn more effective ways of dealing with his anger. Covey states, "What we all need is a 'pause button'—something that enables us to stop between what happens to us and our response to it, and to choose our own response" (p. 29). Hitting the pause button allows the father to stop and think: Is this how I want to respond or do I want to implement a new strategy? If a new strategy has purposely been planned and thought through, then the father is making a deliberate attempt to change. He is also modeling more effective behavior for his children to emulate.

A second strategy the transitional character can utilize to break the cycle of destructive transmission is to create distinctive family rituals. Often, the negative traits of a family are very pronounced in their rituals—holiday traditions, birthday parties, and family reunions. For example, if drinking and alcoholism are part of a lineage, alcohol is often part of the family's rituals. In one study (Bennett et al., 1987), it was found that when alcohol was deliberately kept separate from the rituals and traditions of the family (distinctiveness of rituals), the likelihood of abusing alcohol in future generations was reduced.

A third way Broderick believes a transitional character wards off the destructive transmission of negative characteristics is to create and maintain a healthy emotional distance between generations. Often, parents want to weave their way into the lives of their children long after the children have grown up and left the family. If children and parents stay highly intertwined, then destructive traditions, attitudes, and values are harder to discard. Completely cutting off from parents is not perceived as healthy, but neither is too much emotional involvement and attachment. As Burr, Day, and Bahr (1993) state, "there can be a moderate amount of emotional attachment and interaction when someone is trying to become a transitional character, but if adult children are highly involved with their parents, it is more difficult to disrupt the transmission" (p. 87).

The likelihood of becoming a transitional character may also be enhanced when partners marry later in life. If a person can wait until the mid-to-late twenties to marry, s/he will have had time to experience more of life. This will expose individuals to new ideas, beliefs, and ways of responding that can broaden their horizons, leading to the realization that things can be different—the past does not have to be repeated. Older and wiser, the individual can set a new course.

Another strategy available to the transitional person involves education. Furthering one's education after high school, especially by taking courses in psychology, sociology, parenting, or family studies, provides knowledge and experience that can affect decision making. Also, self-education is helpful. Reading good books on marriage, family, and healthy family relationships may provide insights that can be put to use in one's own family. Individuals can also join organizations that provide support and guidance for those trying to make constructive life changes.

Then too, as individuals attempt to break destructive patterns in the family, it may be beneficial to develop a meaningful personal philosophy of life as well as philosophies of marriage and family life. Covey (1997) suggests that partners and parents develop marriage and family mission statements. Partners and parents will be better able to take a leadership role in developing these statements if they have thought through their philosophy of life. Then with a personal philosophy of life and marriage and a family mission statement in hand, the parents may find that destructive behavior will be easier to change since these behaviors are inconsistent with the marriage and family mission statements.

- Have you been a transitional character in your family? Do you know anyone who has played this role in his or her family? If you have taken on this role have you utilized any of the methods mentioned as you have attempted to replace negative characteristics with positive ones?

IMPORTANT TERMS AND CONCEPTS

attachment theory
secure attachment
ambivalent attachment
avoidant attachment
object relations theory
Imago
Hendrix's stages of development
minimizer
maximizer

family roles
roles that bind to the family
roles that push away from the family
emotional philosophy
the dismissing philosophy
the emotion-disapproving philosophy
the laissez-faire philosophy
the emotion coaching philosophy
transitional person

SUGGESTED READINGS

Ambert, A. M. (2001). *The effect of children on parents* (2nd ed.). New York: The Haworth Press.

Cowan, C., & Cowan, P. (2000). *When partners become parents: The big life change for couples.* Mahwah, NJ: Lawrence Erlbaum.

Gottman J. M., & DeClaire, J. (2001). *The relationship cure: A five-step guide for building better relationships with family, friends, and lovers.* New York: Crown.

Hendrix, H. (1992). *Keeping the love you find: A personal guide.* New York: Simon & Schuster.

Napier, A. Y. (1990). *The fragile bond: In search of an equal, intimate and enduring marriage.* New York: HarperCollins.

Chapter 6

EMOTIONS IN FAMILY LIFE

The family environment is an emotional environment. As couples negotiate the rules that become the basis for their relationship, they have strong feelings about how things should be in their new family. When opinions clash, emotions reverberate throughout the family. Initially, the couple may easily create a loving, caring atmosphere because of their positive feelings for each other, but as romantic love fades, they must sustain that caring atmosphere and those loving feelings. If a positive emotional tone can be created, many beautiful and healthy outcomes are possible, but if a negative emotional climate prevails, just as many disabling and unhealthy outcomes can prevail. Thus, how well a couple and family members handle the emotional part of their lives will determine the success of their marriage and family life.

As couples attempt to deal with complex feelings associated with family life, they do so in a private world. This private world, where feelings are expressed behind closed doors, gives rise to some of the most beautiful and loving emotions imaginable. However, this privacy also allows for the worst of emotional expression—child and spousal abuse. Family life has a way of bringing out both the best and the worst in emotional experiencing. Since the success of family relationships depends on how couples and families handle the emotional part of their lives, it is crucial that families manage emotions in a healthy, emotionally intelligent way.

EMOTIONAL INTELLIGENCE

There is growing evidence that emotional intelligence is an important predictor of success in relationships. Daniel Goldman popularized the concept of emotional intelligence in 1995 with the publication of his book, *Emotional Intelligence: Why It Matters More Than IQ*. This book made the public aware of how important mature emotional management is to success in all aspects of life. Goldman, citing the previous work of Salovey and Gardner, views the following five domains as being relevant to the concept of emotional intelligence.

1. Having insight and awareness. Emotionally intelligent individuals are able to monitor their feelings, knowing from moment-to-moment what they are experiencing. Persons with this insight and self-awareness are attuned to their inner emotional life and have a surer sense of who they are.
2. Handling emotions in appropriate ways. Individuals who are emotionally intelligent are not only aware of their emotional experiencing but are able to handle their emotions in ways that are soothing and constructive rather than harmful and destructive.
3. Using emotions as positive motivators. The emotionally intelligent are able to harness their emotions so that these emotions help them achieve appropriate goals.
4. Reading the emotions of others. Successful emotional managers are sensitive to the feelings of others and have the ability to communicate this sensitivity in a caring way.
5. Knowing how to manage emotions so that relationships succeed. Managing emotions successfully is essential for success in both home

and work situations; this skill allows individuals to deal effectively with many types of situations.

Individuals differ in their abilities in regard to these five domains. Even individuals who have skills in one domain may be lacking in others. Also, it is possible that some individuals are able to apply these skills in one area of life but fail to apply them in other areas. One area where individuals often have trouble managing emotions well is in the family.

- Think about a situation where you behaved in an emotionally intelligent way. Describe that situation in relation to the five characteristics of emotional intelligence. Also, think about a situation where you did not behave in an emotionally intelligent way. Describe that situation in relation to the five characteristics of emotional intelligence.

MANAGING EMOTIONS IN THE FAMILY

Why is it so difficult to manage emotions effectively in the family? There are several reasons. First, couples form a family based on an emotion–love. Outside the family, we create relationships based on work, similar interests, and other non-emotional factors. Although these non-emotional factors may play a role in a couple's attraction to each other, later, it is the feeling tone of their relationship that is important. Does this relationship feel right? When the relationship does not have the proper feeling tone, partners are often unhappy. They may be unaware that even happily married couples go through periods of contraction, betrayal, and disillusionment in their relationship and that even these couples must work through feelings of negativity. Since most couples have had no training in dealing with highly charged emotional situations, they are left to drift aimlessly in their sea of despair.

Then too, the close proximity of family members living together elicits strong feelings. This closeness can seem wonderful at first, but it soon leads to irritations based on differences that were previously overlooked. "I never knew you were such a slob around the house" or "If I'd known you were so obsessive about the way the house looks, I would have had second thoughts" are typical spousal complaints. As time and proximity take their toll, even little differences that did not seem to matter early in the relationship, now matter and have a way of destroying the positive feeling tone of the marriage. Partners have expectations concerning how they want things to be and when reality differs from expectations, adjustment can be difficult. What makes it all the more confusing is that partners may be unaware of why they feel so strongly about certain things. Perhaps it is a quirk of personality or maybe a reaction to something that occurred in one's family of origin. Nevertheless, when feelings are strongly felt, it is hard to compromise.

Generational differences also make managing the emotional climate of the home difficult. This is especially true when children are teenagers. Although young children can be difficult to manage, parents may be able to accept their childlike ways as due to immaturity. But with teenagers, parents often expect them to be more like adults. When they are immature, parents confront, lay down the law, and often become emotional. Almost all parents have strongly held opinions about what they want their children to be, to do, and to become. When they see their teenager deviating from this path, panic sets in. From the parent's point of view, they have invested a lot of money and time rearing this child. They want an outcome consistent with their expectations. Parents often forget how difficult it was breaking away from their parents and fail to empathize with their teenager. Generational conflict can be highly emotional and difficult for both parents and children.

In families, partners need to be adept at managing emotions wisely so that relationships develop in healthy rather than unhealthy ways. This is difficult since most parents and partners have not had adequate training in dealing with the emotional side of life. They have gone to school to develop their cognitive skills. They may even have degrees symbolizing their intellectual achievements, but their failed relationships reflect an inability to deal successfully with emotional issues.

TRAINING IN EMOTIONAL MANAGEMENT

The first training children receive in emotional education comes in the home. This training is usually indirect. Parents do not start their day thinking that today is the day to start training their children in emotional awareness and understanding. Rather, it just happens as parents interact with their children in the day-to-day encounters involving emotions. Gottman (Gottman & Silver, 1997) has observed and studied many parent-child interactions, attempting to learn what parents are teaching and what children are learning. He found that parents usually fall into two categories in regard to the emotional training of their children—those who are helpful in teaching their children about the world of emotions and those who are not. Parents who are successful in helping children understand and deal with emotions are referred to as Emotion Coaches. According to Gottman, these parents "don't object to their children's display of anger, sadness, or fear. Nor do they ignore them. Instead, they accept negative emotions as a fact of life and they use emotional moments as opportunities for teaching their kids important lessons and building closer relationships with them" (p. 21).

But how does the successful emotion coach behave? How do parents respond so that they nurture their child's emotional intelligence? Gottman's research indicates five important strategies used by parents who help their children understand and successfully deal with their emotional lives.

1. Emotion-coaching parents are aware of the feelings expressed by their children. They pay attention even to their child's low intensity feelings and attempt to respond to these feelings before they escalate. This awareness involves an attempt to see and feel what their child is seeing and feeling. This is not easy since most of the time parents see the world from their own perspective, so to understand the child's perspective takes time and effort. Parents who do not nurture emotional intelligence often dismiss, ignore, or disapprove of their child's emotions, thinking these feelings are childlike and unimportant. If you recall, the ability to read the emotions of others and empathize is a characteristic of emotional intelligence; therefore, some parents are more adept at this than others. However, this is a skill that parents can improve; they can develop better listening skills and make an effort to see the world from their child's perspective. Gottman wondered if there was a gender difference in empathic ability. Were wives better than husband's at reading the feelings of their partner when both were asked to identify the feeling their partner had expressed? Gottman and Silver (1997) noted that, "surprisingly, we found that husband's are just as skilled as wives at knowing what their spouses feel minute by minute" (p. 77). Why then are men often seen as lacking in feeling? The answer may lie in the way men are socialized; they are expected to be tough and this toughness discounts attention to feelings and emotional expression. This may be why men have been found to be less emotionally expressive than women. Yet men have the ability to become emotionally aware and respond with empathy if they can allow themselves to be attentive to their feelings. "For most men, becoming emotionally aware is not a matter of picking up new skills; it is a matter of granting themselves permission to experience what's already there" (Gottman & Silver, 1997, p. 78).

2. Emotion-coaching parents see times of emotional expression as opportunities for teaching and intimacy. Successful emotion coaches often reframe their child's emotional reactions; instead of seeing negative emotional outbursts as an annoyance, they see them as an opportunity for bonding, closeness, understanding, and teaching. Some of the parents Gottman studied were critical and disapproving of their children's

negative emotional responses. However, effective emotion coaches saw emotional situations with their children as valuable opportunities for intimacy and learning.

3. Emotion-coaching parents sensitively listen and validate their children's emotional expressions, responding to these experiences in a non-critical way. Parents who respond in this way do not tell their children to cheer up; nor do they attempt to talk them out of their feelings through manipulation; instead, they effectively listen and reflect back to the child the emotion the child has expressed. "You're sad because your sister is sick and had to be taken to the doctor." This validation often soothes children and lets them know that all feelings are acceptable.

4. As emotion-coaching parents listen and communicate empathetically, they help their children find appropriate words to label their emotions. Helping children accurately label emotions, such as anger, sadness, fear, or jealousy, has several helpful consequences. It has a calming effect; perhaps this is because labeling is the first step in the process of thinking about the emotion. Also, if these feelings are labeled, children learn that others have experienced these same emotions and dealt with them effectively. Thus, they can learn to deal with them effectively also. Remember that insight and awareness concerning emotions and the ability to self-soothe are important ingredients of emotional intelligence.

5. Emotion-coaching parents help their children understand limits and solve problems. "You're angry because your brother got to go to the ball game and you didn't. That's understandable. But it's not okay for you to tear up his book. What could you have done instead?" Encounters like this help children (1) label their feelings; (2) realize that their feelings are not the problem, rather it is their behavior that is inappropriate; (3) understand that there are limits on behavior; and (4) begin the process of problem-solving. Doing these things helps a child learn that all feelings are acceptable, but some behaviors are unacceptable and lead to negative consequences.

Emotion coaching has positive outcomes for developing emotional intelligence in children. Gottman (Gottman & Silver, 1997) observed families interacting with children over many years. He wondered if emotion-coaching parents would have children who were different from the children whose parents did not handle feelings in an effective way. After a decade of research, Gottman has found some important differences. Emotion-coached children were better at dealing with their own emotions and with emotional situations. They were better regulators of their emotions—they could soothe themselves and rebound faster from distressing emotional experiences. These children were also more effective in dealing with others. They interacted more effectively with friends, were less likely to have behavior problems, and were less violent. In summary, there were definite differences between the two groups of children. The emotion-coached children were better at handling emotions and emotionally charged situations; they were more emotionally intelligent.

- Think about how your parents dealt with emotions. Were your parents effective or ineffective emotion coaches? How were both positive and negative emotions dealt with in your family of origin? Are you an effective emotion coach?

MALE AND FEMALE: DIFFERENT EMOTIONAL STYLES

Even though emotion coaching is helpful in teaching children how to deal with emotions, the world of children's play also reinforces different emotional styles for males and females. Numerous studies (Tannen, 1990; Maltz & Borker, 1982) have shown that boys and girls react differently during play. By about the second grade, children separate from each other as they play, boys playing with boys and girls with girls. These same sex groups may avoid each other–boys telling girls to go away and girls being just as repulsed by boys. Each group seems to play differently. Boys choose more aggressive games that involve running, climbing, and competing in active ways. They do not let disagreements stop the game, for the game is too important. Boys may quarrel about rules or about whether someone was safe or out, but the game must go on even if the play must be "done over" to satisfy everyone. Thus, boys are not likely to let feelings stop the "all important" game. It's as if emotions must be controlled so the game can continue. If a boy gets hurt during the heat of competition, he soon learns to put it behind him, suck it up, return to the game, and suppress tears. Girls seem to bring different values to their games. Girls tend to choose quieter games involving smaller groups where intimacy and communication are important. For girls, it is not the game that is most important, but rather the interaction between the participants. Games give girls something to do as they talk and share feelings. It's as if they enjoy the closeness of their interaction more than the game. If a participant gets hurt, then her friends support and console her. If disagreements occur, the game may stop because the disagreement is more important than the game. If all goes well, disagreements are ironed out, talked through, and friendships restored.

Parents are also likely to reinforce gender differences in emotional expression. Boys learn to suppress emotions; girls become more adept at dealing with feelings and navigating emotional waters. Gottman (1994) has noted these childhood differences and he believes that by the time males and females reach young adulthood, they have been conditioned very differently in regard to emotional expression. Males come to see emotional expression as a sign of weakness, whereas females have learned to be sensitive to their own and other's feelings and have learned to be more comfortable talking about emotions. This may be why wives tend to be more attuned to the emotional climate in the home and why they are more likely to be upset if things "feel" wrong. These different emotional styles set the stage for misunderstandings in marriage.

Past learning experiences may not be the only reason for differences in emotional expression. Biological differences may predispose males and females to respond differently. Even as young children, boys appear to have more difficulty recovering from highly emotional experiences. This may be why boys have more trouble self-soothing when emotions become over aroused. Girls seem to recover more quickly from all types of feelings and return to normal after crying or talking things out. These findings appear to contradict the belief that males are less emotional. Males may simply appear to be less emotional on the outside, while internally they are very aroused. Gottman (1994) has consistently found that in heated marital discussions, husbands differ from their wives in several significant ways: their heart rate and blood pressure elevate more quickly, rise higher, and stay elevated for a longer period of time. When one's pulse rate climbs eight or ten beats per minute beyond the person's normal resting rate, a person becomes over aroused internally. Gottman refers to this overarousal as flooding. When intense flooding occurs, productive discussion is impossible. Since men tend to become flooded more readily in heated discussions, they tend to be the first to become overwhelmed; they need a break from the unbearable heat of the discussion and their own internal responding. Thus husbands, needing to calm themselves from their intense anxiety, learn to withdraw. Gottman calls this withdrawal stonewalling because it involves turning away and shutting down emotionally—becoming a stonewall. Stonewalling is often expressed in comments like, "there's no use going on with this, we never get anywhere" or "it's useless trying to talk to you." Or stonewalling may involve storming out of the room, leaving a wife to fume about her husband's unwillingness to talk to her. In either case, the wife is likely to be infuriated by her husband's behavior, viewing his withdrawal as disapproval and wondering why he cannot work through emotional issues. If a wife is the first to flood and stonewall (Gottman sees this occasionally), the husband is usually not too upset; he seems to understand the need to withdraw in order to reduce tension.

Why are males more sensitive to emotional discussions in the marriage? Gottman (1994) suggests two reasons. The first focuses on possible differences in the nervous system of males and females. It could be that the autonomic nervous system of males is more sensitive than this system in females, thus causing males to respond more quickly and take longer to recover from emotional arousal. Or it could be that as males withdraw, their tendency to think more emotion-arousing thoughts such as, "I've taken her bitching long enough," keeps them stirred up for longer periods of time. Regardless of the reasons for this arousal difference, a husband often avoids intense emotional conflict, finding avoidance preferable to the emotionally charged conflict with his wife. However, this method of dealing with conflict makes it difficult to resolve emotionally charged issues.

- In your relationship with your partner, have you noticed the typical female pursuer-male withdrawal pattern? Who tends to become emotionally over aroused and stonewall in your relationship?

POSITIVE AND NEGATIVE AFFECT IN MARRIAGE

Early systems theorists believed that all systems were similar and followed some general principles in their method of operation. Although they did not understand these principles and how they related to families, they assumed that a system was self-regulating so that it would respond in ways that maintain the homeostatic balance of the system. It was not until Gottman (1999) began studying marital interactions and applying mathematical models to these interactions that the homeostatic system of balance in families was more clearly understood.

In systems theory language, the term steady state is often used. Remember the example of the heating system set at 72 degrees. When the temperature deviates from this set point, the system turns on and off to bring the temperature back to the set point. If the temperature is set at 72 degrees, then the room is comfortable. If the thermostat is set at 52 degrees, the system works to keep the room at this set point even though the room temperature may be uncomfortable and possibly unhealthy. Gottman has found that these concepts can be applied to the marital system. Every marriage has a set point or steady state and marital interactions gravitate to this set point/steady state. This set point may be healthy or unhealthy for the marriage, just as the 72-degree set point may be a healthier temperature setting than 52 degrees. Yet marital interactions will be drawn to the set point be it healthy or unhealthy. Think of 72 degrees as a mixture of both warm and cold air. Since there is enough warm air compared to cold air, the room is comfortable. In marriages, the balance is not between warm and cold air, but rather positivity and negativity. Is there more positivity than negativity and what is a healthy balance in a marriage? This balance was determined from watching marriage partners interact as they attempted to resolve conflict. Gottman (1999) video-taped these interactions and had trained observers code both the kind and amount of positive and negative affect expressed in these discussions. These observers were taught to recognize and code emotional affect associated with facial expressions, gestures, and verbal expressions. They also coded such emotions as joy, humor, interest, affection, disgust, anger, defensiveness, and contempt. In happy, stable marriages, the ratio of positive affect to negative affect in conflict discussions was found to be 5 to 1, known as the 5 to 1 ratio. In unhealthy marriages (marriages where partners are very likely to divorce), the ratio of positive affect expression to negative affect expression in conflict discussion was .8 to 1 (Gottman, 1999). This reflects a tendency for these partners to have slightly more negative affect expression than positive and substantially less positive affect than that found in the happy, stable relation-ships. Gottman (1994) writes, "as long as there is five times as much positive feeling and interaction between husband and wife as there is negative, we found the marriage was likely to be stable" (p. 57).

The marriage partners who could keep their thermostat set on the 5 to 1 ratio in their conflict interactions continued to have satisfying marriages. Actually, in non-conflict discussions, these couples might have ratios as high as 25 to 1. But the marriage partners who could never reach a 5 to 1 balance in conflict discussions or over time allowed their ratio to be reset, with more allowance for negativity, found their marriages in trouble. Remember that regardless of where the marital thermostat is set pertaining to positivity/neg-ativity, couples will gravitate toward this steady state, even if it is unhealthy for the marriage.

But what influences where the thermostat is set? Gottman (1999) believes there are several things. One factor that determines whether an interaction will be positive or negative is what partners bring to the interaction. Sometimes this is referred to as baggage. There is even a comic strip where a couple is in a marriage counselor's office and the wife has brought along her packed suitcase–baggage. It will be difficult to effect change if past inter-actions have been so negative that one partner has one foot out the door. Gottman has found that what we bring to an interaction will influence that interaction. And what we bring can be stored up feelings and memories relat-ing to past interactions with our spouse. These feelings and memories can be overwhelmingly positive (e.g., affection and love) or overwhelmingly nega-tive (e.g., anger, disappointment, and mistrust). We also may bring feelings and thoughts about other recent past experiences (non-marriage related) that can influence marital interactions. A spouse who comes home after a satisfy-ing day at the office may bring home different attitudes and feelings than the spouse who was raked over the coals by the boss. Each spouse also brings a unique personality and temperament as well as different childhood experiences. Therefore, how an interaction will go may depend on what each spouse brings to that interaction. What Gottman (1999) found was that partners headed for divorce brought far more negative affect to the interaction than partners in stable marriages. Certainly this is not surprising. Usually, by the time a couple goes to a marriage counselor, the past history of the relationship has gone sour (the 5 to 1 ratio is now closer to .8 to 1) even before they begin interacting in the counselor's office.

The troubled couple, whether in the counselor's office or at home, is predisposed to bring high levels of negativity to their interactions. Their thermostatic balance in regard to positivity/negativity has been reset. But then, what happens when they communicate? What happens when they begin to influence each other in their present-time interactions? How do they influence each other? Gottman has observed and studied many of these interactions in both healthy and unhealthy marriages. Stable couples in conflict interactions influence each other toward positivity; unstable couples in conflict interactions increase the negativity. In a stable marriage, if a partner registers a complaint or criticism, the spouse does not tend to respond by increasing the negativity (e.g., responding to a complaint with strong defensiveness or criticism); instead, the spouse is more likely to respond in kind or respond in a way which wards off increased negativity and produces more positivity. In unhappy marriages, when a partner registers a complaint or criticism in conflict discussion, the spouse ups the ante in a way that increases the negativity. This is referred to as escalation of negativity–the tendency to increase the negativity in a relationship interaction. When this happens in marriages, it creates a feedback loop and interactions are characterized by more and more negativity. This escalation of negativity pattern is characteristic of unhappy marriages and predicts divorce (Gottman, 2000). But what about those partners who respond in kind (e.g., anger with anger) without increasing the negativity? Do they put their marriage in jeopardy? Recently Gottman's findings (Gottman, Coan, Carrere, & Swanson, 1998)) have led him to conclude that responses in kind do not predict divorce. He (2000) writes: "Longitudinal prediction research showed that the reciprocation of negativity in kind is characteristic of all marriage and does not predict divorce! Only the escalation of negativity predicts divorce" (p. 30).

In stable, happy marriages, partners were able to keep negativity from increasing and maintain the important 5 to 1 ratio. These partners were able to maintain this healthy balance by making and responding positively to each other's repair attempts. In stable marriages, repair attempts tone down the negativity in conflict discussions, keeping things from getting too heated and spiraling out of control. "Let's stop for a moment and calm down" would be an example of a repair attempt. They are self-correcting mechanisms that keep the positive balance in the marriage. Repair attempts are similar to the thermostatic mechanism that senses the balance of cold to warm air, in the room; when there is too much cold or warm air the mechanism kicks in to restore the proper balance. Both happy and unhappy couples make repair attempts. Why do some attempts work while others do not? Gottman (1999) found that the success of repair attempts could not be predicted from knowing how they were stated or from observing anything in the present conflict interaction. Rather, the success or failure of repair attempts depended on what the partners brought to the interaction. If they brought strong marital friendship, respect, and admiration for each other to the interaction, then their repair attempts worked and kept negativity from overrunning the marital system. But if this friendship and admiration has deteriorated and they brought much negativity to the interaction, then their repair attempts were likely to fail and their conflict discussions spiraled out of control. Thus it is important to maintain positivity on a daily basis so that friendship, respect, and admiration continue to exist and positivity far outweighs negativity in the marriage.

• Where is your relational thermostat set? Is there a healthy 5 to 1 ratio? Do you typically bring an abundance of positivity or negativity to relationship exchanges? Are you and your partner good at making and responding positively to repair attempts or is escalation of negativity a pattern in your relationship?

EMOTIONAL EXTREMES IN MARRIAGE

Emotional extremes are often an unhealthy sign in marriages. Several types of emotional extremes have been observed and studied: emotional disengagement characterized by a flat emotional affect–lack of positivity and suppressed negativity (flat emotional affect) and extreme anger that often leads to violence.

Emotionally Disengaged Couples

In some marriages, negativity is difficult to detect. In these marriages (Gottman, 2000; Gottman & Silver, 1999), partners have withdrawn from emotional engagement. After years of conflict, these couples have settled into a marriage with very little positivity and a suppressed negativity that hides tension and sadness. These marriages are characterized by an emotional deadness; there is no affection and very little openly expressed anger and conflict. These partners have lost the ability or desire to soothe each other. They live under the same roof but live parallel lives, no longer experiencing each other as friends. They have adjusted to this deadness as if they are not entitled to have complaints. In the counselor's office, these couples may even indicate that things are better now than in the past.

Some of these couples will eventually divorce. However, some will stay together in spite of their diminished emotional life. Why would partners settle for marriages with an absence of positive affect and such high levels of suppressed negativity? There are probably many factors that influence their decision. Remember the steady state thermostat model. Over time, the ratio of positivity to negativity has changed and they have adjusted, not in a healthy way, but in a way that is familiar to them. Also, for some couples, the agony of confronting difficult issues related to a break up seems more painful than their present relationship. Lauer and Lauer (1986) found that in 15 percent of a sample of 381 long-term married couples, one or both partners were unhappy. The two major reasons these couples gave for staying together related to issues involving children and their sense of duty based on religious or family tradition.

Angry and Violent Couples

Most couples argue, but their arguments do not escalate into violence. However, in some marriages, arguments do cross the line between heated debate and physical assault. Jacobson and Gottman (1998) state that nonviolent partners lock into the withdrawal/stonewalling mode before violence erupts. Yet some partners do not repair or withdraw; instead negativity escalates into violent interaction. Jacobson and Gottman describe this group in their book, *When Men Batter Women*. These researchers brought male batterers and their wives into their laboratory and studied them during conflict discussions. They closely observed these discussions, monitoring each partner's physiological responses as their conflicts escalated. They also rated the conflict interactions for emotional content and affect. These studies were groundbreaking since no prior studies had actually observed batterers and their spouses engage in conflict discussions. It is important to note that these discussions were non-violent since the restraints in the laboratory situation prevented violence. Yet the researchers felt that had these restraints not been in place, some interactions would have become violent. Also, these researchers used a comparison group made up of couples who reported equal amounts of dissatisfaction in their marriage but who had not engaged in violence. Using this control group, comparisons could be made between the two groups. After observing conflict discussions, these researchers also interviewed the batterers and their wives separately. In these interviews, they elicited information about each couple's past arguments and attempted to understand these episodes from the point of view of each partner.

In this research, an interesting finding emerged. There were two types of batterers, each distinguishable by the physiological data. When couples began arguing, some batterers exhibited the expected increase in heart rate and sweating that is typical when battering partners engage in heated debate. But surprisingly, 20 percent of the batterers exhibited a decrease in heart rate during conflict discussions. While externally, they were exhibiting every indication of being angry and aroused; internally, they were calm with heart rates lower than when they had been asked to shut their eyes and relax. As the data analysis continued, the researchers realized that there were other differences between the two groups, differences so striking that they labeled one group the cobras and the other the pit bulls.

The Cobras

The males that lowered their heart rates were called cobras. While this group internally calmed themselves, externally they were immediately aggressive, belligerent, and hostile in conflict discussions. Wives married to cobras were afraid and sad. They had much to fear and it was important that they chose their words and responses carefully since expressing anger could precipitate a violent response. Cobras were violent not only with their wives but also with coworkers and friends. Consequently, hostile and violent behavior was common in these men both inside and outside the marriage. The researchers also noted that the wives of cobras seemed more attached to their husbands and committed to the marriage than wives of pit bulls. While the wives of cobras continued to seek intimacy and commitment in the relationship, the husbands shunned intimacy, wavered on commitment, and continued to engage in violent, destructive behavior. These husbands, unlike pit bulls, encouraged their wives' independence. What they could not tolerant was a wife who attempted to control them in any way. Even reasonable requests on the part of these wives were met with anger and belligerence.

The Pit Bulls

In conflict discussions, pit bulls are not immediately hostile and belligerent. Their heart rates increase as the discussion heats up. As the discussion continues, they are prone to temper outbursts that are difficult for them to control. Pit bulls constantly demand change from their partners. These men are emotionally insecure and seek to completely control their partners in an attempt to alleviate their anxiety and fear of abandonment. They often exhibit extreme jealousy and attempt to isolate their wives from others. While they demand that their partners change, they resist any suggestion of change for themselves. It is the partner who must do more, be more, and give more. Yet no matter how much the wife gives, it is not enough. When the wife of a pit bull demands that her husband change, these demands are ignored or met with violence and abuse. A pit bull also frequently attempts to control by convincing his wife that her perception of reality is false, giving the impression that if she continues with such absurd ideas her sanity is in question.

Similarities between Cobras and Pit Bulls

There are also some similarities between the two types. Wives of both cobras and pit bulls cannot easily predict when physical abuse will occur. Although physical abuse usually follows emotional abuse, it does not always do so. Emotional abuse is so common in these marriages that it cannot be used as a reliable predictor of when physical abuse will occur. Also, wives in these marriages did not give up easily. They continued to hope for a better marriage. Yet the batterers were completely unwilling to give in to any of their wives' requests or demands. Once an argument ensued in these marriages, there were times when the men did not inhibit their violent tendencies by withdrawing as the partners in non-violent marriages did. Rather, these men would not or could not stop their escalating anger and violent tendencies. In the conflict discussions, battering husbands exhibited much more belligerence, contempt, and domination than husbands in nonviolent relationships. These researchers came to believe that when the violence started in the home environment, there was nothing the wife could do to initiate a withdrawal ritual. Although physical abuse did not occur in the laboratory situation, its closest equivalent was the complete domination of one's partner, resulting in a squelching of the partner's attempt to even engage in conversation. The researchers came to believe that when physical abuse occurred outside the laboratory, it served the purpose of reestablishing control for the batterer. The issue around which the abuse occurred is not resolved, but control is no longer in question.

More About Abusive Relationships

Those who study the male abusive personality have found that all abusers do not fit the same profile. Dutton (1995, 1998) describes three types of batterers: (1) the overcontrolled abuser, (2) the psychopathic abuser, and (3) the cyclical/emotionally volatile abuser. Batterers in the overcontrolled group have trouble describing their feelings. When asked to keep an anger journal, they may say that they don't get angry enough to make regular entries in the journal. Their anger often builds up after long periods of internal seething, which these individuals attempt to keep under control. They score high on scales of dominance/isolation and emotional abusiveness. They expect their wives to adhere to rigid sex role behaviors, often treating them like servants and isolating them from outside resources. In an attempt to gain their partner's submission, they withhold affection and use verbal attack. The overcontrolled abuser uses violence less frequently than abusers in the other two groups. The psychopathic abuser seems to fit Jacobson and Gottman's profile of the cobra group. They have psychopathic personalities and may seem charming, but underneath this exterior, they are cold, heartless, and show no remorse.

The cyclical/emotionally volatile batterer appears to be the most studied type and seems to describe the abuser in Lenore Walker's classic book, *The Battered Women*. Since more is known about the background of the cyclical/emotionally volatile batterer, the following discussion will focus on this type. Walker (1979) describes three cyclical phases that are typical in this pattern of abuse–the tension-building phase, the acute battering phase, and the contrition phase.

The Tension-building Phase

The characteristics of this phase are usually hidden from the outsider. According to Dutton (1995), friends and work associates might notice a slight irritation, moodiness, or tension during this phase but very little else. In therapy groups, however, Dutton sees a different picture. There is "a state of irritating excitement: the individual is agitated, tense, frenzied; he can't sit still or relax and feels some inner force will overtake him" (p. 43). Yet he does not know the source of this irritation nor does he know how to describe it with words. There is only an uncomfortable, vague tension that Dutton calls aversive arousal. In looking for the cause of this arousal, the cyclical/emotionally volatile abuser often projects blame. Thus, it is his wife's fault. If she would only be better at pleasing him, these feelings would go away. It is during this phase that these men play what Dutton calls the bitch tape; since it's her fault and she won't change, she's just a bitch. Since these feelings won't subside, these men begin to focus more and more on thoughts of blame, getting even, and even on their wives' perceived sexual infidelity. These men are extremely jealous, fear abandonment, and have strong dependency needs that are mostly unconscious. As these thoughts and feelings increase, so does their sense of anger and rage. As this rage increases, the second phase of the cycle emerges–the acute battering phase.

The Acute Battering Phase

In the acute battering phase, the rage is so uncontrollable that it cannot be contained. In this state, the abuser's desire is to annihilate, terrify, and humiliate the partner; there is little the victim can do to stop the attack. The abuser's behavior at this point is internally driven, pleasurable, and it releases and diminishes the pent up tension and anger. Dutton believes that the tension release and pleasure that comes during and right after the violent attack is addictive; it cleanses the abuser of the tension and bad feeling.

The Contrition Phase

Once the tension is released, the phase of contrition begins. In this phase, some abusers deny their involvement in what happened, while others seek to atone and promise never to behave violently again. If they seek to atone, they often beg, plead, and bribe their way back into the good graces of their partner. Flowers, gifts, and pleas for forgiveness are common. They will do almost anything to get their spouse back. Now they act as if she is "special," putting her on a pedestal as the beloved Madonna, whereas just a few days before, she had been the unfaithful whore. The abuser now appears very vulnerable, needy, and desperate; it's as if he cannot survive without the relationship. He may even threaten suicide to get his wife to take him back. If he latches onto a nurturance need in his wife, she may accept his contrition. Also, if she is isolated, scared, and has no place to go, her options are limited. However, if she does take the cyclical/emotionally volatile abuser back, the cycle will likely begin again. The contrition phase will diminish and tension building will reemerge.

Why do women so often stay in abusive relationships? Ford (2001) believes the answer to this question is complex. It frequently involves some or all of the following reasons: the wife's low self-esteem, her inability to support herself and her children, the difficulty she would have finding another place to live, and her fear that she might be unable to support her children, thus losing them to a social service agency or even to her husband. Then too, even if women leave, there may be further violence since the most dangerous times for women are when they leave, when they seek shelter, and when they are pregnant (Dutton, 1995). Common thought patterns of the abuser are "I'll show her" and "If I can't have her, no one can."

• If you have been involved in an abusive relationship, describe that relationship? Was your abuser more like a cobra or a pit bull? Did you experience the three phases of abuse? Were you able to change the abuser? If not, have you been able to escape the abusive relationship?

What Creates the Cyclical/Volatile Abuser?

As Dutton (1995) attempted to understand the cyclical/emotionally volatile abuser, he noted that cyclical assaultive men displayed the characteristics of post-traumatic stress disorder. The victims of this disorder have been exposed to traumatic experiences and cannot easily recover from the stress associated with these experiences. PTSD symptoms include sleep disturbances, depression, anxiety, and often dissociation such as flashbacks or out of body experiences. Since cyclical/emotionally volatile men had not experienced trauma as adults, it was hypothesized that childhood experiences might hold the key to understanding these individuals. After examining the childhood history of these men, Dutton believes that he has discovered the roots of the cyclical/emotionally volatile abuser's character. The seeds of this disorder seem to involve three things in a child's early development: (1) a very cold, harsh, abusive, violent father who took pleasure in shaming the child; (2) a mother who could not provide the necessary nurturance for the development of a secure attachment with her son; and (3) the direct experience of abuse in the early home environment. Dutton believes that it takes all three of these seeds to nurture and create the cyclical/emotionally volatile abuser.

As Dutton (1995, 1998) probed the childhood experience of these troubled men, it became apparent that their fathers had created a special kind of hell that could not easily be overcome. These fathers had exhibited a pattern of behavior toward their sons that was especially damaging; they had usually been both physically and psychologically violent toward their sons. The fathers' attacks had been global in that they had been directed at the very nature of the child's developing self with statements like "you little piss ant, you'll never amount to shit." These remarks accompanied by physical abuse were delivered at random; they were not connected to any wrong doing on the part of the child. Thus these young children experienced "global attacks on their selfhood, humiliation, embarrassment and shame" (Dutton, 1995, p. 83). Since these children cannot determine what specific wrongdoing has led to such vile treatment, they come to believe that the flaw must be within them. This random punishment and shaming has literally attacked the identity of these boys and they are powerless to stave off the attacks. This is the trauma that leads to the symptoms of post-traumatic stress disorder.

It is common for men who have been abused to have trouble recalling their childhood experiences. They either don't want to talk about the past or their childhood memories seem very hazy. The researchers must often ask probing questions to uncover the events of childhood or talk to other family members about early family dynamics. This difficulty in bringing back the memories of an abusive childhood is not surprising; individuals who have been constantly shamed and humiliated simply do not want to go there–the pain is too great. However, the result of this shame and humiliation is like a festering wound under the surface of the skin; it will not go away and any slight irritation causes great pain. Thus the abuser's personality is hypersensitive to any experience that may reopen the old wounds of hurt and shame. Responses that were held in check as a child–anger, rage, and a tendency to blame others–lie just below the surface, ready to emerge. And since the abuser is shut off from examining the trauma of the past, he knows very little about the source of his rage.

Dutton (1995, 1998) believes that the second seed in the development of the cyclical/emotionally volatile abuser also has its roots in childhood. It is the inability of the child to develop a secure maternal attachment because the mother is unable to provide an environment that allows for the development of a healthy attachment relationship. The experimental psychologist Harry Harlow contributed to our understanding of attachment behavior by studying infant monkeys. Harlow (1971) created surrogate (substitute) mothers for the infant monkeys he was raising. One group of monkeys was raised with a soft terry cloth surrogate and would cling to this surrogate in order to experience contact comfort. The infants attached to these mothers as evidenced by their clinging behavior. Harlow then transformed these substitute mothers into "monster" mothers by having them occasionally blow painful puffs of air onto the infant's face, hurl them in catapult fashion across the room, or stick them with sharp spikes that came out of the mother's body. Surprisingly, this did not put an end to the infant's clinging behavior. Instead the infants continued to cling to these mothers, leading Harlow to conclude that intermittent abuse followed by periods of comfort actually strengthen the infant monkeys desire to attach.

In homes where the father is abusive, the mother often has difficulty properly nurturing her infant. These mothers also suffer at the hands of their abusive husbands. Dutton (1995) uses the object relations theory of Klein and Riviere to explain what he believes happens as these mothers attempt to care for their infants. These mothers, for various reasons, cannot consistently satisfy their child's needs during the early years when secure attachment is so critical. Instead, the mother is often not available for nurturance when nurturance is desperately needed. At best, she is inconsistently available. The young child, realizing that mother is not there, cries, screams and even comes to hate the "bad" mother who leaves him so alone. Yet when she is there, the "good" mother nourishes him in ways that are sustaining. This leads to a split regarding how the mother comes to be perceived. The "good" mother is present and life sustaining, while the "bad" mother is absent and withholding. Dutton notes that, "by preserving this distinction, the child can entertain fantasies of rage toward the "bad mother" without risk of destroying the "good mother" (1995, p. 102). In normal individuals, the bad and good are integrated into a single picture of mother, but in the cyclical/emotionally volatile abuser, this splitting is extended into adulthood so that the female object is either seen as all bad or all good. When the abuser is wooing his wife to come back, he now sees her as wonderful—everything he needs to be whole. It is at these times that wives may say, "He's so sweet the way he talks to me and treats me." But when he is about to explode in rage, he views his wife as the bad mother—the unfaithful slut who deserves punishment. It is at these times that wives often say, "He scares me when he's like that." It is not suprising that these wives often say that their husbands are like two different people. Dutton found these men to be attached in an angry way, "as if they were infants, seeking proximity to mother and simultaneously arching angrily away" (1995, p.115).

The third seed that sets the stage for the development of the cyclical/emotionally volatile abuser is the experience of abuse in the home. Much has been written about the relationship between the abuser and the violence in the abuser's family of origin. Yet not all men who come from homes where there has been abuse repeat the tragedy in their own families. Dutton believes it takes more than the presence of violence in the home. The cyclical/volatile abuser has likely been nurtured in an abusive home where a rejecting father physically and psychologically abused both the son and the mother. The father has been critical and shaming of the child's very personhood and the child feels powerless to defend himself. He is left feeling shameful and believes that he is utterly worthless. Yet he deadens himself to the memory of such horrors and blames others for his unsettling feelings—feelings that are just below the surface, not easily discussed, and not understood. Unfortunately, these feelings are likely to be triggered in adult romantic relationships since these relationships replicate the early bonding experience. Since the cyclical/emotionally volatile abuser has had negative experiences with a mother who has been intermittently available, his early rage for her is later projected onto his spouse as is his desire and need for her as a loving caretaker. Thus, the wife becomes both Madonna and whore. It is these powerful, unconscious feelings that set the stage for the phases of the abuse cycle in the cyclical/volatile abuser.

A Word of Caution

When a partner has problems controlling anger, the spouse is often a target. In the United States, three million partners are physically assaulted each year, with many more being abused psychologically (Gelles, 1997). Most of the reported cases involve men battering their wives or girlfriends, although some husband abuse is also reported. Often abuse begins during the courtship period. One study (Roscoe & Benaske, 1985) found that 51 percent of abused wives reported being physically abused during courtship. Therefore, it is important to pay attention to any signs that predict abuse, even signs that occur before marriage. Experts in the field of abuse often caution women to be apprehensive about dates and partners who behave in any of the following ways:

- Is verbally abusive—calls you names like bitch, says hurtful things to humiliate you.
- Attempts to control—desires to limit your freedom, wants to know where you are at all times, attempts to make decisions for you.
- Tries to isolate you—from family, work colleagues, friends, and is angry and jealous when these attempts are unsuccessful.
- Blames others—nothing is his fault; instead he always points to others and especially you as the person who is at fault.
- Is hypersensitive—becomes overly angry or annoyed at criticism or even problems of daily life.
- Exhibits mood swings—one moment loving, the next angry, hostile, or sulky.
- Has a history of battering in previous relationships—yet has excuses for how it was someone else's fault.
- Threatens violence to you or others—"I'll kick your ass," I'll crush your bones," or "I'll kill you some day."
- Uses violence or aggression in conflict situations—uses force during arguments such as punching, slapping, kicking, or breaks your possessions.

If you see any of these behaviors in your partner before or after marriage— PLEASE BEWARE! Stable marriages are not built on a partner's anger, jealousy, or desire to control.

- Have you seen any of the above characteristics in yourself or your partner? To what extent has anger and control been a problem in your relationship or your marriage?

Abusive and Unhealthy Non-abusive Relationships

When Gottman observed male batterers interact in conflict discussions, he noticed how resistant they were to even reasonable suggestions made by their wives. These men were not going to allow themselves to be influenced by their partners. Even small complaints were met with increased negativity. Gottman (1999) began wondering if a husband's inability to accept influence was predictive of divorce in nonviolent marriages. Thus he began a longitudinal study of 130 nonviolent couples, seeking to determine the relationship between divorce and power sharing. He found that it was the marriages where the husband refused to accept influence by consistently escalating the negativity in conflict discussions that were on a trajectory toward divorce. Conversely, the marriages where husbands were willing to share power and accept influence were the happiest. Gottman (Gottman & Silver, 1999) found that wives in his study rarely increased the negativity in conflict discussions, whereas 65 percent of the husbands ratcheted up the level of negativity when responding to their wives. When husbands increase the negative affect and refuse to accept influence, they put their marriages in jeopardy. Interestingly, when wives escalated the negativity in these marriages, this did not increase marriage instability.

NURTURING A HEALTHY EMOTIONAL CONNECTION

When husbands ratchet up the negativity and refuse to accept influence, they put their marriages in jeopardy. Yet many couples sustain the positive quality of their relationships without increasing negativity. How do they sustain the positive and keep the negative at bay? As Gottman (Gottman & DeClaire, 2001) studied couples interacting in the lab, he realized that happy, stable couples sustained their positive emotional connection by mastering the bid process.

The bid is the most fundamental way in which couples attempt to connect emotionally. It is any gesture or expression that communicates a desire to connect with another person (Gottman & DeClaire, 2001). Partners frequently make bids for emotional connection with each other. "Did you see that our next door neighbor got a new car?" "I would like to go out to eat tonight if that's okay!" "I like that shirt; it really looks good on you." Bids like these are a part of normal conversation in all marriages. Yet happy and unhappy couples differed significantly in regard to the number of bids submitted and how they responded to bids. Happy couples engaged each other on an average of one hundred times during a ten-minute conversation, whereas couples that eventually divorced engaged each other sixty-five times. If this is typical, over a one-year period, happy couples make many more bids and have many more opportunities to connect emotionally than do couples that eventually divorce. Furthermore, husbands in stable marriages disregarded their wives' bids for emotional connection only 19 percent of the time, while wives in these marriages disregarded their husbands' bids only 14 percent of the time. In comparison, husbands in unstable marriages disregarded their wives' bids for emotional connection 82 percent of the time, while wives in these marriages disregarded their husbands' bids 50 percent of the time.

As might be expected, individuals who have trouble connecting during the bid process have more conflict in their relationships. Partners who consistently respond positively to their partner's bids have a reservoir of good feeling that helps them negotiate their differences and keeps negativity from eroding their relationship.

Ways of Responding to Bids

Those who study relationships have found that marriages do not deteriorate overnight. Rather, the good feeling in a relationship erodes slowly, one small missed opportunity at a time. And the missed opportunity involves the failure to respond positively to a partner's bid for emotional connection. Gottman (Gottman & DeClaire, 2001) has found that individuals usually respond to bids by either turning toward, turning against, or turning away from the partner making the bid.

Turning Toward Your Partner

Turning toward your partner means that you respond positively to their bids. Such responses may be verbal such as "tell me more," "that's interesting," or simply "uh huh." At other times, it may simply be a nod of the head or a gesture that communicates listening. Thus, when a partner bids and the spouse turns toward the bidder, bidding is reinforced and mutual bidding usually occurs. This creates a sense of good feeling because partners are connecting emotionally. Evidence indicates (Gottman & DeClaire, 2001) that partners who continue to turn toward each other as they bid for emotional connection develop stable, long-lasting relationships.

Turning Against Your Partner

Turning against a partner's bids is often seen in unhappy relationships. Turning against usually involves a response that is derogatory, sarcastic, demeaning, hostile, or argumentative. When a partner responds to a bid by turning against, this partner has missed an opportunity for positive emotional connection and has increased the negativity in the marriage. If this happens consistently, the important 5 to 1 ratio deteriorates and the bidder may even withdraw from the bidding process. Couples who frequently turned against each other in the bidding process were more likely to have unstable relationships and eventually divorce.

Turning Away from Your Partner

Another way to respond to your partner's bid is to turn away. Turning away usually involves ignoring a partner's bids and acting as if others things are more important. Sometimes turning away involves a response that is entirely unrelated to what the bidder has said. Consistently turning away from a bidder's attempt for emotional connection is especially harmful to relationships. Couples who could not connect because one or both partners frequently turned away were especially vulnerable to early divorce.

What happens when one partner frequently turns toward their spouse in the bidding process while the other frequently turns away or against? Gottman (Gottman & DeClaire, 2001) found that frustrated partners frequently give up; they discontinue their attempt to emotionally connect. Interestingly, partners in stable marriages rebid only about 20 percent of the time and partners in unstable marriages very seldom rebid at all. When partners stop rebidding, conversation diminishes and the relationship is characterized by emotional disengagement.

- In your relationship are you and your partner good at turning toward each other or do you typically turn away or against?

Avoiding Behaviors that Diminish Emotional Connection

Gottman and DeClaire (2001) believe that partners need to be aware of the bidding process and those things that impede emotional connection. This awareness allows partners to avoid behaviors that are harmful to the bidding process and to engage in behaviors that facilitate successful bidding. In their book, *The Relationship Cure,* Gottman and Declaire identify six behaviors that are detrimental to bidding and to healthy emotional connection and they suggest behaviors couples can use to facilitate healthy bidding.

Be Attentive Rather than Inattentive

After the honeymoon, it is easy to become preoccupied with things other than the marriage–work, television, sports, children, computer time. A person's intent is not necessarily evil; instead partners learn to take the marriage and their spouse for granted. However, over time, marriages often deteriorate—one lost opportunity after another. Each lost opportunity involves a failure to respond in a positive way to the bids of one's partner. Even though there are times when a partner does not feel like turning toward his or her spouse in the bidding process, it is important to be mindful of the big picture in the marriage. Over time, if this trend continues, it will lead to an emotional disconnect that can be detrimental to the marriage. Don't expect the good feeling you have in your marriage to continue if you don't turn toward each other in the bidding process on a day-to-day basis.

Use Soft Startup to Conflict Discussion

Gottman (Gottman & DeClaire, 2001) has found that discussions that begin harshly usually end harshly. Therefore, if the bidding process begins with criticism, this is likely to result in defensiveness and countercriticism as partners respond by turning away from or against each other in conflict discussions. Partners need to be positive, express appreciation whenever possible, talk about their feelings without blaming each other, and use "I" rather than "you" when communicating their feelings.

Register a Complaint Rather than a Criticism

Although this may seem trivial, it is extremely important. Criticism often leads to defensiveness and countercriticism; when this occurs, discussions often spiral out of control. A complaint could be registered like this: "I would appreciate your help in the kitchen when I get home, you know like you used to set the table and pour the tea. That was so sweet of you and helped me so much." A criticism would sound more like this: "You never help me in the kitchen any more. All you seem to care about is watching TV. I can never depend on you for anything anymore." Note the "I" in the complaint followed by the expression of appreciation for past help, whereas in the criticism, notice the "you" statement, the blame, and the generalization "never." Registering a complaint is a much softer way to initiate discussion than confronting your partner with a criticism.

Take a Break from Flooding

You will remember that flooding occurs when the body is so physiologically aroused in an emotional situation that productive discussion is impossible. Gottman (Gottman, 1994, Gottman & DeClaire, 2001) has found that it takes at least twenty minutes for the heart rate to calm down enough for productive discussion to begin again. Thus it is important to break for at least twenty minutes before continuing the discussion. Gottman (1994) notes that if one partner returns to conflict discussion before calming down, the other partner will likely take on whatever emotion the aroused partner brings back to the discussion. So if a partner returns angry, the spouse will take on anger. This will again lead to a downward spiral and more flooding and the time-out break will not have enhanced the couple's chances for rational discussion. Therefore, time-out breaks should be long enough for both partners to calm down emotionally. Partners can aid this process by soothing themselves during time-out breaks instead of reinforcing their emotional arousal with negative thoughts.

Be Positive: Look for Good Rather than Bad

Some couples lock on to criticism, point out shortcomings, and make negativity the focus of their marriage. The tendency to be negative may even be related to one's biological makeup. Research (Wheeler, Davidson, & Tomarken, 1993) shows that higher brain activity in the right hemisphere is associated with negative mood states, while higher activity in the left hemisphere is associated with positive mood states. Since these differences in hemispheric activation are found in infants and are consistent over time, researchers suggest that individuals are born with tendencies that predispose them toward positivity or negativity in emotional responding. If a person has a tendency to be critical and focus on the negative rather than the positive, this may be a biological predisposition and this person will need to work harder to change than someone who has been born with a more positive outlook. But regardless of the origin of a person's emotional outlook, research (Gottman & DeClaire, 2001) indicates that couples who are positive toward each other and regularly express this positivity through expressions of appreciation have the happiest, most stable marriages.

Don't Avoid Needed Conversations

Often couples sidestep issues that are too hot for them to handle. These couples are more comfortable avoiding conflict than confronting it. Then too, other couples try to discuss hot topics, but their discussions spiral out of control, resulting in more anger and hurt feelings. Thus the attempt to resolve conflict may lead to further turning away or turning against. Yet Gottman and others have proposed solutions to this dilemma. We will examine several of these proposals in this and later chapters.

Gottman is optimistic about teaching couples the skills needed to emotionally connect. If couples are aware of the bidding process and can avoid mistakes in this process, then they are more likely to maintain the positivity in their relationship. However, Gottman believes that couples need to do more than just avoid mistakes; they need to make a conscious effort to strengthen their emotional connection.

- In your relationship, do you typically engage in behaviors that diminish emotional connection rather than facilitate emotional connection? What areas do you need to improve?

Strengthening Behaviors that Enhance Emotional Connection

After understanding the bid process and avoiding behaviors that interfere with positive bidding, there are proactive steps Gottman and DeClaire (2001) believe couples need to take to foster emotional connection. These include: (1) understanding self and personality in relation to the brain's emotional command centers, (2) examining the past and how the past affects present behavior, (3) communicating more effectively, and (4) uncovering dreams and finding shared meanings in order to increase the "we-ness" in the marriage.

Understand Emotional Command Centers

Understanding differences in nervous system functioning can be helpful when attempting to gain insight regarding one's emotional life. Gottman cites the work of the neuroscientist Jaak Panksepp (1998) in relation to the brain's emotional command centers. Individuals are predisposed to have varying degrees of activity in these centers. Therefore, partners will be different in terms of what these emotional command centers predispose them to be like. Gottman (2001) discusses seven emotional command centers and the way these centers influence behavior in marriage. Three of these centers have a special importance to marriage: the Commander-in-Chief, the Nest-Builder, and the Sensualist. The Commander-in-Chief center is concerned with power and control. It directs action in a confident, forceful way. Overactivation in this center leads to aggression and anger, while under activation leads to passivity and a tendency to shun decision-making. The Nest Building command center predisposes individuals toward affiliation, attachment, nurturing, and affection. When this center is overactivated, a person's affiliation and closeness needs dominate personality, resulting in boundary infringements and separation anxiety. When this center is underactivated, the individual has tendencies toward loneliness and depression. The Sensualist command center specializes in sexual sensation, gratification, excitement, and pleasure. When this center is overactivated, it may result in high-risk sexual behaviors and possibly even sexual harassment and coercion. When this center is underactivated, it results in a loss of sexual interest and a tendency to be depressed. Since activation in these centers varies with individuals, couple mismatches in regard to activation levels can lead to problems in marriage. Partners need to understand their differences in regard to the emotional command centers, to learn how these centers predispose them to behave, and how to create a satisfying relationship even though their emotional programming is different.

Understand the Pasts Influence on the Present

Experience also influences activity in the emotional command centers. Therefore, understanding past experience and conditioning can help couples understand their emotional lives. The previous discussion of the cyclical/emotionally volatile abuser shows how past experience can influence attempts at emotional connection in the abusive personality. Although most individuals will not be as adversely affected by childhood experiences as the cyclical/emotionally volatile abuser, each individual has had experiences that have produced sensitivities and predispositions. The past influences what individuals fear, what they find enjoyable, and how they feel about most of the things that influence marriage—money, work, fun, sex, children, closeness/distance, and household chores. Also Gottman and DeClaire (2001) believe that it is helpful if individuals understand the philosophy of emotion that prevailed in their family of origin. Were parents effective emotion coaches? Or were they emotion distancing (family members were discouraged from expressing emotions), emotion disapproving (family members experienced hostility when expressing emotions, especially negative emotions), or laissez-faire (family members were allowed to express emotions but were given very little guidance and instruction in understanding and successfully managing emotions) in their approach?

Why are insight and understanding so important? Understanding and awareness help couples recognize where emotions originate; with this awareness comes the possibility of responding differently. A case example may illustrate this point. Carol's mother abandoned the family when Carol was four years old, leaving her alone with her father. Times were hard and Carol felt a deep sense of loss. She hungered for affection and felt that without a mother she was not quite whole as a person. Her negative feelings about herself that developed in childhood did not go away easily. Yet as she came to understand their origin, she realized that these feelings did not have to dominate her life–what happened in childhood was not her fault and did not reflect badly on her. Realizing this, she set out to rewrite her script. Today she sees herself differently; she now is a much more competent person, seeing herself as worthy of love and respect. These insights helped her overcome her past conditioning.

Become a Skillful Communicator

Skillful communication in marriage is so important that an entire chapter (Chapter 8) will deal with issues involving family communication. Gottman believes that both verbal and nonverbal communication express emotions and that it is important to understand the subtleties and complexities of this process.

Uncover Dreams and Find Shared Rituals

This step is achieved in two ways. First, partners need to share their dreams with each other by becoming dream detectors–exploring and finding out about each other's personal feelings, ideals, and aspirations. Often there are hidden dreams at the center of perpetual conflict issues. Stable, happy couples learn to manage their perpetual issues by diverting attention away from the conflict and focusing on their partner's dreams that underlie the perpetual issue. This type of sharing involves respect and dignity and creates meaningful bonds of intimacy and connection; it is caring in the deepest possible sense. This sharing makes it easier to find common ground and to compromise. Dream sharing and compromise will be discussed in more detail in Chapter 10.

Second, partners should create meaningful couple and family rituals as they build a sense of "we-ness" in their marriage and family. Rituals give the couple and family an identity. Family members can say, "We are the Smith family and this is the way we do things." As the Smith family describes who they are, many of the things they communicate will involve their rituals. The Smith family goes to the beach every summer. They fish, sail, and play on the beach until they are totally exhausted; then get up the next day and do it again. Rituals develop around almost every aspect of life–meals, bedtime, eating out, vacations, holidays, religious ceremonies, homework, etc. Both couple and family rituals are important. If these rituals are flexible and implemented with each family member's needs in mind, they create a "we-ness" that strengthens emotional connection in the family.

Gottman and DeClaire (2001) believe that each of these steps is important in the process of building healthy emotional bonds in families. These steps describe what happy, healthy couples and families do on a daily basis. Emulating their example holds out the promise that struggling couples and families can achieve greater satisfaction and happiness.

- Are you and your partner aware of those things that strengthen emotional connection? Have you been able to effectively implement any of these strategies?

MURRAY BOWEN'S FAMILY SYSTEMS THEORY

In the 1950s, Murray Bowen, working with families at the National Institute of Mental Health, began theorizing about the nature of emotions in the family. Bowen (1976, 1978) began viewing the family as an emotional system; this system creates bonds that are difficult to disentangle from and to break. He hypothesized that as family members attempt to develop a sense of autonomy, they must break away from the emotional system of their family of origin. Sometimes this is not an easy task. Bowen believed that there were two opposing and powerful forces at work in each individual. One force pushes toward autonomy, motivating the child to grow up, to become a separate individual with the ability to think and feel as a separate mature person. The other force motivates the individual to be close and connected, making separation difficult. Although no one completely breaks away from his or her emotional connectedness to the family of origin, there are different degrees of emotional closeness and separation. Families even differ in their desire for connection and separation, with some families allowing for more separateness and others pushing for more closeness. How a family member handles separation issues and the extent to which the person remains emotionally connected to their family of origin will have an important impact on development. One aspect of development that will be influenced is the individual's level of differentiation.

- To what extent were your parents able to allow you to have your own thoughts and feelings and to behave in ways that differed from their preferences for you? Were they willing to give you space and privacy without being overly intrusive? As an adolescent, did you realize your need to be connected to your parents even as you attempted to separate from them? What made the separation process easy or difficult for you? How separate are you today from your family of origin?

The Concept of Differentiation

Kerr and Bowen (1988) use the term differentiation when discussing (1) the development of a strong sense of self and (2) the ability to separate intellect and emotion. Some individuals are able to break away from the emotional system of their family of origin and use their intellectual system. These individuals develop a strong sense of self and have what Bowen refers to as a high level of differentiation. They know who they are and can say, "This is what I believe . . . . Other people may see things differently, but this is what makes sense to me." These individuals have a solid self and are not likely to compromise this self even in the face of pressure from parents and family. They are not easily drawn into emotional entanglements within the family or with others. The highly differentiated individual can become emotional but does so as a matter of choice. The choice is whether to be guided by emotion or intellect. Even if an emotional response is chosen, emotional behavior is guided by reason rather than an out of control emotional reaction. This allows the highly differentiated individual to be flexible and highly adaptable in emotionally charged situations.

Individuals who experience a low level of differentiation are fused; they have trouble breaking away from the emotional system of their family of origin. These individuals have a fragile sense of self, often looking to others especially family of origin models, for definition and guidance. As adults, they tend to be insecure, somewhat rigid, and they find change difficult. These individuals often have trouble differentiating themselves from others and are intrusive and overbearing in close relationships. Rather than encourage a healthy separateness and individuality, they want to control how family members think and feel in order to create an emotional oneness in the family. These individuals often insist that family members believe and behave the way they believe and behave since this is the "right" way. They have difficulty differentiating between rational thought and emotionally based opinions; their feelings often take over, making it difficult for them to lock into their intellectual system. Of course, differences in level of differentiation vary along a continuum. At one end of the continuum are those who are highly differentiated and at the other end are those who are low in differentiation or fused. In reality most people are somewhere between these two extremes.

Differentiation

High differentiation _____ Low differentiation (fused)

• How differentiated are you from others in regard to a solid sense of self? Can you easily separate emotion from intellect? Are you the person you want to be or the person others want you to be?

Kerr and Bowen (1988) distinguish between basic differentiation and functional differentiation. A person's basic level of differentiation is long-term and is largely dependent on the degree of separation from one's family of origin. It is usually determined by the time an individual reaches adolescence and it tends to stay with the person throughout life, although some change may be possible through therapy. If individuals have great difficulty breaking away from the unhealthy influence of the family of origin and establishing a healthy individual identity, then they are experiencing a low level of basic differentiation—they are fused. Functional differentiation relates to an individual's ability to remain rational in specific situations; thus, it is usually short-term and situation specific. Can a person remain somewhat rational even in emotion-laden situations? If this is possible, then the person is exhibiting a high level of functional differentiation in that specific situation. If individuals lose control emotionally, at that moment, they are experiencing a low level of functional differentiation.

• Give an example of a situation in which you exhibited a low level of functional differentiation-you became fused and lost control emotionally in a specific situation.

Differentiation Applied to Families

Bowen (1978) and Kerr and Bowen (1988) applied the concept of differentiation to both individuals and families. The highly differentiated family encourages a healthy separateness in its members, while providing the closeness and emotional support needed to foster healthy individuality. These families help members think for themselves and choose rational emotional responses instead of out-of-control, emotionally reactive responses. In contrast, the family low in differentiation encourages oneness of thought; togetherness is emphasized over separateness and individuality. Any deviation from this "one-ness" creates anxiety. Therefore, family members are not encouraged to think for themselves, but to follow established, traditional patterns of thinking and behaving. In such families, there is very little flexibility and creating one's own space and individuality is difficult. Again, the concept of a family's level of differentiation should be related to a continuum with most families falling somewhere between the two extreme positions.

Children growing up in a family dominated by a low level of differentiation may find that they are caught up in the emotions and feelings of those around them. Since they are young and their intellectual systems are not well developed, they are engulfed by the powerful influence of the family. As a consequence, these children have trouble differentiating a solid self and remain captives of the emotional system that characterized their family of origin. These children may struggle to extricate themselves from this system, but their struggles often lead to strong counterreactions from family members, resulting in further entanglements. Some adults try to break away from their family of origin by cutting all ties and moving away from their family's corrupting influence. This strategy is usually unsuccessful; their mental and emotional life is still overly influenced by past experiences in the family of origin. Thus, families characterized by a low level of differentiation produce children who tend to be low in differentiation. These children have trouble developing their own individuality based on a solid sense of self. These low differentiated individuals establish families that tend to be low in differentiation, thus passing this characteristic on to their children. Therefore, Bowen believes that a multigenerational process determines a family's level of differentiation, with each generation influencing the next generation.

- Describe your family of origin in terms of differentiation? Was your family of origin high or low in level of differentiation? How did the level of differentiation in your family of origin influence you?

The Family as an Emotional System

The concept of the family as an emotional system is often overlooked; individuals have emotions not families. Yet families create an emotional environment and tone that has a powerful influence on family members. This emotional tone may swing back and forth at times from healthy to unhealthy, controlling to liberating, and tense to relaxed. But in some families, the prevailing tone over long periods of time is unhealthy. This unhealthy emotional atmosphere can be due to many things: abuse or mistreatment of one or more family members, unhappiness in the marriage, a deep-seated personality problem of a family member, unfair rules that govern family behavior, a family member's problem with alcohol/drugs, or a chronic illness that forces an unhealthy role on a family member. If an unhealthy emotional tone persists over a long period of time, this often creates resentment and anger in one or more family members. This resentment and anger is fed back into the system to create more tension and stress. Thus family members seem to be emotionally stuck together in their distress without any escape. Children are especially vulnerable in these families since they do not understand the emotional turmoil affecting them. And the emotional turmoil these family members experience does not go away; the anxiety, resentment, and anger persist. It's as if the family's emotional system has members in its grip and will not let go. When this occurs, unfinished business from the past carries over to present situations. It is this unfinished business that often emerges in the therapist's office.

Kerr and Bowen (1988) believe that these families experience chronic anxiety—an uneasy tension that lingers in the air over a long period of time; its presence is constant and pervasive. Burr, Day, and Bahr (1993) describe this tension by using the analogy of termites eating away at the structure of a house. The termites are invisible, yet they are slowly doing their damage. Long-term tension in families works in a similar way. If unease and tension fester, this tension destroys those things that are essential to a healthy relationship—admiration, respect, and the positive feelings family members have for each other. Kerr and Bowen (1988) believe that this chronic anxiety can be one of the causes of symptom development—e.g., depression, ulcers, headaches, and heart problems—in family members.

It is possible to think of chronic anxiety both individually (the level of chronic anxiety the individual feels) and collectively (the level of chronic anxiety experienced in the family unit). Personality psychologists (Eysenck, 1967, 1990) have found that individuals differ in regard to their anxiety proneness. One individual may be anxiety prone, worrying and fretting in many different situations; another person may be calm and stable, rarely worrying regardless of the situation. In recent years, research (Eysenck, 1990) suggests that these differences are rooted in hereditary factors. That is, individuals are predisposed by their genetic makeup to have different levels of anxiety proneness. But this research does not rule out the importance of the environment. Different environments can have a calming or excitatory effect on one's predisposed tendencies. Kerr and Bowen (1988) propose that one's level of chronic anxiety is greatly influenced by learning in the family during the developmental years. They state: "An individual growing up in a given nuclear family is 'imprinted' with a level of anxiety characteristic of this branch. Anxiety 'rubs off' on people; it is transmitted and absorbed without thinking" (p. 116). With both heredity and environment influencing emotionality, it is reasonable to suggest that partners bring different levels of anxiety proneness to marriage; when they marry, they create a family system that will tend to generate a certain amount of tension and anxiety as they experience the stresses of family life.

Tension and Anxiety in Marriage

Tension and anxiety often surround the issues of differentiation and separateness/togetherness in a marriage. If both partners are highly differentiated, then each partner has a strong sense of self and is not overly dependent on the relationship for emotional support. The partners could be happy living apart, but they choose to live together. In such a relationship, energy is invested in a healthy individuality while at the same time, partners choose to be together because of their love and admiration for each other. The partners are not in the relationship to satisfy immature needs; the relationship is the product of mature choice and is satisfying because both partners bring a strong sense of self to the relationship. Highly differentiated partners are not easily threatened by their partner's individuality and consequently are quite flexible.

As mature individuality and differentiation decrease in a marriage, partners invest more energy in their togetherness. At the togetherness/closeness end of the continuum, partners are motivated by insecurities; they need the relationship and in extreme cases may believe that they cannot survive without each other. They invest high amounts of energy in assessing how the relationship feels. Is he angry? Did she say the right thing? Did things go okay last night? Is our bond, our oneness, as it should be? A "no" answer to any of these type questions increases anxiety and the couple will attempt to restore the proper balance and reaffirm their togetherness. This balance is critical because these partners feel good only when their relationship feels good. Referring to these marriages, Kerr and Bowen (1988) state: "Perceived slights, hurts, criticism, and rejections are progressively more influential in people's responses. There is more preoccupation with whether one has 'gotten enough' and/or 'given enough' in the relationship. As boundaries dissolve, *there is increased pressure on people to think, feel, and act in ways that will enhance one another's emotional well-being*" (p. 77). When this happens, togetherness and oneness are so important that there is little chance of either partner forging a strong, individual sense of self.

Each partner in a marriage struggles with the forces of individuality and togetherness. Partners seek a marriage that provides the proper balance and comfort for them. This balance may change as the marriage changes so the issue of separateness/togetherness may need to be revisited many times during the course of a marriage. Often, partners are on different wavelengths in regard to the amount of separateness/togetherness that they desire. This creates special problems. If one partner desires more closeness and the other more separateness, partners find themselves in a dilemma. Kerr and Bowen (1988) suggest four ways couples deal with this disharmony: (1) The partners may create emotional distance by avoiding each other or withdrawing internally. They may avoid discussing their hot topics, thus reducing anxiety through avoidance. However, this way of reducing anxiety comes with a price—as disengagement increases emotional closeness decreases. (2) Each partner accommodates to relieve the anxiety in the relationship and preserve harmony. These partners work together through give and take as they attempt to find a balance. The success of this accommodation is often based on each partner's belief that each has given about equal amounts. Yet even if this works to create stability in the relationship, the balance will shift toward more togetherness in the marriage. This is because each partner has given up a piece of self to accommodate to the wishes of the partner and the relationship. And there are some risks in this accommodation process since there is a limit to how much giving up of self and individuality each partner can tolerate. (3) Both partners refuse to give in to the demands of the other and they live in continual conflict. If both partners exhibit a low level of differentiation, their desire to convince the other to agree with their position increases. As each partner refuses to go along with the position of the other because it is viewed as an intolerable position, disharmony in the marriage increases. (4) One partner adapts to the demands of the other, while the other partner refuses or cannot adapt in equal measure. Thus there is an imbalance in the partners' adaptation responses. When this occurs, the partner who adapts does so to relieve his or her anxiety and the partner's anxiety. The adaptive partner may desire to please or may in some way feel responsible for his or her partner. Often for the adaptive partner, it is more natural to give in than to endure the tension in the relationship. For example, the emotionally volatile abuser, lacking a solid sense of self, may demand that his wife change and behave in exactly the way he demands. Although internally she may resist, externally she may go along out of fear for her safety and to keep the peace. She loses her individuality and selfhood in this process and her husband feels better about himself and more in control for the moment. Or a husband may give in to the closeness demands of his wife by not going on a hunting trip with his buddies. But for the husband, if there is too much giving up in this way, he loses self to the relationship—he sacrifices himself for the sake of marital harmony. When this happens, there may be less anxiety in the relationship, but more internal anxiety and resentment on the part of the adaptive spouse. And if this internal anxiety becomes chronic, it may manifest itself in symptoms—headaches, fatigue, heart problems, intestinal disorders, a drinking problem, or a nervous tic. Also, tension in a two-person relationship is rarely kept solely in that relationship. It spills over to other relationships in a process known as the triangle.

• Analyze yourself and your partner on the separateness/togetherness continuum below. Where are you on this continuum? Where is your spouse? Have differences in you and your partners separateness/togetherness desires caused problems in your relationship?

Separateness _____ Togetherness

Emotional Triangles and Symptom Development

Many family theorists have written about emotional triangles. A triangle is created when two people, usually husband and wife, have unresolved tension in their relationship. To decrease the tension, they focus on something else, often a child, and this temporarily reduces anxiety in the marriage. Kerr and Bowen (1988) believe that the involvement of a third person reduces anxiety in the two-person relationship by spreading the anxiety out in the three-person system. Spreading out the anxiety keeps the two-person system from becoming too heated. However, the anxiety is like a volcano. Sometimes it is quiet and the relationship is calm; at other times, when there is an increase in anxiety, the volcano becomes more turbulent. This increase in anxiety can occur due to pressures from inside and outside the marriage. A triangle is activated as a way of reducing pressure in the relationship, thus keeping the relationship from erupting in open conflict.

Kerr and Bowen (1988) believe that there are several ways an outsider can be drawn into a triangle. Suppose there is tension between a wife (Alice) and her husband (Brad). One partner (Alice) may actively recruit a third party (Connie). This third party (Connie) then takes the side of the recruiter (Alice) and the two become close, while the spousal relationship remains conflicted. Should the person who has been recruited (Connie) go to Brad and take the side of Alice, then the relationship between Brad and Connie may be conflicted and the relationship between the couple (Alice and Brad) may either calm down or, as Friedman (1985) suggests, become more distant and conflicted. This type of recruiting for side taking is common. The triangled-in recruit is often a friend, relative, minister, or sometimes even a therapist.

Another way a triangle is created occurs when a child realizes that there is unresolved tension between the parents. This child senses the tension and helps the parents refocus by acting out or developing a symptom. The parents calm down as they address their common problem—the misbehaving or sick child. This child has not been directly recruited to create the triangle nor is the child always completely aware of this role. This strategy often works in the short-term since the parents refocus and this reduces the spousal tension. Some children may naturally be more sensitive to the level of tension in their parent's relationship, exhibiting more discomfort when this tension increases. It is often these children who step in to play the sick or misbehaving child.

Triangles also involve different relationship patterns. Minuchin, Rosman, and Baker (1978) identify three dysfunctional relationship patterns—the detouring triangle, the parent-child coalition, and the spirit loyalties triangle. Detouring often occurs when parents cannot directly address some conflict in their own relationship and so they focus attention on a child. These parents are often unaware of the extent of their difficulties and do not consciously involve the child to reduce tension in the marriage. Yet they play out their negative feelings in ways that impinge on the child. Parents who have a sexually estranged relationship may accuse their daughter of being sexually promiscuous instead of confronting their own sexual issues. Or parents who are unhappy with their employment or financial situation may overfocus on their child's school or athletic achievements, pushing for much more than is reasonable. The parent/child coalition involves an unhealthy close alliance between one parent and a child. For example, a husband who is unable to understand his wife's moodiness avoids her emotionality by withdrawing into his hobbies of fishing and hunting. He justifies his distancing by taking his son with him on trips, saying he is educating him to be a man. The father and son joke about the mother's crying spells and emotional outbursts. However, the mother resents this coalition, although the distancing does temporarily ease their tension and fighting. The spirit loyalties triangle involves situations where the child is unfairly caught between the parents in a no-win situation. This often occurs when parents are divorcing and each parent wants the child to take his or her side. Adolescents often act out in these situations to bring the parents back together. Although this may work for a short time, usually when the parents adjust to their adolescent's outrageous behavior, the conflict between them continues and the child is back in the no-win situation.

Kerr and Bowen (1988) believe that the frequency and intensity of triangles will depend upon the level of anxiety and differentiation in the family. When there is high stress in the system and the partners exhibit low differentiation, triangles become more important to the couple as a means of preserving harmony and stability. The greater the stress, the greater the anxiety; the greater the anxiety, the more need for active triangles. Kerr and Bowen (1988) state it this way: "Stress triggers anxiety and as it becomes infectious, the triangles become more active" (p. 139). However, in highly differentiated families, there is less stress and less need to create triangles. In these families, when stress increases, family members can remain more emotionally separate; thus partners can deal with anxiety in a more autonomous way, keeping triangles to a minimum.

In most families, as the level of chronic anxiety increases, both triangles and symptoms increase. Symptoms may be exhibited by a child who becomes ill or develops a problem as a means of restoring balance and harmony to the parental relationship. Or the symptom or problem may occur in one of the other members of the triangle. Remember that chronic anxiety is long-term and takes a toll on bodily resources. The person who breaks down under the stress of chronic anxiety may develop hypertension, headaches, a drinking problem, depression, or some other disorder. Then too, the symptom occurs in a context that involves complex interactions that pull and tug individuals in different directions, as if they were a part of a complicated dance routine. If a symptom becomes a part of this dance, it is embedded in the context of the interactions. Thus the symptom can be best understood by looking at the entire dance rather than focusing on the one step that relates to the symptom. To the systems theorist, it is the interactional processes that are important. Simply focusing on the symptom will only provide temporary relief at best.

After working with families for many years, Friedman (1985) developed several laws concerning how triangles work in families. These laws are presented here more as hypotheses than facts, although some research and a great deal of antidotal evidence from therapists seem to support these laws.

1. A two-member dyad is kept in balance when a third party is triangled into the situation. Thus when a relationship is stuck, a third person or issue is likely to be triangled in.
2. This third person is not likely to bring about lasting change to the dyad relationship using a direct approach—going to the perceived offender or troublemaker and attempting to get him/her to change.
3. The third person who attempts to change the relationship of the dyad pair for the better may have the opposite effect. Trying to increase closeness in the dyad pair by convincing the perceived offender to change may actually increase the distance between partners in the dyad pair. Trying to separate individuals from their symptoms may intensify symptomatic behavior.
4. When a third party takes the responsibility to intervene in the troubled dyad relationship, the stress is passed on to the third party and this person ends up with a lot of the anxiety.
5. Homeostatic forces are at work in relationship systems. When one person is pressured to change, counterforces resist change.
6. In troubled families, conflict tends to be directed toward one point in the triangle—the offender, troublemaker, or identified patient. Although this person is vulnerable, this person is also usually quite powerful.
7. When a third person is brought into a triangle, this third person can be most helpful by behaving in the following ways: developing a non-anxious presence in the triangle, keeping a well-defined relationship with each member of the conflicted pair, and avoiding responsibility for the pair's relationship.

IMPORTANT TERMS AND CONCEPTS

emotional intelligence
emotion coaching parents
positive/negative affect
5 to 1 ratio
escalation of negativity
repair attempts
the cobras
the pit bulls
Dutton's three types of batterers
Walker's three cyclical phases

the bid process
ways of responding to bids
differentiation applied to individuals
differentiation applied to families
basic differentiation
functional differentiation
chronic anxiety
emotional triangle
Friedman's laws of emotional triangles

SUGGESTED READING

Dutton, D. (1995). *The batterer: A psychological profile.* New York: Basic Books.

Goldman, D. (1995). *Emotional intelligence.* New York: Bantam Books.

Gottman, J. M., & DeClaire, J. (1997). *The heart of parenting: Raising an emotionally intelligent child.* New York: Simon & Schuster.

Jacobson, N., & Gottman, J. M. (1988). *When men batter women.* New York: Simon & Shuster.

Kerr, M.E., & Bowen, M. (1988). *Family evaluation: An approach based on Bowen theory.* New York: W. W. Norton.

Chapter 7

LOVE AND HAPPINESS IN INTIMATE RELATIONSHIPS

Seeking happiness has become a goal for many Americans. When Thomas Jefferson wrote that individuals have the right to pursue happiness, the chase was on. Prior to this time, most people had just tried to survive, giving very little thought to happiness. Today, people frequently monitor how happy they feel and they often attribute the level of their happiness to the quality of their relationships. When happiness researcher David Myers was asked whether there was one thing that guarantees happiness, he responded, "you can't guarantee it, but the closest thing that comes to ensuring happiness in somebody's life is marriage" (Parrott & Parrott, 2001, p. 179). Myers (1992) writes: "Compared to those single or widowed, and especially compared to those divorced or separated, married people report being happier and more satisfied with life" (p. 156).

Why does a good marriage enhance one's sense of well-being? Myers (1992) suggests two reasons. First, a good marriage provides support, comfort, and enduring intimacy. When we share life with someone we like, respect, and admire, we have a best friend to help us avoid loneliness and deal with life's difficulties. Then too, marriage offers us two roles that can be very satisfying—the roles of spouse and parent. Although these roles can be difficult at times, they also offer the promise of great joy and are usually the most meaningful roles in life.

Along with greater happiness, good marriages are also associated with other benefits. According to Gottman and Silver (1999), happily married partners live as much as four years longer than do people who divorce. There are several reasons for this greater longevity. Those who are happily married seem to have healthier immune systems. Perhaps this is because they do not experience the turmoil of a conflicted marriage/divorce and the accompanying immune system stress. Also, people who are married tend to make better health care decisions than do those who are single, divorced, or widowed. For example, married people are more likely to eat healthier, exercise more, and maintain a healthier lifestyle (Olson & Olson, 2000).

People who stay married also have more economic assets. Women and children are especially vulnerable to reduced income after separation or divorce. Waite and Gallagher (2000) report a typical finding from a Los Angeles County study showing that the standard of living of wives decreased 27 percent after divorce. Also, a look at median incomes for married couples, singles, divorced couples, and widowed individuals clearly shows that married couples are better off financially. The median income for married couples is more than two and one-half times higher than the median income of these other groups (Olson & Olson, 2000).

Thus, the goal of finding love and happiness in marriage is a worthy goal. Many couples have reaped the rewards of a loving, stable marriage—greater happiness, reduced loneliness, better health, and increased income. But for many couples, this goal has slipped away. What is love? Why is love so difficult to sustain over time? In this chapter, we will examine these and other important questions about love and happiness.

MYTHS ABOUT LOVE

Perhaps no word is more misunderstood than the word love. This word is often used in popular songs and TV programs but is rarely seriously discussed in homes or schools. Yet there is almost an obsessive interest in love as evidenced by the popular songs of our culture. Look at the song titles on almost any popular CD and you will find that the word love is in many titles: *I'll Make Love to You, Love the One Your With, The Power of Love, Can't Make You*

Love Me, I Will Still Love You, Love Can Move Mountains, To Love You More, and When the Wrong One Loves You Right. Even when the word love is not in the title of a song, love often is the theme of the song: *Where Does My Heart Beat Now, Falling Into You, Born to Make You Happy, From the Bottom of My Broken Heart, E-Mail My Heart, One Kiss From You,* and *When Your Eyes Say It.* These titles come from just a few CDs; the list could go on, almost never ending. The titles of popular songs seem to indicate that love does make the world go 'round or at least the music industry go 'round. But what is often depicted on CDs and in popular culture is an unrealistic and partial picture of what love is. Popular culture often reflects some of the following myths and half-truths about love.

Love is a feeling. The depiction of love as a feeling is misleading. There is a strong feeling component to love, but this is only one characteristic of love. And this is the component that experts believe will certainly wane. The important question is—how will partners respond to each other when that loving feeling is not present? It is at this moment that real love will be tested. Is your partner someone you will still want to be with? Lasting love is more likely to be based on friendship and commitment than on strong emotional feelings.

True love conquers all. This myth seems to suggest that any problem can be successfully worked through if you have a loving partner by your side. It helps to have a loving partner, but there are problems that are unmanageable even with the help of such a partner. This saying is frequently associated with the optimism of romantic love. Since the powerful, passionate feelings of romantic love will fade, it may not be around when a couple must conquer many of life's problems. Will the couple be able to work through their problems when romantic love fades—his drinking problem, her critical nature, his terrible temper, her excessive emotionality, his inability to communicate, her spending habits, his in-laws, and her depression?

Love is like falling; when it happens, you can't help it. At times, when we first meet someone, we feel a special attraction for that person. It's as if we can't help having our feelings; we are falling and there is nothing we can do. Yet you make decisions and choices even as you fall. You may decide that he's cute, someone you want to be with, but you ignore his negative characteristics. Focusing only on the positive and ignoring the negative is a choice you make. Another person sees this same individual and has similar feelings but thinks—he's cute, but he drinks too much; he has a two-year-old child and has never been married; he doesn't have a stable job; he seems to have little ambition; and even though he's cute, I'm not interested. In matters of love, don't be slaves to your feelings. You always carry intellect with you, CHOOSE TO USE IT.

There is only one ideal love partner for everyone. Find this soul mate and you will live happily ever after. Reality is not so simple. Some people cannot find happiness with anyone, while others could be content with a number of potential partners. If you are a person who can easily find happiness, there is probably more than one person with whom you can find this happiness.

Once you find true love, it will be eternal and will never change. The divorce records in every state dispute this belief. Certainly those going into marriage should believe that their partnership will last, but for many, it will not. And if your love is to stay vibrant, it must be nurtured; if the flame is to endure, you and your partner must work to keep it alive. And even couples who stay happily married for many years will experience a change in their love, with certain components of love growing stronger as other components diminish. Love may be just as strong after fifty years of marriage, but it will be a different type of love than it was in the beginning.

Sexual chemistry is love. Don't confuse sexual feelings and love. There are several reasons why this may happen. You may have been told that love will be wonderful and when you discover that sex is also wonderful, you may confuse the two. Or perhaps you believe that sex and love should go together and thus when you have good sex, it must be love. Good sex and deep abiding love are two different things. Frequently, they go together in marriage, enhancing the marriage partnership in immeasurable ways. But don't label sexual attraction love. Love involves much more than sexual experience.

When you meet that special person, you will immediately know that this person is the one for you. Love at first sight is something you see in movies or read about in novels. But love involves much more than seeing someone across a crowded room. Perhaps a first sight feeling is attraction or sexual longing, but it is not love. Real love is much too complex and involves knowing another person much more deeply than first sight or casual acquaintance provides. At times, a first sight attraction may lead to love, but just as often, it leads to disappointment.

Love is the key to happiness. When you find love, you will be happy. Partners in a stable marriage do report a greater degree of happiness. However, many couples initially believe that they have found happiness in marriage, but later conclude that they were mistaken. Individuals cannot expect their partners to make them happy, at least not for long. Happiness that is dependent on an outside source or another person is fleeting. Look for happiness from within. Find it there and you will find a source of strength. Make others responsible for your happiness and you will find disappointment.

- Are any of your beliefs similar to the myths and half-truths that are popular in our culture?

THEORIES OF MATE SELECTION

Have you ever wondered why you choose your husband or wife, boyfriend or girlfriend? Why does an individual develop a special chemistry for one person but not another? Why is it that sometimes we choose someone who is so wrong for us, while we reject a more logical choice? Psychologists have also wondered about these questions. While no one would argue that we fully understand the complex mate selection process, we have some interesting theories that provide food for thought.

Several theories attempt to explain mate selection by examining a person's childhood experiences. These theories make the assumption that important factors influencing mate selection are unconscious. These factors relate to what was learned in our family of origin during childhood. It was at this time that we developed dominant ways of feeling, thinking, and perceiving that were associated with home. These theories might even be called the "replicate home" theories and are frequently associated with those who adhere to an object relations explanation of behavior. Our previous discussion of Harville Hendrix has already provided one example of this thinking. DeAngelis (1992) also elaborates on this viewpoint when she discusses the re-creation of childhood experience and the completion of unfinished business. Let's look at these ideas as they specifically relate to mate selection.

Theories Relating Mate Selection to the Past

Re-creation of Childhood Experience

One theory suggests that individuals will be attracted to someone who re-creates the familiarity of childhood. Recalling early memories produces images and associations that help us re-create our childhood experiences, especially images involving parents. These powerful associations and memories are often about feeling loved or rejected, emotionally connected or separate, secure or insecure, and free or restricted. For example, Bob's mother was very sickly. She complained about all sorts of aches and pains that seemed to keep her incapacitated. Bob's father was gone a lot and not very emotionally available when he was present. He had given up on attending to his wife's needs. Thus, Bob was left to care for the one person who expressed any real concern for him—his mother. And try he did. In the short run, Bob felt some success; he cheered her up, she was appreciative, and they felt close. But then the next day, the same scene played itself out again. As Bob thought of his childhood, he thought of his mother's sickness, the love he received when he cared for her, his adult-like responsibilities, his lack of a childhood, and his emotionless, absent father.

In college, Bob fell in love with Audrey and in doing so was able to re-create the "at home" experience he knew best. Audrey, too, was sickly and provided the kind of experiences for Bob that were comfortable—caring for a weak, insecure, dependent woman. He worked hard to make her happy, determined not be like his father. But her needs were insatiable and the years drained him. So after twenty years of marriage, they divorced. But Bob has not given up on his need to find happiness. He is now dating again and has found someone he thinks is different, someone he says "comes in a different package." She is different in some ways from his mother and his former wife, just different enough that during this romantic stage Bob does not see how dependent and insecure she is. So Bob is right on track to re-create that familiar "at home" feeling again.

The "re-create the familiar" approach is often used to explain why someone coming from a certain background marries a certain type of person. Thus, this theory is sometimes used to explain the following mate selection choices:

- a caretaker marries someone who needs constant care
- a person from an alcoholic family marries someone with a drinking problem
- someone from a hostile, abusive home marries someone who is hostile and abusive
- someone whose father was emotionally unresponsive marries someone who is emotionally unresponsive
- someone from a home where there was very little closeness and intimacy marries someone who has trouble being close and intimate
- someone from a home where the father left the mother marries someone who is likely to leave
- someone from a home where love is expressed in a playful way marries someone who expresses love in a playful way
- someone from a home where the mother has been dominant and overbearing marries someone who is dominant and overbearing

On the surface, some of these mate-choice decisions don't appear to make sense. Why would Bob want to marry another weak, insecure, dependent woman? He has already tired of one such wife. One answer is that he is not completely aware of what is happening—he sees qualities in this new partner that he admires, he is romantically smitten, and he ignores what others more readily see. While many of these marriages are not healthy, they do re-create the familiar. They create a familiarity that is known, one that has been experienced before.

Certain feelings, especially feelings about relationships and intimacy, carry over from childhood and are thought to be especially important in marriage. Since an individual first experiences intimacy at a young age and then later seeks intimacy in marriage, what has been learned about intimacy in childhood may influence this important aspect of marital experience. Boys are often taught not to express emotions because emotional expression is a form of weakness. Thus, a boy may grow up in a family where all males are taught to discount emotions, especially soft, tender emotions. Should he marry someone who is more emotional, he will be ill prepared to deal with his wife's emotional side. When she longs for emotional reciprocity, he may find it difficult to contact his soft, emotional side and respond in kind.

DeAngelis also points out that intimacy may be associated with pain or loss. If a child's nurturing parent is hospitalized for a long period of time or dies suddenly, the pain associated with the loss may become associated with fear of closeness. Closeness brings separation and loss. Don't get too close; when you do, bad things happen. Of course, this is processed by the child's unconscious mind and later emerges as a feeling of unknown origin–a vague kind of fear and uneasiness when others get too close. As adults, these individuals may consciously desire closeness, but at the same time push people away. These individuals may even unconsciously choose partners who have trouble getting close, thus protecting themselves from their own fear of closeness.

Some therapists believe that partners are often matched in their ability to tolerate emotional expression, especially those involving emotional tension. Partners may have learned similar things in their families of origin in regard to highly charged emotional expression. Thus, when the emotional thermostat in the family heats up, they can only let it go so far before they unconsciously collaborate to turn it down. This often involves distancing or triangling in a third party to distract attention. While this method of adjusting may seem to have some advantages (things don't overheat and explode), they also have drawbacks–things never get fully discussed and resolved and other problems are created.

Completion of Unfinished Business

Another variation of the re-create the familiar theme is the idea that we marry someone who allows us to complete some unfinished business from our childhood. These unfinished situations usually involve mom or dad. Mate choice decisions based on this premise are also unconscious; we are not aware of this motivation. One young woman had a rather cold, unemotional, unresponsive father. When he did respond to her, he was critical, rarely offering her any praise, and almost always objecting to her choice of boyfriends. On an unconscious level, she longed for his attention and love;

yet during adolescence, she rebelled against his harsh attitude and rules. But in choosing a mate, she married someone very much like her father. He was unresponsive emotionally, lacked communication skills, and generally was unavailable to meet her needs. This theory suggests that her mate choice provided an opportunity for her to work through early childhood frustrations with a father figure. She married someone like her father, worked to get his approval and love, and in this way attempted to complete unfinished business. This choice allowed her to work on problems from childhood; if she is successful in resolving these issues, she completes the unfinished business, becoming more mature in the process. DeAngelis (1992) also suggests another possibility. If she is extremely angry with her father, she may marry someone whom she can berate and, in this way, retaliate against her father through her husband. Thus, at times an individual may marry a spouse and unconsciously hurt the spouse as an indirect way of hurting the parent.

- Do you believe that the re-create the familiar theory or the complete unfinished business theory have any validity as explanations for mate choice?

The ideas mentioned in the above discussion are intriguing but have very little support from scientific inquiry. Many of the proponents of these ideas are marriage therapists who believe that their clinical encounters with clients support such observations. Also, many of them hold to theoretical viewpoints that are consistent with such observations. However, providing solid scientific evidence is difficult since family of origin experiences may be only vaguely recalled, if recalled at all, and there are so many other intervening experiences, past and present, that may have contributed to present behavior. Even when research suggests a relationship between early upbringing and mate selection or attachment styles, this research is correlational and comes with the causal limitations inherent in this approach.

Mate Selection as a Filtering Process

There is a growing body of research on mate selection and love that does not relate mate selection to childhood. The social psychologists doing this research study variables that are more easily observed and assessed rather than focusing on unconscious variables relating to childhood. In the mid-1970s, several researchers were granted more than $80,000 from the National Science Foundation to study the process of falling in love. When Senator William Proxmire, a watchdog for federal spending, found out about this use of tax dollars, he quickly proclaimed that falling in love was not an appropriate subject of science—it was best left to poets who understand that love is too mysterious a process to comprehend. Scientists would agree that falling in love is a mysterious process but would not agree that this process should be ignored by science. Instead, social scientists believe that the subject of love is fertile ground for research; the more knowledge we have, the greater the likelihood that we can understand the mystery surrounding this important emotion.

Much of the research on mate selection can be related to a filtering process model. Both Udry (1971) and Rice (1996) have proposed such a model. Imagine that the mate selection process involves screening potential partners through filters that sort out the appropriate matches from the inappropriate matches. What will determine which potential partners get filtered out and which ones will survive the cut? This filtering process may not sound much like love, but keep reading; the results are interesting.

The Propinquity Filter

Propinquity is another word for being in close proximity, as in living close to someone, working with someone, or going to school with someone. When this happens, there is the opportunity to have contact. For example, two people are in class together, work together, ride the same bus, or eat at the same pizza place. I know you may meet someone named Roy over the Internet who lives in Lower Slovakia, but you are not likely to fall in love and marry Roy if he doesn't move closer. So this is one common-sense idea that has research support.

The Attractiveness Filter

Suppose two students are in a psychology class and they spot each other across the classroom. How likely is it that attractiveness will play a role in their wanting to get to know each other? Would a male be more influenced by physical attractiveness than a female? Research (Feingold, 1990, 1991) indicates that males do place a bit more emphasis on opposite sex physical attractiveness than do females. However, attractiveness also matters to females. After a brief acquaintance date, Hatfield (1966) asked both males and females how much they liked their date and whether they would like to date their partner again. Her findings indicate that both males and females were influenced by physical attractiveness. The more physically attractive the date was perceived to be, the more the date was liked. And the more physically attractive the date was perceived to be, the greater the desire to date this person again. Another interesting conclusion was that at this early point in the acquaintance process, attractiveness was the only variable that seemed to be associated with liking and the desire to date again.

But everyone cannot marry someone who is judged to be beautiful. Research (Murstein, 1986; Berscheid, Dion, Walster (Hatfield), & Walster, 1971) also indicates that there is a matching phenomenon at work in the selection process. Thus, individuals pair up with partners they judge to be about as physically attractive as they judge themselves to be. There are, however, exceptions to this rule. Sometimes an attractive individual marries an unattractive mate. When this happens, often the less attractive partner has some important compensating quality such as money or high status. Often, status, money, and position compensate for a lower level of physical attractiveness.

The Similarity Filter

The two students in psychology class, who find each other physically attractive, have never spoken to each other or been formally introduced. But that is about to change. They strike up a conversation while getting lunch in the student union. As they talk, they take this opportunity to get to know each other and to find out about their similarities and differences. And what they find out passes through the similarity filter. They soon find that they share some similarities–they both like to smile and laugh; they think the psychology class is interesting, but neither is a serious student; they both turned the homework assignment in late; and they are both juniors. If they continue meeting, many pieces of information will be added to the filtering process regarding similarities and differences. Research tells us that partners are more likely to continue their interest in the friendship if there are enough matching similarities–do they both feel comfortable with each other, do they come from similar backgrounds, share similar beliefs, and have many things in common? Everything doesn't have to match, but couples usually want the important things to do so. Things that often fall into this category are social class and economic status; feelings about love, commitment, and children; attitudes about work, sex, money, and professional goals; and beliefs about religion and education. As these two students share information over the course of the semester, they feel that there is something special about the other, something that has not been present in other relationships. As they lie awake at night, they realize that they share many similarities. They wonder if this is a match–is this that special person?

But what about opposites, don't they attract? Haven't you heard that the strong, outgoing type complements the quiet, shy type? Or do birds of a feather flock together? It appears that the two students from class are a lot more similar on important dimensions than they are different. Is this a good or bad sign? Actually, researchers have found very little support for the opposites attract hypothesis. Researcher David Buss (1985) concluded that the belief that opposites marry has never been reliably demonstrated. Happiness researcher David Myers (1993), in reviewing the research, concludes that friends, engaged partners, and married couples are much more likely to share similarities than are people picked at random. And the more similar married couples are, the happier they have been found to be and the less likely they are to divorce.

But what would therapists say about the matching hypothesis? After all, they get to know couples in a more intimate way. The therapist's response would probably sound something like this: Make sure you are similar in many ways, especially in ways that are important to you. Years of togetherness are calmed by similarities and made more difficult by differences. If you are wondering if there will be differences, there certainly will be. When differences do arise, your similarities will allow you to come together and celebrate your common values, beliefs, and dreams. When you can do this, you can usually still love and respect each other in spite of the differences.

The Compatibility Filter

The word compatibility means capable of living together in harmony. Couples often wonder if they will be able to live together harmoniously, especially through many years of marriage. As we have seen, couples having many similarities are happier and are more likely to stay together. We might say that they are more compatible. However, compatibility also can be related to differences. One partner may enjoy details, planning, and keeping track of the finances, while the other wants input but is happy leaving these details to their spouse. One partner may enjoy doing the grocery shopping; the other views it as boring. One may enjoy cooking, while the other is only interested in eating. In these instances, the couple's differences may complement each other. They do not need to constantly decide who will do the grocery shopping or who will pay the bills. They are flexible, each can fulfill the other's roles when needed, but usually their roles complement each other. The two students who have become interested in each other are making some inferences about compatibility. Yes, they are similar in many ways and both conclude that this is a good sign. But can they know that they are compatible enough to have a stable, happy marriage? Or is your skeptical friend correct when he says that marriage is the biggest gamble in town? For most couples, the answer probably lies somewhere between the two extremes; you can never know for sure, but if you can keep your head about you as you go through the selection process, you can maximize your chances of having a successful, happy marriage. Here are some characteristics associated with lasting marriages, characteristics that should be considered in the mate selection process (Bee, 1994; Myers, 2000).

- Both partners were twenty years old or older when they married.
- Both partners had known each other for a relatively long period of time.
- Both partners had relatively high levels of education.
- At least one partner had a good job and stable income or at least the prospects of a good job and a stable income.
- Both partners came from the same religious background and shared religious beliefs.
- Both partners had high self-esteem.
- Neither partner was high in "neuroticism"—a tendency to be highly emotional, anxious, and impulsive.
- Both partners liked each other as "best friends."
- Both partners were in agreement about many things, including the roles each would fulfill in the marriage.
- The female was not pregnant when the couple married.
- There were low levels of negativity and high levels of positivity in their interactions.
- Both partners were good at conflict resolution.
- Neither partner had bad habits such as drinking or drug use or disagreeable personality traits such as excessive anger or need to control.
- The couple did not cohabit before marriage.

Can couples know all of this before marriage? They cannot completely know; marriage has an element of uncertainty to it. Yet couples should be aware of the positive signs and not ignore the negative ones. The two students in the psychology class are coming to see their relationship as serious; last night, the subject of marriage even came up in their conversation. But doesn't their feeling of love for each other mean that regardless of their differences, they will be able to pull through together? Not necessarily! All couples usually believe this, but about 50 percent of their marriages end in divorce. But what about cohabitation; isn't it a good idea? Why is it on the list? Our two students wondered if living together would help them find out if they were compatible. Good question!

The Cohabitation Filter

It is no longer surprising to hear that a couple is living together. Cohabiting arrangements are more prevalent than ever before. According to the U.S. Bureau of Census (1997), the rate of cohabitation increased by eight-fold between 1970 and 1996–from half a million to four million couples. Cohabitation has been found (Amato & Booth, 1997) to be highest among adults from broken homes and lowest among adults from intact, stable families. Duke's research (as cited in Olson & DeFrain, 2000) found that the incidence of cohabitation was also related to religious orientation with the non-religious having approximately twice the rate of cohabitation as Protestants and more than five times the rate of Mormons. Many believe that cohabitants are young college students who are just testing the water. However, Waite and Gallagher (2000) report that over a fourth of unmarried mothers are cohabiting when they give birth and many cohabiting partners have had children from unions that occurred prior to their present cohabitation. Bumpass and Sweet (1989) reported that over a quarter of college students cohabit before they marry and that about half of adults in their early thirties have been in at least one such arrangement. These researchers also found that the cohabitation rate is higher among less educated couples than educated couples.

Ridley, Peterman, and Avery (1978) reported on four common motives behind cohabitation. These motives were emancipation, convenience, Linus blanket, and testing.

EMANCIPATION. This motivation for cohabitation characterizes situations where at least one partner is seeking to break away from the influence of parents. The parents may have attempted to rule with an iron hand as they espoused conservative beliefs or strict views on sexuality. Thus, the partner seeks emancipation by rebelling against the harsh rules and standards of parents. Cohabitation in these situations is fraught with problems. The underlying purpose of the relationship is not to create a stable living arrangement, but to deal with unfinished business and make a statement about self. This makes the relationship somewhat secondary to the independence needs of the emancipating partner.

CONVENIENCE. These relationships serve a purpose for both partners without the risk of long-term commitment. The man usually gets a sexual partner and housekeeper and the woman gets social interaction, a partner to come home to, and limited security. In these relationships, the woman often hopes for marriage, but the man sees no need to change the way things are. Ultimately, these relationships become frustrating for one or both partners. When they go their separate ways, they leave older and perhaps wiser.

LINUS BLANKET. In this relationship, one partner is extremely dependent and insecure. This partner grabs on to the relationship the way Linus grabs on to his blanket. The dependent partner prefers almost any relationship to the feeling of anxiety and loneliness. The neediness of the insecure partner often pushes the less dependent partner away, leaving the insecure partner more fragile and insecure. When the relationship ends, the insecure partner usually feels depressed and hurt, while the stronger partner feels somewhat guilty about leaving but happy to have escaped.

TESTING. Sometimes couples cohabit as a way to test the strength of their relationship. These couples may believe that marriage is in their future, but to be sure, they want to test it out by living together. If the test goes well, they marry; if it does not, they part ways, usually glad they saw the flaws in the relationship before they got married.

An assumption that many couples make is that cohabitation will improve the chances of a successful marriage since it will allow them to live together in a marriage-testing situation. For couples who are highly committed to each other and plan to marry, there are findings (Brown & Booth, 1996) that suggest cohabiting is much like marriage–the partners act and behave like married couples. But for those cohabitants who are unsure of marriage, the picture is different. Waite and Gallagher (2000) see these arrangements as differing from marriage in two important ways–commitment and time expectations. In marriage, there is the vow of permanence. The couple starts with the expectation that it will work and a commitment to make it work. Less committed cohabitants have a different attitude and it is reflected in their behavior–they do not pool financial resources in the same way as married couples and they place more emphasis on individualism. As a group, they are also more nontraditional in beliefs about sexual roles, are less likely to attend church, and are more likely to believe that if a marriage isn't working, partners should not stick with it (DeMaris & Leslie, 1984). These differences between cohabitants and noncohabitants may explain why cohabitants who do marry have higher divorce rates than noncohabitants who marry and why cohabitants are less satisfied with their marriages than are noncohabitants (Booth & Johnson, 1988; DeMaris & Reo, 1992). Of course, cohabitation may prevent some potentially bad marriages from occurring, thus protecting the partners from some later pain and suffering.

Therefore, the group data on cohabitation indicates that those who cohabit before marriage are less likely to be satisfied with their marriages and are more likely to divorce than couples who do not cohabit before marriage. However, very few couples base their decisions on group data. Perhaps it is best to closely evaluate your motivations for wanting to cohabit and realize that if it is a happy marriage that you want, the road from cohabitation to happy marriage can be treacherous.

- Relate your relationship experience to filter theory. Did you consciously use these filters in choosing your relationship partner?

And so the two students in psychology class are becoming serious about their relationship. There seems to be a special chemistry between them, but is this feeling based on anything more than sexual attraction? They are similar in many ways and when they are together, it appears that they are quite compatible; in some ways, they even seem like best friends. They know couples who are cohabiting, but for now, they have decided not to do so because of their religious upbringing and the desire to find out more about each other before taking the next step. They have heard about programs that attempt to prepare couples for marriage and they are wondering if such a program would be helpful. Certainly they do not want to make a serious mistake and end up divorced seven years down the road.

MISTAKES PEOPLE MAKE ON THE ROAD TO MARRIAGE

Many marriage therapists and family life educators have written about mistakes people make in the mate selection process. And many partners wish that they had not ignored signs that were present even before marriage. Prior to marriage, when romantic feelings are powerful, individuals are likely to overlook a partner's negative qualities or interpret these qualities in a positive way. Later, these same qualities are often seen differently. Here are a few examples:

- Before marriage, she liked him because he was assertive; after marriage, she resented him because he was too domineering.
- Before marriage, he was drawn to her because she was so soft and gentle; after marriage, he disliked her sensitivity and hesitancy.
- Before marriage, she liked his flamboyancy and free spirit; after marriage, she could not stand his immaturity and playfulness.
- Before marriage, he liked her because of her outgoing, talkative nature; after marriage, he hoped for a little peace and quiet.
- Before marriage, she liked him because of his ambition; after marriage, she resented him because he put his work before family.
- Before marriage, he was drawn to her planning and organizational skills; after marriage, he thought she was too uptight and compulsive.

Even if one partner sees characteristics in the other that are troubling, this partner may believe that after marriage the spouse will be easy to reform. After all, their love talk implies that they would do anything for each other. Be careful! Ingrained habits do not change easily. DeAngelis (1992), a well-known author and relationship expert, cautions her readers about common mistakes that put marriage at risk. You may have heard of some of these mistakes and possibly have made some of them yourself.

Not Asking Enough Questions

Before marriage, individuals are often blind to their partner's past and to their flaws. If you were hiring a housekeeper or administrative assistant, you might conduct a more thorough investigation. But in matters of love, it's the feelings that count. It's not until romance fades that flaws of character become more apparent. DeAngelis (1992) even provides questions that partners should ask each other in the different stages of their relationship: the first three months, the second three months, and after six months. She even suggests bringing up topics such as: Tell me about your ex-girlfriends and why you broke up? How do you feel about religious faith and God? How do you feel about seeking help for problems? Later, partners should attempt to find out about any flaws that might harm a relationship, such as problems with drinking or drugs, anger control, or immaturity. You should also be asking whether this person has the positive qualities you desire in a partner, such as integrity, maturity, responsibility, and a positive self-image. Sharon Hanna (2000) suggests that couples consider the following questions before deciding to marry.

- How long have you known each other? Knowing each other for a relatively long period of time predicts success in marriage.
- What are your motivations for wanting to marry? Have you asked whether you are marrying for the wrong reasons?
- Do you have realistic expectations about love and marriage?
- Do you and your partner agree on the roles you both will play in the marriage?
- Do you and your partner have compatible beliefs about careers and personal goals? Will both of you have careers? What potential problems will dual careers present in regard to schedules, finding time for your relationship, and child-rearing? Will you be able to cooperate and work as a team when conflicts over gender issues arise?
- Do you and your partner agree on money and finance issues? Will you share financial resources equally? How will you determine how money is spent?
- How similar are your religious values? If there are differences in religious beliefs and values, how will these differences be handled?
- Do you share many of the same interests—sports, hobbies, and leisure time?
- Do you and your partner have compatible life styles? Do you like each other's friends, like to go to the same places and do the same things?
- Have both of you broken away sufficiently from your families of origin? Are you and your partner mature enough to create a healthy separateness from outside family and friends?

- Do both of you look forward to establishing your own family rituals? How will you celebrate birthdays, holidays, your anniversary, and other special occasions?
- If you decide to have children, do you share the same child-rearing philosophy? Will you be able to work together as a cohesive team as you rear your children?
- Do you agree on issues regarding sexuality? Can you talk openly about your feelings in this area? Are there differences that may cause problems?
- Have you made an attempt to find out about each other's faults, bad habits, and problems instead of pretending they do not exist? Does your partner have a flaw of personality that may cause problems, such as anger control, a workaholic nature, excessive sloppiness or neatness? Will you be able to accept differences that exist without having them constantly irritate you?
- Do you enjoy being together in non-passionate moments? Is your partner someone you would want as a best friend?
- When crises come, will you know how to help each other—how to comfort, when to listen, and how to nurture?
- How will you manage conflict? Will your styles make it difficult for you to work through issues?

Couples will not be able to discover the answers to all of these questions before marriage. Some answers may not be apparent until a couple has children, meets their partner's relatives, or experiences a major conflict. And nothing a couple is presently experiencing, not even cohabitation, can simulate the seventh year of marriage. However, don't be totally blind to differences, potential problems, and trouble spots. If there are too many red flags— be careful! Also remember that marriage is a contract. Although partners might not want to make it as public and legally binding as a written prenuptial agreement, each partner needs to know what their partner expects. Unfortunately, important matters are often not discussed before marriage. Thus partners are surprised when they find many issues that divide them. If partners go into marriage having different expectations about many things, they will certainly discover these differences, more likely sooner than later.

- Did you use a questioning approach in your search for a relationship partner? If so, what questions were important to you? See if you avoided other mistakes mentioned below, mistakes that Delangelis (1992) believes are all too common.

Ignoring Warning Signs–Focusing Only on Feelings

Sometimes, individuals want to be in love so badly that they go strictly by their emotions and bypass intellect. They say things like, "we are soul mates, meant to be together forever" or "I've found my one and only, we will never part." This may even be the third or fourth time they have said this about a relationship. Be careful with your commitment; it should not come easily. When partners commit to each other, it should be based on some feeling but also a good dose of reason–I've checked it out, we are similar and compatible in many ways.

Compromising Your Beliefs and Value System

In an attempt to find acceptance and romantic love, some individuals are too quick to compromise their beliefs. Do you want to drink that much? Do you want to go to those places, watch those videos, compromise in those ways? Do you want to give up valued relationships with family and friends? If you must become someone else during the early part of a relationship to satisfy your partner, you may realize that the person you have become is not the person you want to be. If you find that you avoid certain issues in order to keep the peace and protect the relationship, you may be trying to create an illusion of compatibility that does not exist.

Overemphasizing Physical Attraction and Sexual Desire

In our culture, there is often too much emphasis placed on sexuality and physical appearance. Partners are tempted to think about sex and physical attraction before anything else. Sexual chemistry and physical attraction draw partners together, but this feeling and attraction is not love. Partners who are physically attracted to each other may be very incompatible. Attempt to get to know your partner before being so influenced by appearance and sexual desire.

Being Unduly Influenced by Outside Pressure

Social psychologists have found that people are very influenced by what is going on around them. If friends are getting married and parents encourage marriage at a certain time, then marriage may occur for the wrong reasons. Hopefully, individuals now realize that there is no set timeline and pattern for everyone. Also, marriage is not the life style for everyone. For some, marriage would be a stumbling block to happiness rather than a rewarding life style. Society must value individuals who choose to stay single.

Responding to Loneliness and a Sense of Emptiness

Some people struggle with loneliness. They think that fulfillment comes through love and being with someone. Therefore, they are constantly searching for that someone who can work magic, fill the void, and reduce loneliness. Certainly love does have the power to transform us for a time and initially make us feel better about ourselves. But in popular music and in life, we often attribute too much power to the power of love. The theme of the popular song, *The Power of Love,* is that the world is too much for one person to handle alone, but with that special someone, loneliness and emptiness can be overcome. The trouble with this philosophy is that if you feel desperate and lonely before marriage, there is no guarantee that you will feel any different after marriage. The magic power is not in having someone to love or be married to, but rather learning how to love yourself so that you can feel contentment and satisfaction regardless of your marital status. Thus, every person contemplating marriage should first learn how to be satisfied with self and with life so that s/he does not bring needs to marriage that are impossible for a partner to fulfill.

Avoiding an Important Issue or Situation

Some individuals use a love relationship as a way to escape an otherwise miserable, boring life. Others use marriage or living together as a way to escape difficult living conditions in their family of origin. And some attempt to forestall the psychological growth process by finding someone who will take care of their needs like mother and dad did. None of these motivations provide a sound basis for a stable marriage.

- Have you made any of the above mistakes in your search for a relationship partner?

WHAT LOVE IS

Passionate and Companionate Love

Love is not a simple emotion, nor is love easy to understand. Most experts agree that there are different types of love and in order to understand love, it is necessary to understand the different types. Some researchers (Hatfield, 1988; Walster & Walster, 1978) distinguish between passionate love and companionate love. Passionate love is highly intense and emotional. It is a state of longing for one's partner with a feeling of great elation and joy if that longing is reciprocated. However, if that love is not returned in kind, there is great pain and misery. Some have even called passionate love a chemical high, comparing it to intoxication caused by brain chemicals. When two people are passionately in love and this love is reciprocated, the world is a brighter place, obstacles seem surmountable, and optimism abounds. No wonder people long for this type of love; it makes them feel alive in a very special way.

According to Lauer and Lauer (2000), passionate love is a relatively new type of love that first emerged in twelfth century Europe. Prior to this time, marriages were contracted arrangements, not for love, but for other reasons such as security, status, economic benefits, and procreation. The contract likely stated that the partners would work together, making sacrifices for the common good, but said nothing about romantic or passionate love. In the musical, *Fiddler on the Roof,* the Jewish father, Tevye, is bemoaning the fact that his daughter is resisting the choice of the matchmaker for her. Instead, she is pleading her case for a young man she says she is "in love" with. The father knows nothing of this new type of love since his marriage to Golda, his wife, was a contracted arrangement. As he thinks about established traditions and new ways of doing things, he asks Golda something he had never asked her before. "Do you love me"? Golda responds as if that is a strange question. "Do I what?" But then after thinking, she responds with an answer that reflects the contract. She has washed his clothes, cooked his meals, and shared intimately in every aspect of his life, and she says, "If that's not love, what is?" Of course, in many countries today, times have changed and people have adjusted to the idea of passionate love as a prerequisite for marriage.

But no matter how hard couples try, they cannot sustain the intensity of passionate love indefinitely. This reality is so important that it is restated throughout this book. However, passion may not disappear entirely; it simply lessens in intensity. Experiencing the waning of passion can be troubling for some couples, especially if they do not know to expect it. Perhaps the phrase, "the honeymoon is over," depicts this realization best as partners reflect on their changing relationship. Will this new, changing relationship be a satisfying one? Are the partners really as compatible as they thought they were? Will they want to be together for the rest of their lives? As the years pass, couples begin discovering the answers to these questions.

Even in the beginning, marriages are usually characterized by another type of love–companionate love. This type of love lacks the intensity of passionate love; companionate love involves the sharing of intimate experiences and the deep connection that comes with this sharing. At first, passionate love may overshadow companionate love, but as the relationship endures, companionate love often sustains the relationship. In many ways, companionate love is like a deep friendship. It usually has the eight dimensions of friendship identified by Davis (1985) in his study of love versus friendship. These eight dimensions are:

1. Friends usually enjoy being together.
2. Friends are able to accept each other as they are.
3. Friends trust each other and have the other's best interest at heart.
4. Friends respect each other's decision making, believing it is based on good judgement.
5. Friends help and assist each other, providing support when needed.
6. Friends share feelings and experiences together.
7. Friends understand each others values, feelings, and way of thinking.
8. Friends are free to express who they are with each other without having to play a false role.

Lauer and Lauer (1986) asked happily married couples, couples who had been together for many years, to select from thirty-nine factors the ones that had most contributed to the success of their marriage. The first two selected by both husbands and wives were—my spouse is my best friend and I like my spouse as a person.

• In your search for lasting love, were deep friendship and genuine liking qualities that were important to you?

Sternberg's Triangular Theory of Love

You may be wondering if there is not more to love than just two types—passionate and companionate. Robert Sternberg (1988) describes seven kinds of love, including passionate and companionate in his triangular theory of love. His research reveals that many of the aspects of love are manifestations of three related but distinct components. These components are passion, intimacy, and decision/commitment and they make up the three tips of the triangle.

Passion = Infatuation

The passion component of love is highly emotional and sexual, involving strong physiological arousal. This component of love correlates with a preoccupation with the partner, a powerful desire to be together, a tendency to perceive the partner as perfect, a desire to be loved in return, and a deep sadness at any thought of terminating the relationship. In some relationships, the passion component may develop almost immediately. It is also the component that partners often feel they have little or no control over. Thus, sometimes words like "falling into" this type of love are used to describe what happens, as if the person has no control over the falling process. If love includes passion but none of the other two components, it is called *infatuation.*

Intimacy = Liking

Intimacy is another tip of the triangle. This component of love relates to those things that promote closeness and bonding in a relationship. Many experiences promote intimacy: looking out for the partner's welfare, enjoying happy times together, being there for the partner during times of special need, giving and receiving emotional support, listening and sharing important feelings, and showing that the partner is held in high esteem. As partners share these type experiences, this sharing promotes closeness and they become friends. Intimacy without the other two components of love is referred to as *liking*–the feeling one has for a true friend. The basis for intimacy probably develops as individuals break down barriers through self-disclosure. This may even be easier for friends who have no romantic attachment since in a love relationship one has more to lose by intimate self-disclosure. If too much is disclosed, one's separateness may be threatened. If too little is disclosed, intimacy may fail to develop. Therefore, couple relationships involve a balancing act between autonomy and intimate self-disclosure.

Decision/Commitment = Empty Love

The third component of love in Sternberg's model is decision/commitment. This component includes both the cognitive decision to love and the decision to extend commitment over the long term. It is strong commitment that allows couples to get through the hard times in marriage. The commitment component is reflected in the "till death do us part" statement in the marriage ceremony. However, in contemporary marriage ceremonies, this statement may be omitted, modified, or viewed only as an ideal. Couples often do not discuss their views of commitment with each other; they believe that their romance will be enough to sustain the relationship. If beliefs about commitment are not articulated, one partner may think of commitment as forever binding, while the other may think of commitment as binding as long as the relationship feels right or until it no longer works well. Even if partners initially agree on the "till death do us part" definition, this does not mean that both partners will continue to adhere to this view; circumstances and marital experience often change partners' beliefs about commitment. Love that is characterized by decision/commitment only, without the components of passion and intimacy, is referred to as *empty love.*

In Sternberg's triangular model, a relationship can evolve that is characterized by just one component, a combination of two components, or all three components. Different combinations result in different types of love.

Passion + Intimacy = Romantic Love

Passion combined with intimacy results in *romantic love.* Here strong physiological arousal creates a powerful attraction and intimacy creates a strong friendship bond. This is the type of love often depicted in movies or literature—the passionate summer romance where lovers are physically attracted to each other and share details of their lives but without the commitment necessary for a long-term relationship.

Passion + Commitment = Fatuous Love

When passion combines with commitment, Sternberg calls this *fatuous* (foolish) *love.* The passion is present in the relationship and the couple makes a decision to be together, perhaps they even get married, but the relationship is like a whirlwind courtship that develops without the experiences that build intimacy. Since intimacy takes time to build and is achieved through sharing experiences, it cannot be quickly manufactured and added to the relationship. As these partners spend time together, they often realize that many of the shared beliefs and experiences that help cement a relationship are missing. Since passion can develop very quickly and decisions can be made on the spot, these relationships are often short-lived due to incompatibility.

Intimacy + Commitment = Companionate Love

A long-term relationship is more likely to occur when intimacy combines with commitment. Sternberg calls this combination *companionate love.* Companionate love is built on a deep friendship that intimacy often creates and on a strong desire and commitment to continue the relationship. When many of the strong passions associated with romantic love have waned, partners will discover whether there is enough liking, friendship, and commitment to make the relationship a lasting one. The research of John Gottman (1999) indicates that as couples struggle to repair the negativity that creeps into their relationships, the success or failure of their repair attempts depends upon the strength of their marital friendship. Couples who had the advantage of being good friends could repair the negativity. Therefore, a strong bond of friendship created by intimacy and a desire to continue the relationship (commitment) are extremely important in marriage; these are the ingredients of many lasting relationships.

Passion + Intimacy + Decision/Commitment = Consummate Love

The ultimate type of love occurs when the three components of love—passion, intimacy, and decision/commitment—are combined in equal measures. Sternberg refers to this as *consummate love* and believes that it is difficult to sustain. He suggests that it is like a weight loss program—one may reach an ideal weight but then must work to maintain that weight. Just as there are no guarantees that the ideal weight will be maintained, there are no guarantees that consummate love, if attained, will be sustained. Consummate love often fades—its disappearance becoming evident only after it is almost gone. If couples value consummate love, they must work to maintain it.

- Draw the triangle depicting Sternberg's triangle of love. Write each of the seven types of love in the proper place around the triangle. As you examine your relationship, how would you describe it in relation to Sternberg's triangular model and the seven types of love that make up the triangle?

A Closer Look at Commitment

Many marriage educators view commitment as the most important component of a lasting relationship. However, William Doherty (2001) believes that many young people today view marriage as consumers view products. We trade cars every three years, redecorate the living room periodically, and search for a better deal on our home mortgage. In our throwaway society, very few things are permanent. Some people now talk of starter marriages in the same way they talk about a first home or first car. This consumer attitude downplays the role of commitment. It emphasizes staying in marriage only as long as it feels good, meets self-centered needs, and is satisfying. Consumer-oriented couples fail to make the distinction between things that are unacceptable in marriage, such as physical abuse and infidelity and things that are simply bothersome such as a spouse working too much, not talking enough, or showing enough interest in a partner's concerns. Things that are troublesome have now become unacceptable; a spouse must change or greater satisfaction will be sought elsewhere. What the person with this consumer attitude does not usually understand is that all marriages have their irritating moments.

According to Doherty, couples need to develop "intentional marriages." These are marriages where each partner has a strong commitment to the relationship–a commitment to consciously make the marriage relationship a priority in their lives. Sound easy? It is not easy because gradually work, children, and other things interfere and are given a higher priority than the marriage. Doherty believes that couples must be mindful, self-disciplined, and adamant as they struggle to keep their marriage at the center of their lives. This is accomplished by developing rituals of marital connection and intimacy, developing good communication skills, learning how to effectively and lovingly resolve conflict, and by adapting the attitude that nothing will make you put your marriage on the back burner for long–it is just too important to be shoved aside. Doherty also suggests couples find a support group where they can talk about their marriage relationships with others and support each other in their effort to be intentional.

Markman, Stanley, and Blumberg (1994) also make the topic of commitment an important part of their Prevention and Relationship Enhancement Program (PREP) seminars. This program helps partners learn the skills and attitudes needed to sustain healthy marriages. These educators view commitment as the glue that holds a relationship together. However, couples often fail to understand the different types of commitment. PREP program participants are helped to analyze commitment and to assess the level and type of commitment in their marriage. In the PREP program, participants learn that two motivating forces characterize commitment–constraint and dedication.

Constraint Commitment

Constraint commitment exists when a spouse feels tied to a relationship because negative consequences would occur if the relationship ended. Often, constraint commitment has a moral tone. Some partners believe that divorce is morally wrong; thus, they are tied to a relationship by the desire to avoid breaking an important moral agreement. For these individuals, breaking up would lead to guilt and moral anguish. Others believe that quitting is unacceptable; it is just not part of their nature to give up easily. Still others stay together for the sake of the children.

Other constraint factors pertain to gains and losses–what would be gained and what would be lost if divorce occurred. The things that might be lost, such as the house, car, and furniture, are often very important to each partner. Then too, there are other economic losses that often accompany divorce. If a couple divorces, will there be enough money to continue the present life style? Women are especially vulnerable to a decline in standard of living after divorce. And neither partner may want to go through the hassles of a divorce–lawyers, bickering, expense, and all the other unpleasantries. Divorcing couples also lose a predictable pattern to their lives–to be single again increases the uneasiness that accompanies change. Also, there may be social pressures to stay together coming from parents, colleagues, and friends. When we add all the constraint factors up, they are usually considerable and they form a kind of negative bond that keeps partners together. Both happy and unhappy couples have marriages that are characterized by constraint commitment. Happy couples may experience constraints as adding stability to their relationship, while unhappy couples usually feel trapped by them.

Dedicated Commitment

Happy and unhappy couples also differ in their levels of commitment based on dedication. Constraint commitment exists when partners stay together because negative consequences would occur if the relationship ended; dedicated commitment exists when partners feel drawn to each other because they want to be together and they want their relationship to last. Usually when marriages begin, there is an abundance of dedicated commitment. When high levels of dedicated commitment continue to characterize a marriage, partners want to grow old together. These couples often speak of how important their relationship is to them–it is a top priority, often coming before work, children, and other pursuits. There is a "we-ness" in these relationships that honors togetherness, while at the same time protects individuality. These couples form a team, working together to meet each other's needs so that neither partner gains the upper hand, feels hurt, or left out. Each partner is willing to work hard, even sacrifice if need be because their partner and marriage is important to them. Couples with high levels of dedicated commitment still enjoy everyday togetherness even after many years of marriage.

Why does dedicated commitment wane in many marriages over time? Perhaps John Gottman (1994) explains it best. When conflict is not handled well and criticism, contempt, and other undesirable characteristics consistently characterize a relationship, marital satisfaction declines. Togetherness is no longer pleasant. Dedicated commitment checks out, leaving only constraint commitment. Although constraint commitment does add some stability to a relationship, it cannot create a happy, stable marriage. The best marriages are fueled by dedicated commitment. Couples with high levels of dedicated commitment have more satisfying marriages, experience less conflict, and report higher levels of intimacy (Markman, Stanley, & Blumberg, 1994).

A Closer Look at Intimacy

Couples seek both closeness and separateness in their relationships. At times, partners enjoy sharing intimate feelings with each other, yet at other times, too much closeness is suffocating. There is a story about two porcupines huddling together on a wintry night. As it gets colder, the porcupines come closer to share warmth, but as their closeness increases, their sharp quills prick each other and cause pain. So they move back and forth to increase warmth and reduce pain until they find a comfortable balance–a place where they can share warmth while minimizing their pain. Couples are somewhat like these porcupines, shifting back and forth to achieve a satisfying intimacy while minimizing the discomfort of too much togetherness.

As men and women experience this dance of intimacy, they learn of their differences. Women often enjoy discussing the personal details of their lives; men may avoid such details, believing that disclosing intimate details is boring and an invasion of privacy. Women are more comfortable talking about their feelings, while men talk about things and are more action-oriented. These differences often lead to problems as couples attempt to manage their intimacy needs. The pursuer/distancer dance often reflects this struggle, with the wife pursuing for more emotional intimacy and the husband withdrawing to a safer place. In most marriages, couples play out this drama in some form with partners even shifting roles from time to time. Women usually desire more emotional connection; husbands back off. Men often pursue intimacy through sex; if wives feel abandoned emotionally, they may withdraw sexually. Partners, especially husbands, need to understand that "without the intimate exchange of thoughts, feelings, desires, even the most fiery of sexual relationships will soon dry up" (Block, 2003, p. 176). What happens in a couple's sexual relationship is related to what happens in the other aspects of their lives. If there is satisfying intimate talk and affection on a day-to-day basis, there is usually a satisfying sexual relationship.

Thus, it is important for a couple to nurture intimacy in their marriage, although doing so is sometimes difficult. Work and children often become the focus of a couple's attention and their private time together disappears. Also, in every marriage, some anger and resentment build up, making intimacy more difficult. Brock (2003) believes that anger is a real threat to a couple's love and intimacy, especially when anger is not worked through. Unresolved anger and resentment remain in a relationship often on a hidden level and suck away positive energy. If partners cannot adequately address the issues surrounding their anger, it festers and destroys opportunities for intimacy. This usually happens slowly, one day at a time, so that when intimate moments completely disappear, partners wonder what happened to their marriage. The following comments (Block, 2003) tell the story of lost intimacy over the course of a marriage.

- We talked continually in the beginning of our relationship. We were so enamored with each other that we communicated every detail of our lives.
- We were best friends, consulting each other about everything. It was wonderful!
- We became busy with work and children and only occasionally touched base with each other about "us." We fought over our differences.
- He rarely called me any more from the office to see how I was doing. When he did, I was busy with work or the children so our conversations were short. He worked too much. I rarely saw him. We continued to argue.
- There were fewer enjoyable conversations, just routine things about schedules, work, and children. Our intimacy continued to slip away.
- We stopped sharing our thoughts and feelings. We were like two ships passing in the night; we hardly recognized each other's existence.

Couples must find time to nurture their intimacy. Without finding time each day and each week for the "us" in marriage, intimacy will slip away. In good marriages, couples turn toward each other everyday, sharing the intimate details of their lives. They listen, show interest, and continue to support each other as they keep their marriages vibrant and alive. In the process of nurturing marriage, Block believes that there are specific tasks for both husbands and wives.

Tasks for Husbands

Husbands need to counter their tendency to back away from emotionally charged situations. They must listen to their wives expression of feelings and avoid giving advice when it has not been asked for. Wives frequently just want to be understood. Husbands also need to contact their own feelings and learn to share these feelings. Even though past experience and training have not taught men to be emotionally sensitive, they need to learn these skills for the sake of their relationship.

Tasks for Wives

Wives need to understand that men are socialized in childhood to avoid feeling talk and that they are likely to flood and stonewall in emotionally charged situations. Thus, wives need to address emotionally charged issues in a gentle way; they should use soft words so that husbands do not withdraw or become defensive. This soft approach helps husbands deal with emotionally charged issues and reduces defensiveness, anger, and resentment.

Scott Peck's Definition of Love

In the last twenty-five years, one of the most widely read and discussed definitions of love is one written by Scott Peck (1978) in his best selling book, *The Road Less Traveled.* Peck writes about love, knowing that it is mysterious, hard to define, and that one definition will be somewhat inadequate. He uses the word spiritual in his definition but qualifies this by saying that he sees no difference between the mind and the spirit, thus equating the process of achieving spiritual and mental growth. He writes, "love is the will to extend one's self for the purpose of nurturing one's own or another's spiritual growth" (p. 81).

There are several things to note about this definition. (1) The first is that there is a purposeful nature to love, that purpose being growth. (2) Second, when one extends self, growth occurs because the act of extending produces change in self even though this extension may be directed toward the growth of another. (3) Then too, Peck has included self-love in his definition since he believes that it is impossible to love another without love of self and that one cannot nurture another unless it is possible to nurture the strength in oneself. (4) Also, the use of the word "extend" suggests stretching beyond; becoming more than one is at the present. Since this involves effort, it is work. (5) And lastly, the use of the word "will" implies an intensity that goes beyond desire; it motivates action, and choice—we consciously decide to behave in loving ways. Thus, Peck's definition of love involves effort or work, requires action based on choice, and is characterized by behavior that extends self even though the action or work undertaken may be directed toward the growth of another. Before looking more closely at these characteristics of love, we will examine what Peck believes love is not.

What Love Is Not

THE FALLING IN LOVE FEELING IS NOT LOVE. Peck (1978) contrasts the above definition of love with several common false ideas of love. Many people believe that falling in love is love. This type of love does not fit Peck's definition because falling in love in a romantic way does not involve a conscious choice. Romantic love may even come upon us at inopportune times and be directed toward someone with whom we are quite incompatible. At other times, when a suitable person becomes a part of our life, no amount of effort will bring on that "loving feeling." What then is this falling in love feeling? Peck suspects that it is a part of our genetic makeup, built into our system to motivate sexual behavior for the survival of the species. Since this intense sexual and romantic feeling will fade, in some ways it is false. It deceives our mind into thinking that the euphoria of romantic love will last forever and that this love will conquer all. Peck believes that a loving person will make decisions to behave in loving ways even when there is no loving feeling present or even when negative feelings exist. This is important for couples to understand since romantic love based on intense feelings will fade. When this occurs, the couple begins to discover whether their relationship has the qualities of genuine love. Peck (1978) writes: "It is when the spouses no longer feel like being in each other's company always, when they would rather be elsewhere some of the time, that their love begins to be tested and will be found to be present or absent" (p. 118). At this point, partners must make a decision concerning commitment–they must decide to behave in loving ways even when the loving feeling is not present.

LOVE IS NOT DEPENDENCY. While love is not a feeling, love is also not based on dependency. The statement "I could not live without him/her" reflects parasitism, not love. While most of us have dependency needs, these needs do not rule us and are not the sole purpose for our relationships. While extremely dependent relationships may superficially appear loving, a closer examination reveals sickness. Peck (1978) believes that "two people love each other only when they are quite capable of living without each other, but choose to live with each other" (p. 98). Thus, for Peck, "a good marriage can exist only between two strong and independent people" (p. 104).

LOVE IS NOT ALWAYS SELF-SACRIFICE. Self-sacrifice and excessive nurturing are not necessarily love. The father who gives his children everything they desire or the mother who always sacrifices for her family may think this reflects love, when in reality, this behavior is based on fulfilling a deep-seated inner need. The need to be the perfect giver and provider is based on a false picture of what love is. It may come from the heart, but love also involves the head–the realization that excessive caring, giving, and overprotection do not nurture maturity and growth, but rather reinforce infantilism and dependency. Love is not just giving but is also the strength to say "no" when giving is inappropriate. At times, teaching children to be independent is more loving than nurturing them, especially when they need to learn to care for themselves. Peck uses the terms "judicious giving" and "judicious withholding" to imply that difficult decisions are involved in determining when to give and when to withhold; both are necessary to nurture the growth of another.

What Love Is

If love is not a feeling, if it is not based on dependency, and is not necessarily rooted in self-sacrifice, then what is love? Peck (1978) answers this question by discussing his definition of love.

LOVE IS WORK. Since love involves extending self and is effortful, it involves work. The work of love requires overcoming laziness. Just as going to a job requires exerting ourselves by getting out of bed, driving to work, and even staying late if our work demands, the work of love also requires exerting ourselves against the tendency to be lazy. But what is the nature of this work and how do we get lazy in relation to the work of love? This work involves attending to our own growth and the growth of the person we care for. If a person loves someone, s/he will make a conscious decision to set aside time and energy to attend to that person's concerns. The most fundamental way of doing this is by listening. However, in marriage, partners usually listen very poorly–they often attempt to listen while doing something else such as watching television, reading, or driving. Listening deeply to what another person says requires our full attention as well as tremendous effort and energy. Although it is not always appropriate to listen–as when a child rambles on when our attention must be focused elsewhere, paying attention through listening is essential to a loving relationship with a spouse or child. It is important because it is evidence of your esteem for that person. When you listen to your children, they know that you value them; they are also more likely to listen to you, thus showing you the same degree of esteem. Of course, there are other ways of attending, such as playing games with children or helping a spouse with work-related activities. However, since listening reflects love, it is crucial in a marriage. Peck believes that true listening in a marriage is so difficult and takes so much energy that couples need to schedule time to be together just for listening.

LOVE REQUIRES COURAGE. Just as we must work to defend against laziness, if we are to love, we must also overcome our fears. Overcoming these fears requires the courage of love. This courage requires risk. Taking the risk to love one's spouse or one's children can result in great pain. If partners and parents invest themselves in the life of another, there is always the possibility that this other person will reject or disappoint them. But if partners and parents avoid all risk, fearing potential disappointment and pain, they also deprive themselves of the potential for great joy. Thus, the courage to risk is inevitable if one is to marry and have children.

LOVE REQUIRES COMMITMENT; IT IS A STRUGGLE. As partners risk themselves in relationships, they make commitments. The level of this commitment is the most important factor in assuring the relationship. Thus, Peck (1978) believes that, "commitment is inherent in any loving relationship" (p. 140). In the family, as you attempt to nurture another's growth, you can do so only if there is the expectation that the relationship will be constant–it will be there even after the struggle. Peck states, "couples cannot resolve in any healthy way the universal issues of marriage–dependency and independency, dominance and submission, freedom and fidelity, for example–without the security of knowing that the fact of struggling over these issues will not itself destroy the relationship" (p. 141). There is a risk to this type of commitment that requires courage–the courage to endure the struggle with the hope that on the other side of struggle, things will be better, but also knowing that there are no guarantees. Without a high degree of commitment to the relationship, partners rarely have the determination necessary for the struggle.

LOVE REQUIRES SEPARATENESS. Just as love requires courage, mature love also requires separateness. The romantic feeling type of love emphasizes the union of two individuals becoming one. However, mature love makes the distinction between self and other. Whether it is husband and wife or parent and child, each individual in the relationship is unique and strives toward growth; each needs to realize that his or her uniqueness and separateness is appreciated and understood. Thus, mature love respects and encourages separateness and individuality. This requires courage since the spouse or child may develop in ways previously unimagined. Mature love then is the will to extend oneself for the purpose of nurturing growth, even if that growth leads to some of those unimagined places.

- Comment on Peck's definition of love. Do you possess the characteristics he writes about: the willingness to nurture growth in self and others (spouse and children), the willingness to do the work of love–to give time to listening, to exhibit the level of commitment needed to work through struggles, and to be courageous enough to allow others (spouse, children) to be separate from you?

Love and Happiness: The Conscious Marriage

Another way of looking at love and happiness comes from the work of Harville Hendrix. Hendrix (1988, 1992) works with couples to help them create a conscious marriage. When couples marry, they are unaware of how they have been wounded in childhood and how these wounds surface in the choice of a partner and in their relationship problems after marriage. Partners, intoxicated with love, go through the romantic stage of marriage blinded to many realities. They are unaware that they have found an Imago match–someone whose unique qualities replicate those things that are needed to recover from wounding and complete the journey toward wholeness. But the wonderful feelings associated with romantic love will fade. Yet romantic love serves an important purpose–to bring partners together and to keep them together long enough to work on important issues that must be confronted if individuals are to sustain and continue the growth process. According to Hendrix (1992), "we unwittingly choose someone like our caretakers, who we expect to love us as they never did" (p. 219). Then this person opens old wounds and irritates us as our parents did. Yet paradoxically, this person–our imago match–also has the potential to provide the environment we need to work through our wounding. However, the journey toward healing is long and hard. It leads through the valley of the power struggle–a valley that claims many victims either through divorce or the acceptance of an unfulfilling marriage. Hendrix believes that the hard work necessary to get beyond the power struggle is worth the effort; on the other side of struggle is where real love exists. It is found in the satisfying relationship known as the conscious marriage.

Hendrix (1988, 1992) describes a number of essential ingredients and characteristics of a conscious marriage. First, the conscious marriage is based on the understanding that couples come together to heal old wounds that originated earlier in life. For example, a person wounded at the attachment stage of infancy may fear separation due to abandonment and inadequate caretaker love. To keep the feelings associated with abandonment from reoccurring, this person becomes a clinger, a demanding fuser who attempts to avoid the anxiety associated with abandonment. Frequently, this person's overbearing attempt to fuse drives partners away, especially if this person marries an avoider–someone who was wounded at the same stage but has adopted an avoidance style. Thus, a conscious intent to understand a partner's wounding and one's own wounding is essential to a quality marriage; this understanding is the first ingredient necessary to create a healing environment in marriage. Therefore, partners in a conscious marriage attempt to educate each other concerning their unique needs. This education effort allows a partner to say, "I was hurt in this way as a child and the pain is still there. I guess that's why I feel the way I do and why I am so demanding of your attention. Because of who I am, these are the things I need." The partners' up-front conscious effort to educate each other results in a clearer picture of the other. It allows partners to see and understand each other's needs without having to guess what those needs are.

With this understanding comes valuing. A spouse comes to value his or her partner's needs as highly as s/he values his or her own needs; the partners are separate individuals who place equal value on each other's way of thinking, feeling, and viewing the world. This respect for the other causes each partner to relinquish a self-centered attitude and frees up energy to listen, to empathize, and to understand. This unconditional acceptance and love dedicates itself to providing for the needs of the partner, needs which if satisfied heal psychological wounds and lead toward growth and wholeness. Thus, partners in the conscious marriage give each other unconditional acceptance and love without asking for favors in return.

When unconditional love exists, partners can communicate their needs in an open, honest way. The old strategy of criticism and blame that was previously used to coerce a partner to change is no longer necessary because the couple has learned new ways of satisfying their needs through constructive communication. Thus, in the conscious marriage, partners bring their concerns to each other in a direct way rather than blaming, criticizing, or withdrawing.

Also, in the conscious marriage, partners recognize and accept their negative traits. This makes it less likely that they will project these traits onto their partner and provoke a negative response to the projection. Accepting one's negative feelings, such as anger, is especially important. Anger is usually an expression of pain resulting from wounding in childhood and needs to be understood; it should never be expressed uncontrollably or in an insensitive way. Instead, it should be expressed in a contained, controlled manner. In order to prevent spontaneous and hurtful outbursts of anger, Hendrix (1992) suggests that anger be expressed by appointment. He believes "expressing their anger in a contained way leads to its conversion into passion and deeper bonding" (p. 246).

Partners in a conscious marriage also become aware of their personality deficiencies. They have married someone with the strengths that they lack, hoping this will lead to their own completion. These partners must realize that another person cannot make them complete; they must help each other find wholeness from within. Thus, partners in a conscious marriage help each other as healing partners, cooperating to develop the missing parts of their personalities. Hendrix (1992) notes, "When we give our partner what he or she needs in order to heal his or her wounds, we have to call upon the parts of ourselves that have been suppressed. In pushing the limits of our habituated behavior to heal our partner, we heal ourselves, for we reactivate our own evolution toward wholeness" (p. 239). This process of healing is never easy. However, an individual's Imago match partner is especially well suited to provide the environment necessary for growth and healing.

Then too, in the conscious marriage, partners realize and accept the hard work that must be done to create a good marriage. Much of this work must be done on the self, so partners must help each other through this process.

This work takes commitment, dedication, and courage. The courage is necessary because each partner must change. Previously, each partner demanded that the other change; in the conscious marriage, both partners must change. And the change that is needed is often the most difficult change to make. As couples make these changes together, Hendrix believes that their energy is directed outward and they become more loving and caring toward others and the world.

To summarize, Hendrix believes that in the conscious marriage, each spouse must gain insight into past wounding, share this insight with the other, and overcome this wounding. This occurs by stretching into new behaviors that provide what one's partner needs for growth—a stretching that also stimulates one's own personal growth.

Family Love

Couples considering marriage should give some thought to the concept of family love. This is the type of love that parents often have for their children and family members have for each other. It is certainly similar to the type of love Peck discusses—a love that is concerned with the growth of others. Burr, Day, and Bahr (1993) suggest a model of family love, even though they realize that words alone cannot capture the full spirit of what love entails. Yet this model is important to examine, especially at a time when so many families fail to understand the nature of mature, healthy love. These educators suggest that family love has four characteristics: (1) it is oriented toward fostering the growth of others; (2) it emphasizes overt behavior and action over feelings and sentiment; (3) it is unconditional; (4) and it is enduring.

The Other Orientation of Family Love

The other orientation of family love means that family love involves some sacrifice—sacrifice that is needed for the growth and development of another. Yet this sacrifice does not deprive the giver in a way that diminishes him or her, but rather it enriches the giver. Parents who give up sleep night after night to feed and attend to their baby are temporarily deprived of sleep, but the focus is not on them, it is on their child. By attending to their baby's needs, they are fostering their child's growth and their own growth by engaging in new behaviors for the sake of another. This giving behavior can be exhausting for the giver, but in the long run, it enriches both the giver and the receiver. This paradox is often played out in families; many things that are difficult and painful are ultimately satisfying and growth producing. If a child gets hurt, parents take the child to the doctor even though the treatment may involve some pain. However, the temporary suffering is necessary. Similarly, if a child cries and protests the reasonable limits set on bedtime, standing firm may be difficult and painful; yet the parent knows that standing firm is best since children need reasonable limits. Healthy family love endures the pain for the long-term gain, even when it is difficult to do so.

According to Burr, Day, and Bahr, being other-directed also involves humility. In this case, humility involves entering another person's world by listening because this is what the other person needs. The mother attentively listens to her child even when the child prattles on about things the mother already knows. The mother does not need this information; yet she attentively listens to what she already knows in order to nourish the relationship with her child. And when she does this, she also nourishes herself. Certainly this takes the ability to come down from our know-it-all position and to become humble for the sake of the relationship.

The Action Orientation of Family Love

Family love gives priority to overt acts of behavior over feelings. This action-oriented love involves behaving in loving ways even when a loving feeling is not present. A parent may feel tired, upset, sad, or angry and these emotions may show, but the parent's loving actions transcend these feelings. Family tasks, such as diapering a baby, washing clothes, and fixing meals, may be boring, tedious, and tiring, but the parent unselfishly gives these gifts out of love. And a loving parent also provides opportunities for a child to behave in loving ways toward others because one learns to give loving acts of service by serving, not by always being served. Thus, knowing the level of a child's ability in relation to service and providing the child with opportunities to perform acts of service are not only loving but they also teach a child the joy of engaging in loving behavior.

The Unconditional Nature of Family Love

Family love is not contingent on how a child or family member behaves. It is given unconditionally. This does not mean that it is indulgent or permissive. Often family love must say "no" but it does so in a loving way, emphasizing that the parent or family member has the best interest of the child in mind. Unconditional love is given simply because the other person is and because the other person is family, not because of something the other person does or accomplishes.

The Enduring Nature of Family Love

Family relationships extend into the future without end. The roles of father, mother, and child endure forever and the feelings and memories that one has for family members are enduring. These memories linger in our hearts and minds. Love that has the possibility of ending is suspect and fragile; enduring love is sturdy, constant, and ever present.

If individuals have been exposed to a healthy family love, this love has been a positive influence on their lives—it has so enriched them that they can give the gift of family love to their partners and children. Family love is so important that couples thinking about marriage and having children should ask certain questions about their ability to provide this kind of love. Is each partner able to unselfishly focus on the needs of the other even if it involves sacrifice? Can each partner behave in loving ways toward others even when the loving feeling is not present? Does each partner have the strength to say "no" and to set reasonable limits even when it is difficult but loving to do so? Does each partner have the ability to love unconditionally in spite of the faults and blemishes of family members? And can each partner provide this love on a day-to-day basis, never ending through time?

- Have you seriously thought about the ingredients of family love? Do you and your partner have the determination and ability to provide love in these ways?

IMPORTANT TERMS AND CONCEPTS

theories relating mate selection to the past
filter theories of mate selection
the propinquity filter
the attractiveness filter
the similarity filter
the compatibility filter
the cohabitation filter
passionate love

companionate love
Sternberg's triangular theory
Sternberg's seven types of love
constraint commitment
dedicated commitment
Peck's definition of love
Hendrix's conscious marriage
family love

SUGGESTED READINGS

DeAngelis, B. (1992). *Are you the one for me.* New York: Dell.
Peck, S. M. (1978). *The road less traveled: A new psychology of love, traditional values and spiritual growth.* New York: Simon & Schuster.

Sternberg, R. J. (1988). *The triangle of love: Intimacy, passion, commitment.* New York: Basic Books.

Waite, L. J., & Gallagher, M. (2000). *The case for marriage: Why married people are happier, healthier, and better off financially.* New York: Random House.

Chapter 8

COMMUNICATION IN FAMILY LIFE

Effective communication is especially important in families. Yet it is in families where individuals often feel least understood. Couples often cite communication problems as their major complaint in marriage. However, it is usually difficult for partners to explain the specific nature of their difficulties. They often give superficial explanations, such as "He would not listen" or "She complained all the time." For communication experts who study the complexities of the communication process, it is not surprising that couples have trouble understanding their communication problems. Communication is an intricate process full of subtleties, many of which are outside awareness. Therefore, miscommunication in families is inevitable. However, if couples have a better understanding of the dynamics of the communication process, perhaps mistakes can be minimized.

Galvin and Brommel (1991) define communication as the process of creating and sharing meanings. This process is symbolic and transactional. Looking at specific words in this definition will explain what Galvin and Brommel mean by process, symbolic, transactional, and shared. The word process implies continuous and changing. Effective communication does not develop instantly and get turned on and off like a light switch. Instead, it is continuous, developing with time and experience. Nor is communication static; rather, it is ever changing with the ebb and flow of feelings, situations, and time. Galvin and Brommel note that "relationships no matter how committed, change constantly, and communication both affects and reflects these changes" (p. 15).

The word symbolic means that individuals use symbols to communicate. Words make up most of the verbal symbols that are shared, but a wide range of nonverbal behaviors also contains symbolic meaning. Thus, gestures, facial expressions, tone of voice, inflection, and posture also have important communication value. Transactional means that in the communication process, individuals have an impact on each other. They are influencing the other and being influenced by the other as communication occurs. The words shared meanings indicate that each party involved in the communication exchange must understand these symbols if meanings are to be shared. Thus, a mutual understanding of symbols is important for effective communication.

THE MESSAGE BEYOND THE WORDS

The complex process of communication involves much more than words. The real meaning of a message is usually expressed in the body language, facial expression, pitch, tone, volume, rhythm, and tempo that accompany the words. It is these things that tell us what the words mean. In communication, the words are labeled the digital message, while the more subtle part of the message contained in body language, facial expression, and the way in which the words are spoken make up the analogic message. Since this analogic message goes beyond the words and provides important information concerning the meaning of the message, it is also referred to as the metamessage. It is estimated that over 90 percent of the impact that a message has on the receiver comes from the metamessage—the body language, facial expression, pitch, tone, etc. that accompany the words (McKay, Davis, & Fanning, 1983). When the digital and analogic messages are incongruent, we often sense that the metamessage is a truer expression of the speaker's intent. For example, if a speaker says, "You're so smart," the words seem to convey a compliment, but if the words are said in a sarcastic way, the real meaning conveyed is not positive but rather negative–meaning that the person is really obnoxious and silly.

Even if a person remains silent, his or her silence carries meaning. A blank stare or distant gaze provides information and others may attach meaning to this information–the person is bored or disinterested and would rather be somewhere else. Communication experts often say that it is impossible to not communicate for even one's silence conveys a message.

Gottman and DeClaire (2001) discuss an interesting exercise to help couples become more aware of the metamessage aspect of communication. In this exercise, one person is designated the sender and the other person is the receiver. The sender is given a question, such as "Are you okay?" The sender is then asked to transmit this message to the receiver. However, the sender is given three different context meanings (e.g., the receiver has been terribly hurt by something, the receiver has just suggested a bizarre plan of action, or the sender is asking whether the receiver is ready for a difficult, physical challenge). The sender is to select one of the context meanings and send the message using the tone of voice and other metamessage qualities that accurately convey the meaning. The receiver is then asked to guess which of the three meanings the sender was attempting to transmit. As couples participate in this exercise, they become more aware of the metamessage qualities that convey meaning. Some individuals are excellent senders and receivers–they effectively communicate the intended message and correctly interpret the intended meaning.

With all of these subtleties occurring when we communicate, both the speaker and the receiver can make mistakes that lead to miscommunication. It is helpful if family members, especially the adults in the family, have an understanding of the complexities of language and some training in how to speak clearly. Perhaps the information in this chapter will help you better understand the communication process and avoid some of the mistakes in communication that frequently occur in families.

- Do you recognize the important role that metamessages play in the communication process? Give some examples of the use of metamessages in your communication with others.

WHAT WE ATTEMPT TO COMMUNICATE

McKay, Davis, and Fanning (1983) have divided communication into four types of expression. The four types of information we attempt to communicate are (1) needs, (2) feelings, (3) thoughts, and (4) observations. Frequently a person communicates information about one or more of these during a brief exchange.

The Communication of Needs

Human needs are often categorized as either biological or learned. Biological needs, such as the need for food, are rooted in the tissue needs of the body. Learned needs are not as directly involved with biology, but rather are often associated with personality characteristics. Years ago, Henry Murray (1938) categorized twenty-seven important learned needs that he thought characterized individuals to various degrees. These needs include the need to achieve, to affiliate, to be aggressive, to be autonomous, to nurture and be nurtured, to be dominant, and the need for order. What individuals attempt to communicate is often related to the important needs that make up their personalities. For example, a person with a powerful need to affiliate will often communicate in ways that will reflect this powerful need.

The Need to Affiliate: Involvement and Independence

Deborah Tannen (1986), in her book, *That's Not What I Meant! How Conversational Style Makes or Breaks Relationships,* discusses how differences in involvement and independence needs influence communication. Tannen (1986) writes: "We need to feel close to each other to have a sense of community, to feel we are not alone in the world. But we need to keep our distance from each other to preserve our independence . . . ." (p. 17).

Partners often differ in relation to their involvement/independence needs. One partner may have a strong involvement need, while the other is motivated more by the need for independence. And the strength of these needs will be reflected in the couple's communication. "How was your work today?" "I took Cara to the doctor and let me tell you what he said." "Let me tell you what happened to me this afternoon." This is the language of involvement. If partners are alike in the strength of their involvement and independence needs, then things may run smoothly. However, if differences exist, misunderstandings are likely to occur. For example, if a wife uses the language of involvement and her husband uses the language of independence, then their needs may clash. The wife's persistent talk to me/listen to me style makes the husband uncomfortable. This increases the husband's desire for independence (to be left alone). Thus, the more the wife expresses involvement through talk, the more the husband withdraws, superficially communicates, or responds without even hearing what his wife has said.

What is interesting about this process is that the couple may not talk about their needs openly and may be only partially aware that these needs are being expressed in their communication. We do not say to our partner, "I am powerfully driven by my need to feel supported, connected, and close to you and I want you to do those things that help me satisfy this need." Instead, we are more likely to talk about events of the day, knowing that these events are not earth shattering, but hoping that our partner will listen and attempt to understand. If this happens, we feel confirmed—we have a close relationship that is intimate and caring. Conversely, if the need to be independent, separate, and autonomous is more powerful than the need to be connected, one's demeanor will likely reflect this need. However, we are not likely to say, "Right now I have a strong need to be left alone." Rather, we may superficially listen, curtly respond, and exhibit body language and facial expressions that communicate our need to be left alone.

But why are partners not more direct? Why all the body language and metamessages? Tannen (1986) suggests several reasons. First, partners often want and expect others to know what they need without having to tell them. If this happens partners are on the same wave link and this feels good—our partner understands us. However, a spouse should not always expect his or her partner to be this intuitive. A common mistake couples make is to think that their partners will always understand their needs even when these needs are not communicated directly. And even if our partner does understand, this does not mean that s/he will attend to our needs. Partners also have needs and they are often better at attending to their own needs than to the needs of others.

Also, in close relationships, it does not always feel right to communicate a need in a direct way. Such direct communication may be interpreted as hurtful. Therefore, the husband is hesitant to say, "I need to be left alone for awhile" because he fears that his wife will misinterpret this message—something must be wrong with our relationship. Also the wife may not tell her husband "Pay attention to me now, I need your attention and closeness." Telling a partner to pay attention and to care (listen to me) and then having that partner display attention and caring is a suspect kind of caring. What good does it do for you to tell someone to care when what you want is for that person to exhibit caring without having to be told to do so? Then too, if a spouse is asked to exhibit caring (to listen and understand) and s/he refuses, the partner who asked might feel hurt and rejected. This kind of direct rejection might seriously damage the relationship. Therefore, a partner may ask in indirect ways and if the spouse does not exhibit the attention and caring desired, then the partner who asked can say that s/he didn't really ask. The spouse may be miffed at the partner's inattention but probably not as hurt as s/he would have been if the need had been directly expressed and rejected. Self-protection may also be the reason for the initial questions we sometimes ask. "Would you like to go out to eat tonight?" This question is an indirect way of communicating one's desires, yet it allows a partner to refuse without provoking a direct conflict. Therefore, directness in communication is often avoided when partners express needs; it is safer to indirectly express these needs.

The Sexual Need

Partners often have different perceptions regarding their sexual relationship. In the Woody Allen movie, *Annie Hall*, two lovers are asked how often they have sex. The woman's response was "constantly," while the man's response was "hardly ever," however, both agreed on the number of times– "three time a week." One reason for sexual problems and dissatisfactions in marriage is that men can usually separate sex from other aspects of the relationship. Men are often on go sexually even if the marriage relationship is on lousy. Women are more focused on the characteristics of the relationship. If a woman feels loved and emotionally cared for in the relationship, she is more likely to desire sexual intimacy. Men need to learn that what goes on in the nonsexual aspects of the relationship has a lot to do with the quality of the couple's sexual experience.

When couples have sexual problems, they often have difficulty openly discussing their problems. This hesitancy may be due to past conditioning concerning sexuality. If members of one's family of origin had been more direct and open about sexual matters, then perhaps communication about sex would be easier. Also, McKay, Davis, and Fanning (1983) believe that there are several myths that influence the ability of couples to openly communicate about sex. One myth is based on the belief that sex should be spontaneous and natural in a loving relationship. Therefore, talking about sexual desires makes sexual experience less natural, spontaneous, and romantic. Couples who allow this belief to interfere with sexual communication may not understand that there will be times in marriage when sexual passion wanes. This does not mean that partners love each other less, but means that sex will not be as spontaneous as it once was. At these times, honest discussion of sexual needs may help invigorate sexual passion.

Another myth that interferes with open communication about sex is the belief that if our partner were really sensitive to our needs, then s/he would know what is satisfying without our having to communicate this directly. This belief makes two false assumptions: (1) that our partner can know what is satisfying without our having to communicate our desires and (2) that if our partner fails to sense our needs, then this failure is due to his or her lack of sensitivity and consideration. Both assumptions are somewhat invalid. Partners cannot always read minds correctly or detect unstated desires. Thus, not knowing preferences and desires cannot always be attributed to a lack of sensitivity and consideration. However, here again there is some safety in indirectness. Should partners directly express their desires, they may be seen as perverted, insensitive, or extreme and this may make future sexual encounters more difficult. Thus, most couples weigh the advantages and disadvantages associated with direct, open communication in the area of sex.

A third myth involves the belief that when it comes to sex, the best course of action is to back off and avoid conflict. This belief is based on the assumption that if partners are direct and open about their desires, things could get a lot worse. What exists is better than what might be. Also, most partners do not want to impose their beliefs in an area of life where individuals have strong feelings and where there is not one attitude and behavior that is universally agreed upon as acceptable. Yet if there is no honest discussion, nothing gets resolved and on-going sexual dissatisfactions may persist. Sexual therapists often believe that if sexual issues can be discussed in an open, sensitive, and caring way, then it may be possible for new understandings to be reached, leading to a more satisfying relationship for both partners as they learn to respect their differences and love each other in spite of these differences.

The Need to Love and Be Loved

Several prominent theorists (Maslow, 1970; Glasser, 1965) have made love a central focus of their theories. There is a powerful desire to feel that someone loves us and that we return that love in a mutual way. Chapman (1992) has popularized the idea that there are different languages of love and to feel loved in a relationship, partners must communicate with each other in their preferred love language. This message has touched a responsive note as evidenced by the popularity of Chapman's books and seminars. According to Chapman, there are five love languages and it is important for partners to know their own preferred language and the preferred language of their partner. If partners have different preferred love languages and they are unaware of their differences, then problems may arise not because they do not love each other but because their love is not expressed in the preferred way.

Chapman believes that an individual's primary love language is based on his or her unique psychological makeup. Although individuals may also develop a secondary love language, they will always be more comfortable with their preferred style. Furthermore, Chapman believes that partners seldom have the same preferred love language and this difference leads to confusion and misunderstandings in relationships. If partners are to communicate their love for each other effectively, they must learn to express love in their partner's primary love language. Chapman believes that a spouse's criticism provides important clues to his of her primary love language. Find the request behind the criticism and it may lead to the love needs that your partner is expressing.

The five love languages are words of affirmation, quality time, receiving gifts, acts of service, and physical touch.

WORDS OF AFFIRMATION. This language is spoken with encouraging words, kind words, humble rather than demanding words, and words of appreciation. If you are an individual who finds words of encouragement and appreciation hard to express and your partner's primary love language is words of affirmation, then you may need to learn to express your love using words of affirmation.

QUALITY TIME. This language is expressed in several ways–giving your partner undivided attention, having quality conversations, doing quality things together in a wholehearted way, being together and really listening without giving advice. Too often partners are in close proximity but never really focus on each other exclusively; you cannot watch TV or read the newspaper and provide this kind of quality time. Even when partners do talk to each other, one partners often fails to really listen and communicate understanding. If your partner's primary love language is quality time and you are too busy to give him or her quality time through undivided attention, then you need to stop and reevaluate; if you fail to learn and speak your partner's primary love language, your marriage will suffer.

RECEIVING GIFTS. This language is communicated by giving your partner gifts. Gifts serve as a symbol of your love and tell your partner that you are thinking of him or her. A gift may be found–a beautiful flower you picked on the way home because it reminded you of your partner, made–a poem you wrote and framed as a reminder of your love for your partner, or bought–that mantelpiece your partner admired and thought would go so well in the living room. If your partner's primary love language is receiving gifts and you have never been inclined to be a gift giver, then you need to learn this language. It is one of the easiest languages to learn and the giving of gifts will add immensely to you and your partner's emotional bank account

ACTS OF SERVICE. This language is expressed by doing things for your partner. Love is often communicated through acts of service. What can I do to help you? This question can warm the heart of a spouse whose primary love language is acts of service. And noticing what needs to be done without even having to ask and then doing it is especially comforting to someone who appreciates acts of service. If this is your partner's primary love language and you are too busy to express love in this way, you need to rethink your priorities.

PHYSICAL TOUCH. This language is exhibited in many different ways–holding your partner close, touching her cheek, running your hand through his hair, kissing, massaging, sexual intercourse. If your partner's primary love language is physical touch, then learning how he or she needs to be touched and learning to touch in this way will help him or her feel loved in a special way.

If partners think of the need to love and be loved in relation to these five different love languages, then it becomes more apparent why this need often goes unmet in marriages–partners simply do not speak the same love language. Learning to speak the preferred love language of your partner will add positive feelings to the emotional bank account of your marriage.

The Need for Respect and Worth

Just as partners want to feel that they are loved, they also want to know that they are respected and that what they do is valued. Often, when hard work goes unnoticed, a partner concludes that this work is not valued. A failure to communicate using words of appreciation may communicate disrespect–the many things you do are not important enough even to be mentioned. Thus, a husband who fails to notice that his wife washes and irons the clothes, cooks the meals, cleans the toilets, gets the kids ready for school, takes the kids to the doctor, while also having a full-time job, may give her reason to feel that he does not respect the many roles she plays to provide for her family. When wives and husbands work together to divide household chores fairly and express appreciation for each other's contributions, then they feel valued and respected. When this happens, the marital satisfaction of the wife usually increases. This influences the quality of the marriage, thus benefiting the husband as well.

The Need for Power and Control

Some individual's feel they must have their way–they must dictate the way things are done. They know best how to spend money, how to discipline the children, where to go on vacation, and on and on the list goes. Sometimes the need to control how things are done is divided–for example, the husband believes he knows best about money, the wife believes she knows best about the children. The language of power and control is the language of demand–you demand that your partner see things your way. Criticism and coercion are the dialects of this language. Whereas one partner may be powerful enough to dictate how things are done, winning in this way often leads to defeat by driving wedges between the partners. One thing a partner cannot dictate and coerce is his or her partner's love. Love is a choice each partner makes and the language of criticism and coercion often leads to the withdrawal of love. The language of requests and compromise–a language that will be further discussed later in this chapter–is oftentimes needed if love is to be sustained.

The Communication of Feelings

Feelings are an important part of everyone's experience. The language of feelings is used to express happiness, sadness, boredom, fear, anger, disgust, surprise, and the other emotions that are such an important part of everyday life. Feelings are often conveyed in metamessages that accompany the verbal message. The listener is often told much more about feelings by body language, voice tone, and word inflection than by the actual words. At times, partners are not very aware of their feelings. This may be due to a childhood where the expression of feelings was discouraged–feelings of anger were punished, feelings of disappointment were condemned, or feelings of desire expressed over wanting a toy led to a lecture and feelings of guilt. Thus, some individuals learn in childhood that it is best to avoid the expression of feelings and they become detached from their feeling selves. Males are often exposed to childhood environments that reinforce the denial of feelings. When they marry, their wives often complain that they never talk about how they feel. Thus, women are more likely to engage in feeling talk while husbands struggle to get in touch with and express their feelings.

Yet at times, it is difficult to hide true feelings for these feelings show through in our metamessages. Gottman and DeClaire (2001) discuss a University of Oregon study in which unhappily married couples were asked to fake happiness. They were told to pretend that they had been given a large amount of money and that they were to discuss with their spouse how this money would be spent. Cameras recorded the couples' discussions, picking up both their verbal and nonverbal expressions. If independent raters only read transcripts of a couple's verbal comments, the raters judged the couple as happy. However, if raters observed the couple's videotaped comments and saw the metamessages along with the words, the raters' judgments were very different. The partners' facial expressions and nonverbal delivery gave them away. How the words were spoken made it clear that they were unhappy even though they were trying to fake happiness. Feelings are difficult to hide; they often leak through regardless of our words. Yet even though feelings leak through, it is possible for the receiver of a message to misinterpret this leakage. The husband who responds unenthusiastically to his wife may not be feeling disinterested or upset, but rather tired from a difficult day at work. Partners usually do not preface what they say with the words I feel ... nor do they comment on their feelings before beginning a conversation. Partners may not even be fully aware of their feelings as they converse; yet they often sense that many of their relationship problems involve misunderstandings in the area of feelings.

During the romantic stage of courtship and marriage, partners are often aware of their positive feelings for each other, openly expressing these feelings in words and metamessages. But as the years pass, expressions of love, concern, and politeness give way to the full range of feelings. Now partners allow the expression of irritation, frustration, disgust, and anger to create problems in their relationship. And arguments usually end the way they begin—harsh startups, harsh endings. Therapists who help couples communicate often suggest that rather than criticizing one's partner for behaving in an irritating way, the partner should communicate how he or she feels. "I feel brain dead right now from a stressful day at work; could you give me a few minutes to relax." "I feel overwhelmed right now with the kids and supper preparation; could you watch the kids for me while I get through this?" This direct expression of feelings without blame and criticism allows one's partner to respond without feeling attacked. When partners respond angrily, using attack and criticism, they are more likely to provoke responses that lead to more anger and criticism. When this happens, one or both partners may withdraw, realizing that attack and criticism gets them nowhere. Yet withdrawal has consequence—anger may be suppressed and an opportunity to share feelings openly and honestly has been lost. When partners and family members learn to express how they feel and also exhibit understanding and caring, relationships often improve. But there are also risks involved in sharing feelings. What if a partner fails to listen, makes fun of one's feelings, or decides that s/he cannot live with someone with such feelings? In marriage, there are significant risks. Every feeling should not necessarily be shared. Knowing what feelings to share, and how and when to share these feelings takes a high level of emotional intelligence. However, if couples can navigate the emotional waters of their marriage by learning to intelligently communicate their feelings, greater understanding and intimacy can enhance their relationship. Since this is so important in a satisfying marriage, much of the remaining material in this text will address how to communicate effectively when emotions and feelings are intense.

The Communication of Thoughts

Sometimes our goal is to communicate thoughts, beliefs, and opinions. These expressions may come after much deliberation and serious consideration or off the top of our head. Sometimes thoughts are prefaced by I think . . . I believe . . . or I have concluded. . . . However, frequently thoughts are spoken without being introduced by these identifying words. "It would be best to pay for that with the credit card rather than cash" is such a remark. It reflects a belief, which may or may not be well thought through. Nevertheless, it reflects an opinion based on some degree of thought. At times, we may express thoughts in ways that hurt others; at other times, we may attempt to disguise our thoughts so as not to hurt others. When a wife asks, "What do you think of my new dress?" the husband may hesitate and choose his words carefully, especially if he does not care for her new attire. So the husband's words may say one thing, but his hesitation, facial expression, choice of words, and the way he responds says something quite different. So the metamessage wins out again. However, if any reference is made to how he responded, he can accurately claim that he said, "I think it looks lovely."

The Communication of Observations

McKay, Davis, and Fanning (1983) label another type of expression as observations. This type of communication simply involves facts. Often the communication of factual information is straightforward and direct. "The catalogue says that the payment must be received in the business office by the second Friday in August." "The meeting ran thirty minutes longer than the schedule indicated." Usually problems in relationships are not caused by information of a factual nature. Instead, problems may be caused by differences in how individuals feel about the facts, what they infer from the facts, and how they interpret the facts.

It should be clear by now that when partners communicate, they often express more than one thing; they may express observations, thoughts, feelings, and needs in one brief exchange. As this occurs, communication becomes more complicated. Add to this the probability that metamessages contain the real meaning of the exchange and it becomes more apparent how sophisticated we must be to communicate effectively. The complicated nature of this process may also explain why communication so often seems to miss the mark, to be misunderstood, and be a cause of so many relationship problems.

- In which of these four areas—needs, feelings, thoughts, and observations—are you most likely to experience communication difficulties? Give some examples of how these difficulties have led to misunderstandings in your relationships.

ANALYZING AND UNDERSTANDING COMMUNICATION

Communication is often a spontaneous process. Partners usually do not give a great deal of thought to composing their messages. Only in certain circumstances, such as a speech, a job interview, or a proposal of marriage, do individuals attempt to craft their message using just the right words. Rarely do we think about volume, pitch, tone, facial expression, and the other subtle mannerisms that may be more important in expressing meaning than the words. Very few family members take the time to analyze communication to see what can go wrong. When experts study communication, they find that both the sender and the receiver can make mistakes. Fincham, Fernandes, and Humphreys (1993) have charted the course of communication from sender to receiver as they have analyzed communication problems. Here are some common mistakes they believe partners make when communication breaks down.

Mistakes Partners Make

Failure to Communicate Intent Clearly

Since very little time is spent composing the verbal message, mistakes can be due to the sender's failure to communicate clearly his or her intent. For example, the husband who wants to go out to eat may say to his wife, "What do you want to do about dinner?" This is not a clear expression of his intent. The wife, not knowing the intent, may think her husband is being critical of her for not having dinner prepared and responds with a defensive comment, "Why is it always my responsibility to fix dinner?" This husband might correctly respond, "I didn't say anything about your fixing dinner?" Then the argument about what he said and what she said begins. This confusion might have been avoided if the husband had more accurately communicated his intent, perhaps in the following way: "I would like to go out to eat tonight since it's so late and we're both so tired. What do you think?" The wife, hearing this, would not have had to infer intent and their communication might have gone more smoothly. Many problems in communication begin when the speaker does not accurately encode the message.

Incongruent Verbal and Nonverbal Messages

Another sender mistake occurs when the verbal and nonverbal messages do not match. For example, a sender's words may be complimentary, but because of a facial expression or the way the words are stated, the metamessage is not complimentary. Such errors may be unintentional—the sender may not be attempting to mislead. The sender may even be unaware of this mismatch. When the receiver responds to the nonverbal message, the sender may be puzzled by the receiver's reaction. However, at other times, the sender may be well aware of the mismatch, even hoping that the receiver will understand the metamessage. Conflicting messages—the digital message and the underlying metamessage are in opposition—are called paradoxical messages. Since these messages may be difficult to interpret, paradoxical messages can lead to confusion and misunderstanding in relationships.

The Words Do Not Explain Underlying Motivation

Another source of confusion occurs when the sender's words correctly reflect thoughts and intent, but the words do not explain underlying motivation. If this occurs, the receiver may attempt to infer underlying motives. For example, the husband who says, "I'm going back to the office to work tonight" is clearly communicating his thoughts and intent. However, if he fails to explain his motivation, his wife is left to infer an explanation. She may think—he's mad because I didn't call his mother and tell her she could come visit. Communicating the reasoning behind the words helps eliminate mind reading and false inferences. "I have to work late because I am writing a big report for the sales meeting on Monday. I sure wish I could be here with you." Sometimes we just assume that family members can accurately read between the lines without our having to explain. At other times, we are preoccupied with our own concerns or in a hurry and fail to adequately explain. Communicating the thoughts behind the words can often add clarity and prevent misunderstandings.

Mood States Influence Sending and Receiving

Current mood and feeling states can also influence the communication process. If a husband or wife has had a difficult day, feelings that carry over from events of the day may influence communication. One's partner can easily misinterpret negativity that is due to events of the day (a frustrating day at work) and draw false inferences. "Why is he angry at me? What did I do?" Thus, the sender's mood state may influence how a message is delivered, but just as often, the receiver's mood state may determine how a message is received and interpreted. Innocent words, such as "Have you called my mother yet about this weekend?" may be interpreted differently by an irritated spouse than by a spouse whose mood state is positive. Awareness of one's feelings and how these feelings can cause problems in communication can often prevent miscommunication or at least allow clarification before things get out of hand. "Oh! I'm sorry, I didn't mean to sound angry with you. I'm really ticked off about what happened at work." Such a repair attempt can lead to clarification and can often get communication back on track.

Inattention

Another frequent reason for miscommunication is inattention. If the receiver of a message is watching television, reading, or thinking about something other than the sender's message, then communication problems are inevitable. Good listening is difficult and requires one's full attention. Even though all family communication does not require one's full attention, it is essential that couples and families give full attention to each other some of the time. Full attention to what a spouse or child is saying is an expression of respect—something that everyone needs to give and receive in his or her close relationships. Some therapists suggest that couples make appointments with each other so that they can listen without distractions. Other therapists suggest scheduling family meetings so that each family member can be heard.

In summary, problems in communication can occur when the sender and/or the receiver make mistakes. The sender may encode the message incorrectly or send conflicting messages. Both the sender and the receiver are influenced by mood states as they send and receive messages; this can lead to misinterpretation and confusion. And the receiver simply may not be paying attention to the sender's message.

- Can you recall times when these communication mistakes created problems in your marriage and family life?

Helping Couples Understand Impact

With so much going on in the communication process, how can couples better understand the impact their messages have on each other? Notarius and Markman (1993) have helped couples better understand communication by explaining the concept of the relational bank account and using an interesting feedback technique to help couples understand the impact of their messages.

The Relationship Bank Account

The relational bank account is composed of both positive and negative feelings. Deposits and withdrawals from the relational bank account are made on a daily basis during a couple's interactions. Soon after marriage, there is usually an abundance of good feeling stored up in the account. As time passes, both deposits and withdrawals occur. Any positive word or act of kindness adds to the account, whereas any irritating gesture or negative message results in a withdrawal from the account. In good marriages, there is a healthy bank balance (many more positive feelings in the account than negative) that the couple can fall back on when they encounter hard times. However, for the struggling couple, there is very little reserve in the account to help them through their difficult times. Their fights, harsh words, and silent stares have used up most of the emotional good feeling that once was there. When we think in these terms, we can better conceptualize the things that add to and deplete this important bank account.

The Positive (+) and Negative (-) Feedback Technique

Often, couples are unaware of the effect their communication has on their partner. Was a comment perceived as an addition to the account or as a withdrawal? Remember, how a response is interpreted depends on many factors that relate to both sender and receiver characteristics. Notarius and Markman use a floor exercise to give the sender feedback as to how a message was interpreted. They start by giving each partner three cards: a plus card (+), a neutral card (0), and a minus card (-). Then they designate another card the floor (floor) card. As the couples talk about an issue, the speaker has the floor card. The listener will provide the speaker with immediate feedback using the (+), (0), or (-) cards with the (+) being a positive interpretation of the message received, a (0) being a neutral interpretation, and a (-) being a negative interpretation. After short, brief comments, the floor is exchanged and the roles reverse. From this exercise partners learn whether their comments are interpreted as positive (adding to the relational bank account) or negative (subtracting from the relational bank account). Using this technique, the sender is getting immediate feedback concerning how the receiver interpreted the sender's message.

This feedback technique has been used to understand the nature of communication in both good and bad marriages. Couple interaction is video taped and later observed and analyzed by researchers and the participating couples. Specifically, the researchers look at the intent of the message from the speaker's point of view and the impact of the message from the listener's point of view. Would the speaker's intent have the intended impact and effect upon the listener? These researchers believe that as a message flows from one partner to another, it often passes through a filter. A filter is something that changes the nature of a substance. For example, water may pass through a filter that purifies it. However, if the filter is clogged with impurities, it makes the water toxic. Communication also often gets filtered on its way from sender to receiver. One filter that Nortarius and Markman describe is the "romantic love" filter. The young couple in the pangs of romantic love may interpret almost any message as positive. Whereas, another couple whose marriage is on the rocks may use the "hate" or "passionate dislike" filter and interpret most every message in a negative way.

As these researchers used this technique to study communication patterns in happily married couples, they found that there was usually a match between speaker intent and receiver impact. Even in conflict discussions, most of the messages sent by the speaker had either a neutral or positive intent and the receiving partner perceived these messages in that way. Even the objective observers watching videotapes of the interactions tended to agree with the sender in regard to intent and the receiver in regard to impact. Since the speaker's intent was often positive in these discussions and the listener interpreted intent correctly, this amounted to many more deposits in the relational bank account than withdrawals.

But as the researchers analyzed the data from unhappy couples, they noted very different results. There was much disagreement between intent and impact among husbands, wives, and objective observers. For example, even when a husband's stated intent was positive, the wife might interpret the message quite negatively. With unhappy couples, a general pattern emerged. Wives in these unhappy marriages interpreted their husband's comments as negative even if the comments were meant to be neutral or somewhat positive. For these wives, the interpretations of their husbands' comments were even more negative than the interpretation of objective observers. It's as if these wives interpreted their husbands' intent using dark colored glasses. In contrast, husbands in the unhappy relationships tended to interpret their wives' negative comments as neutral or positive. Even when the objective observers saw a wife's comments as quite negative, the husband frequently did not infer negative intent. It was as if the husband was living in another world–a world of denial, not seeing what was happening before his eyes. Husbands often respond to this discrepancy by saying that their wives are making a mountain out of a molehill–things are really not that bad. This may explain why some authorities speak of two marriages–the marriage the wife perceives and the marriage the husband perceives. And this may be why more wives file for divorce. At least when the wife files for divorce, the husband may finally realize that there is a serious problem. He realizes that the inflated currency in his relational bank account is bogus–not worth the paper it's printed on.

- How aware are you of the impact your communication has on your partner? What characterizes your relational bank account? Do you have a substantial positive balance that can see you through difficult times?

How long does it take for at least one partner in a struggling relationship to note that the positivity in their relational bank account is eroding? These researchers (Notorius & Markman, 1993) noted: "It takes about two and a half years for the withdrawals from the relationship bank account to deplete the positive balance that usually is present in the marriage-planning stage of a relationship" (p. 88). When a couple struggles early on in their relationship, why does it take over two years for at least one partner to notice the negativity in their communication? Notarius and Markman suggest that the warning signs are ignored. Perhaps they are still interpreting their spouse's comments using the "romantic love" filter or the "denial" filter that allows them to see things as better than they really are.

These researchers and many marriage therapists believe that couples need to be aware of the early warning signs that characterize faulty communication; couples should use language that promotes deposits in their relational bank account (e.g., listening, validation, empathy) rather than withdrawals–criticism, defensiveness, and mind reading. Thus therapists often help couples learn the difference between positive talk and negative talk and apply positive ways of communicating in conflict situations. A systematic approach to teaching these skills, developed by Markman and his colleagues, will be discussed later in this chapter.

How Not to Talk about Difficult Issues

You may be wondering how it is possible to listen when you are in a heated argument. How do you de-escalate tension when you are angry and can feel nothing but your anger? Most therapists believe that it is very difficult to do. Dan Wile (1988) writes that even if you make communication errors, you can benefit from these errors if you can see them as clues to your communication problems. In his book, *After the Honeymoon*, Wile reviews some common mistakes couples make and then suggests how couples can benefit from their mistakes even if they cannot always prevent them.

Suppose that when a husband comes home from work each day he goes directly to his computer. After giving his wife a ritual kiss and a superficial hello, he's off in his computer world for at least thirty minutes. He even takes his computer on vacation and uses some of his vacation time as computer time. This irritates his wife, although she is hesitant to say anything because at other times, he is attentive and supportive. But she is becoming more and more irritated, feeling slighted and even somewhat jealous of her husband's computer time. Finally, after a trying day, she blurts out, "You don't spend any time with me any more. You're always on that damn computer. You obviously don't care about me. You never have time to talk to me about my day." Feeling attacked and responding without thinking, the husband defends himself and all of this leads to the biggest argument they have had in years-an argument in which he calls her a super-sensitive neurotic and she calls him cold and uncaring. And in the process, both make one communication mistake after another. Wile's (1988) list of common communication mistakes will illustrate what has gone wrong.

Common Mistakes in Conflict Discussions

USING "YOU" STATEMENTS RATHER THAN "I" STATEMENTS. Using "you" statements rather than "I" statements is a common mistake in conflict discussions. A "you" statement ("you obviously don't care about me") often sounds accusatory and this accusation usually sounds like criticism. And the typical response when criticized is to defend and refute. "Honey, that's not true! I do care about you. We had a long talk last week." Had the wife used an "I" statement, it might have sounded like this: "Honey, I wish we could sit down and talk for a little while when you come home from work. After a long day, I just need someone to listen to how my day was. We used to do that and I felt closer to you." Here the wife is expressing how she feels and it is harder for the husband to refute her feelings. Nor is this "I" statement an attack, so it is not likely that he will become defensive. However, Wile (1988) believes that most couples make some "you" statements in the heat of the moment. When partners make this mistake, they should realize that there is something they need to talk about, perhaps at a later time, when tempers have cooled. When they have this discussion, it would be helpful if they could use "I" statements.

USING THE WORDS "NEVER" AND "ALWAYS". The words "never" and "always" when used in conflict discussions ("you never have time to talk to me about my day") are usually exaggerations. The wife knows that her husband does talk to her and that he is not always on the computer. That's just how it seems to her in the anger of the moment. So it is an easy statement for the husband to refute–"you know that's not true, we had a long talk last weekend." The wife probably uses these words because of her immediate frustration, her desire to make a strong case, and her high level of irritation.

The natural response to these exaggerations is for the husband to become defensive and point out the fallacy in his wife's statement. However, Wile believes that if you have occasionally used the words "never" and "always" in conflict situations, you can still benefit from knowing several things. First, the words "never" and "always" reflect significant frustration and both partners need to be concerned about this frustration. Also, this frustration is usually based on important feelings that the partners need to explore together.

RESPONDING BEFORE SHOWING EMPATHY AND UNDERSTANDING. If the husband could have shown empathy for his wife's point of view, he first would have listened and then paraphrased or restated what his wife had expressed. This paraphrasing is often a reflection of both words and feelings. The husband might have responded by saying, "Wow, you sound really upset and irritated. It sounds like you're feeling ignored. Can we talk about it?" Empathic responses are not natural responses and are especially difficult to make when one is under attack. Yet these responses are important to make—they exhibit understanding and de-escalate tension. However, even if you fail to paraphrase, Wile believes you can benefit from your mistake. First, realize that your partner wants you to listen and when you don't do so, more tension is added to the mix. Also, if you are unable to make empathic responses during the heat of conflict, at least make these reflective responses when you have calmed down.

MAKING MIND READING RESPONSES. Remember the wife's comment, "You obviously don't care about me." This may have been how she felt at the moment; however, her husband has never said those words and has often been understanding and supportive. Wile believes that in most instances, it does not help to tell people what you think they are thinking and feeling. Responses like, "you don't care about me," "you're angry with me," or "you don't like my relatives" are often either wrong or oversimplified. Even if such responses have a grain of truth to them, generally a spouse does not like to be told how s/he thinks or feels. Mind-reading responses usually put the receiver on the defensive. "I do too like your relatives; I just don't like it when they . . ." or "I do too care about you, remember just yesterday when . . . ." Even if you mind read occasionally, Wile believes that you can learn from this mistake. Often, these responses reflect a concern, worry, or fear on the part of the mind-reading spouse. The response "you don't care about me," stated another way, would come out, "I'm worried that you're losing interest in me." Viewed in this way, it is not a statement to be refuted, but a concern both the husband and wife should take seriously.

NAME CALLING. Partners usually name call when their frustration level is high and they are exasperated. In a more rational moment, partners would realize that blurting out a name such as "neurotic," "crazy," or "stupid," would be harmful, but in their irritation and frustration, name-calling occurs.

And yes, it will usually escalate the tension of the moment. However, in the heat of the argument, the name caller probably doesn't care if it makes things worse. Wile believes that when partners name-call, they should realize the depth and intensity of the feelings that are being expressed and address these issues when they can be more rational.

BRINGING UP OLD GRIEVANCES FROM THE PAST. If you bring up old grievances from the past, Wile suggests that you are trying to find a dramatic example as you attempt to make a point or defend yourself. A comment like, "remember last year when you . . . you'll just never learn will you." Partners should be aware that bringing up old grievances is likely to inflame the situation and make things worse.

OTHER MISTAKES. Wile discusses other mistakes that are difficult to resist in the heat of the moment. These include getting sidetracked rather than sticking to one topic, interrupting when your partner is talking, and mentioning all kinds of dissatisfactions as a way of dumping these irritations into the discussion. Each of these mistakes usually increases the tension level and makes rational discussion more difficult.

- Analyze your conflict discussions in light of these mistakes. Which mistakes are you and your partner most likely to make?

Core Issues that Underlie Conflict

Therapists who work with couples experiencing conflict often note that these couples avoid having important conversations. There are issues that underlie conflict that these couples seldom discuss. Perhaps these issues are too "hot" to talk about or past attempts to talk about these issues have just made things worse. Therapists often provide couples with opportunities to have these conversations in safe situations where there are rules that keep couples on topic, de-escalate tension, and minimize withdrawal.

What would such a conversation be like? Gottman and Silver (1999) would suggest a soft startup on the part of the one who makes the first bid for attention, perhaps a statement beginning with "I" that expresses a concern or complaint. "I have been feeling a little left out and sad lately, especially when you come home and immediately go to your computer. Could we talk about that"? It is important to remember that conflict discussions that begin softly have a much better chance of ending on a positive note. However, even if the speaker's bid for attention begins harshly, the receiver must decide whether to turn toward, turn away, or turn against in response to the bid. "I don't have time right now, can't you see I'm busy." This response does not turn toward but rather away; instead, why not try to connect. "Wow! You sound really upset. I didn't know that you were so upset. Sure, let's talk." This simple response opens up dialogue and has a chance at getting at the real issue that underlies the irritation.

Goldberg (1987) believes that there are six core issue areas that are the basis for many disagreements between couples. Yet many fights are over computer time and other daily events rather than the real underlying issue. According to Goldberg, the underlying issues at the root of many relationship problems are nurturance, intimacy and privacy, power and control, trust, fidelity, and differences in style.

Nurturance relates to caring and love. Do partners feel loved and cared for in the marriage in a way that meets their needs? Intimacy and privacy relates to closeness and distance. Do partners have the freedom and separateness that suits them best? Are their needs for closeness and connection being adequately met? Power and control relates to decision making. Do partners have as much say-so in the marriage as they would like to have? Arguments centering on this concern often relate to money and child rearing. Who controls spending or makes child-rearing decisions? Trust can also be the basis for many disputes. Will my spouse do what s/he says—be responsible, pick up the children, stop drinking, remember to stop at the store, etc? Fidelity relates to commitment. Will each partner continue to be committed to the marriage and the expectations that were agreed upon in the beginning? This issue can cause difficulty because early agreements may have been implicit and not clearly stated; or perhaps circumstances changed in ways that a partner never imagined, causing the partner to rethink initial agreements. Therefore, one or both partners may come to believe that a spouse has reneged on those things that were basic to the marriage. Differences in style often result from personality differences. One partner may be an introvert and the other an extrovert. One partner deals with anxiety head on, while the other backs away. A couple may argue about daily issues such as how often to socialize with friends or what concerns are worth worrying about. Often, these types of disputes are due to fundamental differences in personality style.

Let's go back to the couple fighting over computer time. If the wife can bid for her husband's attention using soft startup and the husband can respond to her bid by moving toward rather than away, then they can have a dialogue that may lead to the underlying issue. After the husband's "Wow! I didn't know you were so upset! Sure, let's talk." The dialogue might go like this:

Wife: I feel angry, sad, and even a little anxious when you do that each night. I don't know why it has come to irritate me so much, but lately, I've been downright angry.

Husband: "I can hear the irritation and I'm wondering what's behind it too.

Wife: It's just that I want your attention at that time. That might sound silly but especially when you come home and we haven't seen each other all day, I think it would be good to just have some time together.

Husband: You know that's interesting because I've been coming home from work to be here with you, thinking that I can finish up my day's work at home on the computer and still be with you even though we are not giving each other our undivided attention.

Wife: But that's not the same. I really don't think that kind of togetherness is very satisfying–you in your world and I in mine. That happens a lot in our marriage now; we share the same space but we don't connect like we used to.

Husband: You know I think that's a difference between us. You feel good when we directly connect–like talking, and I'm often content just being home and knowing you are here too.

Wife: It takes a lot more than that for me. You know this may go back to my parents' marriage. Daddy would come home and just work. I knew mother was irritated at him about something, probably a lot of things, but she hated when he brought work home and ignored us.

Husband: So when I come home and go directly to my computer, it seems like a repeat of what you saw in your family.

Wife: Although I hadn't thought about it much until now, yes, it's like the same thing. And you know in my family how things just went from bad to worse. I was really devastated when my parents divorced.

Husband: I'm not sure my coming home and finishing up my work on the computer is in any way like what your dad did.

Wife: Yes, but can you see how it might seem a little bit the same from my point of view. My parent's marriage didn't all of a sudden come apart; it was a gradual thing–one thing after another.

Husband: Yes, I guess I can see where you're coming from.

This couple has discussed this issue reasonably well by turning toward each other's bids for connection, by listening to each other, by talking about how they feel and trying to understand rather than being critical and defensive. They came closer to understanding that the disagreement was more than just about the husband's use of the computer. It was about the wife's need to feel nurtured and loved in a special way, possibly due to what she experienced in her family of origin. It was about how the husband experienced intimacy differently; just being home together was a way of being intimate for him. If a couple can have this type of discussion, perhaps they can understand their differences and make accommodations for these differences through loving compromise.

• What are the core issues that underlie your typical conflicts? Have you been able to have discussions that uncover these core issues?

The Relationship between Thoughts and Communication

Many therapists and communication experts have noticed the link between thoughts and communication. Some types of thinking are detrimental to healthy communication, while other thoughts have a positive influence on interactions. Gottman (1994) has noted that when couples are in conflict discussion, they often report having thoughts that maintain the stress in the interaction rather than soothing thoughts that might reduce the stress. He discusses two types of stress maintaining thoughts—innocent victim and righteous indignation. Innocent victim thoughts convey the message—I don't deserve this type of treatment; I have done nothing to warrant such harsh attack. Thoughts of righteous indignation are similar but also involve a dose of hostility and perhaps contempt directed toward the partner—he's just a bitch, she's just crazy, no one could put up with this nonsense. These thoughts usually prolong the internal stress.

Aaron Beck (1988) has also examined the mistakes in thinking that are associated with relationship problems. Beck calls these mistakes cognitive distortions. These distortions frequently occur in families and can be troublesome because thoughts influence communication and behavior. Beck believes that when family members use these distortions, they are usually not aware that their thinking is faulty, only later might they benefit from examining their errors. See if any of these mistakes seem familiar.

Cognitive Distortions

TUNNEL VISION. This distortion involves seeing only what fits one's state of mind and ignoring all other interpretations. For instance, the man who abuses his wife interprets his wife's absence from home as evidence of her unfaithfulness—she's out running around. Or a father who has been brought up in a strict home believes that harsh corporal punishment is the only logical way to discipline and he cannot tolerate other viewpoints.

SELECTIVE ABSTRACTION. This distortion involves selecting one piece of information from among many available pieces of information and drawing a false conclusion based on this single piece of information. Perhaps a husband always kisses his wife good-bye in the morning but one morning forgets to do so. His wife concludes from this that he must not love her any more. She has taken one piece of information out of many she could have focused on and drawn an unwarranted conclusion.

ARBITRARY INFERENCE. This distortion occurs when something is inferred without any collaborating evidence. A father may assume that a car accident was his teenage son's fault even before hearing what happened. A wife may infer that because her husband was unusually quiet during their evening out, he must be angry with her for something she has done even though there is no evidence to support her belief.

OVERGENERALIZATION. This distortion involves seeing a behavior that occurs on one or several occasions as typical. Words like "never" and "always" are typical of this distortion. A teenager who misses curfew by ten minutes is now seen as *always* late. A spouse who forgets a partner's birthday is seen as *never* being sensitive to the things that matter.

ALL OR NONE THINKING. This distortion is also referred to as dichotomous thinking or polarized thinking. This mistake occurs when things are interpreted as all good or all bad, all love or all hate, all success or all failure. A wife may accuse her husband of hating her parents without realizing that partners often have both positive and negative feelings toward others. Parents may think of themselves as total failures after hearing of their child's misbehavior at school even though this is the first time their child has gotten into trouble.

PERSONALIZATION. Personalization involves attributing external events, including the behavior of others, to oneself, thus taking responsibility for what has happened. For example, a young child may think he caused his parents' divorce. Or a wife may blame all the problems in the marriage on herself, saying, "If I wasn't such a total failure as a wife, none of this would have happened." Individuals using personalization fail to realize that life is complex and many factors contribute to outcomes.

MIND READING. This distortion occurs when one person believes that s/he knows what a family member is thinking without being told. A husband may say to his wife, "you think I'm being narrow minded, don't you" or a wife may say to her husband, "you think I'm stupid, don't you." In close relationships, partners often resent the negative mind reading of a spouse because they want to believe that their thoughts are their own private domain. Also, the mind reader often oversimplifies the thoughts of the other person by not considering the complexities on which thoughts are based.

BIASED EXPLANATIONS. This distortion is often seen in troubled marriages. It is the tendency to find a negative reason for why a family member has behaved in a certain way. Troubled couples often find unworthy motives behind their spouses' behavior. "He's just a hostile SOB" or "she's just a bitch." Such couples often make these negative attributions because of their biased mindset toward their spouse.

• How typical are these cognitive distortions in your conflict discussions? Are there specific distortions that often characterize your discussions?

DIFFERENT COMMUNICATION STYLES

Why are there so many misunderstandings in communication? These misunderstandings often originate from personality differences and from differences in how individuals have been trained and programmed to use communication.

The Origin of Our Differences

Past Training and Family of Origin

Each family is unique and this uniqueness is expressed through communication. Consider the following example. Nancy comes from a quiet family where family members rarely raised their voices. Nancy's family tends to avoid conflict. When important disagreements occurred in Nancy's family, family members were expected to reason with one another in a controlled way to reach an acceptable compromise. Jake, Nancy's husband of three years, comes from a very boisterous family where disagreements were openly expressed in a loud contentious manner. Jake and Nancy are now experiencing difficulty in their marriage. Nancy does not understand why Jake is so loud and argumentative. She is hurt by some of the things he says and wishes he would tone down so they could talk. Jake says he doesn't mean anything by his raised voice and argumentative style; that's just the way he is and the way it was in his family. To some extent, Nancy and Jake's differences may be due to past experience and family of origin differences that have carried over from their families of origin.

Personality and Temperament Differences

For Nancy and Jake, past experiences in their families shaped their styles. However, innate personality characteristics may have also influenced their communication preferences. Someone with a quiet, calm temperament may be more predisposed to communicate like Nancy; someone with a loud, boisterous personality may find Jake's style more natural. Thus, temperament, personality, and communication background each influence the style that individuals find most comfortable. If partners' styles are different, each partner must attempt to understand and be sensitive to the other's style and perhaps even modify his or her style to accommodate for his or her partner's needs.

Gender Differences

Some very interesting differences in communication style relate to gender. Deborah Tannen (1986, 1990) and others (Fincham, Fernandes, & Humphreys, 1993) have written about gender differences in communication style and the reasons for these differences. Males and females are usually socialized differently beginning in infancy and early childhood. During the preschool years, boys and girls separate from each other in their play. By the age of seven, same sex group play is common and opposite sex play partners are rare. Boys enjoy more aggressive games and a rough and tumble give and take. Girls often enjoy quieter play in smaller groups where the game itself is not as important as the friendships and relationships that develop. Girls usually talk about their feelings and interests rather than the game itself. For boys, the game is more important than relationships and feelings; thus, boys talk about the game rather than emotions and feelings. These differences are likely to be reinforced in the home. If a girl's feelings are hurt, it is usually acceptable for her to cry. Her tears are met with sympathy–"I'm so sorry, tell me about it." When boys are hurt, either physically or emotionally, they are often encouraged to "be a man" and to "suck it up." This is often followed by advice about how to avoid getting hurt the next time. It is difficult to determine if the gender differences that are seen in young children are due more to innate tendencies or to the socializing effect of the environment. Yet many have noted gender differences in behavior at a young age.

As these differences are reinforced during childhood, some very important differences between male and female communication styles emerge. Females learn to move toward others, attempting to become close by expressing their feelings and personal concerns. They seek intimacy and closeness; they experience this closeness when a friend listens and understands. Males tend to avoid close relationships where they are expected to share feelings and the personal details of their lives. Males are more comfortable talking about things–the game, the car, the stock market; they readily give advice when questions arise instead of sharing feelings about personal experiences. These gender differences in communication style are often the source of frustration and misunderstanding in marriage. An awareness of these gender differences can help partners understand and accept each other's styles without inferring evil intent when communication goes awry. Thus, it is important for partners to understand these differences and to keep differences from eroding the good feeling in their relationship. It is also important to realize that research findings in this area are generalizations; each of these differences will not characterize everyone and every couple's experience.

SOME SPECIFIC GENDER DIFFERENCES. Fincham, Fernandes, and Humphreys (1993) list the following gender tendencies in communication style.

Female: Talking about a problem with someone can be helpful. Talking provides relief and leads to support and closeness with the listener.

Male: Talking about problems often sounds like complaining. Complaining is not helpful and leads nowhere.

Female: Talking with someone about problems shows that you value that person and that's important even though the subject of conversation may not be important.

Male: Talking about problems does very little good. Make a decision and move on.

Female: Letting others know that you understand their situation communicates support, closeness, and sympathy and strengthens friendship bonds.

Male: Bringing up someone's problem makes the person uncomfortable. It indicates you feel sorry for them and is viewed as a putdown.

Female: A person shows interest by asking questions and others appreciate such inquiries.

Male: Don't ask questions unless you want specific information. People don't want you prying into their affairs.

Female: Giving a lot of details about a situation is helpful to others as they try to understand what another person is going through.

Male: Providing many details is unnecessary. Get right to the point so as not to bore the listener.

Female: When people share their disappointment, even about romantic relationships, it is a way for them to strengthen their friendship bond.

Male: Sharing disappointment about relationship failures does not help. Talking about things that cannot be changed is pointless.

Female: When there is silence between partners, something is wrong. It is important to explore what it is and talk about it. Problems will only be resolved if they are talked out.

Male: When there is silence, everything must be fine. Why talk so much when talking can make things worse.

Female: When my partner tells me that he loves me and that our relationship is wonderful, then I feel loved.

Male: Actions are what counts. Feelings are difficult to express. She should know that I love her because of the things I do.

Communication differences that are due to gender can lead to significant conflicts in marriage. During the romantic stage of courtship and marriage, these differences are not so obvious; both partners communicate more freely as they experience the wonderful feelings associated with being in love. This romantic state allows partners to overlook differences, while they concentrate on their similarities. As these feelings wear off, couples become more aware of their differences. Tannen (1990) believes that an awareness of these differences is important. Awareness of gender differences allows partners to know that many of their communication problems are common to other couples. If a couple can talk about their differences and be sensitive to them, perhaps they can accept each other in spite of their differences.

• Are any of these gender differences characteristic of your relationship?

Deborah Tannen: He Said, She Said

Deborah Tannen's books and research have struck a responsive chord with readers in regard to male/female communication differences. She is in such demand as a speaker on this subject that recently she videotaped a lecture entitled *Deborah Tannen: He Said, She Said.* This tape (Tannen, 2001) has been popular with university students, especially in classes on communication and relationships. Although some of her insights have already been discussed, a further look at her work through the content of this lecture will illustrate how gender differences can lead to communication misunderstandings in marriage. The structure of her lecture is broken down into seven parts with each part outlining how gender differences influence behavior. The following discussion reflects several of her important points.

Gaze and Communication in Children and Adults

When boys talk to boys and girls talk to girls, Tannen notes an interesting difference in the way they communicate. Girls are more likely to face each other as they talk, looking directly at each other. Boys are much more likely to let their gaze wander and not look directly at the person they are talking to. This gender difference is also seen in adults and can lead to misunderstandings between husband and wife. Since a wife may believe that looking directly at a speaker is part of what good conversation involves, she may conclude that her partner is not listening since he is not looking at her. Yet the husband may be listening even though he is not directly looking at his wife. If partners infer that their way of communicating is the style that all good listeners use, then they set themselves up for communication misunderstandings.

Creating Connection and Negotiating Status

Young girls tell secrets to their best friend. When one girl tells a secret, then the other responds in kind. Thus, they share and this sharing becomes an intimate bond between them. With boys, sharing specific details of life is less likely; boys engage in activities that they can experience together. During these play activities, their conversation often relates to status—which boy can best the other in what is said. One boy may say: "One time I threw a rock that went all the way over the fence." Another may respond: "One time I threw a rock that went so far no one could even find it." Then a third boy may say: "I threw a rock that went so far that it went to the moon and didn't come back." These responses are like a game of "who can top this" with the winner giving the response that cannot be topped. These different girl/boy styles also characterize adult conversation. Women use conversation to create connection and closeness in relationships, while men use conversation to negotiate status. Men are concerned that they hold their own so that they are not in a one-down or inferior position.

This basic difference may explain several things that husbands and wives encounter—why men are hesitant to ask for directions and why wives frequently say, "I'm sorry." Asking directions for a man puts him in an inferior position to the other person, thus making him feel uncomfortable—something he wants to avoid. Saying "I'm sorry" for a woman is natural in light of her desire for connection. She is not implying that what happened is her fault; rather, she is attempting to show empathy for the other person and is saying she is sorry the person has had an unfortunate experience. Men, not viewing "I'm sorry" in this way, would be more likely to interpret "I'm sorry" as a statement of apology, something that puts the speaker in a one-down position.

Being Direct and Indirect in Conversational Style

When decisions are to be made, husbands and wives often have different ways of using conversation. Wives, who are more concerned about feelings and creating connection, often begin with a question, such as "Would you like to . . . ?" The husband's response is often a very direct "yes" or "no." What the husband does not realize is that his wife's indirect use of a question to start the discussion is her way of considering his desires. She does not want a "yes" or "no" response because her question is a way of beginning the discussion and finding out about her husband's feelings; they then can begin to negotiate in light of his feelings. However, since her husband is more direct and doesn't understand what she expects, he gives a direct "yes" or "no" answer. He believes that if she doesn't like his answer, she will say so and the negotiation will then begin. However, she may be upset, interpreting his answer as the end of the conversation, while he is puzzled about why she is miffed and there is not further discussion. Tannen notes that women are often more indirect in their way of getting others to cooperate and do things, while men are more indirect when it comes to apologizing, saying they made a mistake, and admitting to hurt feelings.

Talking at Home and in Public Groups

Wives often complain that their husbands won't talk to them at home. The typical picture is of the husband in front of the TV reading the newspaper while the wife is talking and trying to get her husband to talk. This often characterizes how things are at home–the wife talks, the husband has very little to say. Tannen interprets this difference in this way. The wife has been guarded all day in what she has said, not wanting to say the wrong thing and hurt someone's feelings. But at home, she is safe and now can express herself more freely in her bid for connection. Her husband has been at work using language to get his point across, to argue his position, and to display his authority. When he gets home to his safe haven, he no longer has to talk to compete and achieve status, so he is content with silence. Tannen's research indicates that women talk more at home to make connection (private talk) and men talk more in public groups where there are people to impress (public talk). Therefore, a wife, wanting connection at home with her husband, begins to talk. She is hoping that her husband will listen and share conversation about his day. This would make her feel connected. But the husband, not having this strong need for connection, views his home as a safe environment where he does not need to impress; therefore, much to his wife's chagrin, he falls silent.

As this pattern emerges, it often takes a particular form. Women often feel connected by sharing what Tannen refers to as troubles talk–talking about a problem that is then matched by a friend responding in kind. Women bond through this sharing and they feel connected. When wives talk troubles talk to their husbands, it's as if their husbands' don't understand the script. They are not comfortable talking about their feelings in regard to troubles talk. Rather, when someone comes to a man with a problem, this reflects a difference in status; the one with the problem is seeking help from a person higher in status and authority. Thus, it is time for advise giving and problem solving. Whereas this may be what another male at work wants, it is not what a wife is usually seeking. Therefore, a husband who gives advice misses an opportunity to respond to his wife's bid for connection and a wife who hears advice is frustrated because she wants connection.

Ritual Play

Play for boys often involves teasing, or what Tannen calls "play fighting." This ritual opposition is a way for boys to express friendship and make a bid for connection. Certainly not all teasing is for this purpose, but some ritual opposition serves this purpose. Young girls rarely use teasing in this way, nor do they interpret boys' teasing as a bid for connection. Therefore, men may tease women with the intent to build friendship and connection; however, the result may do just the opposite. The man's teasing may alienate a woman, making connection with her more difficult.

Nagging and Self-Initiative

Husbands often say that their wives nag them. Tannen has an interesting interpretation of nagging. Because men are more concerned with status in relationships, they do not like being told what to do by their wives. Being told what to do puts them in a one-down position; what they want is to be seen as independent. Thus, when a wife asks her husband to do something, this causes a dilemma. If he does it immediately, it seems as if he is taking orders from his wife; so he decides to wait a little while before responding in order to claim self-initiative. But his wife, believing that her husband did not hear her request, feels compelled to tell him again. Thus, a cycle involving asking and waiting begins. Finally, the husband complains, "I might do it if she wouldn't nag me all the time." They are unaware that each is responding to different internal commands: he is saying—don't let her be one up in the relationship and she is saying—connect with him, he must not have heard or understood.

• Have you noticed any of these gender differences in your relationships?

Tannen believes that there is a danger in overgeneralizing these findings— all males are not one way and all females another. Yet if research does not describe the typical gender differences, this too has its drawbacks; couples may inaccurately attribute these differences to sinister causes and blame each other for their communication difficulties. Hopefully, knowledge of typical gender differences will result in better understanding, which will lead partners to a greater respect for each other's style.

CONFLICT RESOLUTION: THE PREP APPROACH

Knowing about gender differences and cognitive distortions may be interesting, but this knowledge does not provide direct help for couples who are experiencing conflict. Couples need rules for conflict situations that will help them manage intense emotional situations. Typically, men tend to withdraw or shut down when heated conflict arises, while women are better able to stay with the conflict. This leads to the pursuer/distancer dance. The wife pursues, attempting to bring some closure to a situation, while the husband withdraws, hoping to control emotions that are too hot to handle. If couples are not given training on how to manage conflict, this unproductive pattern is likely to continue.

Markman, Stanley, and Blumberg (1994) provide conflict management training in a program for couples called the Prevention and Relationship Enhancement Program (PREP). In this program, couples are taught how to use rules of engagement as they discuss heated topics so that conflict discussions do not spiral out of control. The PREP developers believe that if couples use these rules, marital conflict can be contained and compromise can be achieved. Although utilizing these rules may seem artificial at first, couples should be persistent as they implement the PREP strategy because managing conflict successfully is crucial to marriage.

The PREP Strategy

Rules for Handling Conflict

Couples are often surprised by the amount of conflict they encounter in marriage. Many couples initially believe that love will somehow magically dissolve their differences. Instead, they find that conflict seems to dissolve their love. As couples attempt to communicate about their differences, words and feelings escalate. They have the same argument over and over and it leads to the same hurt feelings and slammed doors. If only he would listen! If only she would stop complaining! Couples need to realize that conflict occurs in all marriages; it is how couples manage conflict that will determine the success of the relationship. Thus, the developers of the PREP program state: "Contrary to popular belief, it is not how much you love each other that can best predict the future of your relationship, but how conflicts and disagreements are handled" (1994, p. 1). With this in mind, the PREP developers attempt to teach the rules and the communication skills that are needed to successfully negotiate conflict.

First, the PREP program urges couples to control the difficult issues of marriage rather than allowing these issues to control them. The first step toward gaining control is to set aside time for conflict discussion so that difficult issues can be addressed during specified meeting times. Either partner may ask for a meeting and these meetings should be scheduled at a time convenient to both partners. During these meetings, the couple should use the Speaker-Listener Technique. This technique is a central feature of the PREP program; it helps couples discuss difficult issues within a contained framework of rules. This keeps the discussion from escalating out of control, making it less likely that one partner will withdraw while the other pursues. Since emotions are contained by the rules and structure, difficult problems can be discussed without escalating tension.

The Speaker-Listener Technique

The Speaker-Listener Technique has rules for both the speaker and the listener. One person is first designated as the Speaker. This person is said to have the floor–it is this partner's time to speak. Often, a small piece of carpet or linoleum is given to the speaker to reflect this "floor" designation. The Speaker is to talk about how s/he feels and perceives and is not to talk about the Listener's motives or viewpoint. The Speaker's statements are to be brief, clearly reflecting the Speaker's point of view. These statements will often begin with "I," as in "I felt upset when I learned that you withdrew money from our bank account . . ." or "I felt hurt when I learned about our plans for the weekend from our neighbor. . . ." After the Speaker's concise statement of feeling or point of view, the Listener then responds to the Speaker by paraphrasing both the feeling and content of what the Speaker has communicated. So the Listener must pay close attention to what the Speaker says and mirror this back to the Speaker. This mirroring often involves a reflective statement such as "You feel that . . . I hear you saying that. . . . It seems to you that..." For example, the Listener might say, "You're upset because you did not know about the money that was withdrawn from our account." It is important that the Listener does not give his/her opinion or viewpoint at this time. Rather, the Listener is just to reflect back what the Speaker has said. If the Listener's paraphrase is not correct, then the Speaker should clarify and the Listener should try again.

As the Speaker-Listener Technique continues, it is important that the Speaker share the floor. Usually what happens is that the Listener, after having listened and paraphrased, wants the floor. As the floor is handed over, it is now the Listener's time to talk about feelings and the Speaker-Listener role is reversed. As this process continues, it is important that neither party attempts to solve the issue or problem. The Speaker-Listener Technique simply provides a safe environment so that issues can be discussed and points of view can be understood without censure, criticism, or blame. Without the use of the Speaker-Listener Technique, partners frequently do not listen to each other and may never try to communicate understanding of their partner's point of view. The developers of PREP believe that many of the problems couples face do not actually need to be solved; they just need to be discussed so that each partner's viewpoint is understood. The Speaker-Listener Technique provides the rules and framework for this understanding.

Problem Solving in the PREP Program

In marriage, there will always be issues that need more than a Speaker-Listener-type discussion. Some conflicts need to be resolved. When confronting these conflicts, the PREP approach suggests that couples not rush to find solutions; instead, they should thoroughly discuss the issue using the Speaker-Listener Technique. Then when all points of view are understood, effective problem solving can begin. When partners move too quickly toward problem resolution, often solutions are superficial and will not last. Also, when addressing a difficult problem, it is essential that partners work as a team to find the best possible solution rather than working as adversaries in a win-lose situation. Happily married couples work together as they attempt to resolve their difficult issues.

Just as problem discussion is facilitated by the Speaker-Listener rules, the problem-solving phase also benefits from structure. The problem-solving phase of the PREP program involves (1) agenda setting, (2) brainstorming, (3) agreement and compromise, and (4) follow-up. Agenda setting means that partners have clarified each element of the specific problem that needs to be discussed at the next problem-solving meeting. For example, the problem of how to handle money has many elements. These elements may include how much cash is needed for a specified period of time, when and for what checks will be written, when credit cards will be used, who will keep track of the checkbook balance, and how the details of this will be accomplished. Just this one problem involves many elements, each needing to be addressed. Having an agenda during conflict resolution meetings breaks the problem down so that all of the elements are on the agenda.

Once partners are clear on the agenda, they begin brainstorming. During this phase of the process, each partner suggests possible solutions without either partner evaluating the suggested solutions. This is a time to be creative, to have fun, and to let the mind conjure up possible solutions without being critical. One partner should write down all brainstormed solutions. Remember, during this phase, there should be no criticism of brainstormed solutions. After the brainstormed solutions have been recorded, agreement and compromise can begin.

Agreement and compromise involve finding a solution or perhaps a combination of solutions that is acceptable to both partners. This requires compromise as the partners work together to find an acceptable solution. It is important that both partners agree on a solution and that they try the solution for a specified period of time. It is best to write the solution down so that both partners can refer to it during follow-up—a time to meet again to assess how the plan is working and to make modifications if needed. The PREP developers caution that if debate gets too heated during the problem-solving phase, a "time out" should be called. The couple should either revert back to the Speaker-Listener Technique where feelings can be dealt with in a controlled environment or schedule a meeting at a later time so that the Speaker-Listener Technique can be used for non-judgmental discussion.

- Do you think the rules of the PREP approach would increase understanding and facilitate conflict resolution? How difficult would it be for you to use these rules and techniques in your conflict discussions?

Distinguishing Between Events, Issues, and Hidden Issues

Markman, Stanley, and Blumberg (1994) also teach couples to distinguish between events, issues, and hidden issues. Each of these has the potential to influence communication in negative ways if partners cannot make these distinctions and make appropriate responses. Events are occurrences or happenings in daily life. Some events trigger issues that lead to conflict. These issues are usually fairly apparent to couples because they are aware of their differences over these issues. Common issues include money, children, housework, sex, religion, relatives, recreation, friends, and the use of alcohol/drugs. Many different events can trigger an issue and lead to an argument: a spouse coming home to find a messy house (housework), a phone call from a mother-in-law at an inconvenient time (relatives), a spouse's request that a partner attend church (religion), one partner drinking excessively at a party (alcohol), or one partner buying a child an expensive gift without consulting the spouse (money, children). Often when these events occur, arguments immediately ensue even if the time is inconvenient and the argument totally unexpected. The developers of PREP do not recommend that couples talk about issues immediately after the event has triggered the issue. Rather, it is better to say, "Can we talk about this at our meeting tomorrow night?" or "That really ticked me off and I need to talk about it, but now is not a good time. Can we talk when you get home tonight?" Then when the partners talk, it is very important that they use the Speaker-Listener Technique. Using these rules has several advantages: (1) a special time is set aside to deal with hot issues, (2) the rules provide controls so that hot issues can be rationally discussed, and (3) the rules assure that both partners will listen and attempt to understand their partner's point of view before problem solving begins.

It is important that couples not only distinguish between events and issues but also recognize hidden issues that underlie event/issue disputes. Hidden issues are the deeper more fundamental issues that may be at the heart of a dispute but are not discussed. Often, partners do not verbalize their hidden issue needs and therefore their words do not contain the most important meanings. These underlying meanings remain hidden and may be difficult for partners to infer. They may argue over money, but the real issue is power and control. Or they may argue over household chores, but the real issue is whether a spouse is sensitive enough to notice that his or her partner is overwhelmed and needs help. Hidden issues are likely to be involved when an argument occurs again and again without being resolved. Couples often have hidden issues that they avoid discussing because it is easier to talk about the event without going deeper into the more volatile and sensitive hidden issue. PREP provides the rules and communication skills that couples need to discuss their deeper issues. Markman, Stanley, and Blumberg (1994) have noted several common hidden issues in relationships. Their list includes: (1) power and control, (2) needing and caring, (3) recognition, (4) commitment, (5) integrity, and 6) acceptance.

John and Barbara frequently argue about the issue of money. When John comes home, he notices that Barbara has again spent money on clothes for their young daughter (event of the day). John believes such spending is unnecessary since she has a closet full of clothes and she will soon outgrow the clothes she has. This event sets off another one of their arguments about money—what is necessary and unnecessary spending. John grew up in a home where there was not much extra money to go around and frugality was a virtue. He managed to get along without any extras, learning that careful control over spending was important. John always felt loved even though his family lived on a tight budget. In John and Barbara's marriage, there is more money to spend since they both work, yet John insists on controlling the purse strings even though Barbara earns some of the money.

In Barbara's family of origin, money was more plentiful and was used as an expression of love. Barbara's father would often bring her little gifts and tell her how much he loved her. Birthdays were celebrated with gifts to show love. Barbara felt hurt when John only bought her a card for her birthday and did not enjoy giving gifts either to her or their daughter. So they argued over events of the day involving money and how it should be spent. Yet they never mentioned or attempted to understand the hidden issues fueling their disagreements. For John, it was the issue of control over something very valuable (money) and the ability to live happily without having extra things. He never interpreted his attitude as unloving. For Barbara, it was the issue of caring and love. She interpreted John's frugality as evidence he did not care deeply for her or their daughter. How could he care when he did not enjoy giving gifts of love to his wife or daughter? The PREP program helps couples become aware of their hidden issues so that these issues can be more directly addressed using the rules, techniques, and communication skills of the PREP approach.

The Origins of Conflict

When arguments are triggered by events that pertain to issues and hidden issues, communication often becomes embroiled in conflict. The developers of PREP believe that disagreements often occur when there are unfulfilled expectations in the marriage. When couples fall in love and contemplate marriage, they each have expectations about what their togetherness will be like. However, the partners often fail to discuss their expectations since they are "in love" and everything seems so perfect. Yet it is these differences in expectations that often create problems in relationships.

John expected Barbara to accept his strict discipline concerning money and control. Barbara believed that John would want to express his love for her with gifts as her family had done. Each partner has a mental picture of what the ideal marriage would be like. If our partner's mental picture is very similar to ours, then there is compatibility. If there is a mismatch, then problems are likely to occur. Many things shape our expectations and mental pictures: our family of origin, our previous relationships, our cultural background, and even our temperament and personality traits. It is important that couples contemplating marriage understand some of their similarities and differences so that they will not be caught unaware.

The developers of the PREP program help partners become aware of each other's expectations by having couples talk and write about what they expect in regard to sexual fidelity, sexual practices, love, caring, children, work, togetherness, communication, power and control, household tasks, religion, sharing feelings, and what happens when there is a disagreement. PREP leaders believe that clarifying one's expectations and finding out about a partner's expectations can be helpful. If partners explore expectations together, there is a chance that they will respond to each other in a loving, caring way even when their expectations are different. One should not expect a spouse to automatically know about a partner's expectations, nor should partners believe that asking about expectations is somehow wrong. The PREP developers (1994) write, "When you ask and your partner responds, that's evidence of your partner's love and commitment" (p. 157).

Partners also need to examine whether their expectations are reasonable. When disagreements over reasonableness occur, each spouse must attempt to understand their partner's feelings and point of view, preferably by using the Speaker-Listener Technique. Then the couple is ready to move on to problem solving and compromise. Remember that using the PREP approach should make resolving differences easier because it provides structure and builds listening and understanding into the interactions. By using the PREP method, partners are more likely to approach disagreements as a team, working together to find acceptable solutions rather than as adversaries intent on winning.

- Analyze one of your relationship problems in terms of events, issues, and hidden issues. Do these concepts help you understand what is happening in your relationship?

The developers of PREP realize that problems in marriage do not magically disappear. However, they believe that difficult problems can be managed effectively using understanding and compromise. Therefore, problems do not have to jeopardize the relationship. In Chapter 10, other suggestions for handling conflict, even when the conflict is irresolvable, will be presented.

IMPORTANT TERMS AND CONCEPTS

metamessage
digital message
analogic message
Chapman's love languages
common mistakes when
  communication breaks down
sender errors
receiver errors
relationship bank account
the positive (+) negative
  (-) feedback technique

Wile's common communication
  mistakes
Goldberg's core issues that underlie
  conflict
Beck's cognitive distortions
gender differences in
  communication style
The PREP Approach
the speaker-listener technique
difference between events, issues,
  and hidden issues
common hidden issues in
  relationships

SUGGESTED READING

Beck, A. T. (1988). *Love is never enough. How couples can overcome misunderstandings, resolve conflicts, and solve relationship problems through cognitive therapy.* New York: Harper & Row.

Chapman, G. (1992). *The five love languages: How to express heartfelt commitment to your mate.* Chicago: Northfield.

Fincham, F. D., Fernandes, L., & Humphreys, K. (1993). *Communicating in relationships: A guide for couples and professionals.* Champaign, IL: Research Press.

McKay, M., Davis, M., & Fanning, F. (1983). *Messages: The communication skills book.* Oakland, CA: New Harbinger.

Markman, H., Stanley, S., & Blumberg, S. L. (1994). *Fighting for your marriage.* San Francisco: Jossey Bass.

Notarius, C., & Markman, C. (1993). *We can work it out: Making sense of marital conflict.* New York: G. P. Putman.

Tannen, D. (1990). *You just don't understand: Women and men in conversation.* New York: Ballentine Books.

Wile, D. (1988). *After the honeymoon: How conflict can improve your relationship.* New York: John Wiley.

Chapter 9

WHEN COUPLES AND FAMILIES STRUGGLE

Marriages fail at an alarmingly high rate. Recent statistics indicate that more than 50 percent of first marriages end in divorce. The failure rate of second marriages is even higher. The divorce rate is highest in the state of Nevada; yet Oklahoma, considered to be a conservative state, has the second highest rate of divorce (Parrott & Parrott, 2001). The governor of Oklahoma was so concerned by this high divorce rate that he recently developed a statewide initiative with the objective of significantly reducing the divorce rate in his state within the next ten years. Furthermore, he has earmarked ten million dollars to the project, becoming the first governor in history to declare war on divorce (Parrott & Parrott, 2001).

Even before initiatives like the one in Oklahoma, some couples have had second thoughts about breaking up their marriages so easily. Perhaps this change in attitude is due in part to a book by Wallerstein and Blakeslee entitled *Second Chances: Men, Women, and Children a Decade After Divorce* (Wallerstein & Blakeslee, 1989). In this book, the authors report on the long-term effects of divorce on both children and spouses. This book and the more recent writings of others have noted that there are some clear disadvantages associated with the breakup of a family. Ford (2001) summarized three of these disadvantages.

1. Toxic patterns of behavior are often carried over from first marriages and repeated in second marriages. Also, people often choose a second partner who resembles their previous spouse. When this occurs, divorce and remarriage usually do not resolve the issues at the heart of the problem. More second marriages end in divorce than first marriages and more third marriages end in divorce than second marriages. Thus, Ford suggests that an individual's best chance of success in marriage is in their present relationship.
2. Divorce creates many new problems that previously did not exist. Looking at divorce from a systems approach, things that occur in families are interrelated in complex ways. The input of divorce and all its ramifications reverberates throughout the family and often the pain caused by divorce is felt for years.
3. Divorce creates many adjustment problems for children. In some cases, children may be better off when the family breaks up but in many cases, it is far less clear. Children of divorced parents can be scarred for years by the damages of divorce.

This focus on the disadvantages of divorce has lead one therapist (Davis, 2001) to write: "unless you are in an extremely dysfunctional relationship–one in which there is physical abuse or chronic infidelity, for example-and your spouse isn't willing to change, you are better off solving your problems than getting out" (p. 14). Davis has written two books, *Divorce Busting* (1992) and *The Divorce Remedy* (2001), with the explicit purpose of helping couples save their marriages.

Why is there such a high rate of failure in intimate relationships? When couples are asked about their reasons for breaking up, typical responses include unhappiness, incompatibility, communication problems, lifestyle differences, boredom, not feeling loved, conflict, and a spouse's insensitivity. How do relationships that start out with such promise end in such disarray? Researchers and therapists attempt to answer this question in several ways. One method used to study struggling couples examines how partners interact, communicate, argue, and relate to each other as their relationship deteriorates. The researchers using this approach often observe couples before they divorce, usually even before they know they will divorce, to understand how couples interact as they communicate. Another approach used to study divorce asks those who have gone through a breakup to describe their uncoupling experience. Much of the research concerning divorce is of this type. A third approach to understanding the divorce process comes from the writings of marital therapists. After working with troubled couples, these professionals often write about what they observe as relationships come apart. Findings and observations from each of these approaches will be presented in this chapter.

However, before we examine what can go wrong after couples marry, we will examine some warning signs that exist even before marriage. These warning signs are often ignored while the partners experience the intense passions of romantic love.

AVOIDING TROUBLING SIGNS BEFORE MARRIAGE

As couples consider marriage, they often ask—Are you the one for me? This is even the title of a book by Barbara DeAngelis. In this book, DeAngelis (1992) attempts to help couples examine some important issues before marriage. If certain characteristics describe either partner, these characteristics may put a marriage in jeopardy. Thus, partners should ask: Does this characterize me? Does this characterize my partner? Yet remember, when partners are in the grip of passionate love, it is difficult to be objective. However, after the passion wears off, partners often wish they had paid more attention to the troubling clues that were present before marriage. Here are some problem issues that DeAngelis believes couples should examine.

Potential Problem Issues

Problems of Self-Esteem

The first person you should examine before marriage is you. If you do not feel good about yourself before marriage, you will probably not feel good about yourself after marriage. The high of romantic love will fade leaving the same old negative feelings. If you expect your partner to fill your emotional emptiness or somehow magically make up for your lack of self-esteem, you will be disappointed. Happiness and contentment must come from within. One of the complaints of an unhappy spouse is that their partner no longer makes them happy. They then begin to blame their partner, believing that if their partner would only change, their happiness would be restored.

Individuals must learn that they are responsible for their own happiness. Therefore, the first person you need to examine is you. Do you feel good about yourself? Do you like who you are? Can you be happy and content without a love partner in your life? If your answer to these questions is "no" or more "no" than "yes," then you may have an emotional neediness that can be harmful to marriage.

Why is a positive, healthy attitude toward self so important in marriage? Many marriage therapists believe that if you do not love and value yourself in a healthy way, you cannot reach inside and find a healthy love to give to your partner. You cannot give away something that you do not have. Any deficiency you have prior to marriage—feelings of loneliness, unattractiveness, inferiority, for example—you will most likely have after marriage. Remember Peck's conclusion—a healthy marriage exists when each partner is strong, mature, and independent and could live without each other, but choose to live together.

Therefore, before marriage, ask yourself how you feel about yourself. Are you a strong person, someone you like because of who you are? Do you have a positive identity and a healthy sense of self, regardless of whether you have a love interest or not? Also, ask similar questions about your partner. Does the one you love have a healthy sense of self? Will s/he expect a spouse to satisfy powerful emotional needs in the marriage that will be impossible to satisfy? Attempt to be aware of problems relating to self-esteem that may signal trouble.

Some years back, a young student shared his concerns about his marriage with a counselor. While this couple was dating, the young man told his fiancé of his love for her. Her response was one he did not understand so he glossed over it without further exploration. She/had responded that no one could love her because she was unlovable. This young man thought this was certainly untrue because he loved her very much. The couple continued to date and later married. After a few years of marriage, this husband came to realize the importance of that statement. Due to an abusive childhood, this wife did not value and love herself and nothing the husband did made her feel loved. They have since divorced and she has gone on to have two other failed marriages. It is important to feel good about yourself before marriage so that you can give and receive love in a healthy way after marriage.

- Have you ever considered how one partner's low self-esteem can impact a relationship? Has this been a problem in your relationship? If so, in what ways has low self-esteem played a role?

Problems with Anger and Self Control

When a partner has problems controlling anger, the spouse is often a target. The result can be physical and psychological abuse. In the chapter on emotions, abuser behavior was described. This behavior includes attempts to control and isolate, extreme jealousy, blaming others, hypersensitivity, mood swings, verbal abuse, and physical violence. If you see any of these behaviors in your partner before marriage, PLEASE BEWARE! Stable marriages are not built on a partner's anger, jealousy, or desire to control. And no matter how much you think you need a relationship and a love interest, you will not be better off in an abusive relationship.

- Have you seen any of these negative behaviors in yourself or your partner? To what extent have anger and control been a problem in your marriage or relationships?

Problems with Addiction

If you marry someone who is an alcoholic or is addicted to some other drug, you will be in a love triangle. The third partner will be the alcohol or drugs. DeAngelis (1992) writes that the addictive substance will take your partner's time and energy and s/he will become a slave. This type of slave, however, does not want to admit that the alcohol or drugs are in control. Thus, they downplay and deny their problem even as its saps away the positive energy of the marriage. One of the first things to suffer is intimacy. Alcohol and other drugs have a numbing affect on feelings and the addicted user becomes oblivious to his or her feelings. As the addicted partner becomes more and more obsessed with alcohol or drugs, expect an increase in irresponsible behavior, arguments, anger, and emotional deadness in the marriage. Even though we live in a society where drinking is socially acceptable, don't be fooled. When drinking and drugs become a problem, marriages suffer. DeAngelis suggests that even while dating, individuals should determine their partner's values in regard to alcohol and drugs. Do not make excuses for your partner's drinking behavior or compromise your own values for the sake of love. Of course, if you are the one with the drinking problem and are able to admit it, seek help. Admitting your problem and seeking help will give your marriage a fighting chance.

- Have alcohol and addiction problems been present in your marriage or relationships? If so, how have you managed in the face of this problem?

Problems from Childhood Experience

Marriage is not made up of two people who start anew. Rather, both partners bring emotional baggage with them from their family of origin. To some degree, everyone has experienced psychological wounds from the past. Also, everyone brings values and beliefs learned in childhood to marriage; these values and beliefs can make adjustment to marriage more difficult. It is not easy for partners to decipher the extent of childhood wounds or the degree to which values and beliefs will get played out in marriage. Dating partners are often too busy concentrating on the present moment and the loving feelings that exist in their relationship. Also, people are not usually trained to know what questions to ask and what signs should garner their attention. Then too, individuals have a way of putting their best foot forward during the courtship period.

Yet you should ask certain questions not only about yourself but also about your potential mate. These questions include:

- Does your partner bring beliefs from his/her background or family of origin that make compromise and flexibility difficult? Does your partner have attitudes and dreams that you can support and share? Does your partner suffer from childhood wounds that will make adjustment to marriage difficult? Is s/he aware of the impact these wounds can have on marriage? Is s/he actively working to repair these wounds?

Of course, wounds from childhood differ in severity just as beliefs differ in terms of their flexibility. Wounds suffered from abandonment or sexual, physical, or verbal abuse may be so severe that healthy adjustment will be difficult. Also strong beliefs can be so inflexible that relationships suffer. Be cautious! No marriage will be without problems, but if partners ask important questions before marriage, they may find answers that will help them in the marriage decision-making process. If there are too many red flags, back off and seek help.

- How cautious are you before committing to a serious relationship? Do you easily commit or are you cautious?

PREPARE: A PREMARITAL PREPARATION PROGRAM

Most couples spend hours preparing for their wedding; some even hire wedding planners to work with them to see that everything about that day is special. But can couples prepare for marriage? The answer, of course, is yes and no! Couples can examine their beliefs, expectancies, and dreams together; they can discuss their similarities and differences and even learn communication and conflict management skills. This knowledge can help couples decide if they are right for each other and help them foresee the marital landscape ahead. Although this preparation does not completely divorce proof a marriage, it can improve a couple's chances of creating a satisfying relationship. One program that has helped many couples examine their relationship before marriage is the PREPARE program.

PREPARE is both a premarital assessment inventory and a marriage preparation program. In the 1980s, David Olson and his colleagues developed a premarital assessment inventory of 125 questions. In the PREPARE program, each partner answers these questions and then, with the help of a counselor, the partners come together for feedback, discussion, and learning. The following relationship areas are assessed in the PREPARE program (Olson & DeFrain, 2000).

The Relationship Areas

COMMUNICATION. These questions relate to how partners perceive their interaction in regard to communication. Are they good at sharing feelings, listening, and understanding each other?

CONFLICT RESOLUTION. Questions in this area relate to how partners perceive their conflict resolution abilities. Do they avoid discussing important issues? Do they have different ways of handling conflict? How capable are they at compromising?

EQUALITARIAN ROLES. These questions relate to how partners view responsibilities in regard to leadership and household tasks. Do they agree or disagree about work roles, chores, and division of labor issues?

IDEALISTIC DISTORTIONS AND REALISTIC EXPECTATIONS. These questions relate to the partners' perceptions of marriage. Are their perceptions realistic? Do partners have distorted expectations? Do they agree on what their relationship should be like?

FINANCIAL MANAGEMENT. Questions in this area relate to money and financial resources. Do the partners agree on money issues such as spending, saving, and credit card use?

PERSONALITY ISSUES. Matters of personality are considered here. Do partners have habits, characteristics, and patterns of behavior that will pose future problems?

SEXUAL RELATIONSHIP. These questions relate to affection, ease in communicating about sex, and sexual interests and expectations.

CHILDREN AND PARENTING ISSUES. Questions in this area address important child-rearing issues. Do partners agree on discipline issues and the roles each partner will play in rearing the children?

LEISURE ACTIVITIES AND INTERESTS. Do the partners share interests in regard to leisure activity? Do they agree on how free time will be spent?

FAMILY AND FRIENDS. Questions in this area relate to similarities and differences regarding family and friends. Do partners perceive family and friends in the same way? Does each desire the same degree of closeness/distance in their relationships with extended family and friends?

RELIGIOUS BELIEFS. Do partners share religious beliefs? Do they desire the same amount of involvement in religious activities? Do matters of religion have the same meaning for both partners?

COHESION IN FAMILY OF ORIGIN. Here attention is directed to the amount of closeness/separation that characterized each partner's family of origin. Also, the PREPARE program encourages each partner to examine his/her own level of need and desire for closeness and separation in the marriage.

FLEXIBILITY IN FAMILY OF ORIGIN. Here attention is directed to the amount of flexibility that characterized each partner's family of origin. Were their families flexible or rigid in handling daily stressors? Also, the program encourages each partner to examine his or her own style in regard to the flexibility/rigidity continuum.

The PREPARE questionnaire and program assesses each partner's attitudes concerning important marital issues in these fourteen areas. When partner's responses reflect agreement in an area, this is considered a relationship strength; when partner's responses reflect considerable disagreement in an area, this area is considered a growth area. Couples are encouraged to talk and learn about both their strength and growth areas. For example, they learn about budgeting, finance, different styles of parenting, communication styles, and methods of improving communication. Couples are also taught a ten-step conflict resolution approach. They also learn the importance of personal goals, couple goals, and family goals and are aided in establishing healthy goals in their relationship.

The developers of the PREPARE program attempt to help couples achieve several important objectives (Olson & Defrain, 2000). These are:

- Identify and discuss strength and growth areas.
- Develop better communication skills.
- Learn problem-solving and conflict management skills.
- Discuss family of origin issues.
- Explore their current relationship styles.
- Learn budgeting and financial planning skills.
- Develop goals in regard to their personal, couple, and family life.

This program has been widely used and researched since its inception in 1980. Over one million couples preparing for marriage have completed the program and more than 30,000 counselors and clergy have been trained to use the program in their work (Olson & DeFrain, 2000). A similar program entitled ENRICH is also used with married couples in an attempt to improve and enrich marriage relationships. Thus, similar programs and inventories have been used with couples preparing for marriage and married couples seeking to improve their relationships.

Research findings relating to both married and premarital couples support the effectiveness of the programs. First, married couples who score high on marriage satisfaction and happiness have many more strength areas (areas of agreement) than do unhappy couples. Happily married couples were much more satisfied with how they communicated and resolved conflict than were unhappy couples. Happy couples in comparison to unhappy couples were more likely to feel good about their partner's personality, to agree on religious matters, and share equalitarian role beliefs. In most of the fourteen areas, there were distinct differences between happy and unhappy couples. But could marital happiness in the third year of marriage be predicted from premarital PREPARE scores? Fowers and Olson (1986) found that those couples who had many areas of agreement and thus high scores on PREPARE before marriage were much more likely to still be together and be happily married three years after marriage than those who had many areas of disagreement on the PREPARE questionnaire. A later replication (Larsen & Olson, 1989) also supported this finding. Since these inventory scores are good predictors, couples attending PREPARE programs should take the feedback seriously. Actually, research shows that 10 percent to 15 percent of the couples who enroll and complete the PREPARE program decide not to marry after receiving feedback (Olson & DeFrain, 2000). These couples had scores on PREPARE that were very similar to the scores of couples who married after the PREPARE program but were separated or divorced three years after taking the program. The researchers concluded that since the never-married couples had few relationship strengths, their decision not to marry was probably a wise one.

The PREPARE program is only one of a number of marriage preparation programs. However, PREPARE is widely available throughout the United States and has solid empirical evidence to support its value. If you are considering marriage and want to know more about this program, log on to www.lifeinnovation.com. Here you will find more information about PREPARE and a list of the counselors in your state who use PREPARE in their counseling practice.

But perhaps you are not in the marriage planning stage. Instead, you have been married for four or five years and now your arguments and disagreements are occurring more frequently. You are beginning to wonder if your marriage is in trouble. What does a troubled marriage look like and what characterizes a happy stable relationship? Next, we will examine some answers to these questions.

RELATIONSHIPS FROM A PROCESS PERSPECTIVE

No researcher has contributed more to our understanding of marriages than John Gottman. His research program began over twenty-five years ago and involves longitudinal studies of newlyweds, young couples in their first seven years of marriage, middle-aged couples, couples with children, and couples in abusive relationships. This research is remarkable for several reasons. First, Gottman and his colleagues have studied and continue to study over 650 couples. Some of these couples have been followed for more than fifteen years. Second, he observes couples while they interact with each other, providing empirical data about what happens in both stable and unstable relationships. Furthermore, these studies go beyond the observation of couple interaction; this research also examines the physiological and cognitive components associated with couple interaction. Then too, there appears to be significant application value to this research in two areas—helping couples improve their marriages and helping counselors develop a more effective marital therapy. Because Gottman's work is so important and comprehensive, the following discussion will look at what happens in his laboratory when he observes couples interacting and what his findings tell us about marriage.

The Love Lab

The love lab is the name given to the apartment on the University of Washington campus for observing couple interaction. Couples participating in this research fill out questionnaires prior to their stay in the lab. These questionnaires assess such things as each partner's view of the marriage, what they argue about, their recollections of the early history of the marriage, and their philosophy of marriage. The couples then live in the love lab apartment for 24 hours. From nine in the morning until nine at night, cameras monitor the couples' interactions and behavior as they go through their day. As couples talk about enjoyable topics as well as topics of disagreement in their marriage, their facial expressions, verbal responses, and movements are recorded on video cameras. Numerous sophisticated measurements of physiological reactions are also closely monitored and recorded. These include heart rate, respiration, blood flow from the heart to ear and hand, and skin conductance. These measurements allow the researchers to know what the body is doing during both relaxed and stressful times.

The researchers also use videotape playback to gather information about the thoughts and feelings each partner was experiencing during their periods of interaction in the lab. For example, as each partner views their videotaped interactions, they are asked about the thoughts they were having when they made specific comments. They are then asked to rate the feelings they were experiencing at that moment. These feelings are assessed by using an instrument dial that allows each partner to indicate where their feelings fall along a continuum from extremely positive to extremely negative. And, of course, the researchers know what physiological responses were occurring at the time of the interaction, which also provides information about emotional states. Using this videotape playback approach, the partners are also asked to indicate what thoughts and feelings they believe their partner was having at any given moment so that later checks can be made concerning the accuracy of these attributions.

The purpose of the videotapes is for detailed study and analysis by the research team. Trained observers rate every response and every emotion. If one partner lodges a complaint, how does the other partner respond? Does this partner follow by becoming defensive and countering with a criticism? If so, does the spouse ratchet up the tension by responding with contempt or does the spouse offer a repair attempt, trying to lower tension and be understanding? If a repair attempt is recorded, how does the spouse counter? Is the repair attempt heard or does the partner ignore this conciliatory response and continue with criticism and contempt? Complex analysis of these interactions provides an in-depth picture of how couples interact. It is somewhat like instant replay of a sporting event where the sportscaster can use slow motion and stop action to review and study the participants' actions. Studying thousands of these interactions involving hundreds of couples, the researchers have learned what characterizes stable relationships and what types of interactions and responses are predictive of divorce. This comprehensive approach to data collection and analysis has led to an amazing amount of information about couples and marriage. Gottman (1994) equates it to "something akin to an X ray or CAT scan of a living relationship" (p. 20).

Healthy Marriage Styles

Gottman (1994) has found that there are three styles of interaction that characterize stable relationships and two styles that reflect unstable relationships. The three stable styles have been labeled validating, volatile, and avoidant. The research indicates that if a relationship settles into one of these three styles, it is likely to be stable and happy. The two unstable styles were labeled hostile/engaged and hostile/detached. A couple's style is determined by observing the couple interacting in the lab as they discuss a difficult issue in their marriage. What do the partners say during the course of the discussion? What tone of voice is used? How intense is the interaction? What facial expressions and physiological responses are present? These observations served as a basis for labeling the different styles and led to the conclusion that partners in stable marriages resolve their solvable problems and learn to live with their unsolvable, perpetual issues. Although this conclusion may seem like common sense, Gottman's observations of stable couples help us understand how these couples solve solvable problems and how they manage to live in harmony with their unsolvable ones. This knowledge may provide valuable information that can be used to help struggling couples with their solvable and unsolvable issues.

Validating Couples

The validating couples were good listeners. They attempted to understand their partner's feelings and point of view even though they did not necessarily agree. Validating couples tend to exhibit a great deal of respect for each other. As they discuss an issue, they listen to each other, state their point of view, and if they cannot convince the other, they are good at compromising. These skills seem natural to partners in validating marriages. They deal with their inevitable differences as good friends who value the we-ness in their relationship more than their own individual needs. A possible drawback for these couples is that partners lose some of their individual selfhood for the sake of a strong marital bond.

Volatile Couples

The volatile couples exhibit a very different pattern. They frequently bickered, squabbled, and disagreed. They seemed to enjoy their skirmishes. They frequently skipped the empathy and listening part and went right to persuasion. Their arguments were often quite heated, loud, and argumentative. If this pattern of dealing with conflict characterized all their interactions, it would signal trouble. However, intense arguments characterize only a small part of their life together. At other times, they are very warm and loving and their love and passion seem to reach the same level of intensity as their arguments. These couples are comfortable with high levels of both negative and positive emotions. After expressing negative emotions, these couples are good at making up. They thoroughly enjoy the emotional highs that come with doing so. Gottman (1999) has found that volatile couples are the only style to sustain a passionate, romantic relationship after thirty-five years of marriage. Yet volatile couples may also be at some risk; a partner may get carried away with negativity, taking it too far and in doing so, create hurt feelings that take time to mend.

Avoidant Couples

The approach taken by couples using an avoidant style is very different from that taken by volatile couples. The avoidant couples seem never to get anything settled. They rarely air all of their differences even when they discuss areas of disagreement. Rather, they are good at dodging head-on confrontation and withdrawing from heated debates. Intense, heated discussion seems very painful for them, so they back off and agree to disagree. They do not explore in detail their differences of opinion or their emotions underlying their differences; rather, they deal with conflict by avoiding or minimizing it. They appeal to their shared philosophy of marriage and their strong love for each other as they concentrate on positives and accept their differences. The drawback for avoidant couples comes when they are faced with conflict that they cannot avoid. When this happens, they may not have the experience and skills needed to work through their dilemma.

Compatibility and the 5 to 1 Ratio

Prior to Gottman's research, experts might have suggested that the volatile and avoidant styles were unhealthy and unstable. Yet Gottman's research finds otherwise. All three types of marriages can be stable and healthy. However, it is important to consider two other factors. First, in each of these marriage styles, each partner seemed to be comfortable with their style. Somehow, probably early in the marriage, these couples were able to negotiate their way of dealing with issues. Finding this compatibility is essential for stability in marriage. Gottman (1994, 1999) believes that when partners prefer different styles, their marriage is more vulnerable to serious problems. Second, Gottman found that a certain balance between positivity and negativity characterized each of the stable styles. As his research team observed these couples interacting in conflict discussions, they charted the number of positive interactions as opposed to negative in their exchanges. As previously noted in Chapter 6, stable marriages had at least five times more positive interactions than negative interactions–literally a 5 to 1 ratio. Even the volatile couples who argued vehemently were found to be stable if they balanced off these negative moments with five times as many positive moments. The research team found this ratio to be a good predictor of outcome in marriage. When couples could maintain the 5 to 1 ratio even in conflict discussions, their marriages were likely to succeed. If the ratio was off balance with more negativity creeping into conflict discussions, it did not bode well for the marriage.

Unhealthy Marriages

Many of the couples the research team observed interacting in the lab did not exhibit a healthy 5 to 1 ratio of responding. They were unable to find a compatible style that allowed them to balance their arguments with sufficient humor, good-natured talk, and affection. These relationships were overrun with negativity and destined to become unhappy. It may be that their personalities and style preferences did not allow them to settle into one of the healthy styles comfortably. This may happen when one partner is predisposed by background, personality, or temperament to need one style while their spouse is predisposed to need another style. Perhaps one spouse is volatile and the other avoidant or one is validating and the other avoidant. Whatever the differences, in these marriages, it may be difficult to keep negativity from overrunning the marriage. As the researchers observed couples interact, they noted two types of unhealthy styles–the hostile/engaged and the hostile/detached. It is not difficult to visualize these two types.

The Hostile/Engaged Type

The hostile/engaged couples have heated arguments, but nothing really gets settled. They continue to go at each other, throwing barbs and insults while failing to listen and empathize. This pattern of responding becomes a way of life for them as negativity moves in and marital bliss becomes a thing of the past. Perhaps one partner tries to be reasonable, but the other partner is too angry, self-centered, or defensive to hear reason. So the relationship spins out of control as conflict and bad feelings prevail.

The Hostile/Detached Type

The hostile/detached couples are also characterized by a certain amount of hostility but in these marriages, there is at least one partner who is somewhat emotionally uninvolved and detached. This partner may attempt to gain control by keeping strong emotions inside, saying very little, or even withdrawing from confrontation almost before it begins. Yet the tone of the interaction in these marriages is negative with a sense of hopelessness added as if to say: "I'm not going over this issue again, my compromising days are over." As Gottman's research team watched couples interact in deteriorating relationships, he recorded in detail the nature of this free-fall. One of the most significant findings to come from this research is the description of what Gottman calls "The Four Horsemen of the Apocalypse."

Signs of Trouble: The Four Horsemen

"The Four Horsemen of the Apocalypse" are four signs of trouble that Gottman observed as couples' relationships deteriorate. These signs reflect four ways of responding that signify troubled times in a marriage. When these four signs take up residence in a marriage, they interfere with the important 5 to 1 ratio of positive to negative interactions in the marriage. The first sign is *criticism*, followed by *defensiveness*. Then come *contempt* and *stonewalling*.

CRITICISM. Criticism can easily creep into a marriage. There are things most partners do not like about their spouse or the relationship. Every spouse has some complaint and these complaints need to be aired. Airing complaints can help resolve issues and make the marriage stronger. However, if complaints go unheeded and troubling issues remain unresolved, a complaint can become a criticism. The difference between a complaint and a criticism may seem minor, but this difference is significant. A complaint is a statement indicating the presence of something that a partner does not like. Sometimes it is a specific behavior that is especially irritating to the partner, such as leaving clothes on the floor. A complaint often indicates how the complaining partner feels about the irritating behavior and what specific changes are desired. Complaints often begin with an "I" statement, such as "I wish you would pick up your clothes. If I have to pick up and organize your things, it's just one more thing I have to do." Note that the statement does not attack the partner but rather addresses a specific behavior. A criticism is a statement that goes beyond a specific behavior. It often is more global in nature, begins with "you" rather than "I", involves an attack on a partner's character, and may infer blame. "You are such a slob when it comes to your clothes. You never clean up anything around here. Don't you care about me and how I feel?" It is evident that this statement goes far beyond a complaint. Gottman (1999) has noted that women are more likely to criticize in a marriage, while men are more likely to respond to criticism by stonewalling, another of the four horsemen we will discuss. It would be a mistake, however, to view the four horsemen in isolation and conclude that women are to blame because they usually start things by being critical. Actually, how men respond to complaints and criticism, especially if they are defensive, unresponsive, or angry, can sustain a continuing downward spiral in a marriage.

There are several reasons why partners criticize rather than just register a complaint. It may just be more natural for some partners to express frustration in a critical way. Many arguments begin with a harsh startup, bypassing complaints altogether, going directly to criticism. Also, if complaints go unheeded, it may be natural to up the ante with the hope that a stronger statement will produce better results. Gottman (1999) has found that what happens during just the first three minutes of problem discussion is usually sufficient to predict divorce. If there was a harsh startup with one partner quickly becoming critical and the other partner responding by being defensive and contemptuous, the marriage was headed for instability. Therefore, it is important how a discussion starts; the ability to register a complaint without taking a critical, harsh approach is an important difference between stable and unstable marriages.

- In your relationship, do you register complaints or are you critical? Have you and your partner discovered the advantages of complaints over the disadvantages of hurtful criticism?

DEFENSIVENESS. When critical statements invade a marriage, defensiveness is likely to follow. When someone is criticized and attacked, he or she has an important decision to make. Do they listen, attempt to understand, and use the criticism as a springboard to accept influence by compromising and initiating constructive change? Or do they defend themselves by countercomplaining, denying responsibility, and perhaps even blaming their partner. Such escalation is common in marriages that are spiraling out of control, heading toward an unhealthy balance in the 5 to 1 ratio. Although defensiveness may seem to be a logical and natural response to criticism, it is seldom helpful in getting a marriage out of its downward spiral. Taking a defensive posture by deflecting criticism, counterattacking, and counterblaming simply do not help re-establish a stable relationship. Rather, it is likely to lead to more criticism and countercriticism, opening the door for contempt– another sign of a deteriorating relationship.

- How quickly do you become defensive when you are criticized? Has it been possible for you to avoid defensiveness and respond positively to criticism for the sake of your relationship?

CONTEMPT. Contempt, the third negative sign, is an especially corrosive response. Partners who are contemptuous see their position as superior, viewing their spouse as inferior, stupid, and incompetent. This can be communicated verbally by insults, name-calling, and mockery. Verbal contempt is not difficult to recognize. Use of words like jerk, bitch, and idiot are clear signs of contempt and reflect a partner's desire to wound and psychologically abuse. Mockery exhibits contempt because a spouse's words or actions are ridiculed as evidence of disrespect and disgust. Body language can also communicate nonverbal contempt. This may be subtle, communicated with facial gestures such as a rolling of the eyes and a curling of the lips. When Gottman's research team (1994, 1999) turned off the sound on the videotaped interactions and simply coded facial expression, they discovered that the number of facially contemptuous responses by husbands was even predictive of the number of infectious diseases wives experienced over the following four-year period. If the husband frequently expressed contempt, the wife reported a higher number of infections.

The negative impact of contempt cannot be overestimated. It takes a toll on the respect and admiration partners have for each other. As conflict goes unresolved and negativity pervades the relationship, partners cease admiring and respecting each other. At first, this may only occur during times of heated conflict, but as disagreements continue unabated, differences eat away at the heart of a successful relationship—the respect and admiration the partners have for each other. When partners are unable to see any positive qualities in their spouse, then criticism, defensiveness, and contempt have overrun the marriage. But the most destructive of these corrosive elements is contempt. According to Gottman (1999), contempt is the best single predictor of divorce and is "in a category of its own." In happy, stable marriages, some criticism and defensiveness occurs; it just occurs less frequently and is dealt with more effectively in these marriages. But contempt is practically nonexistent in stable, happy marriages. For this reason, Gottman calls contempt the "sulfuric acid of love." Therefore, Gottman and his research team believe that successful intervention with struggling couples must focus on repair mechanisms in order to stave off increasing negativity and contempt.

• Has contempt invaded your relationship? If so, what are the signs of contempt you have seen? Have you been able to control this corrosive horseman in your marriage?

STONEWALLING. The fourth horseman, stonewalling, invades the relationship when one partner withdraws from an interaction as a way of controlling overwhelming emotion. This usually happens when a couple is discussing a problem and one spouse becomes silent, looks away, and does not connect with the speaker, either verbally or nonverbally. Stonewalling partners may initially be involved in the discussion; then they disengage. It appears that they can take no more, so they withdraw as if turning into a stonewall. Some stonewallers may even leave the room to get away from the heat of the interaction. Stonewallers often believe that they are being neutral, trying to be objective, or at least not making things worse. This response is less likely in newlyweds and seems to feed off of stored up negativity that has built up due to the presence of the first three horsemen. Gottman (1994) has found that 85 percent of stonewallers are men. When a husband stonewalls, his wife's heart rate usually increases dramatically, reflecting her irritation and upset with her stonewalling partner. When wives stonewall, husbands do not exhibit this increase in physiological arousal, nor do they seem to be so outwardly upset. Although occasional stonewalling was noted in stable couples, it is most destructive when husbands in deteriorating relationships become habitual stonewallers. So as a couple's relationship deteriorates, stonewalling is added to the other signs of marital discord (criticism, defensiveness, and contempt) and the healthy 5 to 1 balance of positive interaction to negative interaction becomes even more difficult to achieve.

• Have you noted stonewalling in your marriage or relationship? If so, are you or your partner most likely to stonewall?

The Physiological Components of Marital Disaffection

One of the most fascinating aspects of Gottman's research is the massive amount of data collected concerning physiological functioning. While behavioral interactions are being videotaped, sophisticated measurements of internal responses are also being monitored and recorded. As has been noted in Chapter 6, findings from this research concern gender differences and the impact of these differences on conflict discussions. These findings are important and worth further review.

This data indicates that during heated arguments, it takes less negativity for husbands to be overwhelmed physiologically. As heated conflict occurs, a husband's heart rate and blood pressure increase more rapidly, tend to rise higher, and stay elevated longer than that of his wife. This seems to explain why husbands are more likely to stonewall. Their physiology is more hypervigilant during times of marital distress, causing physiological overload. This overload is called "flooding," since it feels as if one's system is being inundated by more stress than it can handle. During flooding, emotions are too high for constructive discussion; the discomfort becomes so great that something must be done. The emotionally flooding partner may want to strike out in anger or stonewall in order to escape. If stonewalling lowers the stress level, it is reinforcing and may become a habitual pattern, a kind of stress-lowering mechanism that defends the person from the attacker and lowers physiological arousal. If the partner leaves the situation and the stress level continues to remain high, at least the arousal stimulus (the spouse) is no longer physically present and for the moment, the stonewalling spouse escapes.

After several such painful marital interactions, one partner, usually the husband, may become supersensitive to potential conflict arousing situations. At the first sign of marital conflict, heart rate and blood pressure rise, leading to an almost immediate withdrawal response. This response allows the partner to escape from the aversive situation before it becomes too heated, resulting in a powerful form of conditioning known as escape conditioning. This is similar to what happens with animals in the laboratory when they learn to escape and avoid unpleasant conditions. If a cue, such as a light, is turned on in an animal's cage and ten seconds later an electric shock runs through the floor of the cage, the animal's internal arousal system will be activated by the shock. The animal will escape the shock and lower arousal level by running to an adjacent compartment. Since the light always precedes the shock, the light comes to activate the internal arousal system and cues the escape (running to the adjacent compartment) even before the ten seconds elapse and the shock is turned on. If this escape behavior continues to work to keep the shock from being experienced, then the animal can avoid the shock by running to the adjacent compartment when the light comes on. This is a powerful form of conditioning and is similar to what may happen when marital conflict occurs. One partner, usually the husband, is prone to flooding during periods of heated debate. During aversive situations when the heat from the conflict is turned up, he learns to withdraw to keep emotions in check and avoid continued interaction in the aversive situation. This is similar to the animal learning to run to the adjacent compartment to avoid the shock. The husband may soon learn the cues that precede these heated debates and respond to these cues like the animal responds to the light. For the husband, the cues may be his spouse's negative moods and caustic glances. Paying attention to and responding to these signals may allow him to escape before things get too overheated and out of control. This doesn't mean that the husband will leave before getting in a few zingers of his own, but it does mean that he escapes before too much overload occurs.

As this flooding occurs, the wife has not yet experienced this internal over-load. So the wife continues to pursue engagement while the husband has already withdrawn. This may explain why many observers of family inter-action have noted the pursuer-withdrawal pattern with the wife tending to pursue and the husband tending to withdraw. Gottman (1999) notes that this pattern characterizes both stable and unstable marriages but increases in severity in troubled marriages. And although this sex difference regarding flooding has been empirically verified, it is important to understand that in a small percentage of the observed couples, it was the wife who flooded and stonewalled. Also, individual thresholds for flooding vary greatly. In a few cases, individuals can tolerate criticism and even contempt for long periods of time without flooding. Volatile couples seem to have higher thresholds for heated debate, while avoidant couples back off more readily. And when negativity has built up in a marriage over time, this may also increase the likelihood of flooding.

The Cognitive Component of Marital Conflict

Even when all of the above factors are considered, it is still striking how frequently flooding and stonewalling are related to gender differences. A husband's heart rate and blood pressure tend to be more sensitive to negativity. In exploring this difference, Gottman (1999) and his research team went one step further; they explored another type of internal variable–the thoughts, perceptions, and beliefs of each partner.

After videotaping couples arguing, the research team then asked partners to view the videotape and report what they were thinking as stonewalling and flooding occurred. From this data, several interesting findings emerged. First, husbands were more likely to have stress-maintaining thoughts– thoughts that kept them upset and physiologically aroused. These thoughts fell into two categories: righteous indignation and innocent victimhood. Innocent victim thoughts ("I'm not the one at fault here; why is she picking on me?") most often led to more defensiveness on the part of the husband. Thoughts of righteous indignation go even further; these thoughts were usually accompanied by anger, hostility, and contempt with a desire to get revenge. These thoughts and reactions are likely to lead to more expressions of contempt by the husband. At times of heated exchange, it is difficult for partners to sooth each other by saying things that cool down their negative thoughts. However, a second finding of this research is that women are more likely to think soothing, relationship enhancing thoughts during times of distress. "He's just had a bad day at work. He'll be over this by tomorrow." These thoughts help calm wives down and lower their physiological arousal. Thus, men seem to have more difficulty dealing with stress in the marriage, have a much greater tendency to withdraw and stonewall, and have thought patterns that serve to maintain the high stress levels they experience. Wives are less likely to stonewall and are more likely to lower internal arousal with soothing thoughts.

- Are your thoughts during conflict situations stress maintaining or relationship enhancing? Have you ever attempted to control your internal arousal level by controlling your thoughts?

The Distance and Isolation Cascade

When the four horsemen set up permanent residence in a marriage and stonewalling, flooding, and withdrawal become habitual patterns for dealing with marital conflict, then the marriage begins to slide down what Gottman refers to as the distance and isolation cascade. This is characterized by frequent flooding, followed by distancing and then a shift in how partners' think, perceive, and feel about each other and the marriage. Gottman (1994) noted the following patterns regarding this cascade:

1. The four horsemen, especially contempt, erode positive feelings so that partners no longer feel a sense of respect and admiration for each other.
2. The partners begin to perceive their problems as severe and unsolvable.
3. The partners come to believe their problems are impossible to fix; thus, there is no reason to talk about them. More talk would be useless.
4. The partners begin to live separate lives. Even though they still live together, interactions are ritualistic–involve safe topics that help the couple maintain the household and keep up the appearance of being married.
5. All of these changes are accompanied by feelings of loneliness. The partners still live in the same house, but they are emotionally isolated. Gottman notes that there is a sad irony to these marriages–this isolation and loneliness exist in a relationship that is supposed to offer intimacy, support, love, and comfort.

As this distancing and isolation occur, some couples seek professional help. However, often when they talk about their marriage, they are so emotionally disengaged that their problems do not seem severe. Gottman (1999) describes how these partners talk unemotionally about how they have adjusted to their situation, how they no longer argue, and how things are better than they once were. In these marriages, there is an underlying tension and sadness that does not get directly expressed and a noticeable lack of positive affect in the relationship. These partners no longer seem to share a friendship and there is little effort to soothe each other's hurts. It is not uncommon for one or both partners, experiencing the loneliness of this kind of marriage, to seek affection and closeness by having an affair. Gottman and Silver (1999) believe that affairs are not the root cause of divorce but rather a sign that something is wrong in the marriage. When the four horsemen have invaded the marriage and distance and isolation have taken a permanent seat at the table, one or both partners may attempt to find friendship, intimacy, and support elsewhere.

Other Characteristics of the Cognitive Landscape

As the four horsemen and the distance and isolation cascade begin to characterize a couple's relationship, Gottman (1994, 1999) found some other ways of thinking to be common. As these couples think about their marital history, they change the way they remember and interpret past events. That chance meeting, which in the past was thought of as such a blessing because it brought them together, now is construed as a terrible mistake, an unlucky misfortune filled with regret. Now as they look over their past life together, they rewrite history. They remember the little things that went wrong rather than the big things that went right. The little irritants now become magnified and take on a special significance. The former happy times are de-emphasized, forgotten, or construed in a negative way. This negative recasting of one's past is another important warning sign that the marriage is in trouble. When the four horsemen have taken up residence in the marriage and negativity has overwhelmed positivity, memories of past events are recalled differently; now that which was positive is construed negatively and the memory of good times begins to fade.

As the researchers further explored changes in thinking, they also noted other characteristics. Couples who later divorced saw their early days together as chaotic and out of control. When explaining why they married, they now seldom mentioned their love for each other; instead, they mentioned external circumstances such as needing to leave home or financial difficulties as the reason for the marriage. Also, couples who later divorced did not look back on their difficulties together and take pride in overcoming hard times; nor did they gain strength from their struggles. Rather, hard times brought back memories of disillusionment and an inability to cope.

- If you are in a troubled relationship or have been in such a relationship, have you experienced the distance and isolation cascade and the other cognitive changes noted above?

Failed Repair Attempts

As a marriage experiences the four horsemen and becomes more troubled, why doesn't one or both partners make an attempt to right the ship?

Actually, Gottman (1999) and his research team recorded many such attempts. You may recall from Chapter 6 that he called these attempts repair attempts. They include any communication or action meant to de-escalate the negativity in the interaction or relationship. It can be something as subtle as a smile, a laugh, or a facial expression that breaks the tension. Or it can be something as overt as "I'm sorry, can we start over" or "Let's take a break, I'm too overwhelmed by this right now." As Gottman's research team watched couples discuss difficult issues in their relationships, they observed many repair attempts. Some couples are experts at repairing negativity, while others try but have little success. This is a significant difference between relationships that thrive and those that fail.

Do happy, stable couples make more repair attempts? Actually, it is the opposite. The researchers observed many more repair attempts made by troubled couples. As the four horsemen take up residence in the marriage, repair attempts increase. But the irony is that as things get more negative and partners become more defensive and contemptuous, the repair attempts either are not heard or they cannot break through the negativity and tension. Gottman (1999) and his team have found that divorce can be predicted by watching a short problem discussion to see if repair attempts succeed or fail. When repair attempts work, the couple can get back on track; when they don't work, things continue to spin out of control. You will recall from Chapter 6 that the success of repair attempts could not be predicted by how they were phrased or from observing anything in the conflict interaction. The success of repair attempts was determined by what the partners brought to the interaction. If they brought friendship, admiration, and respect to the interaction, repair attempts were successful. If they lacked these ingredients and brought an abundance of negativity to the interaction, repair attempts failed.

How does a marriage that held such promise come to experience such misery? It is usually a gradual process, one horseman leading to another until the home is more like a battlefield than a place of rest. But perhaps the couple simply had their expectations too high and initially viewed each other through rose-colored glasses. If they would just lower expectations and become more realistic, might things improve? This is the approach that Lucy takes in the Peanuts comic strip when she tells Charley Brown that she has found the secret of life—you just hang around until you get used to it. And most of us do lower our expectations somewhere along the way and get used to things the way they are instead of how we want them to be. But is this good for a marriage? If partners lowered their expectations and accepted higher levels of negativity in their marriage, would they be happier in the long run? Gottman's research (Gottman & Silver, 1999; Gottman, 1999) and that of others (Baucom, Epstein, Rankin, & Burnett, 1996) have not supported this point of view. Instead, partners who continue to have high expectations have the best marriages. What Gottman noted was that in happy marriages, usually wives are sensitive to levels of negativity. This sensitivity is like an early warning system set to detect the first signs of trouble. If couples accept this negativity, adapt to it, and do nothing until it escalates, they are making a mistake. When wives intervened gently and refused to allow the first three horsemen to become pervasive in the marriage, these marriages were more likely to be happy, stable marriages years later. Gottman suggests that every marriage should have an early warning detector and that couples should be trained in how to deal with the first signs of trouble, rather than waiting until the marital house is on fire to seek help.

- Have you been aware of repair attempts in your relationship? If so, what kinds of repair attempts do you and your partner use? Who is most likely to submit these attempts? How successful have these attempts been? Do you have an early warning system in place to call attention to problems before they escalate?

UNCOUPLING: ANOTHER VIEW OF WHAT GOES WRONG

If you have experienced a failed relationship, you may look back and wonder what went wrong. When did the unraveling begin? Were there signs that you should have noticed? Was your spouse practically out of the relationship before you realized there was a serious problem? Diane Vaughan (1987) has attempted to answer these and other questions concerning how partners transition out of intimate relationships. She interviewed 103 individuals whose relationships had failed and thus, each had gone through the process of uncoupling. Her objective was to explore how uncoupling unfolded over time rather than explain why the relationship failed, for even the partners were seldom sure about why. She studied what she referred to as uncoupling in a variety of groups: partners who had been married, partners who had just lived together, and partners who were gay or lesbian. Vaughan has reported her findings in the book, *Uncoupling: How Relationships Come Apart.*

As Vaughan analyzed the taped interviews, she noted a pattern in the process of uncoupling. Both partners go through the same stages but at different times. Usually one partner becomes dissatisfied, while the other partner does not yet define the relationship as troubled. Thus, the uncoupling transition usually begins for one partner before the other senses that something is wrong. This difference in perception may last for some time. When the naive partner realizes that something is amiss, the dissatisfied partner has already left the relationship in some significant ways. It is not until later that the naive partner begins the uncoupling transition. Thus, Vaughan labels one partner the initiator–the one sensing dissatisfaction; the other is referred to as the rejected partner–the one not realizing something is amiss. It is not always easy to ascertain which partner plays which role. This is especially true if the partners stay in a relationship long after both perceive it as troubled. In these cases, the roles of initiator and rejected may be passed around as both partner's struggle with the dilemmas posed by their troubled relationship.

Viewing the Marriage from Different Perspectives

The Viewpoint of the Initiator

Vaughan (1987) began by asking those interviewed to talk about their relationship, beginning with the first hint that something was wrong. As she studied the taped interviews, she began piecing together the chronological order of events. Uncoupling begins with a secret on the part of the initiator–a secret thought or a secret feeling that something about the relationship is not comfortable. This thought or feeling may be fleeting at first, but eventually it returns to disturb the initiator's peace of mind. Perhaps a specific situation or behavioral exchange brought on the discomforting thought and it lingers in the mind as unfinished business. The initiator occasionally revisits these thoughts, while at other times pushes them aside. Then another experience or exchange may again reinforce the negativity, perhaps followed by a positive experience that eases the mind. These negative thoughts create a breach between the initiator and partner–a breach the partner can do nothing about since the initiator's thoughts remain private.

At some point, the initiator decides to communicate this inner discontent and unhappiness. While this communication is important, it is usually difficult to verbalize directly. It is important because negotiation cannot begin until each partner knows that a problem exists. It is difficult because the initiator's thoughts may still be vague, hard to understand, and even harder to put into words. The initiator, being fearful and uncertain and perhaps not wanting to hurt the partner, finds direct verbal expression difficult. Therefore, it is easier to use indirect methods of expression. Rather than saying, "Look I'm unhappy in this marriage and this is why," dissatisfaction is expressed with a complaint, a criticism, a contemptuous glance, long hours of work at the office, an absence of caressing, a forgotten birthday, or in numerous other ways as life goes on. If arguments and disagreements occasionally ensue, they are in the context of everyday life, allowing the partner to interpret them as normal problems that all couples experience in a hectic world. And at this time, even the initiator may not know how serious the problems are.

Even if the initial effort at communicating unhappiness is feeble, the purpose is to make things better. At this point, the initiator's motive is to reshape the relationship, to bring it more in line with what is envisioned as ideal. In this process, the initiator often comes across as wanting to change something about the partner; perhaps it is weight, drinking habits, friends, work habits, laziness, or an argumentative nature. If initiators are unsuccessful at bringing about these changes, they may decide to change some basic assumptions, understandings, and rules on which the relationship is based. The initiator can do this without informing the partner since these assumptions are often hidden and rarely discussed. For example, the initiator may decide that if the partner is not going to live up to expectations, it is acceptable to have an affair, alter ones views regarding commitment, or change beliefs about divorce. The rejected partner, still believing that assumptions and rules are shared, is startled when later the initiator's behavior violates what is perceived to be a shared rule. When the initiator attempts to improve the relationship but fails, the initiator must live with things as they are or invest time and energy outside the relationship.

Not everyone who chooses to invest time and energy elsewhere will eventually uncouple, but most, if not all uncoupling couples, begin to redefine their relationship. Marriage is no longer a place where they find validation; thus, they seek validation elsewhere. There are many alternatives–increasing work load, going back to school, going back to work, having a child, focusing more attention on children, joining a book club, making new friends, having an affair, jogging, volunteering, and whatever else works. What makes this somewhat confusing is that having a strong separate identity, apart from the couple's marital identity, can be healthy; each partner needs a strong individual identity while still cherishing each other and their marital identity. For the uncoupling partner, the development of this separate identity is a reaction to some dissatisfaction in the marriage; there are now fewer positive feelings for the partner and a greater desire to find satisfaction and validation elsewhere.

As nothing gets settled in the marriage, the initiator experiences more discontent. This discontent now becomes more noticeable to the initiator and to others. The initiator's complaints and criticisms continue, but now the purpose is not to improve the marriage but to convince both the initiator and the rejected partner that the marriage is troubled and possibly beyond saving. Some initiators lose all hope and stop complaining, exhibiting discontent by withdrawing or becoming non-communicative, sullen, or angry. For the first time, the initiator expresses discontent to another person, usually someone who is likely to be understanding and supportive. There may even be a special confidant who gets in-depth accounts of the initiator's relationship problems. This transitional person often listens, supports, and even instructs the initiator through the breakup. It is not uncommon for this person to have had relationship problems similar to those of the initiator; this similarity makes it more likely that these interactions will reinforce the breakup.

Going public to a selected audience also allows the initiator to mourn. This mourning recognizes the initiator's loss. Initially, there were such high hopes and now a once-prized relationship has soured. Even the thought of leaving at this point can be filled with grief. No one enjoys loss, but loss becomes more acceptable when the initiator focuses on the negative characteristics of the partner and the relationship. And at this point, leaving the relationship does not feel as much like loss as it does freedom. So the initiator begins the process of reconstructing history. Events that had previously been remembered as happy are now construed as unhappy. The initiator wonders how the partner's selfishness, ill temper, laziness, and irresponsibility could have been ignored for so long. And the partner's failings cannot be construed as just minor digressions; they must be viewed as major flaws; the rejected partner must look like an unsuitable partner. Vaughan (1987) notes: "There is a necessity to dislike, to find the partner's failings unbearable. In the long run, it seems we really cannot leave someone we like" (p. 55).

As these changes are occurring, the initiator explores what life might be like after the breakup. It is common for initiators to read about and talk to others who have made a similar transition. This gathering of information reinforces the belief—if others have done it, so can I. Mentally, the initiator now develops a different mindset—one that excludes the partner. It is a mindset that shifts from "we" to "I". This change in thinking has taken place gradually and seems to involve the following progression: we have so much in common; we have discovered our differences; we don't seem right together; I am no longer happy; I can make it on my own; I can't wait to be free.

Yet even at this point in the transition, the initiator may experience uncertainty. The initiator is still living at home with a partner who does not know that a breakup is on the horizon. Even though the home environment is unpleasant, the initiator minimizes the unpleasantness by withdrawal. Anything to avoid interaction will do: watching television, bringing work home from the office, spending extra time with the children, avoiding lovemaking, jogging, or reading. For both the initiator and the partner, these changes are not abrupt; they have been gradual, taking place over time. Yet often, initiators come to feel separate while at home, like they are outsiders in their own homes. Now long-term plans that include the partner are made with hesitancy and family get-togethers are a source of pain. The initiator spends time in two worlds: the aversive world of home and the world that is separate from the marriage—a world where dreams still have a possibility of coming true.

The Rejected Partner

The rejected partner in this dance is aware without being aware. Just as the initiator has kept secrets, the partner also sees and hears but chooses to deny. Just as the initiator has difficulty clearly communicating the nature and degree of his or her discontent, the partner has equal difficulty receiving such bad news. Because the partner is still committed to the marriage, s/he selectively processes those experiences that reinforce the marriage commitment. In this way, a partner is able to keep the mental picture of an intact marriage and avoid thoughts of a breakup. This allows the partner to sidestep serious problems instead of taking steps to work through difficult relationship issues.

There are several ways that partners deal with the mixed messages of the initiator. Often, the negative signs are defined as normal for couples in long-term relationships. After all, no one has a perfect partnership. Then another way partners delude themselves is to say that the present situation is temporary and will pass; the initiator is just troubled by something at work or with friends. Other partners attribute the negativity of initiators to some mental or physical problem such as depression. The partner hopes that this temporary problem will ease and things will get better. So the cover-up is a collaborative effort. The initiator at this point does not want all out warfare nor does s/he want to embarrass and cause great harm to the partner. The partner goes along since hearing and seeing bad news would be upsetting to the routine of the family and to personal well-being.

The Cover-Up Unravels

At some point, the cover-up becomes unbearable for the initiator. The breakdown of this cover-up takes one of two forms—direct or indirect. Some initiators directly confront their partner by laying the cards on the table. This is usually difficult and comes after much thought concerning what to say and do. But the initiator now knows that the relationship stands in direct opposition to who s/he is and wants to become. Other initiators use indirect methods. These methods shift the blame to the partner, putting the responsibility for saving the relationship directly on the partner. One indirect method begins with increased displays of discontent by the initiator. These displays become so visible that they cannot be ignored. The partner then confronts the initiator and the relationship is labeled as troubled. However, in the

process, the partner makes what the initiator labels a fatal mistake. Perhaps
·the partner sobs uncontrollably, lashes out in anger, refuses sexual advances,
destroys furniture, or demands an apology. The initiator may now use any or
all of these as evidence that the partner is flawed. Or it may be a characteristic of the partner's personality that is now the flaw. Perhaps in heated discussion the partner becomes hysterical, something that has in the past characterized the partner's behavior. The initiator can now point to the behavior
and say, "See you are doing it again." Another indirect method involves a
serious violation of the rules by the initiator. This is such a breach of trust that
it cannot be ignored. Perhaps the partner finds out that the initiator is having
an affair because the initiator carelessly leaves a love note where it can be
found. So the confrontation begins. Whether its beginnings involve direct or
indirect confrontation, the period that follows is usually difficult.

To Try or Not to Try

After the confrontation, it is usually the rejected partner who believes that
trying to save the relationship has merit. The initiator has contemplated life
outside the marriage, learned about what a separate life would be like, and
in many ways has already transitioned out of the relationship. Partners who
have been left behind are just now beginning the process. Initiators feel that
they have already tried; they unsuccessfully attempted to communicate their
discontent months before and now they have moved on. The partner,
unaware that the initiator has mentally transitioned out of the relationship,
believes that with effort the relationship can be saved. The partners are clearly at two different points in the transition. One partner focuses on the positive aspects of the relationship and why it should be saved, while the other
sees the negative and why it is hopeless. Yet the rejected partner may convince the initiator to try or at least make a feeble effort–for the sake of the
children, for the sake of our religious beliefs, for the sake of all the things we
have together as a couple. And the rejected partner attempts to make
changes in the relationship, but old habits are difficult to modify and changes
often seem superficial to the initiator. Vaughan believes that some couples
save their relationship at this point, but that most couples are unable to do
so.

Why do attempts to save these marriages so often fail? There are several
reasons. The initiator is much further along in the process of separation. For
the initiator the marriage may not be worth saving and life on the outside
seems much more attractive. This attitude creates a power imbalance. The
initiator has mentally entered another, more enticing social world. The partner has no substitute social world to fall back on and is left attempting to save

the only social world s/he is familiar with–the marriage. As the rejected partner tries to change for the sake of the initiator, s/he may withdraw from previously enjoyed activities and relationships to invest more time and energy in the relationship. Consequently, with no life outside the relationship, the rejected partner may become even more unacceptable to the initiator. And now the rejected partner has even fewer outside resources to use to reconstruct a new life. Then too, trying to save the relationship takes time and energy and even with effort, old habits often reemerge. These old habits give support to the initiator's belief that things will never change–the relationship cannot be saved.

Sometimes the initiator attempts to try only as a way of proving to the partner that the relationship is unsalvageable. This pseudoeffort may even involve counseling. But this counseling has different goals: the partner is attempting to save the marriage, while the initiator is attempting to prove the marriage is unworkable. Consulting with a counselor may also label the marriage as officially troubled so that the partner can no longer deny the seriousness of their problems. Either the initiator or the partner may even suggest that they separate for a time as a way of mending the relationship. This strategy works well for the initiator who wants out but usually backfires for the partner who still wants to save the marriage.

The Partner Catches Up

As the partner begins to contemplate the end of the marriage, s/he must begin redefining the relationship. Although the good times are not completely forgotten, there is now more emphasis on the difficult times. The partner now wonders how s/he could have been so blind. In order to uncouple, the partner must do what the initiator has already done–define the relationship and the initiator in a negative light. As this happens, it is now the rejected partner's time to mourn the loss of the relationship. This can be a slow process with periods of mourning intermingled with strong longings for the restoration of the relationship. But in the end, the partner must redefine the relationship and the initiator. For just as the initiator cannot separate from someone s/he likes, neither can the partner. Along with this redefinition must come a redefinition of the self; the partner is now struggling to make it in a different world.

- If you have been through the breakup of a relationship, relate your experience to Vaughan's findings. Were you the initiator or the rejected partner? How hard did you and your partner work to save the relationship?

THE DEVELOPMENT OF MARITAL DISAFFECTION

Karen Kayser (1993) is another researcher who has interviewed partners about the process of marital disaffection. She studied the responses of forty-nine spouses who discussed their thoughts, feelings, and behavior as their love turned to disaffection. Kayser (1993) defines marital disaffection as "the gradual loss of an emotional attachment, including a decline in caring about the partner, an emotional estrangement, and an increasing sense of apathy and indifference toward one's spouse" (p. 6). Marital disaffection did not necessarily lead to divorce. Some disaffected spouses stayed together for various reasons, such as the sake of the children or religious beliefs, yet for all participants in this study, love had died and disaffection prevailed. Although some participants later divorced, they were all interviewed prior to becoming legally divorced. Seventy-one percent of the participants were female, 21 percent were male, and none of the forty-nine participants were married to each other. The average age of participants was thirty-seven, with a range from twenty-one to sixty-eight years; the average length of marriage was thirteen years, with a range from two to thirty-nine years.

Kayser began her study by attempting to answer certain questions. Are there stages in the process of disaffection? If so, what are the thoughts, feelings, and behaviors that characterize these stages? Are there warning signs that go along with the process of change? To answer these questions, Kayser used a semistructured interview to learn about the changes in thoughts, feelings, and behaviors that occurred throughout the disaffection process. The participants' responses helped Kayser define a three-phase process of marital disaffection.

The Three-Phase Process

Phase I: The Phase of Disappointment

For some participants, disappointment occurred early in the marriage. Doubts began to appear in the first six months for 40 percent of those interviewed. Another 20 percent had doubts before the end of the first year. Participants were asked whether there were turning points or specific events that preceded a change in their feelings, thoughts, or behaviors toward their partner. Many such events were mentioned, with three being the most common: the partner's controlling behavior, the partner's lack of responsibility, and the partner's lack of emotional support.

Anger, hurt, and disillusionment accompanied these turning points. These feelings related to unfulfilled dreams concerning the marriage–a spouse had not lived up to certain expectations. The disaffected spouse often talked of how his or her partner had changed. For example, a partner's desire to have fun is now seen as childishness or their bubbly personality is seen as extreme emotionality. Several factors may contribute to this change in perception. Romantic love during courtship makes it more likely that an individual will perceive the positive characteristics of a partner and to interpret negative characteristics in a positive or neutral way. Then too, during courtship, partners tend to be on their best behavior, so there may be less negative input to interpret. But as the routine of marriage sets in and romance fades, negative characteristics are more difficult to hide; thus, a more realistic perception develops.

During this initial disappointment phase, there were things the disaffected spouse did to assess and address the problems. Fifty-nine percent of the respondents blamed themselves for what was wrong in the marriage. This self-blame led to attempts by the disaffected partners to please their spouses, to take responsibility for the relationship, and to fix it by changing something about themselves. This response was much more typical of women than men and is consistent with other findings that have portrayed women as the guardian and caretakers of relationships. A drawback to the "I'll please my partner role" is that problems are seldom due to only one spouse. Yet the pleasing spouse establishes a pattern that suggests s/he will take responsibility for what is wrong. Twenty percent of participants reported that they were passive in this early phase. They did not complain to their partners about their initial disaffection, but rather withdrew. Men were more likely to choose this method, averting their attention away from any self-blame or self-responsibility and avoiding discussion of their discontent.

Was the non-disaffected partner aware there was a problem in the marriage? Although this partner was not interviewed, the perception of the disaffected spouse was interesting. Sixty-nine percent of the disaffected partners indicated that their non-disaffected spouse denied the existence of a problem and made no attempt to change. When the non-disaffected partner did notice a problem, it frequently came after a serious argument. At these times, the non-disaffected partner might behave in an appeasing and contrite way. However, these changes were usually not lasting, although in this early phase, they did provide a small measure of hope for the disaffected spouse. According to Kayser (1993), "what was missing from these pleasing attempts by the partner was the sense of real listening to the spouse" (p. 41). Unable to get their partners to listen and take them seriously, disaffected spouses often used silence and denial to cope with their discontent. Also some used self-destructive methods of coping, such as eating, sleeping, shopping, working, or drinking to excess. However, the disaffected spouse did not usually seek professional help for the marriage during this initial phase; if anyone was told of the disaffection, it was usually a close friend or family member. During this initial phase, most discontented spouses were still hopeful about their marriages and reported positive feelings for their partners.

Phase II: Between Disappointment and Disaffection

As time passed and things did not get better, the disaffected spouses reported less disillusionment and disappointment; now they were more likely to experience hurt and anger. During this phase, they expected irritating behavior from their partners and as it occurred, their hurt and anger increased in intensity. The hurt seemed to be related to repeated occurrences of harmful behavior by their partner and often this behavior was seen as intentional. In the earlier stage, this harmful behavior could be passed off as an occasional mishap; now its frequency could not be overlooked. During this middle phase, 70 percent of the disaffected spouses now attributed their partner's irritating behavior to a flaw in the partner's personality.

During this middle phase, 60 percent of disaffected spouses now weighed the rewards of the marriage against the cost. As rewards went down and costs went up, more disaffected spouses began to think seriously about leaving the relationship. In this phase, about 30 percent of the disaffected spouses were planning to leave the marriage and had thought of taking some specific action to bring this about. Yet approximately 33 percent were still hoping the marriage could be saved. Now, however, more direct methods of problem solving replaced self-blame and compliance; a partner was more likely to directly confront his or her spouse about problems. Increased assertiveness was especially seen in the women who were disaffected. Often, their self-confidence increased due to new work, school, or extracurricular roles. Yet still 39 percent of disaffected spouses still engaged in some "pleasing" behaviors.

Another tactic the disaffected spouses used was physical and emotional withdrawal. Some used this as a self-protection strategy, while others hoped that it would change the marriage. About 20 percent of the disaffected spouses left the relationship for several weeks during this time or asked their partners to leave. Although about 33 percent were thinking of divorce during this phase, only about 10 percent took any action to permanently break up the marriage. Interestingly, the disaffected spouses still reported that their partners were in denial or were only offering up short-lived changes as solutions to their marital problems.

Phase III: Reaching Disaffection

The final phase of the disaffection process is characterized by hopelessness accompanied by physical and emotional distance. A sense of apathy was also reported by approximately 50 percent of the disaffected partners. While apathy increased, anger decreased during this final phase, although it did not completely subside. Kayser notes that apathy is the opposite of love. The apathetic partner has no strong positive or negative feelings toward the spouse. Twenty-five percent of the disaffected partners reported sorrow and pity for their spouse and for the lost dreams associated with the marriage. Few (8 percent) were lonely during this last phase, compared to 33 percent during the middle phase. Most had found support from understanding friends and family members.

Thoughts of divorce greatly increased for the disaffected spouses during this final phase, with 80 percent actually reporting actions to get the process underway. For the other 20 percent, there were barriers to taking action, such as problems concerning children or financial constraints. Pleasing behaviors that had been common earlier in the relationship now significantly declined with the disaffected partners no longer blaming themselves or taking responsibility for finding solutions. Since there was very little to lose, disaffected partners became more assertive. They were more likely to seek professional help during the final phase (27 percent sought help) than during the middle phase when 12 percent sought help.

Denial by the spouse of the disaffected partner also declined during the final stage. As the disaffected spouse becomes more assertive, it became difficult for the partner to ignore their marital problems. Some partners now even attempted to make changes, not realizing that it was too late. However, in some cases, disaffection was mutual with both partners happy to take leave of each other.

- If you have gone through the breakup of a relationship, relate your breakup to Kayser's findings.

THE POWER STRUGGLE: A THERAPIST'S VIEWPOINT

Another approach used to discover what goes wrong in marriage is to work with couples in therapy. After listening to struggling couples, therapists often attempt to describe and explain what they have observed. Early personality theories were developed after therapists observed individuals in therapy and it is logical that a similar approach would be used to understand behavior in marriage. One therapist, Harville Hendrix (1988, 1992), believes that every marriage is destined to become a power struggle. Romantic love will diminish; it is what happens after romantic love fades that will determine the fate of the relationship.

The Death of Romantic Love

Powerful forces based on biological drives and unconscious processes bring couples together to experience romantic love. Once this happens, Hendrix believes it is just as natural that the strong feelings of romantic love will diminish. The veil will be lifted and partners will see each other more realistically. Hendrix (1992) points out that since individuals "have chosen partners with their caretakers' failings, it is likely that the partner will fail them as well, in the same devastating ways. Each is doomed to disappoint the other" (p. 229). Partners will begin to see negative traits in their spouse that were not evident in the early days of the relationship. Some of these negative traits characterized one's parents and some are denied traits within the individual that are projected onto the spouse. As individuals come to see their partners in the same ways they perceived their parents, they behave accordingly-forcing partners to respond in ways that resemble parents. And as partners take note of the negative traits in the other, disillusionment sets in and the power struggle begins.

Stages of the Power Struggle

Hendrix (1992) believes that the stages of the power struggle resemble the stages of grief outlined by Kubler-Ross (1969) in her writings on the grief process. First, there is shock, then denial, then anger, then bargaining; then comes despair, and finally acceptance. For some couples, the shock associated with disillusionment develops soon after marriage; for others, it develops gradually over many years. Initially, individuals try to ignore their partner's negative traits, pretend they don't exist, or make excuses for them, but still the traits persist, making them difficult to ignore. As anger sets in, partners ponder how their mate could have changed so much, could be so inconsiderate, and could be the cause of so much pain. When these feelings are compared with the romantic feelings of the past, partners conclude that love has died. Blame and criticism are now leveled at one's partner in an attempt to adjust and survive. Why so much unpleasantness? Why can't couples communicate their feelings and needs in direct and honest ways without all the blame? Hendrix (1988) believes that a pleasant response was not the first imprint on the old brain. If an infant had an unmet need, screaming, crying, and unpleasantness were the responses that resulted in need satisfaction. Thus, blame and criticism are the knee-jerk responses of the old brain. Unfortunately, this old brain response that rescued us in the past does not serve us well in marriage. When partners attempt to get their needs met with increasing amounts of unpleasantness and criticism, the relationship becomes more toxic. But in time, the anger, blame, and criticism subside and the partners begin to bargain. If you do . . . then I'll do . . . is their response, hoping that such a contract will make things better. The partners may not understand that anger and criticism characterize all marriages to some degree. Nor do they understand that they have wounds from childhood that will continue to negatively impact their relationship if these wounds are not understood and worked through. Without this understanding and working-through process, a relationship cannot properly heal. After experiencing much anger and bargaining, many couples divorce. Others reach a deadened state of acceptance, perhaps even trying to be cordial for the sake of peace or for the children. Yet these couples experience an internal sadness over an unfulfilled relationship as they realize that even "their" marriage is troubled. One of the saddest aspects of these marriages is that couples do not know how to make things better and they often fear that doing anything will rock the boat and make things worse. They are stuck in their discontent. They have what Hendrix calls an unconscious marriage–a marriage without any understanding of the powerful forces that have created their problems, forces that keep them locked into cyclical patterns that lead nowhere. Only a fortunate few work their way out of this fog and create what Hendrix calls a conscious marriage–a truly satisfying relationship. So Hendrix is somewhat pessimistic, believing that all marriages will hit the wall of discontent; yet he is also optimistic, confident that with struggle and effort, couples can get beyond the power struggle and experience a better day. We will look at the characteristics of the conscious marriage in the next chapter.

CHARACTERISTICS OF STRUGGLING FAMILIES

So far, this discussion has focused on struggling marriages. Of course, families also struggle. From a systems perspective when a marital dyad is in conflict, the other members of the family are affected. And from this perspective when children have problems, the whole family, including the marital dyad, is influenced by these problems. Thus, feedback loops reverberate throughout the family and influence each family member.

Napier and Whitaker (1978) have identified several characteristics that they see in families seeking help. To some degree, these characteristics describe every family, but for families seeking help, these characteristics are usually extreme and exaggerated. The extreme nature of these characteristics may be what motivates families to seek therapy. Napier and Whitaker noted the following characteristics of troubled families

1. **Stress.** All families experience several different types of stress. There is stress brought on by events and circumstances in life that are difficult to handle–problems at work, not enough money, lack of resources and support, sickness of a family member, a terrible migraine headache. There is enough stress coming from the problems of daily living to stymie everyone at times. There is also intrapersonal stress–the internal battles we fight with ourselves as we deal with our worries and pressures. Will our child be safe today even though he must ride the bus to school? Am I doing the right thing in demanding that my son not play with the neighbor's child down the street? Am I overconcerned about my child's hyperactivity and poor performance in school? The list of worries is long, often with no clear answers in sight. Then there is interpersonal stress that involves conflict with others, usually the individuals with whom we most want to cooperate rather than fight. Some of life's greatest stressors involve family members fighting with each other–husbands with wives, parents with children, and siblings with siblings. This interpersonal stress is usually apparent in marriage and family therapy sessions. Family members come to therapy ready to do battle with each other over all kinds of issues. Although interpersonal stress is inevitable in families, struggling families seem less able to cope with it in effective ways.

2. **Polarization and Escalation.** As unresolved fighting and conflict occur, family members often become more determined to stand their ground. They will circle the wagon one more time, scream louder if necessary, and increase the intensity of their demands. So with polarization and escalation, the conflicting opinions on issues become hardened, even further apart, as the conflict picks up in intensity. Unhealthy families are less able to work out acceptable compromises–compromises that make each family member feel valued as a special person and as an important family member.

3. **Triangulation.** Troubled family members, sensing tension between a dyad pair, usually the parents, seek ways of relieving the tension by focusing on someone or some things outside the pair. This may happen in all families to some degree, but it is most pronounced and chronic in struggling families. In troubled families, there is usually too much tension for the troubled dyad pair to confront directly. Difficult issues are never addressed in healthy ways; instead, children, friends, and other things become a part of the triangle in order to relieve some of the tension.

4. **Blaming.** When there is a conflict or a problem in families, family members usually look for someone to blame. A common tendency is to play the role of victim while blaming someone else. Thus, it is a child

who is to blame or a spouse who stirs things up. Change someone else and the problem will be solved. Everyone points a finger at the other person. In reality, each family member contributes to the problem. Until this is understood, it is difficult for families to break the polarization and escalation cycle.

5. **Stasis.** The dictionary defines stasis as a stoppage of the blood in the body. Of course, when this actually happens, death ensues. However, stasis also means stuck or stagnant as in not being able to work through a problem or crisis. Families that are stuck try the same methods over and over again without success; sometimes this approach even makes problems worse. Some unhealthy families remain in stuck positions for long periods of time without resolving their issues or accepting their differences. They may never seek treatment; instead, they accept the impasse as a fact of life and tension becomes the norm. Some families remain stuck even after children are grown and have left home. Unhealthy families have trouble getting beyond their issues to a healthier place.

6. **Family-Wide Symbiosis.** In many struggling families, members lose their identity. Individuals cannot be themselves due to the overpowering nature of the family–the invisible rules that clash with individual desires and autonomy. When family members think of something they would like to do, they must first think of how this behavior would affect the family. Although taking family considerations into account can be a healthy sign, when the family becomes so powerful that individual desires must always give way to family concerns, the family has an inhibiting quality. Napier and Whitaker refer to this as a family-wide symbiosis–an attachment to family and family principles that is so strong that it blocks the development of healthy individuality. This is especially harmful to children who must give up healthy desires for adherence to the rigid demands of the family system. Although the opposite of this family-wide symbiosis–a loosely organized system with very few rules to adhere to–can also be unhealthy, it may be that more families seeking help are struggling in systems that are too emeshed.

Of course, this short list does not characterize all the ways in which unhealthy families struggle. Many of the unhealthy qualities of these families have been described in previous chapters. These qualities relate to unhealthy rules (Chapter 3), unhealthy ways of dealing with emotions (Chapter 6), deficiencies in the type of love these families provide (Chapter 7), and unhealthy ways of communicating (Chapter 8). One of the purposes for writing this book has been to help readers understand the differences between healthy and unhealthy families.

In the next chapter, we will look at the characteristics of stable marriages and healthy families and see how therapists are trying to help struggling couples and families turn bad situations around.

IMPORTANT TERMS AND CONCEPTS

validating couples   Vaughan's process of uncoupling
volatile couples   the initiator
avoidant couples   the rejected partner
5 to 1 ratio   Kayser's phase I, II, and III
hostile/engaged couples   Hendrix's power struggle
hostile/detached couples   stages of the power struggle
The Four Horsemen of the Apocalypse   polarization and escalation
flooding   triangulation
the distance and isolation cascade   stasis
repair attempts   family-wide symbiosis

SUGGESTED READING

Gottman, J. M. (1994). *Why marriages succeed or fail.* New York: Simon & Schuster.

Gottman, J. M. (1999). *The marriage clinic: A scientifically based marital therapy.* New York: W. W. Norton.

Kayser, K. (1993). *When love dies: The process of marital disaffection.* New York: The Guilford Press.

Napier, A. Y., & Whitaker, C. (1978). *The family crucible: The intense experience of family therapy.* New York: Harper & Row.

Olson, D. H., & Olson, A. (2000). *Empowering couples: Building on your strength.* Minneapolis, MN: Life Innovations, Inc.

Vaughan, D. (1987). *Uncoupling: How relationships come apart.* New York: Vintage Books.

Chapter 10

HELPING COUPLES AND FAMILIES

When troubled couples enter a marriage counselor's office, they have usually been locked in conflict for many months. In some cases, it seems that so much negativity exists in the relationship that positive change is doubtful–the four horsemen have taken over. Steadying the marital ship at this point is not easy. The partners usually realize that the good feelings they had for each other have slipped away. They are often doubtful that therapy can heal their wounds and mend their hearts. In the past, talking about their problems has not helped; it has only made things worse. Frequently, it is not only the marriage that is stressed, but it is the entire family that seems to be coming apart. Therapy may be their last hope. What would therapists want these couples and families to know and what would they need to do to right the ship? We will look at some answers to these questions in this chapter.

THE ATTITUDES THAT MAKE CHANGE POSSIBLE

When couples struggle in relationships, partners often cling to some destructive attitudes and beliefs. These attitudes are usually reflected in behaviors that further destabilize the relationship. In order to strengthen relationships, negative attitudes need to be replaced with positive attitudes. McGraw (2000) refers to the negative attitudes that need to be eliminated as "bad spirit" and the positive attitudes that need to develop as "core relationship values." First, we will look at some of the negative attitudes that McGraw believes need to be eliminated.

1. *Having a fault-finding attitude.* A fault-finding attitude usually leads to criticism that results in defensiveness and counterattack. Gottman's research, discussed in Chapter nine, underscores the destructive nature of criticism. If a spouse has a grievance, it would be much better to use soft startup in the form of a complaint rather than harsh attack in the form of criticism. McGraw even writes about the attack dog attitude that is seen in many relationships. No matter how justified you think your grievances are, criticism and attack rarely get you what you want—a more stable, loving relationship.

2. *Winning through overt control—my way is the only way.* This rigid position allows no room for compromise and negotiation. Counselors and family life educators often point out that the differences couples have are usually not about objective reality (proven facts) but rather subjective reality (opinions and beliefs). Taking a self-righteous attitude and declaring, "I'm always right," protects the righteous partner from any self-examination. When partners blame their spouse and are unwilling to look inward and see the flaws in their own thinking, problems rarely get resolved.

3. *Winning through passive aggression.* Some partners do not aggressively attack but instead passively undercut their partner's position; then when their partner fails, the passive-aggressive partner wins without having to take the blame for their partner's failure. This backhanded approach can be just as destructive to a relationship as overt control techniques.

4. *The belief that you can only discuss safe topics.* When couples accept this belief, they ignore the real issues and substitute safe, superficial topics for discussion. Thus, they argue about events of the day and the impor-

tant underlying issues are not addressed. McGraw (2000) calls this smoke and mirrors. What upsets partners the most never gets discussed and what gets discussed is never what upsets them the most. This deception is set up because one or both partners are afraid to directly confront sensitive, underlying issues in the relationship.

5. *The belief that your partner owes you one.* Some marriages deteriorate into score-keeping arrangements. "I've done this for you; it's your time to return the favor." Partners should do things for each other out of love, not out of a sense of obligation. A score-keeping attitude can quickly lead to fights about who has done what and how much value certain behaviors should be given. This attitude destroys what couples should be striving for—a cooperative relationship where they behave in supportive ways because of their love.

6. *A partner has an unquenchable need for security.* Extreme emotional neediness motivates partners to continually seek reassurance. These partners need a fix of words, attention, and love to temporarily fill them up and make them feel better. But each fill up is never enough; they are soon in need of another fix because of their low self-esteem. An insecure attitude can quickly drain positive energy from a relationship. Work to free yourself from devastating feelings of inadequacy; this will free up energy for more productive uses.

7. *Partners have settled for a comfortable staleness, not a vibrant relationship.* In many unhappy marriages, there is very little arguing and conflict. In these marriages, partners have settled for less than their dream by convincing themselves that taking risks to improve the marriage is too threatening. To change, one or both partners must be willing to move away from this safe, yet unsatisfying place. Getting what you want in life and marriage does not come automatically; it involves effort, work, and the ability to take reasonable risks.

8. *One or both partners have given up.* When couples come to therapy, it is often apparent that one partner has thrown in the towel. This partner comes to therapy only out of obligation, without any hope that the marriage can again be satisfying. Partners who hold this negative attitude will usually find that their expectations are met. Change occurs only when there is a glimmer of hope. That glimmer and that spark can possibly be rekindled to produce a flame, but when there is no optimism and hope, positive change is rarely possible.

9. *One or both partners have an unforgiving spirit.* One of the most difficult things to do is to forgive. But it is also one of the most fulfilling decisions a partner can make. If one partner harbors anger and resentment toward their spouse, this anger is usually more harmful to the unforgiving partner than to the spouse. Partners should not give another person,

even their spouse, the power to control them in this destructive way. Bonding to another person through resentment and anger is a miserable way to live. Forgive, not just for your partner's sake but also for your sake. Choose to take your life back and with it the possibility of making things better in your relationship.

- Has your marriage or relationship been negatively influenced by any of the "bad spirit" attitudes mentioned above?

McGraw (2000) points out that eliminating unhealthy attitudes is just the first step in the healing process. The next step involves developing beliefs that are conducive to building and supporting healthy relationships. McGraw believes that adopting the following personal relationship values will allow couples to move forward as they attempt to rebuild their relationships.

1. *Accept personal responsibility for your relationship.* McGraw gives voice to this by emphasizing the necessity of accepting ownership of your relationship and its problems. Others (Parrott & Parrott, 2001) also concur with this ownership principle, stressing each partner's personal responsibility for what happens in their relationship. Although partners want to blame others—usually one's spouse or children, this victim attitude must be cast aside. Ownership requires that each partner look into the mirror and see how their attitudes and behaviors contribute to the problem. Admitting ownership can be painful but is the only way partners can work together to make things better.

2. *Overcome fears of vulnerability.* Self-examination can be frightening because each partner sees how his or her attitudes and behaviors have contributed to the pain in the relationship. To see this, partners must drop their protective defenses. These protections are not easy to give up; it is often easier to accept familiar pain than to risk new learning through self-examination. Many partners simply refuse to drop their defenses; they refuse to take the risks involved in being open to self and to change. If partners can overcome their fears, then they have a chance to create a more satisfying relationship. But what risks will have to be taken and what changes will have to be made? Each approach to therapy discussed later in this chapter will address this question. Keep in mind that what these approaches advocate will not be easy. But each approach is in agreement; if you are to improve your relationship, you must be open to change.

3. *Learn acceptance.* Acceptance is essential if partners are to reconnect. All partners have their differences; it is these differences that create prob-

lems. After partners stop blaming and criticizing each other, they must learn to accept each other. An accepting, understanding attitude creates a safe environment so that partners can turn toward each other. Thus, many marital therapists have acceptance as an important element of their therapy. However, don't be misled. These therapists also believe that there are some actions such as verbal, physical, and psychological abuse that are so serious that they should not be accepted.

4. *Remember your friendship.* Marriage begins with friendship. However, too often, when partners marry, they fail to nurture their friendship. They treat strangers and friends more cordially than they treat each other. Good marriages are based on a strong friendship. If you have ignored that friendship, go back and nurture it. Focus on the positive qualities that you saw in your partner during the early days of your relationship.

5. *Act in ways that enhance your partner's well-being and self-esteem.* Is it possible for partners to support each other even though they disagree? McGraw (1998) and others believe this is possible. Later in this chapter, attention will be given to the things happily married couples do to keep their marriages on track in spite of their disagreements. If these things work for these couples, they might also work for other couples.

6. *Realize that your goal is to establish a happy, stable relationship; it is not to prove that you are right.* Marriage is not like a sporting event where someone wins and someone loses. Success in relationships occurs when good feelings prevail in the marriage and the family. If you must win the fight, then someone–your spouse or perhaps your son or daughter–must lose. Gottman (2000) discusses the concept of yielding to win. There are times in a marriage when partners must yield–accept influence from their partner–in order to have a better marriage. This does not mean that you accept all behaviors and avoid all arguments; certainly there are times you must take a stand. But remember, if your goal is have a successful relationship, you must learn that proving a point is often less important than responding in ways that enhance the relationship. Happy couples accept influence and in doing so, they put their relationship first.

7. *Partners should value their relationship so highly that they agree that turmoil will not be allowed to transcend the relationship.* In every marriage, there is some conflict. Partners find that there are issues that are unresolvable. As they confront these issues they may be tempted to give up on their relationship. Partners must agree that their disagreements will not threaten the existence of their relationship. No matter how angry partners are, they should not finish their anger off with, "I'm leaving" or "if you are so mad, why don't you just leave." Partners should agree not to put their relationship in jeopardy in this way. They should adopt the

attitude that even if they have problems, their relationship and commitment are strong enough to transcend the difficult times.

8. *Hold yourself and your relationship to a high standard.* Refuse to let your relationship get pulled down by hateful, ugly behavior and feelings. Set the bar high and in so doing, set an example for your partner to match.

• Have you made a conscious effort to bring any of these positive attitudes to your marriage?

HELPING COUPLES IMPROVE THEIR MARRIAGES

Most of the models of marital therapy are based on theories that make assumptions about what is needed to improve troubled relationships. These approaches are usually not based on research describing what healthy, stable couples do to maintain satisfying marriages. John Gottman (1999) has attempted to create such an approach. In his book, *The Marriage Clinic: A Scientifically Based Marital Therapy*, he states: "We ought to give descriptive science a chance, and what I mean by that is we have to do the hard work of description and prediction to find out how people who are doing well with particular problems manage to do the tasks competently" (p. 7). For twenty-five years, Gottman and his research team have conducted the research necessary to learn how successful couples sustain satisfying relationships; he is now using this knowledge to teach couples the skills that successful couples use to keep their marriages strong.

At one time, Gottman (1999) believed that effective intervention strategies could be devised from knowledge of the interaction patterns of troubled couples. Since the four horsemen invaded troubled relationships, he would teach couples how to resolve conflict effectively so the four horsemen would not overrun their relationships. However, he now believes that he did not discover how to help troubled couples until he studied couples interacting in healthy, successful relationships. Thus, knowing what stable couples did right was more important than knowing what unstable couples did wrong when it came to developing intervention strategies.

From the previous chapter, you will recall that there are three types of stable marriages. The validating couples listen to each other, respect each other's point of view, and are very good at compromising. The volatile couples bicker, squabble, and fight but also exhibit much love and warmth for each other. The avoidant couples avoid conflict, rarely airing all of their differences; instead, they agree to disagree. Somehow each of these successful marriage styles is able to keep the important 5 to 1 ratio of positivity to negativity in their conflict discussions. Gottman believes that understanding how these couples accomplish this is the key to understanding successful marriages. Partners who are mismatched in their basic style preferences are predisposed to greater problems because of their natural tendencies to deal with issues differently. An effective marital therapy will help these couples develop an in-between style that works–one that allows them to maintain the 5 to 1 ratio of positivity to negativity in spite of their differences. When partners are mismatched, one or both partners must make fundamental adjustments. This guarantees that there will be what Gottman calls "perpetual problems" in the relationship. When these ongoing problem issues exist, they can lead to anger, hurt, rejection, and pain and eat away at the positivity that characterizes stable marriages.

Yet this deterioration of positivity need not occur just because there are perpetual problems. Even stable couples have problems that fall into this category; these couples have just found ways to successfully manage their problems. Sixty-nine percent of the problems couples face relate to ongoing issues that never get completely resolved (Gottman & Silver, 1999). When Gottman's research team observed couples four years after their first visit to the love lab, they found that these couples were still disagreeing about the same issues, as if only a few days had passed. These healthy couples realized that ongoing problems exist in all close relationships–perpetual problems are normal and partners must make adjustments for them. Stable couples are masters at making these adjustments; unstable couples, possibly because of their mismatched styles, are unable to cope with their gridlocked issues. Thus, analyzing how stable, happy couples manage these issues may be helpful in developing strategies for helping struggling couples. Gottman's approach (1999), simply stated, is to "make this marital magic of the marriage masters clear so that therapists can teach it to other couples" (p. 104). His observation of hundreds of stable couples has led him to conclude that the magic, which characterizes these marriages, is based on seven principles. These seven principles describe stable marriages, whereas unstable marriages fall short in relation to one or more of these principles. Therefore, these seven principles make up what Gottman refers to as The Sound Marital House. Teaching couples how to incorporate these seven principles into their marriages has become the basis for his marital therapy.

THE SOUND MARITAL HOUSE

As you think about what characterizes happy marriages, attempt to visualize a house that has seven floors. The bottom floor serves as the foundation. As the house goes up, each floor is dependent upon a solid foundation and a sound structure on the preceding floor or floors. If each floor is built well, the house is structurally sound. If the foundation and bottom floors are weak, the entire structure is threatened. When couples marry and begin building their marital house, they must build a solid foundation and then add structurally sound floors. But as every homeowner knows, the structure is continually under attack. There is the threat of termites or other pests that can slowly attack the foundation, eating away the solid structure. Thus, the homeowner must be vigilant, making sure that the things that weaken the foundation are kept at bay. If these things go unchecked, the foundation is weakened, slowly leading to the destruction of the house. This can also happen to a marriage. As a couple sets up housekeeping, the four horsemen gradually invade. If these horsemen eat away at the foundation of the marriage and go unchecked, the entire marital house is soon under attack. How long does it take for the marriage house to crumble? Over 50 percent of the marriages that end in divorce do so within the first seven years. What do stable couples do to protect their marital house? Gottman answers this question in two recently published books: *The Seven Principles for Making Marriage Work*, which is written for a general audience, and *The Marriage Clinic: A Scientifically Based Marital Therapy*, written for marriage counselors and therapists. The following discussion provides an overview of Gottman's research-based approach.

According to Gottman, the Sound Marital House is made up of seven floors. Each floor provides both a description of what characterizes healthy, stable marriages and information concerning what needs to be taught to strengthen troubled marriages. Remember that this approach is based on the assumption that applying the principles that successful couples use to maintain stable relationships can be successfully taught to struggling couples who are seeking to improve their marriages. Therefore, each of the seven floors (characteristics of healthy marriages) will be presented along with the seven principles (things that need to be taught).

The First Three Floors and First Three Principles

The first three floors of the Sound Marital House are based on an essential ingredient of stable marriages—a solid friendship. Over and over, Gottman's team noted that stable marriages were based on friendship; the partners liked each other, liked to be together, and regarded each other highly. They expressed this high regard and fondness in little ways throughout their days together. This deep, abiding friendship created a prevailing positivity that was evident in the many pleasant, non-conflictual moments they spent together. But how did they express this friendship? It was expressed in three ways, with each of these ways making up the first three floors of the Sound Marital House.

Floor one, the first and most basic characteristic of stable marriages, is the continuing interest partners exhibit for each other every day. They take time to find out about the details of their partner's life. They know each other's likes and dislikes, hopes and dreams, worries and anxieties. They are aware of each other's schedules, friends, favorite music, and movies, and the many details that define who their partner is. Gottman refers to this knowing as making cognitive room for their partner by developing love maps concerning their partner's life. Psychologists use the term cognitive map to refer to the detailed information we store in memory about places and things. For example, if you have a detailed cognitive map of a city, you do not need a real map to get around in the city because the details of streets and intersections are stored in memory. Happily married couples have a lot of information about their partners in memory and they are frequently adding new details to this memory bank. Remember that this strengthens friendship and friendship is the basis for a strong marriage. Therefore, the first principle for making marriage work is for partners to continue to be interested in each other—leave a lot of cognitive room for learning about your partner's day-to-day experience.

The second floor of the Sound Marital House is made up of the fondness and admiration system. When couples marry, they admire qualities in each other—qualities that make each other special. This fondness and admiration is the glue that holds marriages together. When this glue no longer exists, the bond cementing the relationship deteriorates. The third horseman, contempt, is especially harmful to the fondness and admiration system. As contempt makes its appearance in the marriage, one partner's thoughts shift drastically, turning away from respect and admiration. This is a dangerous shift, so harmful that Gottman wishes that contempt could be banned in marriages. Contempt was almost never observed in stable, happy marriages. A good marriage has a strong fondness and admiration system that keeps contempt and the other horsemen from overrunning the marriage. When couples are struggling, a clue as to whether there is any admiration and positive feeling left in the relationship is how they view their past together. If they still have positive memories of those early days as a couple, there is hope for restoring the relationship. If those positive memories have been completely extinguished, hope fades. A couple should not assume that their initial admiration and respect for each other will last forever; they must work at nurturing admiration so that when disagreements and conflicts emerge, they have a ready reserve of positive feelings to see them through the difficult times. Therefore, nurturing the fondness and admiration system is the *second principle* upon which Gottman's marital therapy is based.

As couples continue to enhance their love maps and nurture their admiration for each other, they are strengthening their friendship and protecting their marital house from destruction. The third floor in the Sound Marital House, turning toward rather than away from each other, continues to enhance the strength of the friendship bond. As couples turn toward each other in little ways each day, they make deposits in what Gottman refers to as their Emotional Bank Account. Some specific ways couples turn toward each other and give support are illustrated by the following examples (Gottman, 1999).

- Express interest by asking questions and clarifying details.
- Exhibit understanding by making empathic responses.
- Develop the philosophy–it's us against the world: "That's awful! You have a right to be ticked off. I'll stand behind you all the way."
- Show solidarity: "We're in this together. You can count on me for help."
- Similarity of experience: "I had something like that happen to me once."
- Communicate affection: touch, hold, and caress to show caring and support.
- Be sure to listen. Letting your partner know you understand is probably better than jumping in with a solution.

Gottman believes that couples should not underestimate the importance of turning toward each other. Each day partners seek attention from their spouses, often in what may appear to be mundane situations. The little moments when a spouse listens, shows interest, asks questions, or just nods or smiles are very important because they add reserve to the couple's emotional bank account. Gottman and Silver (1999) suggest that couples have end of the day conversations about the events of their day so that they can talk about the stress they are experiencing outside the marriage. These conversations should not be aimed at offering solutions but rather their purpose should be to show understanding and support. If these conversations are handled well, they are stress reducing and help keep outside pressure from spilling over into the marriage. Thus, the third principle for strengthening marriages is for partners to continue to turn toward each other in support rather than away in boredom, disinterest, or mindlessness.

In summary, the first three floors and first three principles can be stated in the following way:

First Floor. Partners have a keen interest in each other's lives and exhibit this interest every day.

First Principle. Find out about the details of your partner's life–likes/dislikes, hopes/dreams, worries/anxieties, etc.

Second Floor. Partners continue to have a healthy fondness and admiration for each other.

Second Principle: Take time to nurture your fondness and admiration for each other.

Third Floor: Partners turn toward each other in positive ways each day rather than turning away or against.

Third Principle: Redouble your effort to turn toward each other in support.

• Has your marriage benefited from a strong foundation built around a solid friendship, a healthy fondness and admiration system, and an ability to continue turning toward each other? What ways have you found to turn toward each other each day?

The Fourth Floor and Fourth Principle

The first three floors of the marital house are vitally important. If these floors are built well, the couple continues to nurture their friendship. Often, young couples are so in love that they cannot imagine a time when positivity gives way to negativity. Yet evidence abounds that this happens in marriages. Be aware that this usually happens slowly. Knowing this and being able to recognize the invasion of anger and resentment should alert the couple to the importance of practicing the first three principles. When couples continue to make cognitive room for each other, persist in nurturing their admiration and respect, and keep turning toward each other, this gives rise to positive sentiment override–the fourth floor in the Sound Marital House. An abundance of positive sentiment override means that there is much more positive affect being expressed in the marriage than negative affect; the positive feelings and thoughts the partners have for each other far outweigh the negative and they continue to be optimistic about their relationship. Having this positive sentiment allows couples to get through difficult times because they have an abundance of good feeling in their emotional bank account. This allows some negativity to be processed in the marriage without being interpreted in a personal way and attributed to evil intent. Recent research (Gottman, 1999) has found that how wives interpret their husband's anger is crucial. In happy marriages where positive sentiment override prevails, wives recognized their husband's anger as important but did not interpret it as negative–his anger was not taken as a personal attack. In unhappy marriages where negative sentiment override prevails, wives were much more likely to interpret their husband's anger as negative and as a personal attack. In these marriages, even statements judged to be neutral are often interpreted negatively. There is so little emotional good feeling and so much resentment and anger in the bank account that a partner is hypervigilant–seeing ill intentions even when none exists. Where there is negative sentiment override, repair attempts are seldom successful. Instead, repair attempts go unheard or are ignored, allowing negativity to spiral out of control. Even when repair attempts are repeatedly submitted, they do not seem to get through. In stable marriages where positive sentiment override prevails, repair attempts are heard and serve to de-escalate conflict and negativity. This is critical because it tones down the negativity and allows the 5 to 1 ratio of positive to negative to prevail. Gottman (1999) found that in newlywed relationships, even when the four horsemen were present, if repair attempts were successful, a very high percentage (83.3 percent) of these couples had happy, stable marriages eight years later. If couples experience negative sentiment override, it is not easy for them to reset the thermostat. Just teaching these couples how to relate to each other during conflict situations is not sufficient because the problem runs deeper than just being unable to negotiate a compromise. The marital friendship has eroded. To rebuild the friendship, the first three floors of the Sound Marital House must be strengthened so that positive sentiment override again characterizes the marriage.

When positive sentiment override characterizes a marriage, Gottman has found that partners are more willing to accept influence. This means that a partner is willing to listen to his or her spouse's point of view and allow this point of view to influence decision making. Interestingly, the researchers (Gottman, 1999) found that wives were more likely to accept influence than were husbands. In heated discussions, wives were more likely to match or tone down their husband's negativity, whereas husbands were more likely to escalate the negativity by becoming critical, defensive, or contemptuous. When a husband steps up the level of negativity, it is evidence of his unwillingness to accept influence. In long-term studies of marital relationships, it was found that when husbands were willing to accept influence from their wives by sharing power and being respectful of their wives' point of view, marriages were much more likely to be stable and happy. There are several possible reasons for this finding. Accepting influence, sharing power, and being respectful leads to positive sentiment override. This creates an abundance of good feeling, which in turn influences the discussion of difficult issues. In stable marriages when wives brought up difficult issues, Gottman (1999) found that these wives were not harsh in how they started the discussion. Because of the overall positivity in the relationship, wives are able to present the issue softly, without being critical and contemptuous. This is extremely important because when wives start the discussion by being overly negative, husbands match the negativity or escalate it and soon the four horsemen emerge. Therefore, there is a reciprocal relationship between a husband's willingness to accept influence and the wife's use of a soft startup in conflict discussions. Husbands who have difficulty sharing power and accepting influence have wives who start conflict discussions harshly; husbands who are willing to accept influence have wives who start conflict discussions softly. This sets the stage for compromise. Without respect for your partner and your partner's point of view, compromise is impossible. Therefore, the fourth principle for making marriage work is for partners to accept influence from each other.

In summary, the fourth floor and fourth principle can be stated in the following way:

Fourth Floor: Partners experience positive sentiment override–an abundance of good feeling that far outweighs negativity in the marriage.

Fourth Principle: Allow yourself to be influenced by your partner since marriages where partners accept influence continue to be strong.

- Why does Gottman believe that just teaching conflict resolution skills to struggling couples may not be enough? Is your marriage characterized by positive sentiment override? Have you and your partner been able to accept influence in a satisfying way?

The Fifth Floor and Fifth Principle

If the first four floors of the couple's marital house have been built well and have weathered the storms of marriage, then positive sentiment override will reinforce the upper floors. In these marriages, couples still enjoy being together and their marital friendship is strong. They have kept the four horsemen from overrunning the marriage and contempt has been virtually excluded from their relationship. But these marriages still face problems. How do couples in these marriages make it through troubled waters while others slowly sink? Buttressed by positive sentiment override, these couples regulate the perils associated with conflict by doing three things. Each of these things makes up the fifth floor of the Sound Marital House. Happy couples (1) effectively solve solvable problems, (2) continue to dialogue and talk about perpetual problems (problems that won't go away), and (3) learn to physiologically soothe themselves and each other.

The ability to soothe oneself and one's partner was an important predictor of marital success. When Gottman and his colleagues observed newlyweds interacting, they found that in fifteen-minute conflict discussions, some couples used more positive affect (humor, engaged listening, affection, etc.) as they communicated. Remarkably, this positive affect predicted which couples would be happy and stable and which would be unhappy/unstable or even divorced six years later. Could this small difference in the amount of positive affect make such a big difference in marital outcome? It seems so. Further investigation (Gottman, 1999; Gottman et al., 1998) indicated that in happy, stable marriages, positive affect was used with precision to de-escalate conflict; it moved the couple away from increasing negativity back to a more positive state. This was observed not only in the overt interactions between the couple but also in their physiological reactions. Where this precise positive affect was used, it not only de-escalated conflict but also was related to physiological soothing. This physiological soothing was usually self-soothing, but at times, it also involved partners' soothing each other. De-escalating and soothing is critical; it keeps the couple from ratcheting up the negativity in their marriage and prevents flooding from occurring. As these researchers studied stable, happy, long-term marriages, they were amazed at how easily these couples navigated difficult waters. In difficult conflict discussions, Gottman compares them to skilled athletes or accomplished high-wire performers because they make it look so easy. They use humor, affection, good-natured teasing, expressions of appreciation, facial expressions, and other positive affect responses to de-escalate conflict and physiologically soothe their bodily responses.

But do happy, stable couples resolve all their conflicts? No! The majority of their conflicts were unsolvable–perpetual disagreements that resurface again and again. When the researchers reinterviewed couples years after the first interview, they found that they were still arguing about the same problems. These problems are rooted in basic personality differences–life style needs or important dreams that are basic to the identity of each partner. The researchers found that these couples did not need to resolve these major issues for their marriages to thrive. All marriages will have problems that cannot be resolved. When individuals choose a marriage partner, they are making a choice that will determine the life-long problems that will characterize their marriage. Gottman attempts to teach couples that these problems are inevitable, somewhat like dealing with the aches and pains of aging. These aches and pains do not go away. You must learn to deal with them, minimize their influence on your life, and find ways to be happy in spite of them. This is what the masters of marriage seem to accomplish in regard to their perpetual problems.

However, 31 percent of couples' problems are solvable. Even though these problems do not present the same hazards as the unsolvable issues, they can cause considerable pain. This is especially true if a couple does not have good problem-solving skills. Gottman (1999) believes that much of the advice given to couples about how to resolve problems is difficult to implement. For example, the active listening/validating model teaches couples to listen and show empathy by reflecting the feelings and content of their partner's message while remaining non-judgmental. This is extremely difficult, especially if you are angry or distressed while engaged in conflict. Furthermore, observations of stable, happy couples did not find that these couples frequently summarized their partner's feelings, paraphrased their statements, or empathized with their negative feelings. These couples simply did not use what is sometimes called the speaker-listener technique as a part of their conflict discussions. Therefore, Gottman's fifth principle for making marriages work–to solve solvable problems–suggests a different approach to conflict resolution; his approach is based on what healthy couples do when they confront solvable issues.

Before discussing how to solve solvable problems and how to successfully manage unsolvable problems, we will examine some suggestions that Gottman and Silver (1999) believe are relevant to both types of problems. Remember, these suggestions are an outgrowth of research concerning what characterizes stable, happy marriages.

Partners in stable, successful marriages have found a way to communicate acceptance and understanding. These partners feel that they are understood, accepted, and respected just the way they are. This is critical because of the marital paradox–partners change only when they realize that being loved and respected is not contingent on change (Gottman, 1999). They are loved and respected just the way they are. Once this matter is settled in their minds, then there is the possibility of change. But if partners feel judged or criticized and believe that they are not respected and admired as they are, change is less likely. Instead, there is an entrenchment–a digging in to protect oneself from assault. If couples want to make their marriages better in regard to either a solvable or perpetual problem, each spouse must know that he/she is accepted, loved, and understood even if no change is made. Why would a spouse be more likely to change if loved in this non-contingent way? Perhaps it is because of the strong marital friendship–a friendship based on positive sentiment override, a wealth of stored-up good feeling in the emotional bank account, and a continued fondness and admiration the partners have for each other.

Another suggestion that Gottman hopes couples understand is that marital conflicts are about different points of view. Each point of view seems right to the beholder, but neither is objective reality. The different points of view are simply differences of opinion between partners concerning subjective reality. Gottman (Gottman & Silver, 1999) has found that happily married couples, even after many years of marriage, are able to accept each other–faults, imperfections, different points of view, and all–because of a strong fondness and admiration system.

Gottman's approach makes an important distinction between solvable problems and perpetual problems. This is important because solvable problems need be solved; thus, solving solvable problems is the fifth principle that must be learned. Perpetual problems will never be totally resolved, but they need to be managed in a way that prevents negativity and gridlock in the marriage. Since dealing with these two types of problems requires different management skills, couples need to determine whether a problem is a solvable or perpetual problem.

Solvable problems are usually situation specific and are not rooted in important philosophical and personality differences between the partners. Thus, even though solvable problems may be irritants, they do not threaten the relationship unless they create excessive tension that cannot be reduced. Failure to resolve these problems is usually due to a lack of problem-solving skills. Also, a solvable problem for one couple could be a perpetual problem for another. For instance, one couple may be having trouble balancing their checkbook. It seems that neither spouse is taking responsibility for entering the checks they have written in a common register, so neither partner ever knows the balance in the account. Therefore, the account has been overdrawn several times, resulting in penalty payments that the couple cannot afford. As this couple talk, they realize it is just a matter of forgetfulness. At the end of a busy day, they do not remember to use the common register. They do not blame each other or defame each other's character for the problem, yet it is a problem that needs a solution. With some brainstorming, stable couples with good problem-solving skills usually find a way to resolve this solvable problem without too much trouble.

However, another couple with a similar difficulty may not fare so well. The husband resents writing in a common check register because doing so seems as if he is always reporting to his wife on how he spends money. Often, she has been critical of him for spending money on things he doesn't need. Since they both work and are still having trouble making ends meet, she thinks it's unfair for him to spend money carelessly; she thinks they should agree before either writes a check for more than a certain amount. They have had this argument many times and get nowhere while their penalty payments mount. This problem has been perpetual because it symbolizes deeper issues about control, power, and responsible behavior. If such problems are to be managed effectively, the couple will need to understand the deeper meaning of the conflict. Only then can this perpetual problem be managed effectively.

Even solvable problems can be difficult for some couples; they simply lack the problem-solving skills necessary to navigate their marital difficulties. Gottman (Gottman & Silver, 1999) attempts to teach these couples the skills that come naturally to the marriage masters. However, if you would ask these successful couples how they manage, they might not be aware of the secret behind their success. This is where Gottman's many hours of observation and years of research pay dividends. He has discovered what the marriage masters do when they face both solvable and perpetual problems.

When confronting solvable problems, Gottman (1999) found that there were five steps that happy, stable couples used to solve these problems. First, they brought up difficult issues in a soft rather than harsh way. Gottman discovered that problem discussions usually end the same way they begin. Harsh startups result in harsh endings. Soft startups result in more conciliatory endings. Therefore, successful couples begin their discussion softly, often by registering a complaint in a gentle, diplomatic way. Harsh startups begin with attacks, usually involving criticism and contempt. Harsh beginnings immediately open the door to the four horsemen, usually ending in flooding and stonewalling. Since husbands are more likely to flood, the husband often withdraws before any effective problem solving can take place. Harsh, critical startups in problem discussions do not usually achieve a successful resolution of problems. Gottman (1999) has found that he can predict how a problem discussion will end 96 percent of the time simply by observing the first three minutes of the discussion. Harsh startup leads to harsh endings; soft startup leads to productive discussion.

Second, successful couples hear and respond to each other's repair attempts. Unhappy couples send repair messages, but they do not get through so their discussions continue to spiral out of control. A repair attempt is a statement or action that has the possibility of toning down negativity. Usually troubled couples do not hear each other's repair attempts because the negativity in their relationship is too great. Troubled couples need to know how to make repair attempts, how to recognize repair attempts when they occur, and how to respond to these attempts in ways that tone down negativity. Thus, Gottman's treatment program for troubled couples teaches couples the second step–to make repair attempts and to respond positively to repair attempts when they are made. Frequently, repair attempts are not heard because one or both partners are flooding. When this happens, heart rate escalates to such a high level that productive problem solving is impossible. The body is both emotionally and physiologically overwhelmed; rational thinking is impaired and negative thoughts take over, making it difficult to calm down. If this happens, partners must realize that they have exceeded their limits and repair attempts will not work. Thus, couples are taught a third skill used by stable couples–to soothe themselves and each other. Gottman recommends that couples take a break of at least twenty minutes to allow the body to calm down. During the break, they are to eliminate thoughts of righteous indignation and innocent victimhood. Instead, they are instructed to do something soothing such as listening to music, controlling muscles with relaxation exercises, or utilizing visual imagery in a calming way. If possible, when you have calmed down, get back together and soothe each other. Although this can be difficult, the benefits can be great. If couples frequently argue and flood, each partner can become a trigger for negative emotions in the other. To combat this conditioning, discover what your partner finds soothing and provide this soothing so you are associated with a calming reaction rather than only negativity and tension.

The fourth step to resolving solvable problems is to compromise. Where there are resolvable differences, this is the only road to resolution. But compromise comes after the implementation of the first three steps—using soft startup, responding to repair attempts, and staying calm. These steps set a positive tone so that compromise can be successful. Yet compromise is only possible if partners are able to accept influence. Partners must listen to each other and be open-minded to the possibility of change. This requires flexibility since in compromise neither partner gets exactly what is desired. Yet compromise solutions are well worth the effort if your goal is to have a happy marriage. The masters of marriage are masters of compromise. Yet Gottman and Silver (1999) see compromise as impossible without one other ability. Thus, the fifth step in handling solvable issues is to be tolerant. Learn to accept the flaws in your partner without demanding change. If you cannot do this, you will find compromise difficult since compromise is based on acceptance and conciliation.

In summary, the fifth floor and fifth principle can be stated in the following way:

Fifth Floor: Stable couples solve their solvable problems.

Fifth Principle: Use the skills the marriage masters use to solve your solvable problems.

- Have you and your partner been able to solve your solvable problems? If so, have you done so by using the five steps that Gottman sees in stable marriages?

Gottman's program for helping troubled couples involves teaching them the skills necessary for resolving their solvable problems. However, the skills needed to solve solvable problems will not work to alleviate perpetual problems. Thus, partners must learn how to manage their perpetual issues.

The Sixth Floor and Sixth Principle

Partners must learn to live with their irresolvable issues so that these issues do not erode the foundation of the marriage. Thus, the sixth floor of The Sound Marital House is learning to live with unsolvable problems and the sixth principle is avoiding the marital gridlock that is often associated with these issues. Most problems couples experience will not go away. When confronting these problems, it is important that couples not give up; they must continue to discuss their perpetual issues. Many couples do not know how to do this without putting their marriage in jeopardy. These couples must get beyond the standoff if they are to have a satisfying relationship. The secret to doing this involves understanding the reasons behind their perpetual problems. When two people are in perpetual opposition in marriage, it is because they have important dreams that are not understood and respected by their partner. First, the partners must uncover these dreams—the dreams embedded in the conflict. These dreams relate to needs, hopes, aspirations, and core values that are a fundamental part of one's basic identity. The argument the couple has had for many years is not just about how to spend money or how neat or tidy the house should look; it is about something that goes much deeper. It is about a fundamental life position, possibly coming from one's family of origin and early childhood, which serves as the bedrock of the partner's identity. To understand the importance of the behavior associated with the entrenched conflict, Gottman helps couples reveal their hopes and dreams to each other so that they better understand what their perpetual argument is really about. Yet, just understanding is not enough. It is important that both partners' dreams are recognized and seen as important. Then the couple can work together so that both partners' dreams can be realized in the marriage. To achieve this, partners must be willing to listen to each other, understand the importance of their partner's dream, and accept influence. They must accept each other for what they are and communicate this acceptance. "If your dream is important to you, then it is important to me." Partners must be willing to yield for the sake of the marriage. What good is it to get your way in relation to the conflict if in the process you extinguish your partner's dream?

Gottman teaches couples to detect underlying dreams, to determine where these dreams come from, and why they are so important. Then they are to discuss their dreams with their partner in a non-judgmental way with one partner being the speaker and the other being the listener. According to Gottman (1999), "acknowledging and respecting each other's deepest, most personal hopes and dreams is the key to saving and enriching your marriage" (p. 234). If a couple can be accepting of their partner's dreams, these dreams are no longer seen as threats to the marriage. Rather, they are seen as needs and desires that have importance to the partner. Each partner's dreams are still different and they certainly don't see eye to eye; however, now they can respect each other's dreams and work toward having a marriage where the dreams of both are honored rather than criticized. The key to achieving this involves three steps: (1) each partner needs to define the areas concerning the conflict on which they cannot yield, (2) each partner needs to define the areas concerning the conflict on which they can be flexible, and (3) the partners need to find a temporary compromise which respects each partner's dream. Although this is not an easy process, if couples can work through these steps, it can improve their marriage. The following example utilizes the format of Gottman and Silver and is adapted from their example (1999, p.

238); it shows how this process might work for one couple experiencing a problem.

Problem: The partners are different in terms of the amount of emotional closeness and distance they each desire in their relationship. The wife needs to connect; the husband needs his space.

The dreams of each partner:

Her dream: To feel close by talking and feeling understood; to have a partner who listens without jumping in with a solution; to have a partner who will share his feelings in intimate ways.

His dream: To come home and be able to relax without having to listen and understand; to have his wife understand his point of view—that talking about feelings gets you nowhere, it's actions that count.

Nonnegotiable areas—ways s/he cannot or will not change:

Her: She cannot give up her emotional style since this is who she is as a person. Emotions and feelings are a valuable part of her experiencing.

His: He cannot automatically turn into an emotional person. This kind of talk is not natural for him.

Flexibility—ways s/he can be accepting: Each partner accepts the other and each realizes that this is a fundamental characteristic and difference that neither can totally change.

Temporary compromise: They will develop a respect for each other's styles. He will understand that at times she will need to talk and be emotionally expressive. He will try to be receptive to her needs but she will accept that there will be times when he cannot communicate in this way.

Ongoing conflict: Their different approaches to emotional expression will persist, probably throughout their marriage.

Remember that Gottman's approach is based on what happy couples do as they work through the difficult issues in marriage. He believes that teaching these skills to couples having problems will help them navigate through difficult times. Also, when couples find themselves gridlocked over perpetual issues, it may be due to a deterioration of the lower floors of The Sound Marital House. Some couples will need to go back and work on their fondness and admiration system and strengthen positive sentiment override in their marriage before their relationship is sound enough to withstand the stress of dealing with their difficult issues.

In summary, the sixth floor and sixth principle can be stated in the following way:

Sixth Floor: Stable couples help make each other's dreams come true by not becoming gridlocked concerning their perpetual issues.

Sixth Principle: Learn and use the skills the marriage masters use to keep your perpetual problems from harming your marriage.

• What are some of the perpetual problems you have experienced in your relationship? Have you been able to overcome your gridlock in relation to these problems? If so, how have you done so?

The Seventh Floor and Seventh Principle

There is more to a good marriage than just learning to live with perpetual problems. The seventh floor of the Sound Marital House completes the structure in a way that protects it from the ravages of the elements. The top floor and roof tie into the structure in such a way as to strengthen the marital friendship. When a couple marries, their togetherness creates a small culture of two. When children are born, this culture becomes more complex as the couple defines what "their" family will be like. As this new emerging culture takes shape, customs develop, rituals are created, and shared meanings emerge. Couples need to build on these shared meanings. They need to talk with each other about beliefs, values, traditions, and dreams. All of their dreams will not be shared, but if their marital house is well built, they will know about and respect their differences. If they talk openly with each other, they usually find that many of their visions blend together as they create important shared meanings. When couples learn how to carry out their shared values and goals in the activities of everyday life, they become a team. There is a "we-ness" in their relationship. This "we-ness" is exhibited when they think alike as in "we share," "we see," "we have," and "we value." Couples who have been happily married for many years often find that there is a blending, a moving together through life with a shared belief and purpose in regard to rituals, roles, goals, and symbols. This moving together or "we-ness" strengthens marital and family bonds and must not be overlooked by the couple desiring to build the Sound Marital House. Gottman and Silver (1999) believe that the more shared meanings a couple creates, the more enriched their relationship will be. When couples create this "we-ness," they have a strong marital friendship that will help them cope with conflicts that arise. Therefore, the seventh floor and seventh principle for making marriages work are to create shared meanings so that the "we-ness" in the marriage allows partners to work as a team as they go through life together.

In summary, the seventh floor and seventh principle can be stated in the following way:

Seventh Floor: Stable couples value healthy rituals, customs, common goals, etc.–their "family culture".

Seventh Principle: Create healthy rituals, customs, common goals, etc. and make these important to who you are as a couple and family.

• What are some important values and shared meanings held by members of your family? How do these shared values and meanings get reflected in the rituals and happenings of everyday life? Do you have the "we-ness" in your marriage and family that Gottman believes is important?

THE CONSCIOUS MARRIAGE AND IMAGO THERAPY

Harville Hendrix has been a leader in the marital therapy movement for many years. His insights have come from years of study and work with couples struggling to create a better marriage. Hendrix (1988) believes that couples in the stage of romantic love experience an illusion—marriage will lead to happiness, fulfillment, and eternal bliss. But as the honeymoon fades and reality sets in, happiness often slips away. This realization may come soon after the honeymoon or gradually over many years. And as happiness slips away, reality sets in—our partner does not heal our wounds. Instead s/he now opens old wounds, irritates these wounds, and leaves us wondering how we could have married such a flawed person. Characteristics that were initially seen in a positive way are now interpreted negatively. Her outgoing nature is now too invasive of his personal privacy. His quiet strength is now isolation and he ignores her need for connection. Partners fall back on old established patterns and begin the power struggle. They blame and criticize each other, hoping that their partner will morph into that ideal spouse who will satisfy their needs.

As the initial shock turns into anger and finally despair, there seems no hope for righting the ship. Hendrix (1988) believes that fewer than 5 percent of married couples work through their struggles to create a truly happy, satisfying marriage. But why do so many marriages turn into unsatisfying relationships? Hendrix believes that our partner will remind us in some way of our childhood caretakers. Choosing such a partner allows us to recreate the conditions of our childhood so that we can continue to work on issues that were unresolved in those early years. This work is not easy; it involves confronting our most dreaded fears—fears about self and about change. Hendrix (1988) notes that when he asks couples to risk new behaviors, they often become angry. "There is a part of them that would rather divorce, break up the family, and divide up all their possessions than acquire a new style of relating" (p. 100). However, for partners who undertake the struggle, fight through the despair, and persist through the hardships, there can be a deeply satisfying relationship on the other side—a relationship known as the conscious marriage.

For a couple attempting to improve their relationship, Hendrix (1992, 1988) believes that there are several things each partner must agree to as they undertake the difficult process of change through Imago therapy. They must stop using criticism and blame as a way of expressing frustration. They must also make a commitment to counseling. Specifically, they must agree to come to twelve counseling sessions to work on their problems and not separate or divorce during this time. Since difficult issues come up during the first five sessions, couples are tempted to terminate therapy or separate to avoid the pain of confrontation and change. This no escape agreement helps couples overcome their tendency to avoid the difficult process of therapy. Also, couples must agree to learn and practice new ways of behaving rather than rely on old, unproductive habits. Agreeing to these ground rules establishes the commitment necessary for couples to work on their difficult issues.

Creating a Positive Vision of Marriage

As therapy begins, Hendrix (1988) encourages a positive focus by having partners describe what they would like their relationship to become. The couple is asked to create a positive vision statement for their marriage and this statement becomes the goal for therapy. Such statements might include: we want to enjoy being together, we'd like to talk to each other more, we want to do more fun things together, and we'd like to laugh with each other again. The couple is asked to read these statements each day as a reminder of what they want their relationship to become.

The Couple's Dialogue

One of the best descriptions of what happens in Imago Therapy comes from Rick Brown's book, *Imago Relationship Therapy: An Introduction to Theory and Practice.* Brown is executive director of the Institute for Imago Relationship Therapy, a marriage therapist, and clinical trainer for the Imago Relationship Therapy process. In this book (1999), Brown discusses and illustrates the couple's dialogue–the major skill couples must learn if they are to benefit from Imago Therapy. This dialogue, which is taught to couples, allows them to safely discuss their difficult issues without escalating negativity. Since this way of communicating is not natural, couples must practice the couple dialogue process together. They initially do this in the therapist's office, but later when this dialogue becomes more natural, they can use it at other times.

The couple's dialogue involves learning and using three skills in communication: mirroring, validation, and empathy. These skills are similar to active listening taught by Markman, Stanley, and Blumberg in their PREP approach. However, the way Brown uses these in therapy is unique–he uses these skills to strengthen a positive bond between the partners so they can explore deeper issues that need to be uncovered and healed. Therefore, the goal of Imago Therapy is not simply to seek compromise but to create a safe environment where deeper issues can be uncovered, explored, understood, and worked through. A first therapy session and couple's dialogue might sound like the following interaction.

Therapist: Don (husband) perhaps you could begin by saying why you think Sarah (wife) is here. What is troubling her about the marriage?

Don: Well, I believe that Sarah is dissatisfied because she thinks I spend too much time on the computer and not enough time with her. When I come home, I still have work to do and sometimes it takes me several hours to finish up.

Therapist: Now, Sarah, you have heard what Don has said and you may have a reaction, but I want you to keep your reaction on hold and just try to mirror back what Don has said without stating your opinion at this point.

Sarah: Well, okay. Don thinks I'm unhappy because he spends a lot of time on the computer and not enough time with me.

Therapist: Sarah, ask Don if there is more. (Sarah is prompted to ask this until Don says there is no more.)

Sarah: (after she has been prompted) Don do you think there is more? Are there others reasons why I'm here?

Don: Well, yes. You seem to think that because I don't call you from the office like I used to that I don't love you anymore. And when I want to do things with my buddies, it bothers you. It seems you want more closeness than I have to offer.

Sarah: (mirroring and summarizing) You think I want you to call me like you used to and pay more attention to me than to your buddies. Somehow you think I want more closeness in the marriage than you have to offer. Without the calls and the closeness, you believe I question whether you actually love me.

Therapist: Sarah, you have heard what Don has said and have mirrored it. How accurate is it on a scale from 1-10. At this point Sarah may say it is right on—a 10 or she may say that there is much more. If there is more, she is to communicate this to Don and Don is to mirror it back to Sarah until she is able to say "that's about it—a 10, he's finally gotten it!

Mirroring is a process where the listener must concentrate on the communication of the speaker and cast aside his or her personal judgment and opinion. At this point, the listener does not have to like what s/he has heard or to understand it, just reflect it back to the speaker. This is a skill that does not come easily; it must be cultivated over time. A more natural response would be to defend oneself or be critical. Later in the process, validation becomes a part of the couple's dialogue. The therapist might prompt by saying, "you've heard what Sarah has said, does it make sense to you? Does it seem logical for her to think that way"? At some point, Don may say, "Well, yes, after I've heard what she has said, it does makes sense that she should feel that way." At this point, Don may not like what his wife has said, but he validates it as something that is not crazy or stupid but rather makes sense to him. The next step is for the listening partner to move into empathy. Empathy involves feeling as the speaker feels–literally participating in the partner's feelings. Don might say, "I would suspect that when I come home and immediately go to the computer, you feel left out, lonely, and ignored. I imagine that's hurtful to you!" At that point, Sarah might respond, "Yes, it's very hurtful. It seems that you purposefully ignore me." Don has been able to stretch into feeling the way his wife feels and their empathic connection has been strengthened. As the exchange involving mirroring, validation, and empathy goes back and forth from partner to partner, the couple's dialogue takes shape. The therapist's role is to help this process along by setting limits, coaching, modeling, experiencing validation and empathy, making sure that both partners are engaged in the process, and sometimes using sentence stems that prompt responding, such as "And when he does that, that makes you feel. . . ."

Seeing the Wounded Child Using the Parent-Child Dialogue

One goal of Imago Therapy is to help partners perceive each other differently. When coming to therapy, one partner may perceive the other as a nag or as uncaring. The partners are angry and frustrated with each other for not meeting their needs in a way they had envisioned. Brown believes that the partners' anger and frustration are defenses against hurt. If the therapist can create a safe environment by using the couple's dialogue, then the therapist can help the couple get to the hurt underlying the anger and frustration. Since partners have been wounded in childhood, the hurt goes back to childhood. This hurt can be accessed through the couple's dialogue and the parent-child dialogue. A therapy session with Don and Sarah might sound like this.

Don: (responding empathically) I guess you (Sarah) really feel hurt when I come home and go to the computer and then when I go fishing with my buddies, that even makes matters worse.

Sarah: Yes, I've cried about it until I can hardly cry any more. It's just a big sore spot that won't go away.

Therapist: (using a sentence stem) And when you feel that hurt, you are reminded of ...

Sarah: What it was like for me as a child. Daddy would come home and go straight to his office. He never paid any attention to mother or me. I wanted him to hold me and love me, but he never did. It was as if he wished I had never been born.

Therapist: (who now suggests the parent-child dialogue) Don, let me suggest that you play the role of Sarah's father and Sarah you be yourself as a child. So Don speaks as Sarah's father and say to little Sarah—What would you like to say to me? What would you like to tell me that you never could before?

Don: (talking as Sarah's father) Sarah, I am your father. What would you like to say to me?

Sarah: (as a little child talking to her father) Why don't you love me. I need your love so much, but you turn away as if I don't exist. And then when you left (Sarah speaking as little Sarah starts to cry), it was as if you disowned me because I never saw you again.

Therapist: (talking to Don as Sarah's father) Ask Sarah what she needs from you.

Don: (talking as Sarah's father) Sarah, what do you need from me?

Sarah: (responding as little Sarah) I need you to hold me and love me. To show me some attention and let me know that you are proud of me.

Don: (speaking as Sarah's father is prompted by the therapist to say) What is your deepest hurt from me?

Sarah: (speaking as little Sarah responds) My deepest hurt from you is. . . .

Don: (speaking as Sarah's father is prompted by the therapist to respond) What you need most from me is. . . .

Sarah: (speaking as little Sarah responds) What I need most from you is. . . .

Don: (speaking as Sarah's father mirrors, validates, and expresses empathy) What you need most from me, as a father is . . . that makes sense. You feel hurt because I neglect you so. If I would love you and be there for you that would make you feel safe.

As partners respond in this way with each other, they strengthen their empathic bond around an important childhood wound. The Imago therapist believes that the unconscious is desperately trying to heal this childhood wound. Using the couple's dialogue and the parent-child dialogue, the therapist helps the partners see each other differently. Don may now see Sarah as a person who has been deeply wounded in childhood and his anger and frustration turn to softer emotions such as concern and caring. And Sarah's frustration with Don turns to hope as Don responds with empathy and tenderness.

De-roling and the Behavior Change Request

After Sarah's expression of childhood pain, Don and Sarah are prompted by the therapist to de-role–to come back to the present as Don and Sarah. Then Don might be prompted to respond to Sarah in the following way.

Don: (prompted by the therapist says) Sarah I'm here for you; what do you need from me that will heal the hurt?

Sarah: I need you to pay some attention to me, to greet me as if you are glad to see me, and to talk to me not because you have to but because you want to.

The therapist now guides the couple through the behavior change request process. The partner's must help each other complete the business of childhood by healing each other's childhood wounds. Beneath the anger and frustration in a marriage, there are wounds or sore spots that need healing and a partner is the person who can best facilitate this healing. Hendrix (1988) believes that the criticisms leveled at a partner provide clues for what the criticizing spouse needs in order to heal. Comments like, "you never pay any attention to me" or "I hate it when you yell and scream at me" provide such clues. An Imago therapist might facilitate the healing process in the following way with Don and Sarah.

Therapist: (to Sarah) Don has said he's here for you. Let's take him at his word. Sarah could you tell him what he could do in the coming week that would help you heal.

Sarah: (to Don) This week you could embrace me when you get home and we could talk for a little while about our day before you go off to the computer.

Brown (1999) suggests that a partner's request should be positive, specific, and measurable. After a request has been given, a partner should mirror, validate, and be empathic. Don might respond by saying, "You'd like me to give you a hug and sit down and talk for a little while when I come home (mirroring). That makes sense to me that you should want that (validation). If I did that, you would feel better about our relationship and about yourself (empathy). If Don could stretch into this behavior, he would be giving Sarah a needed gift that would facilitate her healing. Also, without realizing it, Don would be engaging in a behavior that would lead to his own growth. Brown (1999) sometimes provides a sentence stem to help a partner achieve this realization. Thus, Don might be asked to complete the following statement:

Therapist: (to Don) Don could you complete this statement–If I could do these things each day when I come home, it would help me because. . . .

Don: (completing sentence stem) It would help me because I tend to get caught up in my own little world and forget about the feelings of others. I really need to work on that!

Why is it that Sarah (one partner) needs the very things that Don (the other partner) finds hardest to give? Hendrix (1988) states that he puzzled over this for some time before arriving at an answer. Imperfect caretakers wounded us in childhood. Our old brain stored memories of these caretakers and unconsciously motivated us to choose partners who would behave in the same way as those who wounded us. How can marriage help us heal when our partner exhibits the negative characteristics of our early caretakers? How can a wife who needs closeness and intimacy get what is needed from a partner who is distant and silent like her father? Since one's partner is an Imago match, the old brain unconsciously fuses this partner with our parents. It is this very person, our Imago match, who the old brain allows to simulate unfinished situations so that we can work through the impasse and find healing. But if healing is to occur, our partner must do what our parents did not do. Our partner must change and provide the nutrients needed to help us repair the damage of childhood, work through the impasse and pain, and become complete and whole. For example, a distant, quiet husband may need to become more open, intimate, and close in order to help his wife heal. While this change aids the wife in recovering from her childhood wounding, it also stretches the husband in ways that are necessary for his healing. His wife needs the things that are hard for him to give, but if he can give these things, he rediscovers aspects of his lost self that are needed for his own growth. Thus, if partners can change in needed ways, they not only help their spouse, but they also grow in their own search for wholeness.

Brown (1999) usually has one partner send three requests to his or her spouse and the spouse is to mirror these requests back to the partner. The spouse is then invited to choose and commit to at least one of these requests during the coming week. If a partner chooses to honor a request, he or she would state how this request would be honored. For example, Don might say, "During the coming week, I will embrace Sarah like I used to do when I get home from work and we will talk together about our day. I will tell her that I love her at this time like I used to do." If this goes well, Don might be encouraged to plan something that they might enjoy doing together to reintroduce fun into their relationship. Hendrix (1988) writes about how he asks partners to develop a list of specific behaviors that their spouse could engage in that would fulfill their unmet needs and help them heal. For example, there may be ten requests on the list, each beginning with the words—I would like you to. . . . Then each spouse shares his or her list with the other. As they examine their partner's list, they rank each request in order according to how difficult the request would be to fulfill. At no time are they told that they must fulfill any of these requests. The request list simply provides information about their partner's unmet childhood needs, what behaviors each spouse could engage in to meet the other's unmet needs, and a ranking concerning how easy or difficult stretching into these new behaviors would be. If they choose to stretch into any of these new behaviors, they are to do this stretching as a gift to their partner without any expectation that their spouse will reciprocate. However, they are to keep their partner's list, realizing that they have the opportunity to fulfill any or all of the requests if they wish. Hendrix (1988) found that under these conditions, many couples begin the process of stretching into new behaviors, usually beginning with those behaviors that are ranked easiest to fulfill. As couples make these changes, they begin to feel better about each other and their marriage. They are healing old wounds associated with childhood—wounds that have been reopened many time during their marriage.

This stretching process is not easy. Usually, a request that a spouse ranks most important is the hardest for a partner to fulfill. Hendrix (1988) believes that the Imago therapist should expect resistance because changing long-standing patterns of behavior is difficult. Also, sometimes when a spouse begins fulfilling a partner's requests, the partner feels undeserving. This often occurs when spouses learn that they are not worthy of respect and esteem; thus when they get what they want, they reject it. They deny the very thing they need most with comments like, "you don't really care about me" and "nobody can really love me." When this denial occurs, Hendrix (1988) suggests that couples continue to stretch into new behaviors on the behavioral request list because, "given enough time, they learn that the taboos that have been impeding their growth are ghosts of the past and have no power in their present day lives" (p. 167).

Re-romanticizing the Marriage

After partners begin stretching into new behaviors in order to help each other grow and heal, Brown (1999) often begins therapy sessions by asking couples what they have appreciated in their spouse since the last session. Since they have been working to help each other, it is often not difficult for them to find "caring behaviors" that they appreciate. Couples even come to anticipate this question and think about it before they come to the session. Sarah may say, "I really appreciated having that time together on Tuesday after you got home and the special way we talked and embraced." Don then is prompted to use the dialogue process to mirror his wife's response. Then the therapist might use a sentence stem to help Sarah elaborate—"And having that time together made you feel good because. . . ." Sarah might respond, "Because it reminded me of how we used to be and the loving ways we responded to each other right after we were married. It felt good to feel that again." Don might then be prompted to ask, "Were there other things that Sarah had appreciated since the last session"? Sarah might respond, "Well, yes, it helped me to know that you were concerned about me when I was so tired on Thursday evening. I had had such a hard day at work and it was sweet when you. . . ." As Sarah responds, she begins to tear up. The therapist then might direct a sentence stem to Sarah, "And when Don did that, it touched you because. . . ." Sarah might respond, "Because my dad never did that with my mother or me. He never showed any concern for either of us and we needed his expressions of love so much." In focusing on "caring behaviors," the therapist recreates positive energy between the partners and by using sentence stems, partners are encouraged to elaborate on their feelings in regard to the caring behaviors. And occasionally the sentence stems will lead back to the past where a partner was wounded and the partners will be reminded that they are helping each other heal painful childhood wounds. Recreating positive energy is so important to Brown (1999) that he sometimes uses a procedure known as positive flooding. The procedure might be used after a couple has been in therapy for a time and they have already been able to recreate some positive energy toward each other. In this procedure, one partner (the sender) is asked to focus on his or her partner (the receiver). The sender circles the receiver's chair and as he or she is circling the receiver, the sender is asked to focus on three areas–physical traits, behavioral traits, and character traits. First, the sender sends positive messages concerning physical traits by saying things that the sender likes about these traits. "I love your widows peak in your hair. I think you're so cute when you smile and you do your nose like you do. I love the complexion of your skin, it just seems to glow sometimes." Then the sender concentrates on behavioral characteristics. "I love the way you ask me for my ideas about. . . . I appreciate the way you listen when. . . ." And then the sender focuses on character traits. "I love your energy and enthusiasm. I love your steadying influence, never getting too hyper or too down." While the receiver is being showered with these positives, he or she remains silent. Then, when the positive energy reaches a peak, the sender is to let his or her partner know how much he or she is loved and appreciated. Brown (1999) writes: "Sometimes people actually jump up and down or shed tears of joy as they embrace. This is a way to accentuate the positive energy between the couple and is a very bonding experience" (p. 167).

Thus, in Imago therapy, partners learn how to create a safe environment by using the couple's dialogue so that they can communicate about their difficult issues. Using this dialogue and other techniques, such as the parent-child dialogue, partners learn that they have been wounded in childhood and need to heal. They then learn to stretch into new behaviors that foster their own growth and their partner's healing. As they do this, a new positive energy is created in the marriage and they learn to envision each other differently; they come to see each other in more positives ways—as helpmates in the healing process.

- Do you agree that problems in marriage relate to past experiences that often go back to childhood wounding? Do you believe that these wounds need to be addressed in order to help couples deal with relationship problems? Could the exercises of Imago therapy benefit you and your marriage? How difficult would these exercises be for you and your spouse to carry out?

FINDING SOLUTIONS: THE DIVORCE REMEDY APPROACH

Michele Weiner Davis has been helping couples save their marriages for over ten years. As a therapist and author, she educates couples on how to steer an unhappy marriage back to happiness. Her book, *Divorce Busting*, published in 1992, provides a step-by-step program for helping couples save their marriages. A later book, *The Divorce Remedy* (2001), follows up on her earlier work by offering a seven-step program for saving troubled marriages. Davis has been a leader in the development of Solution-Oriented Brief Therapy, an approach that emphasizes present behavior rather than analyzing the past to gain insight and understanding.

Step One

Step one in her program deals with misconceptions about marriage. Often unrealistic attitudes and expectations make it more likely that couples will define their relationship as troubled. For example, many couples believe that if conflict exists in a relationship, the relationship is doomed. Davis points out that conflict exists in all marriages, even those that are stable. Also, the evidence does not support the belief that happily married couples eventually resolve all of their differences. Then too, some partners believe that most people are much happier in second marriages; yet this is not always the case since bad habits are just as likely to invade these marriages. If you expect marriage to make you happy, be it a first or second marriage, you will be disappointed, for happiness comes from within.

Also, Davis wants her readers and clients to know that one person can change a relationship in a positive way. As a couple, you are part of a two-person system and as a partner, your input influences that system. Just as your input can anger your partner and produce negative outcomes, your input can possibly soothe your partner and produce positive outcomes.

Thus, Davis remains hopeful, even if one partner is motivated to improve the relationship and the other has given up or has settled for accepting things as they are. However, Davis cautions her readers not to expect a new relationship to emerge in a day. Relationships gradually deteriorate over time and they don't immediately re-emerge as satisfying. So even if one partner does change and provide new input, this partner should at first be content with small changes.

Step Two

Step two involves learning how to set small goals that are specific, action-oriented, and stated in terms of the positive behaviors you want to achieve. This is very important because without specific goals stated in behavioral terms, a partner will not know if efforts to produce change have been successful. For example, rather than saying that you want your relationship to be more loving, you should ask yourself what your relationship would look like if it were more loving. What behaviors would you begin to see? Following these instructions, a wife might write: I want my husband to call me from work once a week and ask how my day is going; I want to go out together for dinner at least once a month; I want him to embrace me at least two or three times a week when he comes home from work and ask how my day went. These goals involve small steps, are positively stated, and are action oriented; they can easily be evaluated after one or two weeks.

Step Three

The third step in the program is for a partner to ask for what s/he wants in a positive way. As simple as this seems, it is not always easy to accomplish. A husband may come home and sit in front of the TV while his wife works in the kitchen preparing supper. She may wonder why he doesn't help her or she may think how inconsiderate and lazy he is for not helping. By the time she asks for help, she is upset and her comments may be critical and demeaning. "Why don't you ever get off your lazy butt and help me around here instead of watching television all the time." There are several things wrong with such a statement: it implies a character flaw–lazy, it expresses criticism in a way that often provokes defensiveness, and it does not specify the behaviors that would be helpful. As partners ask for what they want, they should state requests in a positive manner, specifying the behaviors they would like to see. Also, when thinking about a request, consider timing. If you are angry or if you know your spouse has an important business call that s/he must make, the timing may not be right to make your request. Later, when the situation is more conducive to discussion, you might say, "Can we talk for a moment?" Then you might ask, "I was wondering if when you get home from work you could set the table for me and pour the tea? That would be so helpful and would ease my mind about supper." Always remember that there is a right way and a wrong way as well as a right time and a wrong time to ask for what you want. You may find that asking specifically for what you want from your partner in a positive way works–gets you what you want; then again, it may make no difference at all. Some marriages have deteriorated to such a low point that the spouse knows not even to ask. If this is the case, the timing is not right, so Davis suggests that you do other things (step four) so that later, your partner may be more receptive to your requests.

Step Four

In step four, partners are told to stop doing what has not worked. If arguing, lecturing, blaming, screaming, or even asking in positive ways has not worked, then try other things. Stop doing what has not worked. This is hard to learn for several reasons. Many partners do the same things over and over because they don't know anything else to do. They conclude that they have not done it enough or for long enough. However, Davis suggests that these partners have probably done these things long enough and hard enough; their behaviors may even be making matters worse. Even if it seems to be the logical thing to do, don't do it if it hasn't worked. Then what should you do? In the next step, Davis suggests some things partners can do.

Step Five

In step five, partners are given some strategies and suggestions that possibly will influence their relationship toward the positive goals they seek. Davis also suggests that the partner desiring change keep a journal to record what works as change strategies are implemented. Writing in a journal encourages close attention to what the partner seeking change did and how the spouse responded. If journal writing is not your thing, then keep mental notes of what worked and what didn't. Some of Davis's suggestions include:

- Concentrate on changing behaviors that are really important to you and not every little irritating issue. Sometimes you will need to count to ten or use some other anger reducing technique to get you past your immediate irritation. Remember that many differences are unresolvable, so choose your battles carefully.
- Do not address a problem when you are angry. Set aside a later time when emotions have cooled down for your discussion time. You may

also remember that this as a suggestion for conflict resolution in the PREP approach discussed in Chapter 8.

- Pay attention to and reward the positive changes your partner makes. The tendency in relationships is to be supersensitive to the negatives–to notice the negative and overlook the positive. Notarius and Markman's (1993) research shows that it takes only one "zinger" to undo many acts of kindness. So concentrate on the good things your spouse does and reinforce these things rather than ignoring the good and criticizing the bad. When a partner complies with a request, praise him/her for complying rather than being critical of the way the task was done. Many partners discourage future help because present help is met with criticism. Remember to reinforce small improvements, realizing that as you reinforce improvements, you will be creating a cooperative environment in which your spouse will be more likely to help in the future.

- Remember what worked for you in the past during the good times in your marriage and get back to doing those things. Both Davis and William Doherty (2001), another marital therapist, have written poignantly about how couples stop doing what worked for them in the past. Partners allow time pressures, work pressures, and the pressures associated with child rearing to take precedence over their marriage. Couples who want to change how they feel toward each other should start doing some of the things that worked for them in the past. Doing what worked in the past can ignite positive feelings associated with past experiences.

- Many times, when a spouse expects negative consequences after an interaction with his or her partner, s/he gets the negative response that was expected. It's as if the expected negative response is brought about by the negative expectation. Instead of expecting the worst, Davis suggests that the spouse "act as if" good things will occur after the interaction. This will change the way you approach the situation and may produce a different outcome.

- Davis suggests that since what you are doing is not producing the results you want, you should try something else. One wife always asked her husband what he wanted to do about supper. This irritated her husband since he had just gotten home from work where he had to make decisions all day. Even though it was difficult, the wife decided to be more assertive. She stated her preference, "I would like to. . . . This worked well since the husband was glad to go along with the suggestion or could use it as a starting point for negotiation. Think of what you are doing that is not working. Then do something different! This may mean that you will do nothing. For example, if your daughter and your husband are fighting and you are tempted to take your daughter's side like you have done in the past, decide to do nothing; stay out of the conflict and let them deal with it. You might also consider doing what Davis calls a "180." That is, do exactly the opposite of what you usually do. For example, if a wife has been pursuing her husband "to talk," "to solve a problem," "to fix something around the house," or even "to help save the relationship," then she might stop pursuing and even distance since pursuing has not worked. The point is that the behavior you have been using is not working so do something different. This is especially important if your relationship is in serious trouble. You may want to continue to confront, argue, and pursue because you are desperate. But your desperate responses are more of the same and may be what your partner wants to get away from. Thus, you may need to concentrate on other things to keep your mind off of your relationship problems. In doing this, you may become more like the person your spouse would like you to be.

• If you are very verbal and have tried to use words to get through to your partner, try another approach. One wife who nagged her husband about fixing the screened porch went to the hardware store and bought some new screen and began the work herself. Her husband, seeing this, immediately stepped in to do the work so it would be "done right." A husband who loved to go sightseeing in the mountains had a wife who was always busy with something else, so the husband went by himself on several occasions. The next time he went, his wife decided to go with him to see what he was enjoying so much. Another example of the try something different approach is to use another medium to present the message. For example, if you have attempted to get your message across by talking but this has not worked, try writing a letter expressing how you feel.

If you try new things, you should realize that this is a trial and error process; some things may work, while others may backfire. Also, it may take up to two weeks for you to tell if what you are doing is having the intended effect and even then, you may note only small improvements.

• How easy or difficult would it be for you to implement these strategies? Have you ever attempted any of these strategies in your relationship?

Steps Six and Seven

In step six, a partner attempts to analyze the effectiveness of the changes s/he has made in light of the specific, action-oriented goals. There are three possible results: (1) you have achieved your goals, (2) you have made some progress, but there is more to do, or (3) nothing has changed. If nothing has changed Davis suggests analyzing why this might be. In some cases, a partner may have decided that the relationship cannot be saved. However, if some positive changes have occurred, step seven addresses the need to sustain these positive changes. Since your behavioral exploration has helped you discover what works, keep doing what works.

HELPING WHEN THE CLIENT IS THE FAMILY

It is very common for therapists to get calls from parents concerning troubled children or teenagers. Often, when the family system has a problem, the problem comes to the attention of a therapist when the child or teenager is identified as the patient. A desperate parent often wants to make an appointment for his or her child or teenager. Perhaps the teenager is skipping school, smoking pot, running away, or engaging in other behaviors that are troubling to the parent or school authorities. Some therapists would see the identified patient individually in an attempt to bring about change in the teenager's behavior. However, a family systems therapist would want to work with the family. Thus there has been a shift in thinking over the years by many therapists about the best way to intervene and provide help. This shift has coincided with the emergence and understanding of the family systems model discussed in Chapter 2.

The family systems approach to therapy is based on several important assumptions. First, problems are system-wide in that the behavior of each individual in the system influences and affects the other members of the system. Therefore, it is likely that the current dynamics in the family are maintaining the symptomatic behavior in the identified patient. It is the interactions in the family that need to be changed if the behavior is to change. Thus, there is a shift away from seeing one person as the patient; rather, the family becomes the patient. However, we have previously noted that families often resist change. Instead, they fall back on old habits and worn out strategies that have failed in the past. Frequently, unhealthy triangles have become a part of the system. Rather than two people dealing maturely with the tensions between them, a third party becomes triangled in to alleviate the stress in the two-person dyad. As these and other unhealthy patterns develop, the system becomes troubled.

Although there are many different approaches to family therapy, most of these approaches attempt to help the family restructure their interpersonal relationships. Various techniques and intervention strategies are used to achieve this goal. The family therapist not only listens and observes but also may serve as a teacher, coach, model, and director. Using a variety of change strategies, the family therapist often attempts to accomplish the following:

- Help families understand how patterns of behavior are past down from generation to generation.
- Help family members understand that they are too emeshed in the affairs of each other and too stuck together as a family. These families do not have enough freedom for members to develop a healthy individuality. Occasionally, a family may be too loosely connected—there is not enough cohesion in the family. Helping a family find a healthy balance between being too emeshed and too disconnected is important.
- Help parents understand that they are too inflexible. As children grow up, rules need to be changed to accommodate the increased maturity of the children.
- Help family members communicate directly with each other rather than through a third person. Prompting a family member to speak directly to another family member in the therapy session is one of the advantages of bringing the whole family together in therapy. This prompted communication, which takes place under the guidance of the therapist, might never occur if the family did not seek therapy.
- Help the family establish healthy boundaries to the outside world.
- Help family members negotiate healthy boundaries within the family so that no one feels unfairly infringed upon.
- Help family members work as a team to achieve common goals rather than working against each other in unhealthy ways.
- Help the family restructure rules so that toxic and unhealthy rules are eliminated.
- Help the family resolve difficult problem issues so that each member's needs are taken into consideration.
- Help family members see that what they are doing is not working. They must try something else.
- Help families stop denying their problems and help each family member to assess his/her individual contribution to the family's problems. No one is to be blamed; they all contribute to the creation of problems.

As family therapists work with troubled families, they attempt to move the family toward greater health. Numerous lists of the characteristics of healthy families have emerged over the years (Whitfield, 1987; Satir, 1988; Curran, 1983). Healthy families create environments that are growth producing and affirming. These families are like experienced gardeners who plant a seed and nurture it carefully, giving it the right amount of sunlight, water, and other nutrients to produce a beautiful flower. So too, healthy families create environments that are conducive to the positive growth of each family member. These families produce a sense of good feeling in family members. The following characteristics have been used to describe what healthy families are like.

- The family develops flexible, healthy, and age-appropriate rules.
- The family respects each member's needs.
- The family supports the mental and emotional growth of its members.
- The family treats individual members with dignity and respect.
- The family communicates in direct, clear, and honest ways.
- The family listens to each other and attempts to understand.
- The family shares responsibility in a fair way.
- The family forgives mistakes and attempts to learn from mistakes.
- The family knows the importance of play and humor.
- The family has a moral belief system.
- The family respects each member's privacy.
- The family fosters and enjoys time spent together.
- The family values rituals and traditions.
- The family admits problems and knows when to seek help.
- The family encourages service to others both inside and outside the family.

Hopefully reading this text has helped you understand the importance of healthy marriages and families. Family life educators see families as vital to the health of individuals and society. An individual's problems can often be traced back to the family. Societal problems frequently have origins in the home. Thus, a society that fails to support worthwhile family initiatives puts itself in peril. And families put their members in peril when they deny problems and refuse to seek help.

ENDINGS

If you have read this book and taken a course based on its content, hopefully you have made progress in your attempt to understand marriage, family, and intimate relationships. You realize that satisfying relationships don't just happen; healthy relationships must be maintained and nurtured. At times, this nurturing is enjoyable, but at other times, it is hard work, even painful. And when the pain comes, it can be difficult to work through. Often, partners are more likely to maintain their cars than they are their relationships. They will fix their cars, but when relationship difficulties arise, they often go it alone, sometimes even hiding problems from close friends. Individuals often take their marital and family relationships for granted, believing these relationships will always be enduring and satisfying even after years of neglect.

It is my hope that the relationships you have with your partner, children, and family are vitally important to you. When you ask elderly persons what they regret most, they are often likely to respond by saying: I wish I'd spent more time with my children, been more forgiving, spoken softly rather than so harshly, tried harder to work out differences, tried to be more understanding, been more loving. During your later years, when you look back on life, hopefully you won't look back with regrets. Nurture your relationships except, of course, those that are abusive or abnormally demeaning. If you don't always know how to nurture, seek professional help. Recently, a man who had been divorced from his first wife for more than twenty years said that his first wife had begged him to go to therapy with her. He had refused, believing that she was the one who needed help. Looking back now over the intervening years of troubled children, unfulfilled hopes, and a failed second marriage, he wishes he had done things differently. He now realizes that he did not accept his part of the responsibility for his relationship problems. For him, it was too late. But for you, standing at a different place along life's road, there are probably still important choices to be made. Choose carefully! Realize that nurturing a cherished relationship is more important than proving that your spouse or child is wrong. Also, choose those personal relationship values that will allow you to succeed rather than fail. Learn from what happily married couples and healthy families do so that you can practice this learning in your own family. For in understanding the success of others, you may find the keys to your own relationship success.

IMPORTANT TERMS AND CONCEPTS

Gottman's Seven Principles
The Sound Marital House
perpetual problems
love maps
the fondness and admiration system
emotional bank account
negative/positive sentiment override
solvable problems
respecting dreams

creating shared meanings
The Conscious Marriage
Imago Therapy
The couple's dialogue: mirroring, validation, empathy
The parent-child dialogue
The behavior change request
The Divorce Remedy Approach
A "180"

SUGGESTED READING

Brown, R. (1999). *Imago relationship therapy: An introduction to theory and practice.* New York: John Wiley & Sons.

Davis, M. W. (2001). *The divorce remedy: The proven 7-step program for saving your marriage.* New York: Simon & Schuster.

Gottman, J. M., & Silver, N. (1999). *The seven principles for making marriage work.* New York: Crown.

Hendrix, H. (1990). *Getting the love you want: A guide for couples.* New York: Harper Collins.

McGraw, P. (2000). *Relationship rescue: A seven-step strategy for reconnecting with your partner.* New York: Hyperion.

GLOSSARY

Acute battering phase. The second phase in the abuse process where abusers are violent and aggressive toward their partner.

Adaptability. The ability of the family to adjust and change to meet the demands of new situations.

Adult consciousness. A term used by Gould to describe a mature, adult like way of thinking and viewing the world.

Ambivalent attachment. A term used by Ainsworth to describe young children who were especially anxious when their mothers left the room and their anxiety was not turned off by their mothers return, thus they continued to be distressed.

Amplifying feedback. Feedback in the family that pushes the family system to change.

Analogic message. The message that is communicated by things other than the words such as the way the words are spoken, body language, and facial expression. Individuals look to the analogic message to determine what the words mean. Sometimes referred to as the metamessage.

Attachment theory. A theory that focuses on the early bond between the infant and young child. The quality of this bond is thought to influence close relationships throughout life.

Attenuating feedback. Feedback in the family that resists change and attempts to adjust the family system back to a previous equilibrium or steady state.

Attractiveness filter. One of the filters individuals use to evaluate potential mates—does this person meet my standards in terms of looks and appearance?

Avoidant attachment. A term used by Ainsworth to describe young children who ignored their mother when she left the room. These children continued to be overtly unresponsive even when the mother returned; yet their heart rates increased when she returned, indicating they were very much aware of her presence.

Avoidant couples. A term used by Gottman to describe couples who avoid discussing their conflict issues, preferring to concentrate on the positives in their relationship.

Basic differentiation. A type of differentiation that is viewed as long-term and largely dependent on the degree of separation from one's family of origin.

Bid. A term used by Gottman to describe any gesture or expression used to connect emotionally with another person.

Boundaries. The barriers–physical, psychological, and emotional–that separate family members or parts of the family system from each other. Barriers also separate the family system from its surrounding systems.

Boundary permeability. The degree of flexibility relating to how well a family system or a system within the family allows information from outside the system to penetrate and influence the system.

Childhood consciousness. A term used by Gould to describe a childlike way of thinking and viewing the world.

Chronic anxiety. A distress and apprehension that persists and endures for a long period of time.

Circular causality. An approach to understanding based on the belief that forces influence each other in a bi-directional or multi-directional way.

Closed family paradigm. An organizational structure that a family uses when their fundamental belief system stresses continuity, established ways of doing things, and a conventional lifestyle.

Cobras. Jacobson and Gottman's term for a type of abuser who is able to lower heart rate and other internal responses when overtly he is expressing more and more anger.

Cognitive distortions. A term used by Beck and other cognitive psychologists to label the mistakes individuals make in thinking.

Cohabitation filter. One of the filters couples may use to evaluate potential mates and marriage partners-does living together increase our desire to stay together or to marry?

Cohesion. This term is used to characterize the degree of togetherness or closeness of a family.

Companionate love. A type of love that is more common in partners who have been together for many years–a love with high levels of commitment and intimacy but somewhat lacking in intense passion.

Compatibility filter. One of the filters an individual uses to evaluate potential mates–will we be able to live harmoniously with each other?

Conscious marriage. A term used by Hendrix to describe a healthy marriage–where partners understand their own and their partner's needs and they work together to meet these needs in a satisfying way.

Constraint commitment. A type of marital commitment that exists when a partner feels tied to the relationship because negative consequences would occur if the relationship ended.

Contraction and betrayal. The second stage in Dym and Glenn's developmental stages of marriage. In this stage, negative feelings replace positive feelings as the prevailing tone of the marriage.

Contrition phase. The third phase in the abuse process in which abusers seek to atone for their violent acts, often by begging, pleading, and bribing their way back into the good graces of their partner.

Correlation coefficient. A statistical measure represented by a number from +1 to -1 that depicts the extent to which two variables vary together and how well either variable predicts the other.

Dance. A series of behaviors performed in essentially the same way by two or more family members on numerous occasions. This complex pattern of behavior is rule governed yet the pattern and the rules are usually outside a family's awareness. (Also see rule sequence and vicious cycle).

Dedicated commitment. A type of marital commitment that exists when partners feel drawn to each other because they want to be together and they want their relationship to last.

Dependent variable. In an experimental research study, this is the variable that the researcher observes after having manipulated the independent variable.

Differentiation. This term is used to describe how successful an individual has been in developing a solid, mature sense of self, that is, knowing what he or she believes and stands for and how this is different from others, even others in the family. Also, this term is used to describe how capable an individual is at separating intellect from emotion.

Digital message. The actual words conveyed in a message.

Emotion coach. A name given to parents who are skilled at helping their children learn about and successfully handle their emotional life.

Emotional bank account. A term used in reference to the amount of positive and negative feelings that marriage partners have stored up and can draw upon as they face problems. In healthy marriages, there is a healthy bank balance–many more positive feelings in the account than negative. (Also referred to as the relationship bank account.)

Emotional intelligence. The ability to effectively perceive, express, understand, and regulate emotions.

Emotional philosophy. A family's belief about feelings and emotions and how feelings should be expressed and dealt with in daily life.

Emotional triangle. Occurs when two members of a family system experience conflict and they focus on something or someone else in an attempt to reduce anxiety and regain stability.

Empirical data. Information that has been obtained by systematically observing, measuring, and recording as a scientist attempts to accurately describe, explain, and predict.

Epigenesis principle. This principle states that what is done in the early stages of an individual's life or relationship will influence what can and cannot be done in the later stages of the individual's life or relationship.

Equifinality. The idea that many events or beginnings can lead to or be associated with the same outcome.

Equipotentiality. The idea that the same event or beginning can lead to or be associated with different outcomes.

Escalation of negativity. When one partner responds negatively (e.g., with criticism) to the other and the other partner responds in a way that increases the negativity (e.g., with contempt).

Exaggeration principle. The tendency for a family under stress to exaggerate its own character, that is, to simply try harder at doing the same thing (e.g., scream louder than before) in an attempt to meet the demands of the situation.

Expansion and promise. The first stage in Dym and Glenn's developmental stages of marriage. In this stage, positive feelings make up the prevailing emotional tone of the marriage.

Experiment. A research method in which the experimenter manipulates a variable (the independent variable), observes a variable (the dependent variable), and controls for extraneous variables by random assignment of subjects to different conditions.

Explicit rule. Family rules that are clear, known, and understood by each member of the family.

Extraneous variables. In an experiment, the extraneous variables are variables that the experimenter wants to control for so that these variables will not influence the outcome of the study.

Family ideology. A family's way of being that is reflected in the family's beliefs, ideals, values, aspirations, worldview, philosophy of life, etc.

Family love. A type of love, different from passionate or romantic love, that is experienced for one's family members and is action oriented, other oriented, unconditional, and enduring. This type of love is often thought to be unconditional, enduring, action-oriented, and oriented toward fostering the growth of another.

Family role. The characteristic social behaviors taken on by an individual in the family. For example, a child may take on the role of caretaker or problem child.

Family science. The scientific study of the family involving scientists from many different perspectives and fields. The work of these scholars combines to create the field of family science.

Family structure. The consistent and somewhat enduring organizational patterns that regulate a family's way of responding after rules have been established.

Family systems theory. A theory that recognizes the interconnectedness of family members; thus, what happens to one member of the system has an impact on everyone else in the family. This approach also views the family as an integrated unit that is more than the sum of its independent elements or members.

Family-wide symbiosis. An attachment to family and family principles that is so strong that it blocks the development of healthy individuality.

Filter theory. An explanation of mate selection that involves a process of narrowing potential partners through consideration of such things as attractiveness and social background until all mismatches are filtered out and only compatible choices remain.

Flooding. Gottman's term for heightened emotional arousal, which occurs in conflict situations with a partner, interfering with successful management of the tension and conflict.

Fondness and admiration system. The second floor of Gottman's Sound Marital House–the good feelings that permeate throughout a stable marriage because the partners hold each other in high esteem.

Four Horsemen of the Apocalypse. Gottman's term for the four destructive forces that attack a marriage–criticism, defensiveness, contempt, and stonewalling.

Functional differentiation. The ability of an individual to be rational rather than emotional in a specific situation.

Homeostasis. The tendency of an organism or family system to maintain a relatively stable internal environment and thus to preserve the status quo.

Hostile/detached couples. Gottman's term for marriages where partners have a great deal of hostility toward each other but tend to withdraw instead of experiencing their anger in open conflict.

Hostile/engaged couples. Gottman's term for marriages where partners have a great deal of hostility toward each other and this hostility is expressed in open conflict.

Humanistic theory. The personality theory that emphasizes positive growth and the fulfillment of one's potential.

Hypothesis. A testable prediction, usually derived from theory, which can be examined through research.

Imago. The mental image of the person, persons, or possibly a composite of the persons who influenced you most during childhood. This mental picture is carried over into adulthood and influences how individuals respond in their intimate relationships.

Imago therapy. An approach to marital therapy based on the ideas of Harville Hendrix concerning the importance of childhood experience and one's imago on the quality of a marriage relationship. From this approach, individuals are seen as having been wounded in childhood and they must understand their own and their partner's wounding in order to provide the experiences necessary for healing.

Implicit rule. Rules that are below awareness, hidden and submerged from view, making them difficult to examine and question.

Independent variable. In an experimental research study, this is the variable that the experimenter manipulates in order to see if the manipulation of this variable has an effect on the dependent variable.

Input. That which is put into a system to be processed in order to achieve an output or result.

Linear causality. The view that one event or person causes another event or person's behavior (A causes B), but directionality does not run the other way (B does not cause A).

Love maps. Gottman's term for the cognitive information we have in memory concerning our partner and the details of his/her life.

Maximizer. A term Hendrix uses to describe how some individuals expend energy; maximizers move toward others, easily sharing their thoughts and feelings.

Metamessage. The message that is communicated by things other than the words such as the way the words are spoken, body language, and facial expression. Individuals often look to the metamessage to interpret what the words mean. Also referred to as the analogic message.

Minimizer. A term Hendrix uses to describe a way some individuals expend energy. Minimizers tend to withdraw, finding it difficult to openly share their thoughts and feelings.

Morphogenesis. The process of change that takes place in the family system.

Morphostasis. The process of maintaining the status quo and resisting change that takes place in the family system.

Naturalistic observation. An approach to research that attempts to accurately describe what exists by observing and recording behavior in the natural setting without trying to manipulate or control the situation.

Negative affect. Negative feeling or feelings that characterize a person's emotional experiencing, often influencing the person's attitudes and behavior.

Negative sentiment override. When there is more negative affect being expressed in a marriage than positive affect.

Object relations theory. A theory that stresses the importance of early relationships in a child's life, proposing that memories of these relationships are retained as mental representations in memory and influence all future intimate relationships.

Open family paradigm. A family with an open family paradigm is one that values input from each family member and attempts to negotiate in order to find consensus.

Operant conditioning. A type of learning that emphasizes consequences—reinforcement and punishment; behavior is strengthened when reinforced and weakened when punished.

Output. That which a system produces; usually a response to some input into the system.

Passionate love. A highly feeling-oriented love with intense longing for one's partner, ecstatic feelings when love is reciprocated, and deep misery when the loved person does not love in return.

Perpetual problems. Problems that persist throughout a relationship because they are based on irresolvable differences.

Pit bulls. Jacobson and Gottman's term for the male abuser who gradually becomes more and more internally aroused and angry during conflict discussion, leading to heightened emotional and behavioral outbursts.

Positive affect. Positive feeling or feelings that characterize a person's emotional experiencing, often influencing the person's attitudes and behavior.

Positive sentiment override. When there is more positive affect being expressed in a marriage than negative affect.

PREP approach. PREP (Prevention and Relationship Enhancement Program) is a program developed by Markman, Stanley, and Blumberg for helping couples resolve conflict by applying a set of rules to problem-solving situations, thus reducing tension so that a compromise can be more easily reached.

Propinquity filter. One of the filters individuals use in the mate selection process—individuals are more likely to choose a partner with whom they frequently come into contact with and frequently see.

Psychoanalytic theory. The approach to understanding personality and behavior developed by Freud that emphasizes early childhood experiences, unconscious motives and conflicts, and the structure of the id, ego, and superego.

Random family paradigm. A family with a random family paradigm is one where there are very few traditions and prescribed forms of behavior, allowing family members to come and go as they please.

Receiving errors. Errors made in the communication process by the person who is the receiver of a message.

Relationship bank account. A term used in reference to the amount of positive and negative feelings that marriage partners store up and can draw upon as they face problems. In healthy marriage, there is a healthy bank balance—many more positive feelings than negative (also referred to as the emotional bank account).

Repair attempt. A response made by one partner to de-escalate negativity in a relationship interaction in an effort to initiate the repair process.

Resolution. The third stage in Dym and Glenn's developmental stages of marriage. A spirit of compromise and negotiation characterizes this stage with partners being more accepting and tolerant as they attempt to work things out.

Ritual. Behaviors that are repeated many times in the life cycle of a family because these behaviors have important meaning to the family; rituals help define the special nature of a family system.

Rule. A regulation that creates predictable and enduring patterns of behavior and interaction in the family.

Rule sequence. A connected series of rules that are carried out in sequence so that when the first rule is followed, the other rules fall into place, thus dictating a complex sequence of behaviors that are rule governed.

Second family. Taffel's term for the child and adolescent's peer group—a group that he believes has more influence today than in the past.

Secure attachment. A term used by Ainsworth to describe young children who cry when their mother leaves the room but are easily comforted when she returns and are able to quickly return to play.

Sending errors. Errors made in the communication process by the individual who is the sender of a message.

Similarity filter. One of the filters individuals use in the mate selection process—individuals are more likely to choose a partner with whom they share many similarities.

Social learning theory. A theory that explains learning as the result of attending to a model such as happens when one individual observes another and is changed in some way as a result of this observation.

Speaker-listener technique. A technique used in the PREP approach—an approach that is designed to help partners deal with heated conflict in their relationship. This technique requires partners to exchange roles as first one speaks and the other listens and restates what has been said and then these roles are reversed. This technique helps partners understand each other's point of view.

Stage. A period of relative stability that occurs between transitions—periods of rapid change.

Stonewalling. Gottman's term for describing the process of shutting down (withdrawing) in conflict discussion.

Subsystem. A system that functions within a larger system (e.g., the sibling subsystem and the spousal subsystem exist within the larger system of the family).

Survey. A technique used in research when the goal is to ascertain the attitudes or behaviors of a certain population; this is usually done by questioning a representative sample of that population.

Tension-building phase. The first phase in the abuse process in which the abuser experiences a gradual build up of tension and irritation without understanding the deep-seated source of this tension.

The Sound Marital House. The term Gottman uses as he describes the characteristics of a satisfying, stable marriage.

Transition. A period of rapid change occurring between stages–periods of relative stability.

Transitional person. A person who changes a destructive family pattern that was experienced in his or her family of origin, replacing this destructive pattern with a more healthy pattern and thus, making it more likely that this new healthy pattern will be passed down to the next generation.

Triangular theory of love. Sternberg's theory of love, a theory that proposes that there are three major components of love–passion, commitment, and intimacy–and that these components combine to various degrees, producing seven different types of love.

Tyranny of the cool. Taffel's term for an attitude that dominates children's thinking during the elementary school years–an attitude that stresses the importance of designer clothes and other "cool" things that advertisers and culture stress as important.

Validating couples. Gottman's term for couples who exhibit a great deal of respect for each other by listening, understanding their partner's point of view, and compromising to maintain harmony in their relationship.

Vicious cycle. A series of rule-governed behaviors engaged in to achieve a goal; however, these behaviors have the opposite effect–they make matters worse.

Volatile couples. Gottman's term for couples who frequently bicker, squabble, and disagree, even seeming to enjoy their skirmishes.

REFERENCES

Ackerman, R. J. (1989) *Perfect daughters: Adult daughters of alcoholics.* Deerfield Beach, FL: Health Communications.

Ainsworth, M. D. S., Blehar, M. C., Waters, E., & Wall, S. (1978). *Patterns of attachment: A psychological study of the strange situation.* Hillsdale, NJ: Lawrence Erlbaum.

Amato, P. R., & Booth, A. (1997). *A generation at risk: Growing up in an era of family upheaval.* Cambridge, MA: Harvard University Press.

Ambert, A. M. (2001). *The effect of children on parents* (2nd ed.). New York: Haworth Press.

Arnstein, H. S. (1985). *Between mothers-in-law and daughters-in-law.* New York: Doad, Mead.

Arond, M., & Pauker, S. L. (1987). *The first year of marriage.* New York: Warner Books.

Bandura, A. (1977). *Social learning theory.* Englewood Cliffs, NJ: Prentice-Hall.

Bandura, A., & Walters, R. H. (1963). *Social learning and personality development.* New York: Holt, Rinehart, and Winston.

Bandura, A., Ross, D., & Ross, S. A. (1963). Imitation of film-mediated aggressive models. *Journal of Abnormal and Social Psychology, 66,* 3-11.

Bank, S. P., & Kahn, M. D. (1982). *The sibling bond.* New York: Basic Books.

Baucom, D. H., Epstein, N., Rankin, L. A., & Burnett, C. K. (1996). Assessing relationship standards: The inventory of specific relationship standards. *Journal of Marriage and the Family, 10,* 72-88.

Beck, A. T. (1988). *Love is never enough: How couples can overcome misunderstandings, resolve conflicts, and solve relationship problems through cognitive therapy.* New York: Harper and Row.

Becvar, D. S., & Becvar, R. J. (1993). *Family therapy: A systemic integration.* Needham Heights, MA: Allyn and Bacon.

Bee, H. (1994). *Lifespan development.* New York: HarperCollins College.

Belsky, J., & Kelly, J. (1994). *The transition to parenthood: How a first child changes a marriage: Why some couples grow closer and others apart.* New York: Delacorte Press.

Bennett, L. A., Wolin, S. J., Reiss, D., & Teitelbaum, M. A. (1987). Couples at risk for transmission of alcoholism: Protective influences. *Family Process, 26,* 111-129.

Berkowitz, L., & Geen, R. G. (1966). Film violence and the cue properties of available targets. *Journal of Personality and Social Psychology, 3,* 525-530.

Berscheid, E., Dion, K., Walster (Hatfield), E., & Walster, G. W. (1971). Physical attractiveness and dating choice: A test of the matching hypothesis. *Journal of Experimental Social Psychology, 7,* 173-189.

369

Blevins, W. (1993). *Your family your self.* Oakland, CA: New Harbinger.

Block, J.D. (2003). *Naked intimacy: How to increase true openness in your relationship.* New York: Contemporary Books.

Blumstein, P. W., & Schwartz, P. (1983). *American couples.* New York: Morrow.

Booth, A., & Johnson, D. R. (!988). Premarital cohabitation and marital success. *Journal of Family Issues, 9,* 255-272.

Bowen, M. (1976). Theory in the practice of psychotherapy. In P. Guerin (Ed.), *Family therapy.* New York: Gardner Press.

Bowen, M. (1978). *Family therapy in clinical practice.* New York: Jason Aronson.

Bowlby, J. (1969). Attachment and loss. Vol. 1, *Attachment.* New York: Basic Books.

Brennan, K. A., & Shaver P. R. (1995). Dimensions of adult attachment, affect regulation, and romantic relationship functioning. *Personality and Social Psychology Bulletin, 21,* 267-283.

Brennan, K. A., & Shaver, P. R. (1993). Attachment styles and parental divorce. *Journal of divorce and remarriage, 21,* 161-175.

Broderick, C. B. (1988). Marriage and the family. (2nd ed.). Englewood Cliffs, NJ: Prentice-Hall.

Brown, R. (1999). *Imago relationship therapy: An introduction to theory and practice.* New York: John Wiley and Sons.

Brown, S. L., & Booth, A. (1996). Cohabitation versus marriage: A comparison of relationship quality. *Journal of Marriage and the Family, 58,* 668-678.

Bumpass, L. L., & Sweet, J. A. (1989). National estimates of cohabitation. *Demography, 26,* 615-625.

Burger, J. M. (2000). *Personality* (5th ed.). Belmont, CA: Wadsworth.

Burr, R. B., Day, D. D., & Bahr, S. B. ((1993). *Family Science.* Pacific Grove, CA: Brooks/Cole.

Buss, D. M. (1985). Human mate selection. *American Scientist, 73,* 47-51.

Carter, B., & McGoldrick, M. (1989). Overview: The expanded family life cycle. In E.A. Carter & M. McGoldrick (Eds.), *The expanded family life cycle* (pp. 1-25). Needham Heights, MA: Allyn and Bacon.

Chapman, G. (1992). *The five love languages: How to express heartfelt commitment to your mate.* Chicago: Northfield.

Chess, S., & Thomas, A. (1987). *Know your child: An authoritative guide for today's parents.* New York: Basic Books.

Christensen, A., & Jacobson, N. S. (2000). *Reconcilable differences.* New York: The Guilford Press.

Collins, N. L., & Read, S. J. (1990). Adult attachment, working models, and relationship quality in dating couples. *Journal of Personality and Social Psychology, 58,* 644-663.

Constantine, L. L. (1986) *Family paradigms.* New York: Guilford Press.

Covey, S. R. (1997). *The 7 habits of highly effective families.* New York: Franklin Covey.

Cowan, C., & Cowan, P. (2000, 1992). *When partners become parents: The big life change for couples.* Mahwah, N.J: Lawrence Erlbaum.

Curran, D. (1983). *Traits of a healthy family.* New York: Ballantine.

Davis, K.E. (1985). Near and dear: Friendship and love compared. *Psychology Today, 19,* 22-30.

Davis, M. W. (1992). *Divorce busting: A revolutionary and rapid program for staying together.* New York: Simon and Schuster.

Davis, M. W. (2001). *The divorce remedy: The proven 7-step program for saving your marriage.* New York: Simon and Schuster.

DeAngelis, B. (1992). *Are you the one for me.* New York: Dell.

DeMaris, A., & Rao, K. V. (1992). Premarital cohabitation and marital stability. *Journal of Marriage and the Family. 54,* 178-190.

DeMaris, A., & Leslie, G. R. (1984). Cohabitation with the future spouse: Its influence upon marital satisfaction and communication. *Journal of Marriage and the Family, 46,* 77-84.

Doherty, W. (2001). *Take back your marriage: Sticking together in a world that pulls us apart.* New York: The Guilford Press.

Donnerstein, E. (1980). Aggressive erotica and violence against women. *Journal of Personality and Social Psychology. 39,* 269-277.

Dutton, D.G. (1995). *The batterer: A psychological profile.* New York: Basic Books.

Dutton, D.G. (1998). *The abusive personality.* New York: The Guilford Press.

Dym, B., & Glenn, M. L. (1993). *Couples: Exploring and understanding the cycles of intimate relationships.* New York: HarperCollins.

Erikson, E. H. (1963). *Childhood and society* (2nd ed.). New York: W.W. Norton.

Eysenck, H. J. (1967). *The biological basis of personality.* Springfield, IL: Charles C Thomas.

Eysenck, H. J. (1990). Biological dimensions of personality. In L. Pervin (Ed.), *Handbook of personality theory and research* (pp. 244-276). New York: The Guilford Press.

Feeney, J. A., Noller, P., & Patty, J. (1993). Adolescents' interactions with the opposite sex: Influence of attachment style and gender. *Journal of Adolescence, 16,* 169-186.

Feingold, A. (1990). Gender differences in effects of physical attractiveness on romantic attraction: A comparison across five research paradigms. *Journal of Personality and Social Psychology, 59,* 981-993.

Fiengold, A. (1991). Sex differences in the effects of similarity and physical attractiveness on opposite-sex attraction. *Basic and Applied Social Psychology, 12,* 357-367.

Fincham, F. D., Fernandes, L., & Humphreys, K. (1993). *Communication in relationships: A guide for couples and professionals.* Champaign, IL: Research Press.

Ford, L. (2001). *Human relations: A game plan for improving personal adjustment* (2nd ed.). Upper Saddle River, NJ: Prentice Hall.

Fowers, B. J., & Olson, D. H. (1986). Predicting marital success with PREPARE: A predictive validity study. *Journal of Marital and Family Therapy, 12,* 403-413.

Freud, S. (1901). *The psychopathology of everyday life.* London: Hogarth Press.

Freud, S. (1924). *A general introduction to psychoanalysis.* New York: Boni and Liveright.

Friedman, E. H. (1985). *Generation to generation.* New York: The Guilford Press.

Furman, W., & Buhrmester, K.L. (1992). Age and sex differences in perceptions of networks of personal relationships. *Child Development, 63,* 103-115.

Garbarino, J., & Bedard, C. (2001). *Parents under siege: Why you are the solution, not the problem, in your child's life.* New York: The Free Press.

Gelles, R. J. (1997). *Intimate violence in families* (3rd ed.). Thousand Oaks, CA: Sage.

Gibran, K. (1923). *The prophet.* New York: Knopf.

Glasser, W. (1965). *Reality therapy: A new approach to psychiatry.* New York: Harper & Row.

Goldberg, M. (1987). Patterns of disagreement in marriage. *Medical Aspects of Human Sexuality, 21*, 42-52.

Goleman, D. (1995). *Emotional intelligence.* New York: Bantam Books.

Gordon, T. (1970). *Parent effectiveness training.* New York: Wyden.

Gottman, J. M. (2000). *Clinical manual for marital therapy: A researched-based approach.* Seattle, WA: The Gottman Institute.

Gottman, J. M. (1999). *The marriage clinic: A scientifically based marital therapy.* New York: W. W. Norton.

Gottman, J. M. (1994). *Why marriages succeed and fail.* New York: Simon and Schuster.

Gottman, J. M., Coan, J., Carrere, S., & Swanson, C. (1998). Predicting marital happiness and stability from newlywed interactions. *Journal of Marriage and the Family, 60*, 5-22.

Gottman, J. M., & DeClaire, J. (1997). *The heart of parenting: Raising an emotionally intelligent child.* New York: Simon & Schuster.

Gottman, J. M., & DeClaire, J. (2001). *The relationship cure: A five-step guide for building better communications with family, friends, and lovers.* New York: Crown.

Gottman, J. M., & Gottman, J. S. (2001, 2002) *The art and science of love: A workshop for couples video manual.* Seattle, WA: The Gottman Institute.

Gottman, J. M., & Silver, N. (1999) *The seven principles for making marriage work.* New York: Crown.

Gould, R. L., (1978). *Transformations: Growth and change in adult life.* New York: Simon and Schuster.

Greeley, A. M. (1991). *Faithful attraction.* New York: Tor Books.

Haley, J. (1964). Research on family patterns: An instrument measurement. *Family Process, 15*, 41-65.

Hanna, S. L. (2000). *Person to person: Positive relationships don't just happen* (3rd ed.). Upper Saddle River, NJ: Prentice-Hall.

Harlow, H. F., & Harlow, M. (1971). Psychopathology in monkeys. In H. D. Kinnel (Ed.), *Experimental psychobiology.* New York: Academic Press.

Hatfield, E. (1988). Passionate and companionate love. In R. J. Sternberg & M. L. Barnes (Eds.), *The psychology of love.* New Haven: CT: Yale University Press.

Hatfield, E., Aronson, V., Abrams, D., & Rottman, L. (1966). Importance of physical attractiveness in dating behavior. *Journal of Personality and Social Psychology, 4*, 508-516.

Hazan, C., & Shaver, P. (1987). Romantic love conceptualized as an attachment process. *Journal of Personality and Social Psychology, 52*, 511-524.

Hendrix, H. (1990, 1988). *Getting the love you want: A guide for couples.* New York: Harper and Row. Originally published by Henry Holt and Company in 1988.

Hendrix, H. (1992). *Keeping the love you find: A personal guide.* New York: Simon and Schuster.

Jacobson, N., & Gottman, J. M. (1998). *When men batter women: New insights into ending abusive relationships.* New York: Simon and Schuster.

Kantor, D., & Lehr,W. (1975). *Inside the family.* San Francisco: Josey-Bass.

Kayser, K. (1993). *When love dies: The process of marital disaffection.* New York: The Guilford Press.

Kerr, M. E., & Bowen, M. (1988). *Family evaluation: An approach based on Bowen theory.* New York: W. W. Norton.

Kubler-Ross, E. (1969). *On death and dying.* New York: Macmillan.

Larsen, A. S., & Olson, D. H. (1989). Predicting marital satisfaction using PAR-PARE: A replication study. *Journal of Marital and Family Therapy, 15,* 311-322.

Lauer, H. L., & Lauer, J. C. (2000). *Marriage and family: The quest for intimacy* (4th ed). Boston: McGraw-Hill.

Lauer, J. C., & Lauer, R. H. (1986). *Til death do us part: How couples stay together.* New York: Haworth.

Lederer, W. J., & Jackson, D. D. (1968). *The mirages of marriage.* New York: W. W. Norton.

Lempers, J. D., & Clark-Lempers, D. S. (1992). Young, middle, and late adolescents' comparisons of the functional importance of five significant relationships. *Journal of Youth and Adolescence. 21,* 53-96.

Levy, K. N., Blatt, S. J., & Shaver, P. R. (1998). Attachment styles and parental representations. *Journal of Personality and Social Psychology, 74,* 407-419.

Linz, D. G., Donnerstein, E., & Adams, S. M. (1989). Physiological desensitization and judgements about female victims of violence. *Human Communication Research, 15,* 509-522.

Linz, D. G., Donnerstein, E., & Penrod, S. (1988). Effects of long term exposure to violent and sexually degrading depictions of women. *Journal of Personality and Social Psychology, 55,* 758-768.

Mahler, M., Pine, F., & Bergman, A. (1975). *The psychological birth of the human infant.* New York: Basic Books.

Malamuth, N. M., & Check, J. V. P. (1981). The effects of media exposure on acceptance of violence against women: A field experiment. *Journal of Research in Personality, 15,* 436-446.

Maltz, D.N., & Borker, R. A. (1982). A cultural approach to male-female miscommunication. In John J. Gumperz (Ed.), *Language and social identity* (pp. 192-216). Cambridge, MA: Cambridge University Press.

Markman, H., Stanley, S., & Blumberg, S. L. (1994). *Fighting for your marriage.* San Francisco: Jossey Bass.

Marlin, E. (1989). *Genograms: The new tool for exploring the personality, career, and love patterns you inherit.* New York: Contemporary Books.

Maslow, A. H. (1970). *Motivation and personality* (2nd ed.). New York: Harper & Row.

McGoldrick, M., & Gerson, R. (1985). *Genograms in family assessment.* New York: W.W. Norton.

McGraw, P.C. (2000). *Relationship rescue: A seven-step strategy for reconnecting with your partner.* New York: Hyperion.

McKay, M., Davis, M., & Fanning, F. (1983). *Messages: The communication skills book.* Oakland, CA: New Harbinger.

Mickelson, K. D., Kessler, R. C., & Shaver, P. R. (1997). Adult attachment in a nationally representative sample. *Journal of Personality and Social Psychology, 73,* 1092-1106.

Minuchin, S. (1974). *Families and family therapy.* Cambridge, MA: Harvard University Press.

Minuchin, S., Rosman, B., & Baker, L. (1978). *Psychosomatic families: Anorexia nervosa in context.* Cambridge, MA: Harvard University Press.

Murray, H. A. (1938). *Explorations in Personality.* New York: Oxford.

Murstein, B. I., Cerreto, M., & MacDonald, M. G. (1977). A theory and investigation of the effect of exchange-orientation on marriage and friendship. *Journal of Marriage and the Family, 39,* 543-548.

Murstein, B. L. (1986). *Paths to marriage.* Newbury Park, CA: Sage.

Myers, D. G. (1992). *The pursuit of happiness: Discovering the pathway to fulfillment, well-being, and enduring personal joy.* New York: Avon Books.

Myers, D. G. (1993). *Social psychology* (4th ed.). New York: McGraw-Hill.

Myers, D. G. (2000). *The American paradox: Spiritual hunger in an age of plenty.* New Haven, CT: Yale University Press.

Napier, A. Y. (1990, 1988). *The fragile bond: In search of an equal, intimate and enduring marriage.* New York: HarperCollins. Originally published by Harper and Row in 1988.

Napier, A. Y., & Whitaker, C. (1978). *The family crucible: The intense experience of family therapy.* New York: Harper and Row.

Nichols, M. P. (1999). *Inside Family Therapy.* Needham Heights, MA: Allyn & Bacon.

Notarius, C., & Markman, C. (1993). *We can work it out: Making sense of marital conflict.* New York: G. P. Putman.

Olson, D. H. (1988). Circumplex model of family systems VIII: Family assessment and intervention. *Journal of Psychotherapy and the Family. 4,* 7-50.

Olson, D. H., & DeFrain, J. (2000). *Marriage and the family: Diversity and strength* (3rd ed.). Mountain View, CA: Mayfield.

Olson, D. H., & Olson, A. (2000). *Impowering couples: Building on your strengths.* Minneapolis, MN: Life Innovations, Inc.

Olson, D. H., Fay, S., & Olson, A. (1999). *National survey of happy and unhappy couples.* Minneapolis, MN: Life Innovations, Inc.

Olson, D. H., McCubbin, H. I., Barnes, H., Larsen, A., Muxen, M., & Wilson, M. (1983). *Families: What makes them work.* Los Angeles: Sage.

Panksepp, J. (1998). *Affective neuroscience.* New York: Oxford University Press.

Parke, R. D., Berkowitz, L., Leyens, J. P., West, S. G., & Sebastian, J. (1977). Some effects of violent and nonviolent movies on the behavior of juvenile delinquents. In L. Berkowitz (Ed.), *Advances in experimental social psychology* (Vol. 10). New York: Academic Press.

Parrott, L., & Parrott, L. (2001). *When bad things happen to good marriages.* Grand Rapids, MI: Zondervan.

Patterson, G. R., & Gullion, M. E. (1968). *Living with children: New metnods for parents and teachers.* Champaign, IL: Research Press.

Peck, S. M. (1978). *The road less traveled: A new psychology of love, traditional values and spiritual growth.* New York: Simon & Schuster.

Peplau, L. A., & Gordon, S. L. (1985). Women and men in love: Gender differences in close heterosexual relationships. In V. E. O'Leary, R. K. Unger, & B. S. Wallston (Eds.), *Women, gender, and social psychology* (p. 20). Hillsdale, NJ: Lawrence Erlbaum.

Pistole, M. C. (1989). Attachment in adult romantic relationships: Style of conflict resolution and relationship satisfaction. *Journal of Social and Personal Relationships, 6*, 505-510.

Rice, F. P. (1996). *Intimate relationships, marriages, and families* (3rd ed.). Mountain View, CA: Mayfield.

Ridley, C. A., Peterson, D. J., & Avery A. (1978). Cohabitation: Does it make for a better marriage? *Family Coordinator (April)*, 129-136.

Rogers, C. R. (1961). *On becoming a person: A therapist's view of psychotherapy.* Boston: Houghton Mifflin.

Rogers, C. R., (1951). *Client-centered therapy: Its current practice, implications, and theory.* Boston: Houghton Mifflin.

Roscoe, B., & Benaske, N. (1985). Courtship violence experienced by abused wives: Similarities in patterns of abuse. *Family Relations, 34*, 419-424.

Satir, V. (1972). *Peoplemaking.* Palo Alto, CA: Science and Behavior Books.

Satir, V. (1964). *Conjoint family therapy.* Palo Alto, CA: Science and Behavior Books.

Satir, V. (1988). *The new peoplemaking.* Mountain View, CA: Science and Behavior Books.

Segal, N. L. (1999). *Entwined lives: Twins and what they tell us about human behavior.* New York: Plume.

Simpson, J. A. (1990). Influence of attachment styles on romantic relationships. *Journal of Personality and Social Psychology, 59*, 971-980.

Skinner, B. H. (1953). *Science and behavior.* New York: Macmillan.

Sternberg, R. J. (1988). *The triangle of love: Intimacy, passion, commitment.* New York: Basic Books.

Taffel, R., & Blau, M. (2001). *The second family: How adolescent power is challenging the American family.* New York: St. Martin's Press.

Tannen, D. (1986). *That's not what I meant: How conversational style makes or breaks relationships.* New York: Ballantine.

Tannen, D. (1990). *You just don't understand: Women and men in conversation.* New York: Ballantine.

Tannen, D. (Lecturer). (2001). *Deborah Tannen: He said, she said.* Videotape lecture. Into the Classroom Media, Los Angeles, CA.

Thomas, A., & Chess, S. (1977). *Temperament and development.* New York: Bruner/Mazel.

Thornton, J., & Lasswell, M. (1997). *Chore wars: How households can share the work and keep the peace.* Berkeley, CA: Conari Press.

Turecki, S., & Tonner, L. (1985). *The difficult child.* New York: Basic Books.

U. S. Bureau of Census (1997). *Statistical abstract of the United States* (117th ed.), Washingrton, DC: U. S. Government Printing Office.

Udry, J. R. (1971). *The social context of marriage* (2nd ed.), Philadelphia: Lippincott.

Vaughan, D. (1987). *Uncoupling: How Relationships come apart.* New York: Vintage Books. Originally published in 1986 by Oxford University Press.

Viorst, J. (1986). *Necessary loses.* New York: Ballentine.

Waite, L. J., & Gallagher, M. (2000). *The case for marriage: Why married people are happier, healthier, and better off financially.* New York: Random House.

Walker, L. E. (1979). *The battered women.* New York: Harper and Row.

Wallerstein, J.S., & Blakeslee, S. (1989). *Second chances: Men, women and children a decade after divorce.* New York: Ticknor and Fields.

Wallis, C. (1987, October 12). Back off, buddy: A new Hite report stirs up furor over sex and love in the 80s. *Time*, pp. 68-73.

Walster, E., & Walster, G. W. (1978). *A new look at love.* Reading, MA: Addison-Wesley.

Wheeler, R. E., Davidson, R. J., & Tomarken, A. J. (1993). Frontal brain asymmetry and emotional reactivity: A biological substrate of affective style. *Psychophysiology, 30,* 82-89.

Whitfield, C. L. (1987). *Healing the child within.* Deerfield Beach, FL: Health Communications.

Wile, D. (1988). *After the honeymoon: How conflict can improve your relationship.* New York: John Wiley.

Williams, W., & Ceci, S. (1998). *Escaping the advice trap: 59 tough relationship problems solved by the experts.* Kansas City: MO Andrews McMeel.

Woititz, J. G. (1983). *Adult children of alcoholics.* Deerfield Beach, FL: Health Communications.

Wynne, L. C. (1984). The epigenesis of relational systems: A model for understanding family development. *Family Process, 23,* 297-318.

Zuckerman, M. (1991). *Psychobiology of personality.* New York: Cambridge University Press.

INDEX

377

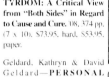

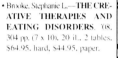

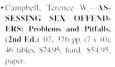
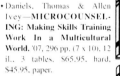
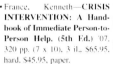

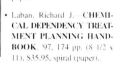